The Taft Court

ABC-CLIO SUPREME COURT HANDBOOKS

The Burger Court, Tinsley E. Yarbrough
The Fuller Court, James W. Ely, Jr.
The Hughes Court, Michael E. Parrish
The Stone Court, Peter G. Renstrom
The Taft Court, Peter G. Renstrom
The Taney Court, Timothy S. Huebner
The Waite Court, Donald Grier Stephenson, Jr.
The Warren Court, Melvin I. Urofsky

Forthcoming:
The Chase Court, Jonathan Lurie
The Jay and Ellsworth Courts, Matthew P. Harrington
The Marshall Court, Robert Lowry Clinton
The Rehnquist Court, Thomas R. Hensley
The Vinson Court, Michal R. Belknap
The White Court, Rebecca S. Shoemaker

Peter G. Renstrom, Series Editor

ABC-CLIO SUPREME COURT HANDBOOKS

The Taft Court

Justices, Rulings, and Legacy

Peter G. Renstrom

A B C CLIO

Santa Barbara, California • Denver, Colorado • Oxford, England

Library of Congress Cataloging-in-Publication Data

Renstrom, Peter G., 1943–
The Taft Court : justices, rulings, and legacy / Peter G. Renstrom.
p. cm. — (ABC-CLIO Supreme Court handbooks)
Includes bibliographical references and index.
ISBN 1-57607-280-0 (hardcover : alk. paper); ISBN 1-85109-537-3 (e-book)
1. Taft, William H. (William Howard), 1857–1930. 2. United States. Supreme Court—History—20th century. 3. Constitutional history—United States. I. Title. II. Series.
KF8742.R483 2003
347.73'26'09—dc21

2003004170

06 05 04 03 10 9 8 7 6 5 4 3 2 1

ABC-CLIO, Inc.
130 Cremona Drive, P.O. Box 1911
Santa Barbara, California 93116-1911

This book is printed on acid-free paper ♾.
Manufactured in the United States of America

To my family:
for providing the opportunity to be a son,
brother, husband, father, and grandfather—
roles I value beyond words

Contents

Series Foreword

There is an extensive literature on the U.S. Supreme Court, but it contains discussion familiar largely to the academic community and the legal profession. The ABC-CLIO Supreme Court series is designed to have value to the academic and legal communities also, but each volume is intended as well for the general reader who does not possess an extensive background on the Court or American constitutional law. The series is intended to effectively represent each of fourteen periods in the history of the Supreme Court with each of these fourteen eras defined by the chief justice beginning with John Jay in 1789. Each Court confronted constitutional and statutory questions that were of major importance to and influenced by the historical period. The Court's decisions were also influenced by the values of each of the individual justices sitting at the time. The issues, the historical period, the justices, and the Supreme Court's decisions in the most significant cases will be examined in the volumes of this series.

ABC-CLIO's Supreme Court series provides scholarly examinations of the Court as it functioned in different historical periods and with different justices. Each volume contains information necessary to understand each particular Court and an interpretative analysis by the author of each Court's record and legacy. In addition to representing the major decisions of each Court, institutional linkages are examined as well—the political connections among the Court, Congress, and the president. These relationships are important for several reasons. Although the Court retains some institutional autonomy, all the Court's justices are selected by a process that involves the other two branches. Many of the significant decisions of the Court involve the review of actions of Congress or the president. In addition, the Court frequently depends on the other two branches to secure compliance with its rulings.

The authors of the volumes in the ABC-CLIO series were selected with great care. Each author has worked extensively with the Court, the period, and the personalities about which he or she has written. ABC-CLIO wanted each of the volumes to examine several common themes, and each author agreed to work within certain guidelines. Each author was free, however, to develop the content of each volume, and many of the volumes advance new or distinctive conclusions about the Court under examination.

Each volume contains four substantive chapters. The first chapter will introduce the Court and the historical period in which it served. The second chapter will examine each of the justices who sat on the particular Court. The third chapter will represent the most significant decisions rendered by the particular Court. Among other things, the impact of the historical period and the value orientations of the individual justices will be developed. A fourth and final chapter will address the impact of each particular Court on American constitutional law—its doctrinal legacy.

Each volume contains several features designed to make the volume more valuable to those whose previous exposure to the Supreme Court and American constitutional law is limited. Each volume will have a reference section that will contain brief entries on some of the people, statutes, events, and concepts introduced in the four substantive chapters. Entries in this section are arranged alphabetically. Each volume will also contain a glossary of selected legal terms used in the text. Following each of the four chapters, a list of sources used in the chapter and suggestions for further reading will appear. Each volume will also have a comprehensive annotated bibliography. A listing of Internet sources is presented at the end of the bibliography. Finally, there will be a comprehensive subject index and a list of cases (with citation numbers) discussed in each volume. ABC-CLIO is delighted with the quality of scholarship represented in each volume and is proud to offer this series to the reading public.

Permit me to conclude with a personal note. This project has been an extraordinarily rewarding undertaking for me as series editor. Misgivings about serving in this capacity were plentiful at the outset of the project. After tending to some administrative business pertaining to the series, securing authors for each volume was the first major task. I developed a list of possible authors after reviewing previous work and obtaining valuable counsel from several recognized experts in American constitutional history. In virtually every instance, the first person on my list agreed to participate in the project. The high quality of the series was assured and enhanced as each author signed on. I could not have been more pleased. My interactions with each author have been most pleasant, and the excellence of their work will be immediately apparent to the reader. I sincerely thank each author.

Finally, a word about ABC-CLIO and its staff. ABC-CLIO was enthusiastic about the project from the beginning and has done everything necessary to make this series successful. I am very appreciative of the level of support I have received from ABC-CLIO. Alicia Merritt, senior acquisitions editor, deserves special recognition. She has held my hand throughout the project. She has facilitated making this project a reality in every conceivable way. She has encouraged me from the beginning, provided invaluable counsel, and given me latitude to operate as I wished while keeping me on track at the same time. This project would not have gotten off the ground without Alicia, and I cannot thank her enough.

—*Peter G. Renstrom*
Series Editor

Preface

The Court era during which William Howard Taft was chief justice followed two decades of progressive politics in the United States. During the presidential administrations of Theodore Roosevelt and Woodrow Wilson particularly, a substantial number of progressive reforms found their way into both federal and state law. Even during Taft's presidency, Congress enacted federal laws prohibiting interstate prostitution and conferring rate-making authority to the Interstate Commerce Commission among others. The period immediately preceding the Taft Court also found the United States engaged in a world war. The war brought with it a greatly expanded federal government, particularly the executive branch, and gave the federal government unprecedented authority over the economy, conscription of men for military service, and political rights.

The election of Warren G. Harding as president in 1920 ushered in a decade of conservative reaction to progressive politics. The country seemed exhausted by all the reforms of the Progressive Era, the severe governmental controls necessitated by the war, and the fear of political radicals that surfaced at the war's end. By contrast, the 1920s was to be a decade marked by what Harding termed a "return to normalcy." By "normalcy," Harding was referring to a time with a diminished governmental presence, nineteenth-century values, and economic prosperity resulting from minimal government regulation of business.

The 1920s turned out to be close to what Harding envisioned. It was a time of great material advance. Most Americans enjoyed economic prosperity, women got the vote, and despite National Prohibition, alcoholic beverages were readily available. It was, indeed, the "Roaring 20s." Many experienced the "good life," although there were groups such as farmers, union members, and immigrants who suffered rather than prospered. Near the end of the 1920s, the country began what was to be a protracted economic depression. The Taft Court era ended just as the Depression replaced prosperity.

William Howard Taft joined the Supreme Court on 3 October 1921 and served as its chief justice until he resigned 3 February 1930. The Taft Court era coincided with a decade during which conservative Republicans controlled the apparatus of the national government. Chief Justice Taft and most of his colleagues were very comfortable with the Republican ascendancy and the political values they brought to the national stage. Indeed, the story of the Taft Court was largely a reflection of those values. The Court gave high priority to protection of private property and it supported freeing American businesses from most forms of governmental regulation.

The Court of the 1920s was largely defined by its chief justice. Taft's impact on his Court began during his presidency more than a decade earlier. Taft was able to "remake" the Court by naming six justices while he was president. His nominees maintained the conservative orientation of the Court into the 1920s. Two of Taft's nominees, Willis Van Devanter and Mahlon Pitney, were still on the Court when Taft became chief justice. Taft was not only instrumental in securing his own nomination in 1921, but was the decisive factor in the three other Supreme Court nominations made by President Warren G. Harding. Thus, Taft essentially "remade" the Court twice. The Harding nominees assured that the Taft Court would reflect the values of its chief justice throughout the decade.

The Taft Court followed the Republican administrations of the 1920s into so-called normalcy; it, too, retreated from progressivism. The Taft Court energized the dual federalism limits on federal commerce and taxing powers, leaving regulation of businesses and private property in the domain of the states and not the federal government. Taft and most of his colleagues believed that the Court must sustain a constitutional system in which protection of property interests was paramount. As a result, the Taft Court took an unyielding stance in support of business interests, greatly restricted the authority of federal regulatory agencies, and exhibited a distinctly antilabor bias. In these respects, the Taft Court was a "maintaining" Court—it affirmed and often extended the jurisprudence of the conservative Fuller and White Courts on property rights and business regulation issues.

The Taft Court also did something that was unexpected. It revealed a sensitivity, however modest, to individual rights. It was the Taft Court that took some initial steps toward a modern jurisprudence of civil liberties. The doctrinal changes were not dramatic, but were nonetheless recognizable as departures from the status quo. Not surprisingly, it was Justice Louis Brandeis who led the way in this development. Even before Taft became chief justice, Brandeis had argued that the Fourteenth Amendment should protect civil liberties at least as extensively as it protected property rights. In cases such as *Meyer v. Nebraska* (1923) and *Pierce v. Society of Sisters* (1925), the Taft Court struck down a state law prohibiting the teaching of foreign languages to elementary-level students and another that required attendance of all students in only public schools through the eighth grade. It was the Taft Court that ruled in *Gitlow v. New York* (1925) that the free speech protection of the First Amendment applied to actions of state governments as well the federal government. This was the beginning of the "incorporation" or "nationalization of rights" process, which would not conclude until the end of the Warren Court era. Although many of the Taft Court rulings did not further either civil liberties or civil rights, it was the Taft Court that commenced serious debate on these issues. To this extent the Taft Court can be viewed as a "transitional" Court—it began the migration to a greatly expanded jurisprudence of constitutional rights.

The Taft Court volume is my second in the ABC-CLIO Supreme Court Handbook series. My first examined the Stone Court. The Stone Court project enabled me to revisit the familiar ground of my dissertation research. The Taft Court project, on the other hand, was a journey into comparatively unfamiliar territory. In contrast to the Stone Court period, the decade of the 1920s was a time when the Court operated free of the exigencies of wartime and economic distress—it was a time of relative peace and prosperity. The project allowed me to stretch historically and focus on the conservative activism of Chief Justice Taft and his associate justices. The Taft Court project was a thoroughly enjoyable professional venture, and I sincerely thank ABC-CLIO for the opportunity to produce this volume for the Handbook series.

This book contains four substantive chapters. The first introduces the reader to the 1920s, which is the Taft Court decade. In addition to providing an overview of the period, the first chapter introduces the members of the Taft Court by sequentially discussing the appointment of each Taft Court justice. The second chapter offers biographical information on the Taft Court justices and attempts to briefly characterize each justice's contribution to the rulings of the Taft Court. The third chapter develops the decisional themes of the Taft Court by representing the Court's most important rulings. The final chapter develops the Taft Court's contribution to American constitutional law—its particular legacy.

There are some additional features of this book that are intended to enhance its value to readers. There is an alphabetically arranged reference section that provides information on selected people, legislative acts, executive actions, and agencies to supplement discussion found in the four main chapters. At the end of the reference section is an appendix containing a term-by-term statistical representation of the Taft Court and its justices. The appendix is followed by a timeline of the period 1918–1932. The timeline represents the dates of important Court decisions, major legislative enactments, personnel changes on the Court, and other noteworthy events. A table of cases and a glossary of legal terms follow the chronology. There is also an extensive annotated bibliography, which includes an annotated list of selected Internet sites containing information about the Supreme Court. Finally, there is a comprehensive index designed to help the reader locate discussion of particular cases and topics treated in the volume.

A number of people contributed to the production of this volume. I greatly appreciate the comments and suggestions I received from people both in the Political Science Department at Western Michigan University and elsewhere in the academic community. They clarified my thinking, and as a result of their comments, I am more confident about my treatment of the Taft Court. Certainly, any remaining errors of commission or omission are mine alone.

The Supreme Court Handbook series would not have happened without the guiding hand of Alicia Merritt, senior acquisitions editor at ABC-CLIO. The series was her idea, and she encouraged me to undertake both the Stone Court and Taft Court volumes in addition to serving as series editor. Our regular e-mail exchanges provided much-needed guidance, humor, and focus. I must also note the contributions of my family—my wife Bobbi; my children Dan, Joelle, Ola, and Michele; and my granddaughters Rowan and Sage. They were invaluable sources of support through the ups and downs associated with writing. My daughter Joelle deserves special mention. She spent countless hours with red pen in hand attempting to make my drafts intelligible. My sincere thanks to you all.

Peter G. Renstrom

The Taft Court

PART ONE

Justices, Rulings, and Legacy

1

The Taft Court and the Period

The decade after the First World War featured conservatism in politics and social philosophy. The Republican Party had a virtual lock on the control of national affairs and it advocated a laissez-faire economic philosophy and made government the instrument of big business. The decade saw changes in manufacturing and business practices and dramatic growth in corporate profits, but the industrial prosperity did not transfer to other economic sectors. Agriculture, for example, not only suffered through the decade of the 1920s, but was particularly hard hit by the effects of the economic depression through the decade that followed. Political liberalism was replaced by a conservatism stemming in part from postwar nationalism. In the view of some, the country "moved into the future with [its] eyes fixed on the past; the 1920s sought to preserve the rural values of nineteenth-century America from the rude intrusion of the great city" (Morison, Commager, and Leuchtenburg 1980, 413). The Taft Court freely embraced these conservative objectives and willingly joined the Republican administrations' attempts to realize them.

Woodrow Wilson and World War I

Between 1900 and the American entry into World War I, progressivism had a substantial impact on American life. Progressivism was a reform movement that developed in response to the rapid industrialization of the late nineteenth century. Progressives held big-city political machines responsible for many of the evils plaguing urban areas and believed the people could bring about needed political and economic reforms if given the power to do so. The progressive agenda included such issues as ending the exploitation of female and child factory workers, unsafe and unsanitary working conditions, urban poverty, political corruption, and the abusive practices of giant corporations (Goldberg 1999, 1). Presidents Theodore Roosevelt and Woodrow Wilson strongly endorsed much of the progressive agenda, unlike William Howard Taft.

Progressive reformers, particularly at the state and local levels, succeeded in achieving much of their agenda during the first two decades of the twentieth century.

The progressive reforms that surfaced during the Roosevelt presidency came to dominate national politics by the election of 1912. The Republicans renominated President William Howard Taft for president, but Roosevelt, who led the progressive wing of the Republican Party, remained in the presidential race by running as the candidate of the Progressive or "Bull Moose" Party. The 1912 presidential campaign focused on corporate trusts and the different solutions advanced by Democratic nominee Woodrow Wilson and Roosevelt. Roosevelt believed that trusts should be extensively regulated while Wilson's New Freedom program advocated breaking up the trusts to facilitate competition within the American economy. Progressivism was advanced with the election of Wilson. Once inaugurated Wilson pursued his New Freedom reform program. By the eve of World War I, progressivism largely defined both the domestic and foreign policy objectives of Wilson's presidency.

The United States was initially able to stay clear of the conflict, but war in Europe was inevitable by 1914. As an international trading power, however, the United States could not avoid being affected by the turmoil. By 1916 the European struggle had prompted a highly contentious debate in the United States between internationalists and isolationists. Wilson was challenged in the presidential election of 1916 by Republican and former Supreme Court justice Charles Evans Hughes. Wilson prevailed in a close election and was generally perceived by the electorate as the candidate who offered the better chance of keeping the United States out of the widening European war. The United States would enter the world war, a conflict Wilson called the "war to make the world safe for democracy," less than a year later, however. Wilson tried to apply progressive concepts to his foreign policy and make American involvement a crusade for a new world order. Wilson had hoped to concentrate on domestic reforms during his presidency, but became a war president when war was formally declared in April 1917.

Mobilization for the war led the Wilson administration to establish a number of new federal agencies such as the Fuel Administration and the War Industries Board. In addition, the federal government took over the operation of privately owned railroads. Progressives hoped that the war would bolster social and political reforms, but instead, the federal government took steps to stifle political dissent, leading to one of the most repressive periods in American history. A number of factors, including concerns about the loyalty of German immigrants and the revolution in Russia, contributed to the demand for restrictions on political freedoms.

The major issue facing the Wilson administration was the organization of public and private resources to support the war effort. The first expansion of federal power occurred in the summer of 1916 when Congress authorized the president to take control of the nation's railroads in the event of war. Congress passed the National Defense Act in 1916 establishing a Council of National Defense to inventory national industrial resources, and on 17 May 1917 enacted a draft law providing for the conscription of American males for military service. The White Court upheld the draft initiative in the *Selective Draft Law Cases* in December 1917.

The need for war mobilization was evident to all, and initiatives to impose extensive regulations on the industrial sector and transportation were widely supported. Even the military draft was recognized as necessary once war was declared. More problematic were attempts by Wilson to extend federal control into such areas as food distribution and retail prices. The Lever Act of 1917 give Wilson extensive authority over American agriculture and the prices of agricultural commodities. Following passage of the act, Wilson created the Food Administration and selected Herbert C. Hoover to direct it. The bases on which prices were established under the Lever Act were unclear, and the vagueness of the law produced constitutional challenges. The "fair price" provisions of the act were struck down by the White Court in 1921, well after the end of the war. Congress assigned additional wartime authority to Wilson early in 1918 with the passage of the Overman Act. This act gave the president virtually unlimited authority to reorganize executive agencies to meet the demands of the war.

The Postwar Period

Woodrow Wilson was determined that the United States would play a decisive role in shaping the peace following World War I. In his Fourteen Points address in January 1918 Wilson not only stated the objectives of the United States for entering the war, but also outlined his vision of the postwar future. The centerpiece of his vision was the League of Nations that would serve as the means for preventing future international conflict. Believing that decisions reached in Paris would define the world's future, Wilson personally led the American delegation to the peace talks, which were held in the elegant palace of Versailles. His participation signaled America's emergence as a world power, but prompted serious political difficulties at home.

Wilson's political problems were largely of his own making. He sought to capitalize on his popularity as a wartime president during the mid-term elections of 1918 by appealing to the American people to elect a Democratic Congress that would support his peace initiatives. The tactic backfired and the Republicans took control of both the House and the Senate. Republican control of the Senate made Henry Cabot Lodge of Massachusetts chair of the Senate Foreign Relations Committee. From this position, Lodge became a major obstacle in the ratification of any peace treaty favored by Wilson.

Throughout the peace conference, Wilson made compromises in order to secure support for the League of Nations. After five months, Wilson achieved his primary goal of a treaty that, among other things, established the League. Wilson returned to the United States and submitted the treaty to the Senate. Although the Republicans controlled the Senate, it was still expected that the treaty would be ratified. Instead, an acrimonious battle ensued that focused almost entirely on the League. Lodge devised the strategy that ultimately led to the treaty's defeat. Members of his committee attached destructive "reservations" (limiting amendments) to the document before the Senate vote. Wilson stubbornly refused to yield any ground in the face of these modifications. Instead, the president undertook a grueling speaking campaign seeking to generate public support for the treaty. Traveling across the country by train, Wilson delivered forty speeches in twenty days. The trip ended in Colorado when Wilson's physician concluded that Wilson was suffering from "nervous exhaustion" and ordered his return to Washington. In early October Wilson suffered a severe stroke that incapacitated him for the duration of his presidency. Senate Republicans, especially those known as the "Irreconcilables"—senators who were categorically opposed to the treaty regardless of the reservations—succeeded in defeating the treaty in which Wilson had invested so much. Rejection of the treaty "signaled American hostility to foreign influences that characterized the increasingly xenophobic and nationalistic postwar period" (Goldberg 1999, 20).

The fight over the Treaty of Versailles was only one aspect of the turbulent postwar period. Wilson disappointed many of his progressive followers by focusing on international rather than domestic matters in his State of the Union message in December 1918. He moved quickly to dismantle some wartime agencies, including the National War Labor Board, and he became preoccupied with his peacemaking role. He indicated no intention of using wartime mobilization measures as the basis for postwar domestic reform. The return of the railroads to private ownership most clearly signaled the retreat from progressive priorities, although some restrictions on the railroads remained under provisions of the Transportation (Esch-Cummins) Act of 1920.

For the most part, the transition from a heavily controlled wartime economy was concluded without serious short-term difficulty. After a very brief economic slump, business began to bounce back. The economic upturn was produced by a number of factors, including pent-up consumer demand and continued government spending and loans for European relief operations. The economic recovery led to a speculative boom but brought serious inflation as well. Prices on most consumer goods rose almost 30 percent. The overriding domestic problem became the increasingly high cost of living. Although inflation brought distress to most of the population, it hurt hourly workers particularly. Labor was anxious to maintain wartime gains in both union membership and real wages, but employers did not increase wages to meet the inflated cost of living. Several million workers resorted to work stoppages including a nationwide coal strike and a bitter steel strike. Government, acting with strong public opinion support, endorsed the interests of ownership over those of labor.

The unions were not the only cause of public concern. Many blamed the labor disputes, the high cost of living, and foreign crises on a radical, Marxist political conspiracy. Late in 1919 Attorney General A. Mitchell Palmer, until then regarded as a progressive, organized a series of raids on alleged foreign radical organizations. Even when the Red Scare began to subside, public fear of aliens, dissenters, and nonconformists manifested itself in race riots and lynchings, anti-Semitic attitudes, and in suspicion of all foreigners. All these tendencies played a part in the marked resurgence of the Ku Klux Klan. Before the end of Wilson's second term as president, many Americans attributed a wide range of problems and frustrations to him. Even Wilson's most loyal supporters agreed that the president who had performed effectively through the war had become a sick old man presiding over an administration that zealously hounded political radicals but was otherwise helpless in dealing with the nation's postwar social or economic problems. It is not surprising that the country was so receptive to the alternative represented by Warren G. Harding and the Republicans in 1920.

Prelude to Normalcy

No single issue divided the progressive movement more than World War I. Progressives split into two groups, one supporting American involvement in the war, and the other opposing it. The prosecution of political dissidents further divided progressives, and Prohibition divided them yet again into rural-urban camps. In other words, the movement faltered after 1918 because progressive solidarity was seriously fractured by the war and its aftermath. The irony was that the progressive Wilson, not Harding and the Republicans, triggered postwar conservatism.

The most significant contributor to the unsettled political conditions of postwar American society was a destabilized economy brought on by the return to peacetime. The war ended more quickly than foreseen by the Wilson administration, which was caught unprepared for demobilization. The economy did not falter immediately, but it was sustained largely by continued government spending and consumer demand for items unavailable during the war. These temporary economic influences had diminished if not disappeared altogether by the time of the 1920 election. In their place came inflation, recession, and serious labor unrest. The gross national product declined by almost 10 percent, upwards of half a million farmers lost their farms, and nearly five million workers lost their jobs. The wage gains made by workers during the war were lost to inflation. The country experienced an unprecedented number of strikes, which involved more than four million workers. These job actions by workers not only produced hostile responses from employers, but also public animosity.

To many Americans, labor appeared, at least in part, responsible for the country's economic and social unrest. The war had upset the balance of power between management and workers that had been in place since the early days of the Progressive Era. As unions grew in size and power, labor's aspirations also expanded. Unfortunately for labor, the public was in no mood to identify with its cause or to tolerate its strikes. When the coal miners went out on strike in November 1919, Attorney General Palmer obtained federal court injunctions against the strikers (Goldberg 1999, 12–14). For the next decade, government's relationship with labor was nothing less than adversarial. The agricultural sector also experienced serious economic hardships as farmers struggled with the familiar problems of both inflation and declining market prices for their crops. The Wilson administration did not offer effective options for the agricultural community. The situation was aggravated by the Esch-Cummins Transportation Act of 1920, which returned the railroads to private hands. A 25–40 percent rail rate increase followed shortly thereafter.

The public saw industrial warfare and increased racial violence as signs of political radicalism. The Russian Revolution in late 1917 made the threat of international communism credible as the new Soviet regime actively sought to export the communist revolution beyond its own borders. National alarm was further prompted by a series of bombings that targeted business and political leaders in the United States. In response to the so-called Red Scare, most states passed sedition laws that criminalized the promotion of revolution. At the national level, Attorney General A. Mitchell Palmer coordinated a series of raids on centers of radical activity throughout the country. The "Palmer Raids" led to the arrest of more than 6,000 persons. The intensity of the Red Scare was not long lasting, but its effects persisted throughout the Taft Court era.

The period immediately preceding Warren Harding's inauguration produced two constitutional amendments—one establishing national prohibition and the other extending the vote to women. Both amendments reflected progressive values. Many progressives saw law as a means for establishing public morality and national prohibition as a moral issue, at least in part. Woman's suffrage reflected the progressive view that democratic processes were enhanced by maximizing citizen participation.

Efforts to restrict the consumption of alcohol dated back to the 1820s. The Ohio-based Women's Christian Temperance Union (WCTU), founded in 1874, elevated the public visibility of the issue. In 1895 the Anti-Saloon League joined the WCTU's campaign against alcohol. The drive against the "liquor trust" won the support of many progressives who viewed abstinence as a way to uplift the urban poor. The prohibitionists triumphed in part because brewers, who believed that beer would be exempted, refused to join distillers in a fight against the proposed amendment. More importantly the cause gained momentum from America's entry into the war. The prohibitionists argued that grains such as barley and rye should not be wasted on the manufacture of intoxicants when there were more pressing war-related needs. Many fervent "drys" won election to Congress in 1918. The debate in Congress focused on the need to conserve grain during wartime. The amendment emerged from Congress with little opposition and was ratified by three-fourths of the states within a year, although neither the Republicans nor the Democrats specifically endorsed national prohibition. Rather, the amendment "intruded into the constitutional system under the cover of the war" and a general feeling by the public that self-denial was in order during the conflict (Swindler 1974, 252). The proposed amendment banned the manufacture, sale, or transportation of intoxicating liquors, but did not define "intoxicating" and many expected Congress to permit the continued sale of light wines and beer. However, the enforcement statute, known as the Volstead Act, categorized any drink containing more than 0.5 percent alcohol as "intoxicating" (Goldberg 1999, 54–56).

Prohibition was one of the few political issues that aroused strong emotions in the 1920s. Prohibition went into effect on 1 January 1920, a year before the conservative Republicans took control of the national government. The White and Taft Courts decided a number of cases relating to prohibition, all of which supported efforts to enforce it. Almost before prohibition went into effect, the country was "rapidly losing its zeal for reform and abstinence which had climaxed in the Wilson years" (Swindler 1974, 258). Although the Republican administrations of the 1920s felt obligated to enforce the Eighteenth Amendment through the Volstead Act, the movement to repeal the amendment rapidly gained strength. "Wets" scored a major victory as early as 1923 when the New York legislature, with the encouragement of Governor Alfred E. Smith, voted to repeal its state enforcement law although federal agents continued to enforce the Volstead Act in New York. By the end of the decade, the issue had become increasingly partisan. Governor Smith, the Democratic presidential nominee in 1928, strongly endorsed repeal. The report of the National Commission on Law Observance and Enforcement—known as the Wickersham Commission after its chair, former Attorney General George W. Wickersham—noted the change in public sentiment about prohibition and the ineffectiveness of enforcement efforts. Although While it did not expressly call for abandonment of prohibition, the commission's findings alluded to such a course. Repeal of the Eighteenth Amendment was a major component of Franklin D. Roosevelt's successful presidential campaign in 1932, and upon his inauguration he reduced the funding of the federal enforcement agency and called for substantial changes in the Volstead Act. A constitutional amendment calling for repeal of the Prohibition Amendment was sent to the states for ratification. The Twenty-first Amendment was ratified by December 1933, bringing to an end the so-called noble experiment.

The second amendment of the period brought about woman's suffrage. Although ratification of the Nineteenth Amendment delighted suffragists, they were disappointed by the low turnout in the November 1920 election, when less than half the eligible female voters cast ballots. In addition to being less inclined to vote than men, a distinctive "women's vote" was not evident—women "cast their ballots much as their husbands, fathers, and male relatives did" (Parrish 1992, 142). Nonetheless, activist women believed that they now had the political leverage to get Congress to act on their legislative agenda. The Women's Joint Congressional Committee pressured Congress to pass laws endorsed by women's groups, including measures to protect women in industry, extend federal aid to public education, and disarmament. The first notable victory came in 1921 when Congress enacted the Sheppard-Towner Act, which aimed at reducing the country's high infant mortality rate. A second victory for newly enfranchised women came in 1922 with the enactment of the Married Women's Independent Citizenship Act, popularly known as the Cable Act. The Cable Act "abolished the legal disabilities suffered by those who married male aliens" (142). However, a cohesive bloc of women voters failed to materialize and few women sought elective office. Coupled with divisions among women activists themselves, political influence of women could not be sustained throughout the decade, and the Cable Act turned out to be the last significant legislative victory won by women in the 1920s.

Immigration had fallen off and the national birthrate had begun to decline by 1920. There was every reason to suppose that the restrictions on immigration initiated during the war would be reinforced by appropriate new legislation. The homogeneity of the American people in religion, education, and language remained far more extensive than generally realized, however. Most notable from the census data collected in 1920 was the rate at which the American people were moving from rural to urban areas. Indeed, the decade of the twenties would see many more millions of country people move to the cities. The shift of population from country to city accurately reflected the growing importance of manufacturing in the national economy as compared to agriculture (Hicks 1960, 3–4).

The 1920 Election: The Triumph of Conservative Republicanism

The Republican Party entered the 1920 election year confident of victory. President Wilson unwittingly played into Republican hands by focusing on ratification of the peace treaty formally ending World War I, rather than attending to domestic issues that were deemed more pressing by the electorate. Senator Warren G. Harding of Ohio was elected president in November 1920. His victory was partially attributable to his "return to normalcy" campaign theme. It resonated with the public's apparent call for a moratorium on progressive reforms and an end to wartime controls. Harding sounded the theme for his campaign in a Boston speech in May 1920. He said that "America's present need is not for heroics, but healing; not nostrums, but normalcy; not revolution, but restoration . . . not surgery, but serenity" (Milkis and Nelson 1994, 256). The word "normalcy" attracted immediate and particular attention. "Normalcy" captured the temper of the times concerning not just public policy but the presidency as well. Harding capitalized on the popular reaction against what Republicans called "executive autocracy" (256). By "normalcy," Harding would later explain he "did not mean reaction or the old order, but a regular steady order of things" (Parrish 1992, 9). He said he was referring to "normal procedures," for conducting the people's business the "natural way, without excess" (9). The Republicans began acting on this sentiment even before the November election. Before adjourning in the summer of 1920, Congress passed an act that repealed most of the laws that had conferred extensive executive war powers to Wilson. The enactment was unanimously approved in the Senate and passed the House with only three dissenting votes. Wilson pocket-vetoed the act after Congress adjourned, which allowed him to retain certain war powers until Congress reconvened after the election. In doing so, Wilson "took one more step which decisively alienated the average American citizen" (Milkis and Nelson 1994, 256–257).

When the Republicans gathered in Chicago for their nominating convention, none of the leading contenders had enough delegates to immediately secure the nomination. Finally, on the tenth ballot, a consensus formed behind Senator Harding. Although Harding was not well known nationally, he presented an appealing alternative to a public tired of Wilson and the Democrats. Governor Calvin Coolidge of Massachusetts was selected as his running mate. Coolidge had gained national visibility for his handling of the Boston Police Strike of 1919 when he declared that "there is no right to strike against the public safety by anybody, anytime, anywhere!" (Goldberg 1999, 45). Coolidge thus came to symbolize uncompromising resistance to striking workers. He added a valuable dimension to the ticket and made and formidable team with Harding.

The Democrats, on the other hand, were rightly pessimistic about retaining the presidency. When they convened in San Francisco, William Gibbs McAdoo, A. Mitchell Palmer, and James Cox were the leading contenders for the nomination. Both McAdoo and Palmer had political liabilities that kept them from gaining additional delegate support at the convention. That left Cox, a three-term governor of Ohio, as the eventual choice—although not until the forty-fourth ballot. Cox, like any other Democratic nominee in 1920, had to run with Wilson's accumulating negatives, a virtually impossible task. In addition, some progressives supported the third-party candidate, California senator Hiram Johnson, which drew additional votes away from Cox.

Harding's pledge of a "return to normalcy" drew a favorable response from most of those who voted in 1920. The Republican ticket won 60 percent of the popular vote and gained control of both the House and the Senate by wide margins. Turnout was less than 50 percent, however, which reflected the disaffection and apathy of many eligible voters. Low turnout notwithstanding, Harding's election was the beginning of the end of the Progressive Era. The election was also a referendum on the League of Nations. Rejection of the League so closely identified with Wilson indicated that voters were expressing a desire for quieter times and the desire to return to "normalcy" in the form of isolationism. In addition, the election brought about a "return to laissez-faire, a partial restoration of the wall that separated government from society before the advent of progressivism" (Milkis and Nelson 1994, 256). Historian Michael Parrish concluded that in choosing Harding, American voters "rejected both the tone and substance of the political movement Roosevelt had galvanized two decades earlier" (1992, 3). In his view, the American public declared itself "weary of crusades and of charismatic leaders who constantly demanded that [Americans] live a political life of great deeds and heroic sacrifice at home and abroad" (3).

The one issue that might have rallied progressive support was the League of Nations, but instead the League accentuated the internal divisions within the ranks of liberals and progressives. The progressive movement fragmented more on foreign policy than any other issue in the postwar era. For a time, the League rode the crest of internationalism that sustained American entry into World War I. It was supported by the same wartime idealism that accompanied American engagement in the war. The League was pushed into the background by diminishing public support and by more compelling domestic issues. Wilson's plea that the election of 1920 be a "solemn referendum" destroyed any hope that the Democrats had of prevailing in the election of 1920.

The Harding Presidency and Normalcy

Harding and his two Republican successors, Calvin Coolidge and Herbert Hoover, took their understanding of executive power from William McKinley and William Howard Taft rather than from the stewardship theory advocated by Theodore Roosevelt. The tenure of these three presidents was generally undistinguished and even regarded by some as the "nadir of the presidency in the twentieth century." Following the executive activism of Roosevelt and Wilson, the presidential administrations of the 1920s were passive and seemed to lack purpose and direction. At the same time, the presidency had developed to such an extent by 1920 that even "Harding's concept of normalcy did not entail turning back the clock entirely" (Milkis and Nelson 1994, 257–258).

Harding was a small-town newspaper editor and a Republican cast in the mold of William McKinley. Aware of his own shortcomings, he announced his intent to staff his administration with the party's "best minds." He was able to bring some high-quality people into his administration. Agriculture Secretary Henry C. Wallace, Treasury Secretary Andrew Mellon, Secretary of State Charles Evans Hughes, and Commerce Secretary Herbert Hoover were able men and their selections were widely applauded. Some of Harding's Cabinet choices, however, confirmed *The Nation*'s observation that this would be the most "material and sightless" administration ever. Too many in his administration were party hacks and political cronies from Ohio. For example, Harding tapped his political mentor Harry Daugherty to head the Justice Department. Daugherty was a man "totally unprepared for such an office" (Goldberg 1999, 49). Interior Secretary Albert Fall, a confidant of oil investors, eventually left the Harding administration in 1923 in the wake of the Teapot Dome oil-lease scandal.

True to his promise as a candidate, Harding made only a limited effort to lead Congress. Harding's model was William McKinley, whose influence on Capitol Hill was achieved behind the scenes and through compromise with his party's leadership. But McKinley-style legislative leadership was no longer possible by the 1920s. Gone was the time when the president and the Speaker of the House could achieve executive and legislative cooperation through quiet consultation. Furthermore, the Seventeenth Amendment had taken effect in 1913, which ended the practice of state legislatures choosing U.S. senators and mandated their direct election. This change undermined party discipline in the Senate even further. Harding's plan for postwar economic recovery, which featured higher tariffs and lower taxes, stalled in Congress as a consequence of his reluctance to press these issues more aggressively. In the absence of presidential direction, Congress became bogged down if not paralyzed by its own disagreements over what to do. Although Harding chided Congress for its inaction, he would not "engage Congress in a bitter and protracted struggle" on these matters (Milkis and Nelson 1994, 258).

Harding had called for "triumphant nationality" during his campaign, and his new administration moved quickly to initiate what amounted to an "America first" policy approach. Once in office, Harding made it clear that the United States would not join a "super government" such as the League of Nations. The postwar labor strikes, many in industries "with large numbers of 'hyphenated Americans,' racial conflicts in the cities, and the equation of political radicalism during the Red Scare intensified the drive to shut out all foreigners" (Parrish 1992, 111). In response to this growing anti-immigrant sentiment, the Republican Congress in 1921 enacted the Emergency Immigration Act, which established stringent immigration quotas. The Emergency Tariff Act of 1921, the protectionist Fordney-McCumber Tariff Act of 1922, and the refusal to grant debt relief also "reflected the prevailing nationalistic anti-European sentiment" (Goldberg 1999, 50).

Harding assigned the problem of rising unemployment to Secretary of Commerce Hoover. Secretary Hoover convinced Harding to convene a conference on unemployment. Hoover's solution was to call for the business sector to stabilize employment and have local governments undertake public-works projects. Consistent with the predispositions of President Harding, Hoover did not propose an expanded role for the federal government.

Of all the pressure groups that operated on the Harding administration, those representing business enjoyed the most support. Other groups, such as labor, farmers, and veterans, scored "occasional victories," but as nearly as a "leaderless administration could be said to have had a policy, the policy of the Harding administration was to do with alacrity whatever business wanted to have done" (Hicks 1960, 50). Business demanded only a "few fundamentals from government, but these were important and it demanded them with great insistence" (50). Business wanted "economy and efficiency in government," which would enhance the prospect of its "other great goal of lowering taxes, particularly on business incomes" (50). Business advocated a free-enterprise system that was free of governmental restrictions on the ability of business "to do exactly as it pleased" (50). Finally, business wanted government help "in the disciplining of labor, the growing power of which it feared and meant to curb" (50).

Congress demonstrated its responsiveness to the pressure from the business sector. Among the first laws it enacted following Harding's inauguration was the Budget and Accounting Act, which was signed by the president on 10 June 1921. The trouble with the budgeting process in place prior to the act was that it "made no provision for an adequate over-all study of proposed expenditures and receipts" (Hicks 1960, 51). Rather, Congress tended to make independent appropriations decisions, "trusting that somehow what came in and what went out would balance" (51). The act of 1921 provided for a director of the budget who should advise the president in the preparation of an annual budget, and a comptroller general who would audit all accounts to ensure that expenditures were made in accordance with the law (51). The Budget Act required an annual, comprehensive executive budget, assigning to the president the responsibility to "estimate both the government's financial needs and the revenues it expected to collect during the coming fiscal year." The Budget Act gave the president "legal authority to influence the allocation of expenditures [from] the executive branch" (Milkis and Nelson 1994, 261–262).

The Budget Act that Harding signed was virtually the same one that Wilson had vetoed. When Harding submitted his first budget proposal to Congress in December 1921, it represented a "program of economy." The budget that Harding recommended for 1922–1923 called for appropriations of $3.5 billion. This lean budget recommendation was certainly welcomed by the business community, but greatly displeased the veterans' lobby, among others, which demanded "adjusted compensation for all servicemen"—the so-called Soldiers' Bonus (Hicks 1960, 52). As the mid-term elections of 1922 approached, a petition campaign was begun asking Congress to embrace the veterans' demands on the "Bonus" bill issue. Congress passed a law providing veterans with a paid-up twenty-year insurance policy based on length of military service.

The proposal was vetoed by the president. By "holding the line as long as they did against the 'Bonus,'" Harding and congressional Republicans won the "undying gratitude of the business community, which hoped almost above all else to translate economies in government to lower taxes" (52).

Secretary of Treasury Andrew W. Mellon was a dependable advocate for business interests. One of Mellon's first initiatives was to press Congress for comprehensive tax relief to American businesses. The reduction of taxation for the country's most wealthy was a "matter of principle with Mellon, and not merely self-interest" (Hicks 1960, 53). He vigorously opposed taxes that would inhibit entrepreneurial initiatives. He saw such taxes as penalizing "wealth in the making." His was the classic "trickle down" argument—if the "wealth producers" were only left alone, they would "create more jobs for more people, and add to the country's prosperity" (53). Despite opposition from the remaining congressional progressives and the representatives of agricultural states, the so-called Farm Bloc, Mellon got a substantial tax reduction for the rich.

The business community did not get all the tax reductions it desired, however, due at least in part to the emergence of the Farm Bloc, a group of House and Senate members representing agricultural states. The Farm Bloc wanted greater tariff protection for agricultural commodities, but it also pressed for the Futures Trading Act designed to "restrict speculation in wheat on the grain exchanges," and the Packers and Stockyards Act, which reinforced the regulatory power of the Federal Trade Commission by giving the Department of Agriculture "substantial powers over the inspection and control of the meat-packing industries" (Hicks 1960, 54–55).

To no one's surprise, members of such regulatory commissions as the Federal Trade Commission (FTC) and Federal Power Commission (FPC) became much more conservative. According to Michael Parrish, Harding, his successor Calvin Coolidge, and their appointees "chloroformed the remnants of the progressive movement" (Parrish 1992, 52). Because government could not itself "create wealth, but only drain it from the private, wealth-producing sector," it was the Harding/Coolidge view that "government should remain small and frugal" (52). The national government, Coolidge said, "should avoid military conflict and promote American trade abroad" while at the same time "encouraging economic expansion at home through policies that allowed businessmen to earn a profit" (52). It was not the role of government to "impose unnecessary regulatory burdens on capital or interfere with the bargains struck by employers, workers, and consumers in the free market" (54).

The FPC was established in 1920 primarily for the purpose of regulating electric power producers. It was composed of the secretaries of war, agriculture, and interior, and it "succumbed immediately to the administration's point of view" (Hicks 1960, 65–66). The conservative fiscal policies of President Coolidge, Treasury Secretary Mellon, and Budget Director Herbert M. Lord "eviscerated other regulatory agencies not subject to direct capture by probusiness appointees" (Parrish 1992, 54). Their philosophy of "balanced budgets and tax reductions" severely diminished regulatory activities by the federal government. For example, "fewer investigators for the Department of Agriculture's meat inspection service and the Food and Drug Administration" (54). "Ruminating on the wreckage of the regulatory system," Senator George Norris wrote that the effect of the Harding-Coolidge appointments was "to set the country back more than twenty-five years" (Hicks 1960, 66).

The economic distress of the early 1920s was particularly acute for labor. Between 1916 and 1919, unions used labor shortages caused by the war to make substantial wage gains. Between 1920 and 1922, business used the high unemployment rate to its advantage. Most major industries, for example, imposed severe wage cuts during 1921. Labor was "pounded into submission" during 1921 and retrenched accordingly. When the economy began to rebound the following year, however, a new round of strikes began. Unlike the job actions of 1919, these strikes were "defensive" in character—seeking to avoid "take backs" of previous gains—and they generally involved skilled workers rather than industrial unions. In the end, the interests of capital "emerged fully triumphant over labor" (Goldberg 1999, 73).

The decisive role of the federal government in union work stoppages was most evident in the strike referred to as the Great Railroad Strike of 1922, the most extensive labor action to hit the nation's railroads since the 1890s. Dismayed by the government's return of the railroads to private ownership, the unions had "hoped for equitable treatment from the Railway Labor Board, established by the 1920 Esch-Cummins Transportation Act" (Goldberg 1999, 75). Instead, the board approved a series of wage cuts and new work rules, among other provisions. The conflict reached the boiling point on 1 July 1922 when more than 400,000 railroad workers walked off their jobs. The situation was aggravated by a strike in the coal industry. The simultaneous work stoppages threatened prospects for economic recovery. After all efforts at agreement had failed, Attorney General Daugherty asked federal judge James Wilkerson of Chicago, a Harding appointee, to grant an injunction against the strikers. In one of the most sweeping injunctions ever written, Wilkerson forbade the officers of unions from "picketing or in any manner by letters, circulars, telephone messages, word of mouth, or interviews encouraging any person to leave the employ of a railroad" (Hicks 1960, 72). The railroad union had little choice but to comply with the terms of the restraining order. It was clear enough from the Wilkerson injunction that "during industrial disputes the government would neither assist labor nor remain neutral; rather, it would throw its influence firmly on the employer's side" (72).

The coal strike began three years earlier than the railroad strike when mine operators refused to renew the existing wage agreement and instead called for substantial wage reductions. As the strike dragged on for months, violence became inevitable. President Harding had chosen not to intervene in the dispute until the violence began, at which point he felt obliged to act. The situation was exacerbated by diminishing reserves of coal, which reached dangerously low levels. The conflict was finally resolved by arbitration, essentially under the terms that existed at the outset of the miners' walkout. As part of the settlement, Congress created a Coal Commission composed of seven persons of Harding's choosing. The report of the commission was not entirely satisfactory to mine operators, but "offended the unions by failing to recommend the checkoff and complete unionization" (Hicks 1960, 71). More importantly, the report was "ignored" by Congress, which had "created the Commission only in support of the agreement to return to work, and after that was accomplished had lost interest in the subject" (71). For the remainder of the decade, the plight of coal miners "tended to become worse rather than better" (71). Among the results was that the United Mine Workers "declined steadily in membership and influence" (71).

In foreign affairs, the Republican Party position was fundamentally isolationist. The approach Harding and Secretary of State Hughes took to foreign policy "spurned internationalism in the Wilsonian sense of full-fledged membership in the League of Nations or support for collective security. But neither did it endorse isolationism" (Parrish 1992, 15). Despite the strength of isolationist feelings, real isolation was impossible, and Hughes was able to function effectively with this reality. He directed the Washington Conference in late 1921 and early 1922, which produced, among other things, the Five-Power Treaty. This agreement froze the naval strength of the United States, Britain, Japan, Italy, and France at "immediate postwar levels." To some extent, the Five-Power Treaty resembled the provisions of the Kellogg-Briand Pact of 1928 that attempted to actually outlaw war. Both agreements reflected an almost naive approach to foreign policy and the agreements themselves "contained many loopholes" (14). At the same time, the Five-Power Treaty "marked the first time in modern history that great nations agreed to curb their military arsenals" (14). Isolationism was also impossible in terms of international economics, and the Republicans responded with policies designed to safeguard American business and industry such as the steeply protective Fordney-McCumber Tariff of 1922.

The Scandals

Harding's performance as president was modest from the outset and deteriorated from there. Rumors circulated about Harding's philandering and about the "flow of liquor at the White House" notwithstanding prohibition (Goldberg 1999, 59). By his third year in office, it was evident that even beyond Harding's own inability to provide effective leadership, some of those he placed in positions of responsibility were corrupt. Indeed, the level of corruption exceeded that of any administration since civil service reforms were enacted in the early 1880s. Harding became ill while returning from an Alaskan junket and died of a stroke in San Francisco on 2 August 1923. Thus he was spared from knowing the full extent of the corruption in his administration.

Congressional investigations of the Harding administration revealed rampant misconduct. Much of the wrongdoing was the result of Harding loading his administration with political cronies, otherwise known as the "Ohio Gang." At the point Harding began his administration, *The Nation* suggested that it was the "most material, the most sightless Administration ever to begin rule in America" (Goldberg 1999, 49). The observation was primarily based on some of Harding's suspect Cabinet choices. One such Cabinet choice was Harry Daugherty. Daugherty was Harding's political mentor and was completely unqualified to head the Justice Department. Daugherty's personal secretary was Jess Smith, whose services as a "fixer and lobbyist were known among insiders to be for sale" (Hicks 1960, 74). Fearful that investigation would reveal that he had received kickbacks from German bankers and other misconduct, Smith committed suicide in Daugherty's apartment. It was later uncovered that Smith had used his association with Daugherty to "arrange favorable deals for gamblers and bootleggers" (Goldberg 1999, 59). Smith was also involved with Thomas W. Miller, Harding's Alien Property Custodian, who was later convicted of bribery in the return of property to foreign owners—Smith received "fees" for expediting disposition of the various claims. Smith's suicide gave the public and media the first indication of scandalous misconduct in the administration.

Another of Harding's appointees, Charles R. Forbes, headed the Veteran's Bureau. It was discovered that Forbes and his second in command, Charles F. Cramer, had defrauded the government of "fantastic sums," in the neighborhood of $200 million. Forbes was imprisoned for his actions while Cramer, like Smith, chose suicide (Hicks 1960, 74).

The worst scandalous revelation was that government oil lands, held for naval needs, had been transferred in a series of maneuvers to a group of private speculators. Interior Secretary Albert Fall persuaded Harding to transfer the naval oil reserve lands from the Navy Department to his department. Transfer of these lands to Fall's control allowed him to lease the Teapot Dome (Wyoming) and Elk Hills (California) reserves to petroleum magnates Harry F. Sinclair and Edward Doheny in exchange for nearly $400,000. Fall's corruption might have gone undiscovered but for the extensive improvements Fall made to his "badly run down" New Mexico ranch, the payment of back taxes on the ranch, and Fall's acquisition of additional property in the area. A Senate investigation conducted by Senator Thomas J. Walsh of Montana brought many of the facts to light and prompted Fall's forced resignation. Fall was convicted of bribery in 1929 and became the first American Cabinet member imprisoned for a felony committed in office. Suits to annul the leases were carried to the Supreme Court, which adjudged the defendants in the Teapot Dome case to be guilty of "collusion and conspiracy," and in the Elk Hills case to be guilty of "fraud and corruption." Not only were the leases canceled, but the leaseholders were required to make complete restitution for their illegal use of government property (Hicks 1960, 76–77). Judged by any standard, the Harding administration was badly tainted with corruption. However, given the "abysmally low ethical standards" of the businessmen who took part in the oil-lease deals, the shenanigans were "seemingly accepted with little resentment, both by the juries that refused to convict them and by the public at large" (77). Rather, the "obvious inference that similar but undisclosed transactions were probably a commonplace of big business," John Hicks suggested, "worried only the liberal journalists and other professional worriers. For the average American all this was taken for granted as just another aspect of normalcy" (77–78). Hicks overstates perhaps, but his conclusion provides perspective on the scandals.

Calvin Coolidge

The Republicans fared badly in the mid-term elections of 1922. The GOP lost seven seats in the Senate and seventy seats in the House. The House losses were particularly damaging because a pro-Harding majority was replaced by a majority differing with Harding on such issues as taxation and increased federal spending for veterans and agriculture. Although neither Harding's performance nor his agenda, limited as it was, were singularly responsible for the election losses, Harding felt compelled to undertake a lengthy trip to "mend his political fences and gain new momentum for the next two years" (Parrish 1992, 27). After maintaining a speech-a-day pace for two weeks, Harding suffered a heart attack while traveling from Alaska to San Francisco. He died in San Francisco three days later.

Calvin Coolidge succeeded to the presidency on 3 August 1923. He was thought by some to be an "unlikely heir to the increasingly public presidency" (Milkis and Nelson 1994, 265). His "public persona was ordinary" at a time when more seemed to be required of a president (265). Nonetheless, "in spite of his limitations, or perhaps in part because of them, Coolidge was one of the most popular presidents in history" (265). Like Harding, he was not an assertive president. When it came to interaction with Congress or exerting his preferences in shaping public policy, Coolidge "felt even less responsibility to act than had Harding" (265). Indeed, his restraint in relations with Congress reflected his "general disdain for programmatic initiatives" (265–266).

In other words, he "out-Hardinged" Harding when it came to demonstrating leadership from the Oval Office. Nonetheless, Coolidge was able to establish a positive connection with the American people. His popularity was based in part on his commitment to corporate America, but he also personified Republican values of the time. Coolidge was also able to present himself effectively to the public by adeptly using the media, particularly the new medium of radio.

Coolidge and Harding had similar views on the role of government, the presidency, and the need to promote the interests of business. On a personal level, the two could not have been more different. Coolidge was plain and aloof, and he would not have been an attractive presidential prospect under most circumstances. Unlike Harding, however, he "made fetish of honesty and propriety" (Hicks 1960, 81). As the corruption of the Harding administration was about to be revealed, the Republicans needed someone completely free of taint. Coolidge was a person of unquestioned integrity.

Most Americans prospered during the five and a half years Coolidge was president. The principal reason for the economic prosperity was an increase in industrial productivity. The most noteworthy examples were in production of electric power and durable consumer goods, and in the construction of suburban housing and skyscrapers in the large metropolitan areas. The prosperity of the time seemed to suggest that the future might be best served by letting private enterprise operate free of government regulation. It was a time that argued against the divisiveness represented by labor unions and political radicalism.

However, certain groups within the population, such as coal miners, textile workers, small farmers, and racial minorities, remained in poverty. Faced with a deepening agricultural crisis, congressional representatives from rural states grouped themselves into the Farm Bloc, also known as the Progressive Bloc. At the initiative of these lawmakers, Congress enacted farm relief laws such the McNary-Haugen Act. McNary-Haugen contained a complex scheme providing for government purchase and sale abroad of surplus farm commodities. Predictably, Coolidge vetoed McNary-Haugen. The most vocal dissenters in the Coolidge era were two widely divergent groups. On the one hand, there were the religious fundamentalists who advocated laws such as the Tennessee anti-evolution statute. On the other were the literary intellectuals who had been alienated by postwar repression and intolerance and who were put off by the materialism and conformity of the Coolidge era. These groups combined with the agrarian discontent to produce a short-term revival of progressivism. The 1922 mid-term election revealed the extent of agrarian discontent in the Midwest particularly, and progressive hopes for the 1924 presidential election were bolstered as the American Federation of Labor (AFL) expressed its displeasure with the antilabor stance of the Harding administration. Organized labor, dissatisfied with the probusiness orientation of the courts, was joined by women's rights activists following the Supreme Court's decision in *Adkins v. Children's Hospital* (1923). In *Adkins*, the Court used a property rights approach to strike down a minimum wage law for women employees. Groups such as organized labor and women's organizations shared the view that business interests possessed extensive if not full control over the Harding administration. In addition to Harding Treasury Secretary Andrew Mellon's uncompromising pursuit of tax cuts for businesses and the most wealthy, Harding's four appointees to the Supreme Court all demonstrated a commitment to the business agenda.

The 1924 Presidential Election: The Democratic Divide and the Progressive Demise

The Republicans were fortunate to have President Calvin Coolidge as their standard-bearer in 1924. A referendum on Harding's performance might have proven problematic for the GOP. Many thought the Harding scandals and possibility of a progressive resurgence foreshadowed an end to Republican government. The Republicans renominated Coolidge and ran on a platform aimed at retaining the status quo. The 1924 election took place during an economic boom period. Because most voters are said to "vote their pocketbooks," incumbents usually benefit from prosperity. By the time of the election, Coolidge had removed those involved in the Harding scandals, and he replaced Attorney General Daugherty with the highly respected Harlan Fiske Stone. Coolidge was also the appropriate choice for a party anxious to demonstrate its faith in American business.

The Democrats had insurmountable problems. The party was deeply divided along agrarian-urban lines, which led to a deadlocked convention. Religion was also a significant factor at the Democratic convention. The party condemned bigotry in its platform, but failed to condemn the antiblack, anti-Catholic, anti-Semitic Ku Klux Klan by name. The Democrats' disarray doomed whatever chance they had at regaining the White House. The Democrats did not choose their party's nominee, John W. Davis of West Virginia, until the 103rd ballot at the nominating convention. Davis was Wilson's attorney general, but an economic conservative and head of a prominent Wall Street law firm.

The Democrats' choice of Davis to run against the big-business candidacy of Coolidge prompted progressives to think that a third-party candidacy might succeed in 1924. Senator Robert La Follette of Wisconsin was the obvious choice. A long-term foe of monopolies and outspoken critic of concentrated wealth, La Follette possessed the appropriate progressive credentials. He saw control of government and industry by private monopoly as the greatest issue facing America and used this theme throughout his 1924 campaign. The Republicans largely ignored Davis and the Democrats and expended most of their energy denouncing La Follette and his supporters as political extremists.

The 1924 election was a bitter disappointment for the Progressives. The La Follette campaign suffered from a lack of organization and a lack of money. The Republicans, on the other hand, had more money than they could reasonably spend on the campaign. The Coolidge campaign focused on the dangers posed by La Follette and the progressives. Despite the initial interest prompted by the La Follette candidacy, less than half of the country's eligible voters voted. Of those who did, 54 percent chose Coolidge, with Davis (28.8 percent) and La Follette (16.6 percent) splitting the remainder.

The 1924 election result can be interpreted in various ways. It marked the last election in which a presidential candidate attempted to run on the monopoly issue; the issue no longer appealed to enough prospective voters. It also marked the end of progressivism as a major political movement and exposed the weaknesses of the political left and of organized labor. The 1924 election affirmed that a new era in American politics had fully arrived—one in which business was ascendant. Coolidge had observed that "the business of America is business" and his name became associated with prosperity. These factors led to the Coolidge landslide, and the result seemed a green light for business prosperity and its political friends.

A number of observers were of the view that the United States had entered an era of labor-management peace following the election. The industrial surge that began in 1923 provided a level of job security for factory employees, and a low inflation rate removed one of labor's rallying points. Reinforcing the notion that the United States had entered a new era, American industrial productivity far surpassed that of international competitors, and the United States could assert that its standard of living was higher than in any other country. Labor activists struggled to understand how the sentiment and energy that had served as the basis for numerous strikes had seemingly evaporated. The Great Depression of the next decade would confirm the vulnerability of the American economy, which, in turn, would revitalize the labor movement.

The issue of immigration remained a major difficulty throughout the 1920s. Following the passage of the Emergency Immigration Act of 1921 (also known as the Quota Bill), Congressman Albert Johnson and other nativists in Congress sought to find ways to further reduce immigration from southern and eastern Europe. With the endorsement of Coolidge, the Johnson-Reed Immigration Act of 1924 effectively ended the chance of many hopeful immigrants to enter the United States. Many thought that the severe restrictions would be loosened once the country emerged from its postwar hysterics about immigrants, but such would not be the case.

Herbert Hoover and the Great Depression

On 2 August 1927, President Coolidge announced to the press that he would not be a candidate for reelection the following year. More accurately, Coolidge gave to each member of the gathered press corps a piece of paper that simply said, "I do not choose to run for president in 1928." Coolidge affirmed his decision several days later, never again to discuss the matter. A number of possible explanations for his decision were advanced, but the most plausible seemed to be those that focused on personal rather than political reasons. Despite his popularity, Coolidge never seemed to enjoy being president. Because he had never offered a broad range of policy goals, he did not have compelling unfinished business to prompt him to seek another term.

Coolidge's withdrawal from the race triggered some scurrying within the Republican Party, but the obvious choice was Herbert Hoover, secretary of commerce in both the Harding and Coolidge administrations. Hoover's first public service came as he directed the nation's rationing program during World War I. Hoover's identification with the Wilson administration and his support of the League of Nations troubled Republican isolationists. Republican progressives thought of him as one of the big business types while the hard-line conservatives did not embrace him as one of their own. Nonetheless, Hoover possessed a remarkable record of accomplishment in both the business and political worlds and was clearly the candidate with the best chance of holding the White House for the Republicans. He was opposed in the 1928 election by four-term New York governor Al Smith.

Hoover was an attractive candidate because his entire adult life was a story of remarkable achievement. The war and Hoover's involvement in Europe played an important role in shaping his ideas. He believed European governments had gotten too fond of state socialism, and he opposed development of governmental bureaucracies that resembled the West European model. Harding had given Hoover full discretion in shaping American economic policy starting in 1921. He performed with effectiveness and imagination in his role as commerce secretary. He was instrumental in convincing the steel industry to move away from twelve-hour workdays to three eight-hour shifts. He was involved in developing the Railway Labor Act of 1926 that recognized collective bargaining rights for unions and established mediation procedures for resolving labor disputes. He encouraged the growth of trade associations and his Department of Commerce was organized to facilitate the growth of foreign markets. He also chaired a special committee whose charge was to deliver relief to victims of the Mississippi River flood in 1927, a role that affirmed the humanitarian reputation he had earned during World War I.

Once the nomination was secured, Hoover immediately became the overwhelming favorite to defeat any Democratic nominee. The Democrats were in terrible disarray. They chose Smith, a contender for the nomination in 1924, as their presidential nominee and Arkansas senator Joe Robinson as his running mate. Some Democratic partisans were unenthusiastic about Smith, particularly those from the South. Smith's campaign failed to appeal to constituencies that might have enabled him to compete with Hoover. Smith abandoned standard Democratic campaign themes and instead sought to dispel fears that he was the enemy of business. He chose not take on either the corporate tax cuts proposed by Treasury Secretary Mellon or Republican tariff policies. In addition, he failed to feature such "natural" issues as farm relief and government-owned power. Smith's campaign strategy created something of a vacuum. The failure to define the campaign in socioeconomic terms allowed Prohibition and Smith's Catholicism to take center stage. Without socioeconomic issues, the campaign became a contest of stereotypes and prejudices.

The Republicans rolled to a decisive triumph in the election. The prosperity enjoyed by most Americans all but guaranteed Hoover's election. The Democrats carried only states in the Deep South. Although Smith did not benefit, the 1928 election marked the beginning of a shift in the fortunes of the Democratic Party. The Democrats made gains in many of the urban areas and among recent immigrants and ethnic minorities because of a stated commitment to the economically disadvantaged. The Democratic coalition that began to form in 1928 achieved full electoral strength with the onset of the Great Depression. The economic conditions that put Hoover in the White House changed so dramatically by 1932 that his reelection was as improbable as Smith's election was in 1928.

Herbert Hoover assumed office under auspices more favorable than those that had attended any other president since Taft. All that ended with the stock market crash in October 1929. The Great Depression exposed weaknesses in the business system that were not widely perceived during the 1920s. Farmers and workers lacked the purchasing power to buy the goods produced by American industry. Management success in stemming the growth of unions meant that wages did not change even though productivity increased sharply. In addition, Europe did not bounce back economically as quickly as expected after the war, which limited that market as an outlet for American goods. The 1930s were thus dramatically different from the 1920s. As a sign of the shift in emphasis from social to economic issues, those opposed to Prohibition gained its repeal in 1933 by arguing that opening up distilleries and breweries would create jobs. In foreign as well as in domestic affairs, the 1920s provided "only a respite for a nation and a world that was slow to recover from [World War I]" (Goldberg 1999, 183).

The economic collapse was devastating in scope. Industrial production dropped by 50 percent, and the gross national product fell by more than 30 percent by 1932. A sizable portion of the workforce was unemployed and many more lived in abject poverty. The congressional elections in 1930 reflected the widespread disillusionment with Hoover's performance. Hoover was not the "do-nothing" president that the Democrats portrayed him to be in the 1932 election. However, Hoover was willing to go only so far with governmental intervention. Rather, Hoover put his faith in traditional and largely voluntary approaches to addressing the country's needs. His unalterable commitment to preserving nineteenth-century American political practices and principles "even in the face of national calamity served only to discredit them" (Milkis and Nelson 1994, 273). In this way, Hoover "unwittingly laid the groundwork for a fundamental break with the politics and policies of the past" (273). Franklin Roosevelt would be elected in 1932, and in the first months of his presidency, Congress would enact much of his New Deal recovery program. The Taft Court would have no role in reviewing the New Deal measures. Rather, the Supreme Court headed by Hoover nominee Charles Evans Hughes would scrutinize the New Deal initiatives. The jurisprudence of the Taft Court, however, would shape the Hughes Court's response to both constitutional and statutory issues for almost a decade after Chief Justice Taft left the Court.

Assembling the Taft Court

Formation of the Taft Court began in the late 1890s. President William McKinley had only one opportunity to nominate a Supreme Court justice in his four and one-half years as president. Part of the reason was that the two presidents who preceded him, Grover Cleveland and Benjamin Harrison, had faced an unusually high number of vacancies and together appointed eight members of the Court between 1887 and 1896. McKinley's single appointee was Joseph McKenna, a close friend and fellow member of Congress. It was widely speculated that McKenna would be nominated at the first opportunity and it was expected that Justice Stephen J. Field would provide that vacancy. Field had served on the Court for thirty-four years, and many thought he would retire at the outset of McKinley's presidency. Field did not retire until a year later, and in the interim, McKenna served as McKinley's attorney general. When Field actually retired, McKenna was nominated on 16 December 1897, taking his seat on the Court the following February. Like Field, McKenna was a Californian and had enthusiastically supported such McKinley priorities as higher protective tariffs. In addition, McKenna was Roman Catholic and McKinley thought this nomination would allay the belief that McKinley was anti-Catholic. The Senate vote on McKenna's nomination was delayed several weeks because of the opposition of antitrust and antirailroad interests, allegations by attorneys that McKenna's lower federal court record was mediocre at best, and by religious bigotry. Opposition notwithstanding, McKenna was confirmed without a formal roll call vote on 21 January 1898, five weeks after his nomination (Abraham 1999, 115–116).

Theodore Roosevelt succeeded to the presidency on the assassination of William McKinley in September 1901. Roosevelt was determined to fill any vacancies on the conservative Fuller Court with individuals who shared his progressive political values, particularly the desire to support trustbusting. In addition to shared political priorities, Roosevelt sought professionally competent lawyers who also exhibited good character. Roosevelt appointed three justices to the Court, two of whom remained on the Court into the Taft era, Oliver Wendell Holmes Jr. and William R. Day.

President McKinley was aware of Justice Horace Gray's deteriorating health and considered Alfred Hemenway of Massachusetts as a replacement for Gray. McKinley was assassinated before Gray left the Court, however, and McKinley's successor, Theodore Roosevelt sought his own nominee. Among those on Roosevelt's short list was Oliver Wendell Holmes Jr. He was from the same state as Gray and had a most distinguished record as a member of the Massachusetts Supreme Judicial Court. Nonetheless, Roosevelt was not immediately convinced to nominate Holmes. There could be no doubt about Holmes's legal or intellectual qualifications. Roosevelt was concerned about Holmes's "real politics"—his political values. Roosevelt sought the counsel of Massachusetts senator Henry Cabot Lodge, who provided the necessary reassurance. Lodge reported to Roosevelt that Holmes was a "constructive statesman," a "broad-minded constitutionalist," and a man blessed with "broad humanity of feeling" (Abraham 1999, 119). Holmes also "seemed right" on issues of race and antitrust. On the strength of Lodge's recommendation, Roosevelt sent Holmes's name to the Senate on 2 December 1902, and Holmes was unanimously confirmed two days later (119). Although Roosevelt was disappointed with Holmes's early record in antitrust cases, Holmes reflected very well on his nominator with thirty years of distinguished service on the Court.

Roosevelt did not fare so well with his next choice, William Rufus Day of Ohio. Justice George Shiras Jr. indicated to Roosevelt that he planned to retire in early 1903. William Howard Taft was Roosevelt's first choice, but as much as Taft wanted to sit on the Court, he chose not to leave his position as governor of the Philippines. Taft's refusal led Roosevelt to seek the advice of such prominent Republican leaders as Mark Hanna and Elihu Root as well as Taft. Hanna had worked with Day in the McKinley administration when Day had served as assistant secretary of state and then secretary of state. Taft had served with Day on the U.S. Court of Appeals for the Sixth Circuit. All three supported Day's nomination. Day possessed solid Republican credentials and had worked extensively on Benjamin Harrison's presidential campaigns in 1888 and 1892. Furthermore, Day was one of President McKinley's closest political advisers. Roosevelt had an opportunity to assess Day's "real politics" for himself when Roosevelt served as assistant secretary of the navy during McKinley's first term. Although denied an opportunity to nominate Taft, Roosevelt was more than satisfied with Day. Day was confirmed by voice vote in the Senate on 23 February 1903, four days after his nomination. Roosevelt also nominated his attorney general, William H. Moody, to the Court in 1906, but Moody's service on the Court lasted less than four years.

In his single term as president, William H. Taft had an opportunity to substantially remake the Court—he appointed six justices, two of whom remained on the

Court during Taft's tenure as chief justice. Taft chose his nominees with little care for their partisan affiliation—three of his six appointees were Democrats, although all three were conservative Southern Democrats. The Taft appointees were all men of integrity, personally known to Taft, and, with the exception of Charles Evans Hughes, all had previous judicial experience. Most important to Taft, however, were the political values of those he would nominate. In the words of Henry Abraham, Taft "wanted no liberals of the stamp of Learned Hand, Louis Brandeis or Benjamin Cardozo," candidates Taft regarded as "destroyers of the Constitution" (Abraham 1999, 125). Rather, he sought ideological conservatives who would protect property rights and minimize regulatory initiatives of both the federal and state governments.

In late March 1910 Justice David J. Brewer died and provided Taft with the opportunity to make what Henry Abraham characterized as his "most important" appointment—Charles Evans Hughes of New York. Hughes was a possible Republican presidential candidate, and Taft doubted that Hughes would accept the nomination. Taft tried to sweeten the offer by indicating that Hughes would be considered for promotion to chief justice when the position became vacant. Whether the possibility of the chief justiceship was decisive or not, Hughes accepted his appointment to the Court. Taft equivocated just two months after Hughes's confirmation when Chief Justice Melville Fuller died. Many, including Hughes, expected that Taft would elevate Hughes to the chief justiceship, but when the nomination was not immediately forthcoming, it was evident that Taft was looking elsewhere for a new chief justice. Taft instructed Attorney General George Wickersham to solicit the views of the Court's members. Their preference was Associate Justice Edward Douglass White. Taft knew that White was an able administrator and expression of support for White from his fellow justices weighed considerably. White's political orientation was also compatible with Taft's. Perhaps Taft's most important consideration, however, was his own "all-consuming ambition to attain the chief justiceship." When Taft considered Hughes's age (five years Taft's junior) and good health, he decided not to nominate Hughes for the position he wanted so much for himself. He nominated the more senior White instead. As it turned out, both Taft and Hughes would serve as chief justice with Taft succeeding White in 1921 and Hughes succeeding Taft in 1930 (Abraham 1999, 128).

White's promotion created a vacancy for an associate justice. Taft selected Willis Van Devanter of Wyoming, at the time a judge on the Court of Appeals for the Eighth Circuit. Van Devanter earned a reputation as something of a progressive during his service in the U.S. Department of the Interior, where he was an attorney specializing in public lands and Indian affairs issues. This had been a substantial factor in Roosevelt appointing him to the court of appeals. Van Devanter served almost twenty-seven years on the Court, including the entirety of Taft's tenure as chief justice. Although more conservative than Taft, Van Devanter was Taft's most important

Court colleague. Van Devanter is perhaps most often remembered as one of the "Four Horsemen," a group of four extremely conservative justices who opposed virtually all of Franklin Roosevelt's New Deal initiatives when they came before the Hughes Court for review. As valuable as Van Devanter was to Taft in facilitating conference discussion, he wrote a lower proportion of majority opinions than any other Taft Court justice. During Taft's chief justiceship, Van Devanter wrote fewer than 100 (6 percent) of the Taft Court's majority opinions.

Taft's fifth appointment was Joseph Lamar, who replaced William Henry Moody. Like Moody, Lamar's tenure was short (1911–1916). Taft's sixth and last Court nominee was Mahlon Pitney, who replaced the first John Marshall Harlan in 1912. Taft began his search for Moody's replacement by considering court of appeals judge William Hook of Kansas, a person under consideration for the vacancy created by White's promotion two years earlier. Taft also thought about Charles Nagel of Missouri, his secretary of commerce and labor. With New Jersey becoming a key state in the forthcoming contest between Taft and Theodore Roosevelt for the Republican presidential nomination in 1912, Taft chose Pitney, a New Jersey state judge. Pitney was an attractive candidate beyond any political boost he might give Taft. He had extensive judicial experience and was a former legislator at both the state and federal levels. Pitney's judicial record reflected his support of most regulatory initiatives. Liberals and organized labor were skeptical, however, and they orchestrated a campaign against his confirmation. The effort only delayed the vote, and the Senate ultimately confirmed Pitney by a vote of fifty to twenty-six. Pitney served an undistinguished decade on the Court and became leader of the Court's antilabor faction. Taft would eventually say of his own nominee that he was a "weak member" of the Court to whom he could "not assign cases" (Mason 1964, 213).

Taft nominated six justices during his four-year term as president, while his successor, Woodrow Wilson, nominated only three justices during his eight-year presidency. One of those nominations went to Louis Brandeis, another to John Hessin Clarke, and another to James McReynolds. Like Roosevelt and Taft, Wilson was concerned with the political values of prospective justices. Wilson sought progressive thinkers who, among other things, had a commitment to breaking up monopolies. Wilson favored individuals he knew personally and did not value previous judicial experience to the same degree as either Roosevelt or Taft—neither McReynolds nor Brandeis had any judicial experience, and Clarke had only two years service on the federal district court.

Horace Lurton died in 1914 during his fifth year on the Court. Wilson immediately nominated James Clark McReynolds, who was Wilson's attorney general at the time. A native Tennessean, McReynolds graduated from the University of Virginia Law School. He gained national prominence as an assistant attorney general in the Theodore Roosevelt administration by leading the Justice Department case against the tobacco industry. McReynolds actively supported Wilson's presidential campaign in 1912 and was named attorney general when Wilson took office. Wilson may have had some doubts about McReynolds's political values at the point of the Court nomination, but McReynolds's incapacity to deal civilly with others made him something of a political liability to Wilson; the McReynolds nomination looked very much like the proverbial "kick upstairs." McReynolds was confirmed by the Senate on a forty-four-to-six vote on 29 August 1914. McReynolds served on the Court for almost three decades. His bigoted and abrasive manner was evident throughout as was his ultra-conservative jurisprudence. He was one of the "Four Horsemen" who steadfastly opposed Franklin Roosevelt's New Deal program as a member of the Hughes Court. He was the reactionary anchor of the Taft Court.

Wilson offset the McReynolds nomination with the selection of Louis Dembitz Brandeis, who is generally recognized as one of the Court's great justices. His greatness was not a certainty when Wilson nominated Brandeis on 28 January 1916, and the confirmation battle that followed the nomination was one of the most intensely contested in the Court's history. Wilson's selection of the so-called people's lawyer triggered significant opposition, especially from the business community. In Henry Abraham's words, Brandeis was "no enemy of capitalism, free enterprise, or profits," and while he consistently supported efforts to regulate corporate trusts, he never wrote an opinion in favor of the government in an antitrust case. At the same time, Brandeis was "acutely conscious of maldistribution of power, reward and opportunity, and he dedicated his life to a rectification of that condition" (Abraham 1999, 136).

Brandeis worked on Wilson's presidential campaign in 1912 and was instrumental in developing the Wilson platform positions on domestic policy. Brandeis subsequently became a political adviser and close friend of Wilson. It was Wilson's intention to offer Brandeis the attorney generalship, but he decided against it when substantial opposition developed. When Wilson subsequently considered Brandeis for nomination to the Court, he proceeded with caution, recognizing that a Court nomination would likely prompt similar opposition. When the Brandeis nomination was announced in January 1916 the opposition Wilson had feared materialized. The opposition focused on Brandeis's social activism and his sociological jurisprudence, but anti-Semitism was a factor as well. Among those opposing the nomination were members of the organized bar, such as its president Elihu Root, former Attorney General George Wickersham, and William Howard Taft. There were Brandeis supporters as well, including Harvard Law School faculty member Felix Frankfurter and several of his colleagues, journalist and commentator Walter Lippmann, president of the AFL Samuel Gompers, and a number of publications including the *New Republic* (Abraham 1999, 136).

The confirmation process was particularly acrimonious. Through it all Brandeis kept his silence. On 1 June 1916, more than four months after his nomination, Brandeis was confirmed in a highly partisan vote of forty-seven to twenty-two. All but three of the votes for Brandeis came from Democrats, and only one of forty-five Democrats in the Senate voted against his confirmation. Two of the three Republicans supporting Brandeis were the notable progressives, Robert La Follette of Wisconsin and George Norris of Nebraska. Twenty-seven senators, including William Borah of Idaho, had enough misgivings about Brandeis to abstain on the confirmation vote (Abraham 1999, 137).

Associate Justice Charles Evans Hughes resigned from the Court to run for the presidency shortly after the Brandeis confirmation vote. The Hughes vacancy gave Wilson his last opportunity to name someone to the Court, which he used to nominate John Hessin Clarke of Ohio. Clarke was serving as a U.S. district court judge at the time of his nomination and had established a liberal progressive record both before and after taking the bench. Once satisfied that Clarke "could be depended upon for a liberal and enlightened interpretation of the law" (Abraham 1999, 138), Wilson sent his name to the Senate on 14 July 1916. Wilson's nomination of Clarke, so closely following Brandeis, "thrilled the Left and infuriated conservatives" (Clements 1992, 80). Nonetheless, the Senate unanimously confirmed Clarke ten days later, despite non–Senate member William Howard Taft's opposition.

Clarke served on the Court for only six years. Wilson expected that Clarke would join Justices Holmes and Brandeis, and this expectation was largely fulfilled. Clarke's record was progressive—for example, he was the only justice to support the child labor tax law before the Court in *Bailey v. Drexel Furniture Co.* (1922). He was a civil libertarian, but was not as supportive as either Holmes or Brandeis of the free speech claims arising out of World War I. He fully met his judicial responsibilities while on the Court, but he was generally unhappy as a justice. He resigned in 1922, saying he wished to devote his life to the cause of world peace, but Henry Abraham suggests that he had grown "increasingly disillusioned" by the Court's rulings. In addition, he became "unwilling to ignore and unable to cope" with the abrasive personality of Justice McReynolds (Abraham 1999, 138). Clarke's resignation from the Court created the opportunity for President Harding to nominate George Sutherland, who would personify the diametrically opposite political and judicial outlook from that of Clarke.

Harding's victory in the 1920 presidential election enabled him to nominate four men for the Supreme Court during his brief tenure as president. Each met Harding's qualifying criteria—political conservatism, a probusiness orientation, and experience in public life. These criteria were not entirely Harding's, but were suggested to him by Taft. Of the four Harding nominees, William Howard Taft and George Sutherland served with distinction. The other two, Edward T. Sanford and Pierce Butler, fell far short.

Taft exercised great influence over Harding, particularly on judicial appointments. He decisively influenced his own selection and, once confirmed in 1921, Taft was thereafter Harding's principal adviser on matters relating to the Court. Taft was not only able to succeed in getting those he preferred nominated by Harding, but was also able to keep potential nominees with whom he disagreed from being chosen. Taft was determined to keep any prospective candidate who might join Holmes and Brandeis and side with that "dangerous twosome" from being nominated. He fully supported the nominations of Sutherland and Butler and found Sanford an adequate addition to the Court. He was satisfied that the three Harding nominees besides himself were "sound economic conservatives with proved antagonism toward contemporary liberal progressive elements" (Abraham 1999, 140).

Taft intensified his pursuit of the chief justiceship from the moment Harding won the presidency. Taft might have been satisfied with a nomination for an associate justiceship earlier in his life, but by 1920 only the chief justiceship would suffice. Indeed, he directed those working on his behalf to "dispel any notions Harding might have of appointing him to an associate justiceship," and he communicated directly with Harding emphasizing that his interest "lay solely in the post of Chief Justice" (Abraham 1999, 140). Chief Justice White, who had suffered poor health for some time, was able to remain on the Court until Harding was inaugurated, which enabled Harding (rather than Wilson) to nominate his replacement. White died near the end of the 1920 term of the Court (19 May 1921) and Taft was nominated on 20 June 1921. He was confirmed the same day by voice vote of the Senate.

On 4 September 1922, Justice John Hessin Clarke resigned from the Court. The next day President Harding nominated his friend and political adviser George Sutherland to fill the vacancy. A former senator, Sutherland was unanimously confirmed by the Senate on the same day the nomination was received. Seldom in history had a prospective nominee been such an obvious choice. Not only was Sutherland a personal friend of the president, he also received endorsements from a number of influential Republicans, including an enthusiastic endorsement from Chief Justice Taft. Sutherland became the "intellectual-philosophical leader of the Four Horsemen" and proved himself a worthy successor of the Field-Brewer-Peckham wing of the Fuller Court era" (Abraham 1999, 142). During the Hughes Court era of the 1930s Sutherland became the "scourge of the New Deal, heading a majority that struck down more than a dozen pieces of domestic legislation fundamental to the New Deal" (142).

Harding's third nominee was Pierce Butler of Minnesota. The vacancy arose when Justice William Rufus Day retired from the Court on 13 November 1922. A field of three prospective candidates emerged—New York governor Nathan Miller, John W. Davis, and Butler. Davis, Taft's preference, and Miller both withdrew from consideration for financial reasons. That left Butler, a conservative Democrat and Taft's second choice. Taft suggested to Harding that the Court had become "too Republican" in composition and that the next nominee ought to be a conservative Democrat. Butler had become wealthy by serving as counsel for several western and midwestern railroads.

The Taft Court in 1921 (left to right front row): William Rufus Day, Joseph McKenna, William Howard Taft, Oliver Wendell Holmes Jr., and Willis Van Devanter; (left to right back row): Louis Dembitz Brandeis, Mahlon Pitney, James C. McReynolds, and John Hessin Clarke (Clinedinst, Collection of the Supreme Court of the United States)

He was politically active, but typically out of the public eye. He was, in Henry Abraham's words, "sternly moralistic and inflexible and although he had a sense of humor and could be a convivial companion, he was neither charming nor tolerant" (Abraham 1999, 143). Butler gained national notoriety while a member of the Board of Regents of the University of Minnesota, where he urged the dismissal of all "unpatriotic," "pro-German," and otherwise "radical" faculty (Danelski 1964, 118–119). Taft did not see Butler's actions as a liability and vigorously endorsed Butler's nomination. Beyond Butler's ultraconservatism and party affiliation, Harding also found Butler's religion, Roman Catholicism, to be a constituency asset. Butler's candidacy encountered resistance in the Senate, especially from progressives such as Robert La Follette and George Norris. They were particularly troubled by Butler's inflexible probusiness orientation and the intolerance he displayed while a University of Minnesota regent. Attorney General George Wickersham orchestrated a strategy during the Senate Judiciary Committee hearings that overwhelmed the opposition and eventually led to Butler's confirmation. The final vote, delayed for almost a month, confirmed Butler by a sixty-one-to-eight margin, but the margin concealed the level of doubt that existed in the Senate; twenty-seven senators abstained.

The fears of those who opposed the Butler nomination were on the mark. In Henry Abraham's words, his record during seventeen years on the Court "was wholly and unswervingly in the Darwin-Spencer mold." He was "consistently intolerant" of First Amendment claims and his "reactionary reading of the Constitution was second only to that of McReynolds." Rated as a "distinct failure" by most Court observers, the "aggressive, domineering and stubborn Butler hardly merits a kinder treatment than that historical evaluation has accorded him" (Abraham 1999, 144).

Harding's final opportunity to nominate a Supreme Court justice resulted from the retirement of Justice Mahlon Pitney in late 1922. Harding considered Henry Anderson of Virginia; William Marshall Bullitt, his former solicitor general; and Charles M. Hough of the Second Circuit Court of Appeals. Each seemed to have political downsides, however, that ultimately prompted Attorney General Harry Daugherty to suggest Judge Edward T. Sanford of the U.S. District Court for the Eastern District of Tennessee. Sanford was not Taft's first choice, but Taft supported the selection largely on the basis of Sanford's extensive federal judicial experience. Sanford was also conservative enough to satisfy those involved in the selection process. Sanford was nominated on 24 January 1923 and was easily confirmed by voice vote in the Senate several days later. Sanford served only seven years on the Court and made no distinctive impact. He was typically found voting with the Four Horsemen on most issues. He died 8 March 1930, the same day that Chief Justice Taft died.

The last justice to join the Taft Court was Harlan Fiske Stone. He was nominated by President Calvin Coolidge on 25 January 1925. Stone was an academic when he came to Washington in 1924. He was summoned by his Amherst classmate Calvin Coolidge, who was attempting to deal with the aftermath of the oil-lease scandals that occurred late in Harding's administration. Coolidge wanted to remove Attorney General Daugherty, whose Justice Department had failed miserably in dealing with the Harding scandals and replace him with someone of undoubted integrity. Stone not only served Coolidge's reelection effort in 1924, but was effective in restoring the image of the Daugherty–tarnished Justice Department. When Justice Joseph McKenna left the Court in 1925, Stone was the obvious choice to replace him.

The nomination was met with "all-but-universal approbation" although some opposition developed among the progressives in the Senate, particularly Senator Burton Wheeler of Montana (Abraham 1999, 147). Prior to the confirmation vote, the Senate recommitted the nomination to the Judiciary Committee. Stone made a personal appearance before the committee—the first Court nominee ever to do so. Stone effectively responded to the questions of committee members and the committee unanimously recommended his confirmation. He was confirmed on 5 February 1925 by a vote of seventy-one to six.

The Taft Court in 1925 (left to right front row): James C. McReynolds, Oliver Wendell Holmes Jr., William Howard Taft, Willis Van Devanter, and Louis Dembitz Brandeis; (left to right back row): Edward T. Sanford, George Sutherland, Pierce Butler, and Harlan Fiske Stone (Towles, Collection of the Supreme Court of the United States)

Stone seemed a safe choice for Coolidge. He had been a corporate attorney in his private practice prior to becoming dean of the Columbia Law School. In other words, he had solid Republican credentials. Once on the Court, Stone did not perform quite as Coolidge anticipated or wished. Stone was expected to closely follow the lead of Chief Justice Taft. By his second year, however, he had begun to "slide away from Taft's shadow," and often attempted to distance himself from the conservative Four Horsemen (Johnson 1994, 426). Taft Court dissent rates were low, but Stone's dissent rate over the last three years of Taft's chief justiceship ranked behind only the dissent rates of Holmes and Brandeis (Goldman 1991, 100). Stone aligned himself with Justices Brandeis and Cardozo on the Hughes Court typically in support of New Deal initiatives. Stone was in the minority on the ultraconservative Hughes Court until the doctrinal revolution that occurred in 1937 created a more liberal majority that included Stone. During the 1935–1936 terms of the Hughes Court, the period just preceding the advent of the Roosevelt Court, Stone supported government regulation of the economy in 97.7 percent of cases. Only Cardozo's support rate of 97.9 percent was higher, with Brandeis a close third at 95.8 percent. By comparison, the so-called Four Horsemen voted in support of economic regulation in less than one case in four—Van Devanter (25.5 percent), Sutherland (20.8 percent), Butler (12.5 percent), and McReynolds (10.4 percent) (Goldman 1991, 101).

Taft as Chief Justice

Chief Justice White once suggested that a chief justice can influence the performance of the Supreme Court by making administration an "exercise in maintaining power and perpetuating influence" (White 1976, 204). Taft was unusually skilled at the internal management of his Court. A second way a chief justice can lead is by facilitating "scholarly exchange" among colleagues. Taft was able to lead in this way, although Justice Van Devanter assisted in this function. Finally, a chief justice can lead through the utilization of political influence. Taft was extraordinarily well connected politically and was an especially effective political leader. In each of these areas the twentieth-century chief justice was "better suited to exert influence than any of his colleagues. He stood for and could shape his Court" (204). Taft greatly preferred his judicial role over those in elective office. Ironically, without the experiences Taft gained during his years in electoral politics, he may not have been able to perform as ably as chief justice. Taft aggressively sought the chief justiceship because, in his view, that was the only position that could serve as a fitting conclusion to his public life.

Taft was the second of three consecutive strong chief justices, serving between White and Hughes. Taft brought to the chief justiceship executive experience that no previous chief justice possessed. Taft's performance was also affected by the Court's rapidly expanding caseload. The Court's caseload had increased so extensively that administrative demands on the chief justice became critically important. Beyond the Supreme Court's caseload, Taft believed that the entire federal judiciary needed reorganization. His concern for improving the operations of the federal judiciary developed during his time as a federal appellate judge. Congress had created courts of appeal in 1891 as an intermediate appellate court positioned between the federal trial courts and the Supreme Court. In addition, Congress gave the Supreme Court discretionary jurisdiction—authority to select at least some of the cases it would review. By the time Taft became chief justice, the certiorari power had become the Court's principal means of keeping abreast of its work. At the same time, administrative skill in the hands of the chief justice was still essential for the Court to function effectively (White 1976, 202).

Edward Douglass White's chief justiceship immediately preceded Taft's and revealed the increasing importance of administrative leadership by the chief justice. Charles Evans Hughes, who would succeed Taft as chief justice, was an associate justice during the first six years of White's chief justiceship. During this period Hughes learned from White the importance of sound Court management. One clear lesson was that a "well-organized chief justice could not only manage his docket but increase his power in the process" (White 1976, 203). Taft was an effective advocate for additional reforms to the federal judicial process. He was largely responsible for writing the Judiciary Act (Judges' Bill) of 1925 and securing its passage by Congress. The Act not only continued the reorganization of the federal courts, but also expanded the Court's certiorari authority. During Taft's tenure as chief justice, each justice was assigned a law clerk to facilitate review of certiorari petitions and generally to assist with legal research and the drafting of opinions.

Taft insisted that his Court stay current with its caseload and he tried to facilitate achievement of consensus in the Court's decisions. Indeed, he was preoccupied with "massing" his Court—leading it to unanimous rulings as often as possible. In G. Edward White's view, Taft's performance as chief justice demonstrated how "twentieth-century chief justices could exercise or fail to exercise leadership." The most important manner in which leadership could be exercised was "through administration of the Court's internal business" (White 1976, 203). It was certainly Taft's legal background and personality that allowed him to function effectively as chief justice, and the executive experience made him a distinctive chief justice.

References and Further Reading

Abraham, Henry J. 1999. *Justices, Presidents, and Senators: A History of the U.S. Supreme Court Appointments from Washington to Clinton.* Rev. ed. Lanham, MD: Rowman and Littlefield.

Braeman, John, Robert H. Bremner, and David Brody, eds. 1968. *Change and Continuity in Twentieth-Century America: The 1920s.* Columbus, OH: Ohio State University Press.

Clements, Kendrick A. 1992. *The Presidency of Woodrow Wilson.* Lawrence, KS: University Press of Kansas.

Danelski, David J. 1964. *A Supreme Court Justice Is Appointed.* New York: Random House.

Fausold, Martin L. 1985. *The Presidency of Herbert C. Hoover.* Lawrence, KS: University Press of Kansas.

Ferrell, Robert H. 1998. *The Presidency of Calvin Coolidge.* Lawrence, KS: University Press of Kansas.

Goldberg, David J. 1999. *Discontented America: The United States in the 1920s.* Baltimore, MD: Johns Hopkins University Press.

Goldman, Sheldon. 1991. *Constitutional Law: Cases and Essays.* 2d ed. New York: HarperCollins.

Hicks, John D. 1960. *Republican Ascendancy: 1921–1933.* New York: Harper and Row.

Johnson, John W. 1994. "Harlan Fiske Stone." In *The Supreme Court Justices: A Biographical Dictionary.* Melvin I. Urofsky, ed. New York: Garland Publishing.

Mason, Alpheus T. 1964. *William Howard Taft: Chief Justice.* New York: Simon and Schuster.

Milkis, Sidney M., and Michael Nelson. 1994. *The American Presidency: Origins and Development, 1776–1993.* 2d ed. Washington, DC: Congressional Quarterly Press.

Morison, Samuel Eliot, Henry Steele Commager, and William E. Leuchtenburg. 1980. *The Growth of the American Republic.* Vol. 2. New York: Oxford University Press.

Noggle, Burl. 1962. *Teapot Dome: Oil and Politics in the 1920s.* Baton Rouge, LA: Louisiana State University Press.

Parrish, Michael E. 1992. *Anxious Decades: America in Prosperity and Depression, 1920–1941.* New York: W. W. Norton.

Schlesinger, Arthur M., Jr. 1957. *The Crisis of the Old Order, 1919–1933.* Boston, MA: Houghton Mifflin.

Soule, George. 1947. *Prosperity Decade: From War to Depression, 1917–1929.* New York: Rinehart.

Swindler, William F. 1974. *Court and Constitution in the Twentieth Century: The Old Legality, 1889–1932.* Indianapolis, IN: Bobbs-Merrill.

Trani, Eugene P., and David L. Wilson. 1977. *The Presidency of Warren G. Harding.* Lawrence, KS: Regents Press of Kansas.

White, G. Edward. 1976. *The American Judicial Tradition: Profiles of Leading American Judges.* Oxford, UK: Oxford University Press.

2

The Justices

Thirteen justices nominated by six different presidents served on the Taft Court. Justice Joseph McKenna was the senior justice at the time William Howard Taft became chief justice. McKenna, appointed in 1898, was President William McKinley's only Supreme Court nominee. In 1925, after sitting during the first four terms of the Taft Court period, McKenna retired from the Court. President Theodore Roosevelt placed three justices on the Court, two of whom served on the Taft Court—Justice Oliver Wendell Holmes Jr. and William R. Day. Holmes was one of five justices to serve through the entire nine terms of the Taft Court period, while Day served for only the first term of the Taft Court era. Taft was president from 1909 to 1913, and is the only person to serve both as president and as a Supreme Court justice. During his tenure as president, Taft nominated six justices for the Court, two of whom, Willis Van Devanter and Mahlon Pitney, subsequently served during his chief justiceship. Van Devanter served for all nine Taft Court terms, while Pitney sat for only the 1921 Term and the start of the 1922 Term.

President Woodrow Wilson nominated three justices to the Court, all of whom served for at least a part of the Taft Court era. Justices James C. McReynolds and Louis D. Brandeis served for all nine terms, and Justice John H. Clarke served for only the first Taft Court term. President Warren G. Harding appointed four Taft Court justices, including Taft himself. Taft, of course, sat for the full period. Justices George Sutherland and Pierce Butler were both nominated in 1922 and sat for all but the first term of the Taft Court era. Harding's fourth nominee was Edward T. Sanford, who joined the Court in early 1923 and sat for the duration of the Taft Court period. The last justice to join the Taft Court was Justice Harlan Fiske Stone, who would later become chief justice. Stone was the only nominee of President Calvin Coolidge, and he sat for the last five terms of the Taft Court.

Table 2.1 summarily represents some basic information on the thirteen Taft Court justices—their birth dates, dates of appointment, age at the time of appointment, age span during the Taft Court, the nominating president, and the justice whom they succeeded.

Table 2.1 Taft Court Justices

	Birth Year	App't Year	App't Pres.	App't Age	Age Span Taft Court	Replaced
BRANDEIS	1856	1916	Wilson	59	65–74	Lamar
BUTLER	1866	1923	Harding	37	37–44	Day
CLARKE	1857	1916	Wilson	59	64–65	Hughes
DAY	1849	1903	T. Roos.	54	72–73	Shiras
HOLMES	1841	1902	T. Roos.	61	80–89	Gray
McKENNA	1843	1898	McKinley	55	78–82	Field
McREYNOLDS	1862	1914	Wilson	52	59–68	Lurton
PITNEY	1858	1912	Taft	54	63–66	Harlan
SANFORD	1865	1923	Harding	58	58–65	Pitney
STONE	1872	1925	Coolidge	53	53–58	McKenna
SUTHERLAND	1862	1922	Harding	60	60–68	Clarke
TAFT	1857	1921	Harding	64	64–73	White
VAN DEVANTER	1859	1910	Taft	51	62–71	White

The William McKinley Appointment

Joseph McKenna (1843–1927)

President William McKinley had only one opportunity to nominate someone to the Supreme Court. His choice was Joseph McKenna of California. McKenna was born in Philadelphia, Pennsylvania, on 10 August 1843. He moved to California with his family in 1855. McKenna was admitted to the California Bar in 1865, but practiced law for only a brief time—he was much more interested in a pursuing a political career. Beginning in 1866 until his appointment to the U.S. Court of Appeals bench in 1892, McKenna served as Solano County district attorney, California state legislator, and as a member of the U.S. House of Representatives from 1885 to 1892.

During his four terms in the U.S. House, McKenna was able to gain the support of such influential Republicans as Leland Stanford and William McKinley. A staunch Republican, McKenna basically followed the party line during his tenure in Congress and was instrumental in establishing high protective tariffs and, with the exception of the Interstate Commerce Act, forestalling virtually all forms of railroad regulation. McKenna was able to secure congressional appropriations for projects in his district, including federal funding for improving the port facilities of San Francisco and appropriation of federal money to Stanford's Central Pacific Railroad for military transportation. Stanford subsequently recommended McKenna to President Benjamin Harrison to fill a vacancy on the Ninth Circuit Court of Appeals in 1892. After his elec-

Joseph McKenna (Harris and Ewing, Collection of the Supreme Court of the United States)

tion in 1896, President McKinley made McKenna his attorney general. Less than a year later, McKinley nominated him to the Supreme Court to fill the vacancy created by the departure of Justice Stephen Field.

Opposition to McKenna's nomination was immediate and loud, but in the end had little effect. His critics pointed to his extensive connections with the railroad industry, his limited educational credentials, his Roman Catholicism, the short duration of his time in legal practice, and what some thought was a less-than-distinguished record on the court of appeals bench. His nomination was called "weak" by several newspapers, and a number of federal judges from the northwest wrote to Chief Justice Melville Fuller to "protest McKenna's unfitness" for the Supreme Court (C. Cushman 1993, 284). Although most of these criticisms were politically motivated, they were credible nonetheless. Notwithstanding the criticisms, McKenna had sufficient support in the Senate to be confirmed by voice vote on 21 January 1898. Aware of his own limitations, McKenna attended courses at Columbia Law School for several months before assuming his seat on the Court in an effort to sharpen his legal skills.

McKenna served on the Court for almost twenty-seven years, during which time he wrote 659 opinions. He served for almost four years of the Taft Court period. He was a member of the Taft Court for 699 (43.31 percent) of its decisions and wrote eighty-five opinions during that time: sixty-seven majority opinions and eighteen dissents. Richard Hamm suggests that his tenure broke into three distinct periods: an "early period" during which he was learning his new role; a "middle period" during which he was an "important (though somewhat erratic)" member of the Court; and a "late period" during which failing physical abilities limited his effectiveness. His career, especially his middle period, essentially showed him as a "politician dressed in judicial robes" (Hamm 1994b, 289).

McKenna was a substandard lawyer when compared with other justices at the time of their appointments to the Supreme Court. His limited practice of law probably accounts for his lack of a coherent legal philosophy at the time he began his judicial career, and despite his long tenure on the Supreme Court, he never developed a philosophical foundation for his work. The absence of a guiding philosophy was manifest in the "inconsisten[cy of] his decisions and reasoning," and the "tentativeness" of his opinions, which were "weighed down with heavy loads of precedent and irrelevant case law," especially at the outset of his tenure on the Court (Hamm 1994b, 289).

As is often the case with justices who come to the Court without a well-developed judicial philosophy, McKenna located himself near the center of the conservative Fuller Court. Although some exceptions or "inconsistencies" are evident in his record, he was generally deferential to legislative policy preferences and tended to support federal regulation of business and industry. He saw the Sherman Anti-Trust Act, for example, as a permissible exercise of federal commerce power and he wrote the Court's majority opinion in several early antitrust cases.

McKenna seemed to adapt his to his role as a Supreme Court justice after several years of service. His opinions became more confident and clear, characteristics not evident during his early years on the Court. His opinions in *Hipolite Egg Co. v. United States* (1911) and *Hoke v. United States* (1913) are illustrative. The Pure Food and Drug Act prohibited the use of interstate commerce to transport impure foods and drugs into the states. McKenna wrote in *Hipolite* that the question before the Court was whether articles that are "outlaws of commerce" are outside the jurisdiction of the national government "when they are within the borders of a state." To give such immunity "would defeat . . . the provision for their confiscation" (*Hipolite*, 58). The Mann Act prohibited the transportation of women across state lines for the purpose of "prostitution and debauchery." In *Hoke*, McKenna rejected the contention that women are outside the reach of the commerce power because they are not "articles of merchandise." He acknowledged that women have rights, but "their rights cannot fortify or sanction their wrongs." If they employ interstate transportation as a "facility of their wrongs, it may be forbidden to them" (*Hoke*, 323). Both opinions strongly support the use of the federal commerce power to promote the general welfare.

Some of McKenna's opinions focused on practical application of federal law. McKenna wrote the majority opinion for the Court in *United States v. United States Steel Corp.* (1920) in which he said that the Sherman Act did not prohibit the "mere existence" of the power to achieve monopoly status in a particular industry. He suggested that corporate behavior was presumed reasonable in the absence of an overtly monopolistic action. McKenna also joined Justices Brandeis, Holmes, and Clarke in a dissent in *Hammer v. Dagenhart* (1918), which featured a vigorous criticism of the doctrine of dual federalism. McKenna supported extending federal regulatory power to child labor. It was his view that if a statute was a "proper exercise" of the commerce power, it was "immaterial how it affected the persons or the property within the States" (McDevitt 1974, 159). McKenna was convinced that the commerce power was "sufficiently broad to prevent evils occurring before, as well as after, interstate transportation" (159).

McKenna's occasional lack of consistency can be seen in cases involving state and federal liberty-of-contract cases. He was in the majority in *Lochner v. New York* (1905), a ruling that struck down a state law establishing maximum hours of work for bakers on substantive due process grounds. Just three years later he was part of a unanimous majority in *Muller v. Oregon* (1908), which upheld a state limit on the hours for women industrial workers. In *Bunting v. Oregon* (1917) McKenna's majority opinion sustained a state law limiting work days to ten hours. In *Adkins v. Children's Hospital* (1923), however, he joined the majority in striking down federal minimum wage legislation for women, returning to the position he took in the *Lochner* case eighteen years earlier.

McKenna voted with the "liberal bloc" of Holmes, Brandeis, and John Clarke on occasion. McKenna was unwilling, however, to apply the Bill of Rights in the same way Holmes and Brandeis did, believing instead that its provisions had only narrow application. This view was evident from McKenna's votes in the First Amendment cases that grew out of attempts to limit expression during World War I. In such cases as *Schenck v. United States* (1919), *Abrams v. United States* (1919), and *Gilbert v. Minnesota* (1920), McKenna joined the majority in upholding both federal and state restrictions on expression. In times of emergency such as wartime, he felt that restrictions on speech and press were "justifiable and necessary for the protection of public safety and welfare" (McDevitt 1974, 178).

Overall, McKenna's performance on the Court was better than his critics had predicted at the time of his confirmation. He served at a time when the Court made some significant rulings, but few of his opinions endured. During the Taft Court years, McKenna's mental acuity began to deteriorate. He failed to recognize the effects aging had on his mind, and he stayed on the Court beyond the time he could function effectively. His colleagues, realizing as early as 1922 that he often missed the central issues in the Court's cases, agreed among themselves to postpone decisions in those cases in which McKenna's vote would be decisive. Finally, after considerable urging from Chief Justice Taft, McKenna retired from the bench on 25 January 1925 and died two years later in Washington.

The Theodore Roosevelt Appointments

Oliver Wendell Holmes Jr. (1841–1935)

Two of President Theodore Roosevelt's appointees to the Court served on the Taft Court. His first nominee was Oliver Wendell Holmes Jr., who is universally regarded as one of the greatest justices ever to serve on the Court. Roosevelt nominated Holmes on 2 December 1902, and he was confirmed by voice vote two days later. He served on the Court for almost thirty years, retiring on 12 January 1932. During his tenure on the Court, he wrote 873 opinions—more than any other justice. Holmes sat for the entire Taft Court period and participated in 99.69 percent (1,609) of the cases decided with opinions between 1921–1930. Holmes wrote the opinion of the Court in 215 Taft Court decisions (13.32 percent), wrote or joined concurring opinions in 14 cases, and dissents in 68 (4.21 percent) cases.

Holmes was born in Boston, Massachusetts, in 1841. He attended Harvard as an undergraduate, where he became an outspoken abolitionist. He attended Harvard Law School following two years of military service during the Civil War. Holmes was admitted to the bar in 1867 and began a private practice in Boston. During this time, Holmes began writing extensively on the common law. He presented his work as part

Oliver Wendell Holmes Jr. (Harris and Ewing, Collection of the Supreme Court of the United States)

of the Lowell Institute's lecture series in late 1880 and eventually published his lectures as a book entitled *The Common Law*. The book was a critical success in both legal and academic circles, which prompted his appointment to the Harvard law faculty and to the Massachusetts Supreme Judicial Court in 1882. He sat on the Massachusetts court for about twenty years, the last three as chief justice. In September 1902 a vacancy occurred on the U.S. Supreme Court when Justice Horace Gray died. Although Holmes was highly regarded as a legal scholar and jurist, President Theodore Roosevelt was not certain that Holmes was sufficiently committed to the progressive agenda. Those supporting Holmes's nomination allayed Roosevelt's uncertainties and he nominated Holmes in December 1902.

Holmes is often described as a progressive and civil libertarian, although that was not evident during his first fifteen years on the Court. Indeed, in the view of G. Edward White, the "principal attributes of his later images—that he was an enlightened judge in his deference to progressive legislation and that he was a supporter of civil liberties—are hard to square with the thrust of his decisions" (White 1994, 226). In some of his early opinions, including *Lochner v. New York* (1905), Holmes expressed the view that judges should not second-guess the policy judgment of legislators, at least on matters involving economic policy. It would have been premature to label Holmes a progressive during this early period, however. Similarly, "his early decisions on civil liberties were equally inconsistent with a later stereotype of Holmes as a liberal" (227). White suggests that the progressive and civil libertarian labels are derived from Holmes's later years on the Court—the postwar period through the end of the Taft Court period. He consistently rejected substantive due process, an approach used by conservative majorities to limit the reach of state regulation of property. One explanation for the apparent contradiction between Holmes's image and his early decisions is to suggest that his judicial stance changed with time; that he became more "liberal" as he aged (228). White points to evidence suggesting that Holmes's more "progressive" friends had a direct impact on the way he conceptualized speech issues in the last years of his tenure. Notwithstanding his free speech opinions, Holmes's jurisprudence remained largely unchanged during his career on the Court. The perception of Holmes as a progressive and a liberal does not generalize across all issues. Even Holmes's libertarian posture on speech, which emerged late in his career, rests more on selected sentences in his opinions than on a comprehensive jurisprudential theory (229).

Two groups of Holmes's opinions require closer examination. The first group is composed of opinions in cases that review such social policy initiatives as the regulation of wages and hours of work for women and children (e.g., *Adkins v. Children's Hospital*) or compulsory sterilization for mentally retarded persons (*Buck v. Bell*). This group of cases reflects Holmes's opposition to substantive due process—judicial review of the reasonableness of legislative actions. In cases such as *Adkins*, Holmes effectively rebutted the "liberty of contract" doctrine and supported state regulatory power. Holmes began with a presumption that legislatures, as both "majoritarian and positivist institutions, could do what they wanted: the scope of judge-created constitutional review was narrow" (White 1994, 230).

The second group of opinions come from First Amendment cases, in which Holmes typically defended unpopular speakers and the arguments they brought to the marketplace of ideas. These were perhaps the most important and controversial of Holmes's opinions. When the federal government prosecuted thousands of people for resisting mobilization for World War I, Holmes vigorously disagreed with criminal prosecution that targeted political beliefs rather than actual conduct. He was "contemptuous of Socialism, but he hardly felt threatened by it, or by any other isms that some of his acquaintances believed were fouling the air in 1919" (Baker 1991, 519). Holmes saw free speech protection in utilitarian terms. There was "nothing necessarily good about speech as such; what was good was the fight among competing ideas" (Strum 1984, 317). Holmes also saw the free speech protection as conditional rather than absolute. For example, he acknowledged in *Schenck v. United States* (1919) that Congress had the power to forbid political expression that interfered with the military draft. The "clear and present danger" standard Holmes articulated in *Schenck* was subsequently modified by the Court, prompting Holmes to object strongly to the use of the test to support successful prosecutions of political dissidents. Beginning with *Abrams v. United States* (1919), Holmes dissented in virtually all free speech cases that involved convictions for so-called dangerous expression. In Holmes's view, expressions of opinion must be given nearly absolute immunity from prosecution. Only speech uttered for the deliberate purpose of doing harm and having a clear and present danger of succeeding could be criminalized. On balance, Holmes's free speech opinions were not so much evidence of a progressive sensibility as they were evidence of the "unique complex of values, which composed his judicial posture" (White 1994, 233). Holmes was interested in "exploring the philosophical foundations of legal issues and identifying his philosophical stance toward those issues" (233). He was less interested in "doctrinal or analytical consistency, and his philosophical views, rendered in terms of the political ideologies of his day, did not easily mark him as a progressive, a liberal, or a conservative" (233).

Holmes believed that the U.S. Supreme Court possessed only limited jurisdiction and that the Court should usually defer to legislative judgments. He believed that English common law principles were embodied in the general terms of the Constitution. This view, in turn, provided the basis for his belief that the Constitution was continually evolving. The Constitution's provisions "are not mathematical formulas," but are "organic living institutions transplanted from English soil." Their significance is to be "gathered not simply by taking the words and a dictionary, but considering their origin and the line of their growth" (*Gompers v. United States* 1914, 610). He strenuously objected to governmental actions that, among other things, encroached on personal privacy or people's political ideas, however radical or unorthodox. In any case in which individual rights were involved, the decisive issue for Holmes was the procedural fairness of the government's action. He would allow government interests to prevail over individual rights, but only if procedural due process of law was fully observed.

Often called the "great dissenter," Holmes wrote proportionately fewer dissents than many justices. His dissenting opinions were particularly forceful, however, and often embraced in later decisions.

William Rufus Day (1849–1923}

The second of Roosevelt's Taft Court nominees was William Rufus Day. He was nominated to the Court on 19 February 1903, a little more than two months after the Holmes nomination. He was confirmed by voice vote in the Senate four days later. Day left the Court in November 1922 after almost twenty years of service. During his tenure on the Court, Day wrote 430 majority opinions and 22 dissents. His service on the Taft Court was less than a year, and he participated in only 171 (10.59 percent) of the Taft Court cases in which an opinion was issued. He wrote 15 majority opinions during the 1921 Term, accounting for 8.77 percent of the majority opinions that term, and 0.93 percent of the total Taft Court majority opinions.

Day was born in Ravenna, Ohio, on 17 April 1849. It was no surprise that he pursued a career in law, as both his father and grandfather were attorneys and served on the Ohio Supreme Court. After studying law at the University of Michigan, Day began a practice in Canton, Ohio, in 1872. He lived in Canton for twenty-five years and became increasingly involved in Ohio Republican politics. It was during this period that Day developed a close friendship with William McKinley, who would become the country's twenty-fifth president. After McKinley's election as president, Day agreed to serve as assistant secretary of state under John Sherman. Sherman proved to be wholly ineffective as secretary of state, however, and much of the burden of the office fell to Day. The outbreak of the Spanish-American War in April 1898 prompted Sherman's forced resignation and the naming of Day as his replacement. The war was of short duration, and Day resigned the position at the war's conclusion. Day led the American delegation that went to Paris to negotiate the accord that formally ended the war. Included in the treaty was American acquisition of the Philippine Islands, Puerto Rico, and Guam.

Day returned from Paris with every intention of resuming his legal practice, but instead accepted McKinley's appointment to the U.S. Court of Appeals for the Sixth Circuit where he joined, among others, William H. Taft and Horace H. Lurton, both of whom later sat on the U.S. Supreme Court. Day "thoroughly enjoyed" his four years

William Rufus Day (Harris and Ewing, Collection of the Supreme Court of the United States)

on the Sixth Circuit Court and "felt comfortable in the presence" of both these colleagues on that bench (Watts 1995, 893).

President McKinley was shot on 5 September 1901 and died several days later. A year after McKinley's death, Justice George Shiras Jr. left the Court and Theodore Roosevelt, who had succeeded McKinley, first offered the position to Taft, then governor of the newly acquired Philippine Islands. When Taft declined, Day was nominated to fill the vacancy.

Historian Richard Hamm has characterized Day's record on the Supreme Court as that of a "liberal formalist." Day generally favored government action with respect to regulation of the economy, but "at the core of Day's constitutional philosophy was the concept of dual sovereignty, especially as expressed in the Tenth Amendment" (Hamm 1994a, 139). Day believed that both the federal and state governments could extensively regulate the economy, but the sphere of federal authority was substantially more limited; the federal government did not possess police power similar to that of the states. The interstate commerce power, however, enabled some federal regulation of the economy. In Hamm's words, Day "never countenanced the unlimited growth of the commerce power, and was unwilling to expand it beyond its late nineteenth century bounds" (Hamm 1994b, 139). Day supported federal legislation that regulated those specifically engaged in interstate trade, so such federal statutes as the Interstate Commerce Act and the Sherman Anti-Trust Act were constitutionally acceptable to him. Day saw the federal commerce power sufficient to ban certain harmful products, such as impure food or drugs from interstate transport. Similarly, he voted in *Hoke v. United States* (1913) to uphold the federal Mann Act, which banned the transport of women across state lines for prostitution.

Day viewed federal commerce power as limited. Implicit was the belief that "commerce does not comprehend production in any of its forms." Instead, "the production of articles intended for interstate commerce is a matter of local regulation" (McLean 1946, 76). Day accepted the production-commerce distinction developed by Chief Justice Melville Fuller in *United States v. E.C. Knight Co.* (1895). Day's literal acceptance of this principle emerged in a number of cases. In *Delaware, Lackawanna & Western Railroad Co. v. Yurkonis* (1915), for example, Day argued that even if products were made for the singular purpose of interstate shipment, their manufacture or production could not be reached under the commerce power before the goods actually crossed any state lines.

Day's views on the federal commerce power and dual federalism often came together, as in the Court's decision to strike down the Keating-Owen Child Labor Act of 1916. The law outlawed the interstate shipment of products made by child labor. This congressional initiative attempted to utilize the commerce power to regulate the practice of child labor. Day wrote the opinion of the Court in *Hammer v. Dagenhart* (1918), a sharply divided five-to-four ruling that invalidated the law. Day's opinion reflected his narrow view of the federal commerce power. He drew heavily on the *E.C. Knight Co.* opinion, which distinguished acts of commerce from acts of manufacturing. Under this doctrine, interstate commerce did not begin until items actually crossed state lines. Regulation of any aspect of production, including conditions of labor, was exclusively reserved for the states. The Child Labor Act did not regulate interstate commerce as such, but instead was to regulate the age when minors could be employed in manufacturing. As Day argued that the Tenth Amendment limited the extent to which the federal government could regulate the economy, he actually added the word "expressly" to the Tenth Amendment in an apparent attempt to create a more substantial hurdle for federal regulatory initiatives.

Day was not among those justices of this period who engaged in substantive due process review of state economic regulations. Instead, he generally deferred to the use of the state police power. He voted, for example, to uphold a maximum hours of work statute in *Lochner v. New York* (1905), the establishment of more stringent mine safety regulations in *McLean v. Arkansas* (1909), and a prohibition on yellow-dog labor contracts in *Coppage v. Kansas* (1915). His dissents in *Lochner* and *Coppage* revealed his belief that state promotion of public welfare could override individual claims of liberty of contract and the right to work—concepts at the center of substantive due process. Consistent with his attitude toward the state police power, he generally approved the exercise of the state taxing power, proving himself a "sincere exponent of states' rights" (McLean 1946, 155).

In Day's view, the federal government did not possess authority comparable to the state police power. At the same time, he believed that the commerce clause in the U.S. Constitution conferred sufficient power on the federal government to regulate monopolies; his distrust of large corporations led him to support federal antitrust regulation. Princeton political scientist Joseph McLean reports that Day favored enforcement in forty-nine of seventy-five antitrust cases decided during his tenure on the Court. These numbers indicate that Day was "one of the strongest, if not the strongest, of the judicial supporters of vigorous enforcement of antitrust laws" (McLean 1946, 82–83). Day's most forthright defense of the Sherman Act occurred in 1920 in *United States v. United States Steel Corp.*, in which the Court ruled that U.S. Steel's dominance of the steel industry did not constitute a violation of the Sherman Act. Day's dissent was a scathing attack on giant combinations and rebutted the notion that such combinations were either "inevitable or desirable." This dissent, which called on the federal government "to do no less than reverse the basic results of the American industrial revolution," clearly contrasted Day's refusal to sanction the use of federal power to "undo the blatant evils of child labor in *Hammer v. Dagenhart*" (Watts 1995, 899). Day's jurisprudence, "shaped in rural, pre-industrial America, carried a strong dose of nineteenth century liberalism well into the urban, industrialized twentieth century" (900). He was able to adjust his legal philosophy, at least marginally, during his tenure on the Court. Except for his "stubborn reliance on Melville Fuller's odd definition of commerce, Justice Day generally cast his vote on the side of the twentieth century" (900).

Day resigned from the Supreme Court on 13 November 1922. He left the Court before the 1922 Term was really underway, thus he sat for only a single year as a member of the Taft Court. McLean speculates that had Day remained on the Court for a longer period, his "harmonizing influence" as a "middle-of-the-road justice" might have prevented a "splitting of the Court into doctrinaire extremes" in the 1920s and 1930s (McLean 1946, 163). He was asked by President Harding to serve on a commission created to resolve financial claims arising out of World War I. Day agreed to serve, but resigned shortly thereafter because of poor health. He died on 9 July 1923.

The William H. Taft Appointments

Willis Van Devanter (1859–1941)

Willis Van Devanter was one of President Taft's six Supreme Court nominees and one of two Taft appointees to serve during Taft's chief justiceship. He was nominated on 12 December 1910, one of three persons nominated that day by Taft (Edward D. White and Joseph R. Lamar were the others). Van Devanter was confirmed by voice vote three days after his nomination. He retired in June 1937 after more than twenty-six years of service on the Court. During that period, he authored 360 majority opinions, one concurring opinion, and four dissents. Van Devanter participated in all but two of the 1,614 Taft Court decisions in which opinions were issued (99.88 percent). He wrote 98 majority opinions for the Taft Court (6.07 percent) and dissented in 20 (1.24 percent) of the Taft Court decisions.

Van Devanter was born in Marion, Indiana, on 17 April 1859. He moved to Wyoming in 1884, three years after he earned his law degree from Cincinnati Law School. He soon began a political career as the Cheyenne city attorney, territorial legislator, and chief judge of Wyoming's territorial court. When Wyoming gained statehood in 1890, Van Devanter served briefly as the state supreme court's first chief justice. He returned to private practice, where he spent most of his time representing the Burlington and Union Pacific Railroads. Van Devanter's Republican Party affiliation led to his appointment as assistant attorney general in the U.S. Department of Interior in 1897. Six years later in 1903, he was appointed to the U.S. Court of Appeals for the Eighth Circuit by President Theodore Roosevelt. President William H. Taft chose him to replace retiring Supreme Court Justice William Moody in December 1910.

On average, Van Devanter wrote only thirteen majority opinions a year during his twenty-six years of service on the Court. He suffered from what observers have

Willis Van Devanter (Harris and Ewing, Collection of the Supreme Court of the United States)

called "pen paralysis." His service was notable nonetheless because of the role he played in the Court's conferences and as a critic of his colleagues' opinions. Although he authored comparatively few opinions during his tenure on the Court, he had a well-developed jurisprudence that featured an unyielding commitment to the principles of limited government. He categorically opposed the use of federal commerce and taxing powers by the 1930s, and he used substantive due process to insulate private property and business from state regulation.

Van Devanter was not only put on the Court by President Taft, but was Chief Justice Taft's close confidante during the 1920s. They shared views on virtually all legal and political issues, and both were dedicated to reforming the American court system. Van Devanter's knowledge of jurisdictional and procedural matters led Chief Justice Taft to choose him to play a leading role in drafting the Judiciary Act of 1925 and presenting the proposal to the Congress. Many observers considered Van Devanter the foremost intellectual conservative on the Court during the 1920s and 1930s. Along with James McReynolds, Pierce Butler, and George Sutherland, collectively known as the "Four Horsemen," he consistently opposed New Deal economic and social programs in the 1930s. He was described by colleague Harlan Stone as the "Commander in Chief of Judicial Reaction" (Shoemaker 1994, 486).

Van Devanter's conservative judicial philosophy was not immediately evident when he joined the Court. Indeed, he could have been mistaken for a progressive at the outset of his tenure. For example, he voted to uphold the Federal Employers' Liability Act of 1908 in *Kiernan v. Portland* (1911) and wrote the Court's opinion in the *Second Employers' Liability Cases* (1911), which made railroads legally responsible for workers injured on the job. Similarly, in *Southern Railway Co. v. United States* (1911), Van Devanter wrote for the Court as it upheld the federal Safety Appliance Act of 1893, which banned the interstate use of railroad cars that were not equipped with automatic couplers. In *Southern Railway*, Van Devanter spoke of the federal commerce power in broad terms that extended beyond the mere transport of goods. He suggested the federal commerce power could legitimately reach every instrument and agent by which such commerce is carried on, including intrastate incidents of that commerce. The federal act under review in *Southern Railway* was designed to "promote the safety of [interstate] traffic and of the employees engaged in its movement," a reasonable objective in his view (*Southern Railway* 1911, 24). He spoke of the railroads as "highway[s] of interstate commerce," and saw the commerce power as "not confined to vehicles used in moving interstate traffic, but embrac[ing] vehicles used in moving intrastate traffic" as well (26). Opinions such as these prompted David Burner to conclude that Van Devanter did not intend to broaden federal regulatory power beyond all limits, but offer a "particular conception of commerce itself, as inherently national in scope" instead (Burner 1995f, 973).

One of Van Devanter's most important opinions came in *McGrain v. Daugherty*

(1927). The case involved a general challenge to the power of the Senate to conduct investigations, specifically the authority to subpoena witnesses and the power to have witnesses taken into custody for failure to comply with subpoenas. Information is critical to the effective exercise of the legislative power. Van Devanter suggested that the power to secure needed information by means of subpoenas "has long been treated as an attribute of the power to legislate" (*McGrain* 1927, 161). He concluded that the "power of inquiry—with power to enforce it—is an essential and appropriate auxiliary to the legislative function." Van Devanter went on to point out that "mere requests for such information are often unavailing," thus "some means of compulsion are essential to obtain what is needed" (175).

Such cases notwithstanding, Van Devanter became, in the words of David Burner, the "most intractable of the reactionary justices of the 1930s" (Burner 1995f, 976). Historians have referred to Van Devanter as "unimaginatively conservative," and he has been ranked as one of the "failures" among Court justices. Such criticism is perhaps too harsh. It has been suggested that Van Devanter has fared poorly with evaluators "because he is best known as a reactionary conservative in a period dominated by liberal writers" (Shoemaker 1994, 487). Taft regarded Van Devanter as "far and away the most valuable man on our Court" because of his thoughtful deliberations in the justices' "closed conference" (C. Cushman 1993, 314). Van Devanter's decision to retire came in 1937 after the Court began to expand the regulatory authority of the federal government. His retirement gave Roosevelt the opportunity to remake the Court, beginning with the appointment of Hugo Black. The timing of Van Devanter's retirement was also calculated, at least in part, to "create maximum embarrassment" for Roosevelt because it made obvious that a "little patience would have enabled Roosevelt to avoid the political fiasco engendered by his Court-packing proposal" (Shoemaker 1994, 487). Van Devanter died early in 1941.

Mahlon Pitney (1858–1924)

Mahlon Pitney was the last of President Taft's Supreme Court nominees and the second who served into the period of Taft's chief justiceship. He was nominated to replace John M. Harlan on 19 February 1912 and confirmed by a Senate vote of fifty to twenty-six on 13 March 1912. Pitney retired on 31 December 1922 after serving a little less than eleven years. He wrote 249 majority opinions while on the Court and issued 19 dissenting and 5 concurring opinions as well. His tenure during the Taft Court period was limited to one term in which he participated in 166 (10.29 percent) of the Court decisions issued with an opinion. He wrote eleven majority opinions during that year (6.63 percent) and accounted for less than 1 percent (0.68 percent) of the total number of majority opinions written during the Taft Court era. During his single term on the Taft Court, he wrote or joined four dissents and two concurring opinions.

Mahlon Pitney (Harris and Ewing, Collection of the Supreme Court of the United States)

Pitney was born in Morristown, New Jersey, on 5 February 1858. He attended private schools in Morristown before enrolling at what is now Princeton University, where he was a classmate of Woodrow Wilson. He graduated in 1879 and practiced law in Dover, New Jersey, until 1894, when he began the first of his two terms in the U.S. House of Representatives. He left Congress to serve a term in the New Jersey state senate, which he believed would better position him for a gubernatorial bid. He was among the leading contenders for the governorship in 1901, but a short time before the election, Pitney accepted appointment to the New Jersey Supreme Court where he served eight years. He was appointed chancellor of the New Jersey court system—the highest judicial position in New Jersey. As chancellor, Pitney presided over the law and equity courts and was administrator of the state's entire judicial system (C. Cushman 1993, 323).

President Taft nominated five associate justices and one chief justice, of which Pitney was the last and most controversial. His confirmation by the Senate took twenty-three days. Senate liberals and union leaders were put off by what they saw as Pitney's antilabor and antiprogressive judicial record. His former Princeton classmate and then governor of New Jersey, Woodrow Wilson, crossed party lines to support Pitney's nomination. With this and other endorsements, Pitney was confirmed.

Pitney was particularly knowledgeable in tax law, and he represented the Court's thinking in cases involving federal or state taxes quite frequently. Perhaps his most notable opinion on the taxing power came in *Eisner v. Macomber* (1920), in which the Court held that stock dividends were not taxable income despite seemingly contrary language in the Sixteenth Amendment. Pitney articulated the Court's conclusion in *Eisner* that investment gains are not taxable income until actually realized, which remains relevant today. Pitney is probably more often remembered for his opinions in labor cases, however. He came to the Court with something of an antilabor reputation, and his opinions in several prominent labor cases reinforced that view. He wrote the majority opinion in *Coppage v. Kansas* (1915), for example, offering the rationale for the Court's ruling that struck down a state prohibition on "yellow dog" contracts. Such contracts required workers to agree not to join a union as a condition of employment, and in the Court's view, impermissibly impaired the employer's freedom of contract. Similarly, in *Hitchman Coal & Coke Co. v. Mitchell* (1917) Pitney spoke for the Court when it held that employers could seek restraining orders to keep union organizers from recruiting employees working under "yellow dog" contracts.

Pitney generally deferred to state judgments on matters of property and contract. Although antagonistic toward unions, Pitney was quite supportive of unorganized workers, repeatedly upholding state labor regulations designed to protect their interests. He supported, for example, state initiatives regulating hours of work for both men and women. He wrote for the Court several times strongly supporting state workers' compensation laws, and he was generally sympathetic toward programs designed to provide benefits to workers injured on the job. Nonetheless, Pitney had a reputation as not only anti-union, but anti-union to a "reactionary" degree (Belknap 1986, 408). Pitney believed that employers whose products were boycotted by a labor union were entitled to injunctive relief under federal antitrust laws. Indeed, in *Duplex Printing Co. v. Deering* (1921), he disregarded provisions of the Clayton Act that were designed to exempt unions from the antitrust laws in order to sustain a restraining order banning a secondary boycott. In cases arising under the Federal Employers' Liability Act, he consistently ruled in favor of railroad employees injured on the job and against the companies for which they worked. Most notable of all was his steady support of state workers' compensation laws (411–412). He joined the Court's opinion in the first *Coronado Coal* case (1922), however, refusing to invoke the Sherman Act against striking coal miners. Pitney supported zealous enforcement of antitrust laws against businesses engaged in monopoly-building practices. Like other justices of this time, Pitney brought to the Court the "atomistic, competitive world view of nineteenth century liberalism, which distrusted economic combinations of any kind" (B. Cushman 1994, 355).

Pitney had a strong antimonopoly bias long before he joined the Court, and this view carried over to his tenure on the Court. Generally, his judicial position in cases arising under antitrust laws and some other federal and state regulatory measures reflected something akin to progressive attitudes. He strongly disagreed, for example, in *United States v. United Shoe Machinery Co.* (1918) when the Court held that the exclusive leasing agreements used by United Shoe to dominate the shoe manufacturing industry did not violate the Sherman Act. Similarly, he dissented from the Court's ruling in *United States v. United States Steel Corp.* (1920) when it refused to order the dissolution of the steel company (Belknap 1986, 418–419).

Pitney was far less supportive of civil liberties and civil rights claims. Pitney consistently joined the Court in upholding convictions of wartime dissenters under the Espionage and Sedition Acts. Pitney wrote for the Court in *Pierce v. United States* (1920) as the Court upheld Espionage Act convictions of several Socialists for, among other things, distributing a pamphlet characterizing American participation in World War I as driven by capitalistic objectives. He also joined the Court majorities upholding Espionage Act convictions in *Debs v. United States* (1919), *Abrams v. United States* (1919), and *Schenck v. United States* (1919). Although generally unreceptive to civil liberties claims, Pitney joined the Court majority in creating the exclusionary rule for federal criminal cases in *Weeks v. United States* (1914), and he voted against a city ordinance mandating segregated housing in *Buchanan v. Warley* (1917). He also wrote a concurring opinion in *Newberry v. United States* (1921) supporting broad federal power to regulate elections.

There are discernible patterns in Pitney's judicial record, but he is difficult to classify with precision. Indeed, legal historian Barry Cushman asserts that the "complexity of Pitney's record exposes the folly of using vulgar political taxonomy as a means of explaining the judicial behavior of his era" (B. Cushman 1994, 355–356). Although Pitney certainly could not be labeled a liberal, at least by contemporary standards, referring to him as a reactionary is not accurate either. Pitney served on the Court for 10 years and participated in all but 19 of the Court's 2,412 decisions rendered during his tenure. During that period he authored 244 majority opinions. He died in December 1924 at his home in Washington.

The Woodrow Wilson Appointments

James C. McReynolds (1862–1946)

All three of Wilson's Court nominees served on the Taft Court. Two of these nominees, James C. McReynolds and Louis D. Brandeis, sat on the Court for the entirety of Taft's chief justiceship. Wilson's first nominee was his attorney general, James C. McReynolds. He was nominated on 19 August 1914 and confirmed ten days later by a vote in the Senate of forty-four to six. McReynolds served on the Court for twenty-six and one-half years, retiring 1 February 1941. During his lengthy tenure, McReynolds wrote 488 majority opinions, 65 dissents, and 7 concurring opinions. He participated in all but 4 of the 1,614 cases decided with opinion during the Taft Court period. He was responsible for writing 183 (11.83 percent) of the Taft Court majority opinions. During that same period he wrote or joined 80 dissenting opinions (4.96 percent of Taft Court cases) and 11 concurring opinions.

McReynolds was born in Elkton, Kentucky, on 3 February 1862. He graduated valedictorian from Vanderbilt University in 1882 and subsequently studied law at the University of Virginia. Following his graduation from law school, he established a law practice in Nashville, Tennessee. McReynolds joined the Vanderbilt law faculty in 1900 to teach commercial and business law. Although McReynolds was a Democrat, he was appointed assistant attorney general by Republican president Theodore Roosevelt in 1903. He regarded monopoly as "essentially wicked" and considered full enforcement of the Sherman Act a "moral obligation." As a result, he was put in charge of conducting the tobacco trust litigation. During this period, he established a reputation as an effective trustbuster (Burner 1995c, 1009). McReynolds left the Justice Department in 1909 and joined a prestigious law firm in New York City. He was called back to Washington by President Taft to complete antitrust proceedings in the tobacco and anthracite coal industries, but resigned when Attorney General George Wickersham compromised on the final settlement in the tobacco case. His support for Wilson in the 1912 campaign prompted Wilson to appoint him attorney general in 1913. His career as head of the Justice Department was both "brief and disastrous," a

James C. McReynolds (Harris and Ewing, Collection of the Supreme Court of the United States)

result produced by his "intemperate manner," at least in part (1010). The Supreme Court vacancy caused by Justice Horace Lurton's death in 1912 had never been filled. As Lurton also came from Tennessee, considerations of geography and politics led Wilson to elevate McReynolds to the Court in 1914. Appointing McReynolds to the Court also solved Wilson's political problem by removing him from the Cabinet.

Some Court observers expected McReynolds to join the liberal wing of the Court, but by the end of his tenure, he had become its most conservative member. As a Supreme Court justice, McReynolds opposed the growing regulatory power of government, both federal and state, and believed that the Constitution committed the nation to a policy of laissez-faire capitalism. McReynolds is probably best remembered as one of the so-called Four Horsemen, a group of laissez-faire justices who sat during the 1920s and 1930s. The group also included Justices George Sutherland, Pierce Butler, and Willis Van Devanter. The four voted as a bloc against every New Deal initiative. After the "constitutional revolution" that occurred in early 1937 until his retirement in February 1941, McReynolds was a shrill dissenting voice on the Hughes Court against what he considered the unconstitutional exercise of power by the federal government. He was the last of the Four Horsemen to leave the Court, retiring after Roosevelt won his third term in 1940.

McReynolds was probably the "most reactionary and easily the most tenacious" of the Four Horsemen (Burner 1995c, 1007). He was the single negative vote in the case that tested the constitutionality of the Tennessee Valley Authority (TVA) in *Ashwander v. Tennessee Valley Authority* (1936). He bitterly dissented from the Court's decisions in 1935 (*Gold Clause Cases*) that approved Roosevelt's decision to devalue gold, saying that the Constitution as he knew it was "gone." McReynolds was known to be both racist and anti-Semitic. He snubbed both Louis Brandeis and Benjamin Cardozo because they were Jewish. He also refused to sign the customary letters on the retirement of both Brandeis and Clarke, and for many years would not speak to Clarke, whom he considered stupid. More generally, McReynolds was frequently "intolerably rude" (1007). He wrote just over 500 majority opinions during his 27 years on the Court, most of which dealt with narrow and technical legal points. In the view of historian David Burner, his opinions generally "reflect the directness, even the abruptness, of his personality. Pungent or sarcastic language appeared not infrequently in remarks aimed at his fellow Justices" (1010).

McReynolds believed in fair access to competitive markets, and he consistently saw the Sherman Act as an effective device to combat monopolies. This value was driven by his trustbusting days as a federal prosecutor. He was at the same time a laissez-faire devotee, believing that markets ought to be free not only from monopolies but also from government regulation. In other words, the American economy must be free enough to "enjoy the interplay of natural forces." To some extent, however, McReynolds reflected both a conservative and a progressive side on these questions.

He opposed monopolistic practices of big business, but even more strongly opposed big government and big labor.

McReynolds's civil liberties record also reveals some contradictions. He could take libertarian positions. He was the only dissenter in *Carroll v. United States* (1925), for example, a case in which the Court upheld the warrantless search of a car stopped on a highway. He was in the Court majority that struck down state efforts to dictate content taught in public schools. He wrote the majority opinion in *Meyer v. Nebraska* (1923), which invalidated a state law prohibiting the teaching of foreign languages before the ninth grade. McReynolds wrote for a unanimous Court in *Pierce v. Society of Sisters* (1925), which struck down an Oregon compulsory public education law, concluding that the law unreasonably interfered with the liberty of parents and guardians to direct the upbringing and education of their children. Two years later, in *Farrington v. Tokushiga* (1927), McReynolds struck down a Hawaii statute that sought to ban the teaching of Japanese (Burner 1995c, 1012).

The period that is most often recounted when discussing McReynolds is not the Taft Court years, but rather the New Deal Court (Hughes Court) years. It was during this period that McReynolds was known for his unrelenting opposition to the New Deal reforms. His opposition certainly was based on his categorical rejection of governmental interventionism, but also on his literal hatred of Franklin Roosevelt, someone he considered "utterly incompetent," a "fool," a "bad misfit—a megalomaniac," and someone who was simply "bad through and through" (Burner 1995c, 1014). McReynolds was not careful in concealing his contempt for Roosevelt, with vitriolic language frequently appearing in his Court opinions. As McReynolds read his dissent in *Norman v. Baltimore & Ohio Railroad,* one of the *Gold Clause Cases* (1935), he is reported to have caustically remarked that as a result of the ruling, "shame and humiliation are upon us" and that "anarchy and despotism are at the door." This is "Nero at his worst. The Constitution is gone" (Wolf 1994, 449). McReynolds voted against more New Deal measures than any other justice. Between 1933 and his resignation in 1941 he wrote 146 dissents, 119 of them in the years after the Court had shifted to upholding New Deal measures (Burner 1995c, 1014). McReynolds was not a constitutional literalist as such, but it is clear that he did not view the Constitution as a document subject to judicial adaptation.

McReynolds left a judicial legacy that featured almost categorical opposition to government regulations, especially those emanating from the federal level. His jurisprudence frequently rejected the exercise of even enumerated powers at the federal level. He put these views into effect by functioning as a judicial activist—inquiring into the wisdom or reasonableness of federal legislation. Many consider McReynolds one of the worst justices who ever sat on the Court, and he has become the embodiment of the laissez-faire conservatism of the Four Horsemen. The fundamental criticism of McReynolds is that he allowed his defense of wealth and privilege to drive his interpretation of the Constitution. As a result, McReynolds has come to represent uncompromising opposition to progressive public policy. In fairness, McReynolds conscientiously sought to defend and protect the Constitution as he understood it, but during the last decade of his tenure his vantage point seemed altogether outdated in twentieth-century America. Believing that he had failed his judicial obligation to protect citizens in the exercise of their inalienable rights, McReynolds retired from the Court as the isolated figure marginalized by the more liberal Hughes Court.

McReynolds retired in 1941 and spent his final years in Washington. He died in 1946. McReynolds was not married, and he left much of his estate to a number of charitable and educational institutions. His will contained substantial bequests, for example, to the Children's Hospital in Washington, the Salvation Army, the Washington National City Christian Church, Vanderbilt University, and the University of Virginia.

Louis Dembitz Brandeis (1856–1941)

Louis Dembitz Brandeis was President Wilson's second and most controversial nominee for the Supreme Court. He was selected to succeed Justice Joseph Lamar on 28 January 1916. The nomination triggered a lengthy and acrimonious confirmation battle during which conservative opponents unsuccessfully sought to prevent his joining the Court. Although Brandeis was the first Jew to sit on the Court, the problems surrounding his confirmation resulted not from his religion, but his political and legal philosophy, both of which were considered unacceptably radical by the leadership of the business and legal communities.

Brandeis was finally confirmed by the Senate on 1 June 1916 by a vote of forty-seven to twenty-two. He served on the Court until his retirement on 13 February 1939. In his almost 23 years on the Court, Brandeis wrote 455 majority opinions and 65 dissents. He participated in 99.32 percent of the Taft Court decisions with opinions (1,603). He wrote 201 majority opinions for the Taft Court, 12.45 percent of the total for the period. He also wrote or joined 87 dissenting opinions or 5.39 percent of the Taft Court rulings. This was the highest rate of dissent of any Taft Court justice.

Brandeis was born in Louisville, Kentucky, on 13 November 1856. He enrolled at Harvard Law School without a college diploma at the age of eighteen and graduated at the top of his class. He joined a St. Louis law firm, but left after less than a year to begin practice in Boston with Samuel Warren, a law school classmate. Brandeis was an unconventional lawyer from the outset of his practice. He felt that many lawyers had become adjuncts of large corporations and had lost touch with the obligation to work on behalf of the public interest. His own sense of public responsibility led to his involvement in a broad range of public causes, such as the legalization of labor unions, women's suffrage, and the preservation of natural resources for the

Louis Dembitz Brandeis (Harris and Ewing, Collection of the Supreme Court of the United States)

public rather than private benefit. He often chose not to accept compensation for his services, preferring instead to act pro bono or "for the public good." This led the media to refer to Brandeis as the "people's attorney."

Brandeis introduced something called the "Brandeis brief" in *Muller v. Oregon* (1908). His brief in support of an Oregon law setting maximum hours of work for women devoted only two pages to legal precedent and more than 100 pages to sociological data demonstrating that lengthy work days had negative effects on women and their families. This marked the beginning of sociological jurisprudence.

In 1914 Brandeis accepted the leadership of the American Zionist movement, largely because he envisioned a Jewish state in Palestine that would be small-scale, egalitarian, and protective of the rights of Jews and non-Jews alike. Brandeis shared most of Woodrow Wilson's progressive views and assisted in fashioning Wilson's New Freedom program. His political connection to Wilson made him a candidate for solicitor general, but Wilson instead nominated him to the Supreme Court to succeed Justice Lamar.

Brandeis believed that judges should defer to legislative judgments in matters of economic policy, although he took a different approach when governmental actions affected individual liberties. Brandeis suggested in *Gilbert v. Minnesota* (1920), that the liberty guaranteed by the Fourteenth Amendment went beyond property rights to include personal freedoms as well, the first time that a justice had suggested that the Bill of Rights imposes limits on the states through the Fourteenth Amendment. Brandeis is well known for his advocacy of limited judicial intervention in policy making; such restraint was a central element of his jurisprudence. Brandeis believed it was both undemocratic and unwise for judges to substitute their views for those of elected legislators. Perhaps his most comprehensive statement about the limits of judicial review came in *Ashwander v. Tennessee Valley Authority* (1936).

Brandeis's sociological jurisprudence was based on his philosophy of democracy. In his view, law should reflect the public's perception of societal needs. As these needs change, laws adapt accordingly. Not only should statutes change, but judges should adapt the Constitution on the basis of current societal needs. Brandeis is also well known for his judicial opinions in the areas of social experimentation and civil liberties, among others (Strum 1994, 40). Brandeis's opinions differed from those of his colleagues because they included "discussion of the social realities leading to the legislation that was under review by the Court" (44). He felt legislatures ought to be free to engage in social experimentation to meet societal needs. This approach led Holmes to call Brandeis's opinions "those of an advocate." Indeed, said political scientist Philippa Strum, "they were the opinions of an advocate of state experimentation" (Strum 1984, 314).

Brandeis distrusted concentrations of power in either the public or private sectors. This is evident in his unrelenting opposition to monopolies. He opposed concentrated power in government as well and steadfastly maintained the separation of powers doctrine. He dissented, for example, in *Myers v. United States* (1926) as the Taft Court held that a president could remove a civil servant without Senate consent. Chief Justice Taft argued for the Court that it was more efficient for presidents to act unilaterally against employees, at least those in the executive branch. Brandeis declared that the "doctrine of the separation of powers was adopted by the Constitution of 1787 not to promote efficiency but to preclude the exercise of arbitrary power" (*Myers* 1926, 293). The purpose of separation of powers, he continued, "was not to avoid friction, but, by means of the inevitable friction incident to the distribution of the governmental powers among three departments, to save the people from autocracy" (293). He held to this principle even when it meant "infuriating Franklin Roosevelt, most of whose New Deal programs Brandeis endorsed" (Strum 1994, 43). He was not willing to permit the emergency of the Depression to be used as "an excuse for concentration of power within the executive branch" (43).

Brandeis was as "impassioned and influential in the area of civil liberties as he was in the economic sphere" (Strum 1994, 44). He viewed free speech as an essential component of an enlightened citizenry, and was influential in shaping contemporary free speech doctrine. Brandeis was part of the unanimous Court that upheld an Espionage Act conviction in *Schenck v. United States* (1919). The next year, he wrote several dissenting opinions that clearly communicated his free speech jurisprudence. One of these dissents was in *Schaefer v. United States* (1920), a case that involved an appeal from a conviction under the 1917 Espionage Act for printing critical articles about the American war effort. Brandeis argued that the constitutional right of free speech should be the same in wartime as in peacetime. He was particularly concerned that an "intolerant majority" may be inclined to "stamp as disloyal opinions with which it disagrees." Wartime provides the conditions where intolerance may be produced "by passion or by fear" (Strum 1984, 318). His *Schaefer* dissent revealed that Brandeis rejected the contention that wartime was itself enough to make certain speech unlawful.

Another of his 1920 dissents came in *Gilbert v. Minnesota* in which the Taft Court reviewed a Minnesota law that prohibited interference with military enlistment. Joseph Gilbert had been convicted for statements denouncing World War I and the military draft used to support it. Brandeis said in *Gilbert* that congressional war power was exclusive and that enactment of the Espionage Act preempted similar legislation by the states. Brandeis went further, however, concluding that the Minnesota law was an "act to prevent teaching that the abolition of war is possible," and unlike the Espionage Act it "applies equally whether the United States is at peace or at war" and precludes the "teaching of the doctrine of pacifism and . . . in effect proscribes it for all time" (*Gilbert* 1920, 334).

Perhaps Brandeis's most eloquent contribution to free speech came in *Whitney v. California* (1927). Anita Whitney had been convicted under a California law for her association with the Communist Labor Party. Brandeis suggested that a state does not have the power to "prohibit dissemination of social, economic and political doctrine which a vast majority of its citizens believe to be false and fraught with evil consequence" (*Whitney* 1927, 374). Those who won the nation's independence, he continued, believed that the "freedom to think as you will and to speak as you think are means indispensable to the discovery and spread of political truth" (375). He saw public discussion as a "political duty," and the right to speak and assemble freely affords "protection against the dissemination of noxious doctrine" (375). Brandeis "transformed" Holmes's "clear and present danger" standard by defining "present" as meaning that the "incidence of the evil apprehended is so imminent that it may befall before there is opportunity for full discussion" (377). Brandeis also rejected Holmes's assumption that the government could act against speech "presenting a danger of any evil the government had the right to prevent" (Strum 1994, 46).

Brandeis substantially influenced privacy jurisprudence, although the impact of his view was not fully evident until the 1960s. In *Casey v. United States* (1928), for example, the Court reviewed a federal drug conviction. Casey, an attorney, was suspected of supplying some of his imprisoned clients with illegal narcotics. Recordings were made of conversations between Casey and two prisoners, and the prosecution used the disclosures in Casey's trial. Brandeis concluded that the evidence against Casey would not have existed but for the government's misconduct.

Similarly, Brandeis objected to a conviction under the National Prohibition Act, obtained at least in part through the use of evidence gathered by the government tapping telephone lines. The Court held in *Olmstead v. United States* (1928) that wiretapping did not constitute the kind of physical trespass or seizure prohibited by the Fourth Amendment's search and seizure clause. Brandeis contended that the objective of the Fourth Amendment was to protect privacy, and that those who wrote the Bill of Rights intended to include, among other things, the "right to be let alone." Protection of people's privacy requires that every "unjustifiable intrusion by the Government upon the privacy of the individual, whatever the means employed, must be deemed a violation of the Fourth Amendment" (*Olmstead* 1928, 478). It was immaterial to Brandeis that the wiretapping had been undertaken in the name of law enforcement. "Experience should teach us," he suggested, "to be most on our guard to protect liberty when Government's purposes are beneficent" (478–479).

In Brandeis's view, it was one thing for legislatures to limit such things as hours of work, but "when government action curbed these liberties, [he] became a judicial activist" (Mason 1995a, 1030). His perception of the law as a dynamic, changing entity, and his delineation of the right of privacy have become "embedded in American jurisprudence" (Strum 1994, 47). His defense of freedom of speech and the right to privacy were adopted and expanded subsequent to Brandeis leaving the Court. So, too, was his deference to the legislative branch's economic policy judgments.

Like Holmes, Brandeis was known for his dissents, although his dissent rate was not unusually high. His dissenting opinions are significant, however, because many of these dissents would subsequently be incorporated into majority opinions. Constitutional scholar Alpheus T. Mason suggested that Brandeis's most significant qualities were "restless curiosity, thirst for knowledge" (Mason 1995a, 1034). It was not learning "for its own sake but knowledge to put to some use." His curiosity drove him to "toil over every inch of the complex segments of modern life. Much of his own scope and power came from infinite capacity for taking pains" (1034). Brandeis left the Court on 13 February 1939. Although he probably could have continued his distinguished service, he thought that at the age of eighty-three, the "years have limited the quantity and intensity of work possible, and I think the time has come when a younger man should assume the burden" (Strum 1984, 416).

John Hessin Clarke (1857–1945)

President Woodrow Wilson's third and final Supreme Court nominee was John Hessin Clarke. He was nominated on 14 July 1916 and confirmed by voice vote ten days later. Clarke retired from the Court on 18 September 1922 after only six years of service. He participated in only 10.10 percent of the Taft Court decisions with opinions (163 cases). Clarke wrote the majority opinion in twenty (12.27 percent) of those cases. Clarke's twenty majority opinions in the 1921 Term accounted for only 1.24 percent of the total Taft Court rulings. Clarke also wrote or joined thirteen dissenting opinions and six concurring opinions during his year on the Taft Court.

Clarke was born in New Lisbon, Ohio, in 1857. He attended Western Reserve College, where he studied law as an undergraduate. He was admitted to the Ohio Bar in 1878 and practiced law in his hometown for two years. He moved to Youngstown, Ohio, in 1880, where he both practiced law and was an owner of a weekly newspaper. Clarke was a political liberal and a partisan Democrat, and despite a number of conservative corporate clients, he continually supported progressive policies. Clarke left Youngstown to join a prominent corporate law firm in Cleveland in 1897. He also participated in Democratic politics and unsuccessfully sought the Democratic nomination for the U.S. Senate in 1904. Clarke favored direct election of U.S. senators, protective workers' compensation policies, and full campaign finance disclosure. Although his views were not considered mainstream, a number of his policy priorities were articulated in Woodrow Wilson's presidential campaign in 1912. Clarke sought the Democratic nomination for the U.S. Senate again, but could not muster sufficient support and eventually withdrew. This led him to abandon elective politics, which made him available for nomination to the federal district court. President Wilson used the lower federal courts as a training ground for a number of progressives judges to prepare them for subsequent elevation to the Supreme Court. Charles

John Hessin Clarke (Harris and Ewing, Collection of the Supreme Court of the United States)

Evans Hughes left the Supreme Court in 1916 to run for president, and Wilson nominated Clarke as his replacement. Wilson's selection of Clarke was intended to provide Justice Louis Brandeis with a dependable liberal voting ally. Clarke's voting record shows that he generally performed as Wilson had hoped, although Wilson did not anticipate that Clarke would serve on the Court for only six years.

Clarke joined a conservative Court presided over by Chief Justice Edward D. White. In addition to Brandeis, Clarke found a consistent ally in Justice Oliver Wendell Holmes. Clarke was an antitrust expert and wrote a number of strongly worded opinions favoring federal regulation of monopolies. Clarke biographer Hoyt Warner suggests that Clarke had the "typical progressive's concern about the abuses of Big Business and the menace of the trusts" (Warner 1959, 46). His majority opinion in *United States v. Reading Railroad Co.* (1920) is illustrative. He asserted that the railroad's extensive holdings created a monopoly that constituted a "menace to and undue restraint upon interstate commerce," and his rationale provided, at least in part, the foundation for the more aggressive enforcement of federal antitrust laws in the 1930s (46). Clarke believed child labor was a social evil that could be reached by federal commerce or taxing power and he dissented in both *Hammer v. Dagenhart* (1918) and *Bailey v. Drexel Furniture Co.* (1922) as the Court struck down two congressional initiatives designed to regulate child labor.

Clarke, along with Brandeis, subscribed to the theory of sociological jurisprudence. Clarke was "not so concerned as Brandeis with factual data," but neither was he "preoccupied with precedents" (Burner 1995b, 1042). With the exception of Brandeis, his colleagues were "unimpressed" with this outlook. Chief Justice Taft complained that Clarke was "prone to decide some cases by the parties rather than the issues" (1042).

David Burner characterizes Clarke's civil liberties record as "mixed." Clarke warned in *Gouled v. United States* (1921), a Fourth Amendment ruling, that only actual contraband, not corroborating evidence, could be seized by government agents. Clarke believed that the Fourth and Fifth Amendments should be liberally construed to prevent "stealthy encroachment upon or gradual depreciation of rights secured by them, through imperceptible practice of courts or through well-intentioned mistakenly over-zealous executive officers" (*Gouled* 1921, 304). Warner concludes that Clarke was "clearly a 'liberal' in zealously defending the individual's right to a fair trial and to every protection from arbitrary legal procedure" (Warner 1959, 94).

Clarke's liberal predispositions were also reflected in his support of working people. He consistently upheld restrictions on the number of hours workers could work in a day and voted against the use of "yellow dog" contracts, which forced workers to promise not to join unions as a condition for getting and keeping their jobs. Clarke also joined Brandeis and Holmes in dissenting from the Court's ruling that unions are subject to prosecution under antitrust laws if their boycotts restrain a company's commerce.

Clarke took a markedly less liberal position in cases involving the First Amendment. *Abrams v. United States* (1919), for example, examined provisions of the Espionage Act of 1918. Clarke voted in *Abrams* to uphold the convictions of Russian-born anarchists and socialists accused of encouraging weapons workers to strike in protest of the U.S. government sending troops to Russia in World War I. The case was argued during the postwar Red Scare period and the White Court, including Clarke, were inclined to rule against political agitators such as Abrams. Clarke had, in Warner's view, a "decent respect for the liberal tradition in preserving civil liberties—at least in time of peace" (Warner 1959, 96). All the significant free speech cases during Clarke's tenure originated in wartime, however, and in these situations Clarke consistently voted to uphold convictions (96). It was only in these cases that he "fail[ed] to uphold the liberal position but instead supported the suppression of speech which had a tendency to subvert the established order or to interfere with the war effort" (106). In *Milwaukee Social Democratic Publishing Co. v. Burleson* (1921), Clarke again rejected a liberal application of the First Amendment, voting to uphold the denial of mailing privileges to the socialist *Milwaukee Leader*.

Clarke did not particularly enjoy his time on the Court. He found much of what the Court did "tedious," and he generally viewed the Court itself as a "restraining" institution. This was reflected in the opinions he wrote—typically brief because he did not want to "obscure the obvious" by discussing it at length. In September 1922 he decided to leave the Court. In his letter of resignation, Clarke indicated that he wanted to "serve some public causes." Among the causes he wished to take up was American participation in the League of Nations. He is said to have told Brandeis that he would be happier promoting American entry into the League of Nations than continuing to devote his time to "determining whether a drunken Indian had been deprived of his land before he died or whether digging a ditch in Iowa was constitutional or not" (Burner 1995b, 1045–1046). Wilson had anticipated that Clarke and Brandeis might deflect the Court from its "extreme reactionary course," but Clarke thought the Court was spending too much of its time on "trivial matters." There is also evidence that Clarke left the Court because he was too often the object of James McReynolds's continued criticism, even harassment. By the time Clarke joined the Court, Chief Justice White, for reasons of diminishing physical capacity, was unable to alleviate the harsh personality clashes on the Court. These factors all contributed to Clarke's decision to resign in 1922.

Clarke supported most of Franklin Roosevelt's New Deal initiatives and fully supported Roosevelt's "court-packing" proposal in 1937. In the time between Clarke's leaving the Court and his death—a period of twenty-three years—Clarke supported efforts to break up corporate trusts, improve working conditions, and promote world peace. Clarke died in 1945 as World War II was concluding and just several months before the discussions leading to the creation of the United Nations began.

The Warren Harding Appointments

William Howard Taft (1857–1930)

William Howard Taft wanted to be chief justice more than anything else in his political life. This was true both before and after his term as president. He finally had the "hope and ambition" of his life fulfilled by President Warren G. Harding, who nominated Taft for the chief justiceship on 20 June 1921. He was confirmed by voice vote of the Senate the same day. The only opposition to his nomination came from several progressive Republicans. Taft retired from the Court on 3 February 1930 after eight and one-half years service. He died a month after he left the Court. During his tenure as chief justice, Taft participated in all but six of the Taft Court decisions issued with opinions. He wrote 252 majority opinions during this period, the highest number (15.61 percent) of majority opinions by any Taft Court justice. Taft said that "somebody has to do the work," and from 1921 to 1928 he wrote over thirty opinions per term—ten more than the average for his colleagues (Mason 1964, 231). He also wrote or joined nineteen dissenting and three concurring opinions.

Taft occupies a unique place in the history of American government as the only person to serve as both president and chief justice. Taft was born in Cincinnati, Ohio, on 15 September 1857. He was the son of a prominent Ohio lawyer, Alphonse Taft, who was attorney general and secretary of war during the Grant administration. Following his graduation from the law school at Cincinnati College in 1880, Taft embarked on a remarkable political career. Between 1881 and 1913, Taft served as a local prosecutor, county solicitor, judge of the Ohio superior court, U.S. solicitor general, U.S. Court of Appeals judge for the Sixth Circuit (1892–1900), governor of the Philippines (1900–1904), secretary of war (1904–1909), and president (1909–1913). Despite his great desire to serve on the Supreme Court, Taft declined Roosevelt's offers to appoint him in 1902 and again in 1906. He declined nomination because he believed the exigencies of duty required that he remain in his executive positions (Post 1994, 457). "It seems strange," Taft remarked sadly while the matter of Chief Justice Fuller's successor was pending, "that the one place in the government which I would have liked to fill myself I am forced to give to another" (Mason 1995b, 1054). The choice was between Associate Justices Charles Evans Hughes and Edward Douglass White. Hughes's name figured more prominently in press speculation as the likely choice. Alpheus T. Mason suggests that Taft overlooked nothing that might diminish his own chances of one day becoming chief justice. White was twelve years older than Taft, and seventeen years older than Hughes. The selection of Hughes would almost certainly have precluded any possibility of Taft becoming chief justice; the elevation of White would not (1055).

Taft brought to the Court a clear sense of purpose and the energy to vigorously achieve it. Taft believed that the primary mission of the judiciary, particularly the

William Howard Taft (Underwood and Underwood, Collection of the Supreme Court of the United States)

Supreme Court, was to actively dispense justice. He is also recognized as the father of modern judicial management. According to Mason, the federal courts were "in dire need of modernization," because they were "decentralized and encumbered by a staggering variety of outmoded procedures" and the system had become characterized by "clogged dockets and delayed judgments" (Mason 1995b, 1056). At the Supreme Court level, much of its "time and energies" were being "frittered away on inconsequential issues" (Mason 1964, 89).

Taft came to a Supreme Court that was both badly divided and far behind in its work. Taft's greatest contribution to the federal judiciary was to address the workload problems of the Supreme Court and lower federal courts. He used his personal political connections to propose reforms intended to simplify court procedures and reduce the continuing backlog of pending cases. Two Taft initiatives stand out. The first was a federal law enacted in September 1922 that established a conference composed of the chief justice and nine circuit senior judges. The conference, which was the predecessor of the present Judicial Conference, established a means by which the federal judiciary might better monitor, coordinate, and improve its performance. The second major reform legislation achieved by Taft was the Judiciary Act of 1925 (also known as the Judges Bill), which significantly reduced the mandatory appellate jurisdiction of the Supreme Court by allowing it to pick and choose the bulk of its cases through the discretionary writ of certiorari.

Taft had unprecedented influence on federal judicial selection from the outset of his presidency. During his tenure as president he appointed six members to the Supreme Court. When he later became chief justice, he sought to advance his own political and judicial philosophy by counseling President Warren Harding on persons to select for federal courts. Harding's victory in 1920 provided the opportunity to make the Court "staunch and strong" (Mason 1995b, 1059). Taft aggressively pursued his own selection as chief justice, and once he achieved his goal he continued to "bombard Harding with suggestions and recommendations" (1059).

Taft brought a clear image of the chief justiceship to the Court. He had a passion for "teamwork"; it alone could give "weight and solidarity" to judicial decisions. "Massing the Court"—seeking unanimity—was a consuming objective. To this end "he persuaded by example, frowned on dissents, exploited personal courtesy and charm, maximized the assignment and reassignment powers and relied on the expertise of his associates" (Mason 1995b, 1060). Taft went to great lengths to establish working conditions and relationships among the justices that were conducive to bringing "weight and solidarity" to the Court's rulings. Taft's ability to accurately gauge and effectively utilize his colleagues is seen in his assignment of opinion-writing responsibilities. The opinion assignment authority, in turn, promoted unanimity as much as possible (1061). During the eight full terms of Taft's tenure as chief justice, almost 85 percent of the Court's decisions decided with written opinions were unanimous.

Taft's jurisprudence was dominated by his conception of property rights. Taft believed that private property provided the means by which human selfishness might be mitigated. Private property is the "keystone of our society," and impairment of property rights threatens the "social fabric by undercutting the motive of enlightened selfishness that today is at the basis of all human labor and effort, enterprise and new activity" (Post 1994, 460). Taft thus took the lead in the Court's effort to limit the ability of governments to regulate property, and he generally orchestrated the Court's use of the Due Process Clause of the Fourteenth Amendment to invalidate social legislation. Taft's defense of private property was directly linked to attempts to bring about court reform. He believed that revision of judicial processes would enable the courts to forestall the social reforms that he believed threatened private property (Mason 1995b, 1052).

Taft's first major opinion came in *Truax v. Corrigan* (1921), a landmark ruling that generated more criticism than any other decision in his first term. In *Truax*, the Supreme Court struck down a state law that prevented the state's courts from issuing injunctions in labor disputes. In Taft's view, injunctions were needed to protect the property interests of business owners. Taft suggested that a law that makes such "wrong[s]" as picketing and secondary boycotts lawful "deprives the owner of [a] business and the premises of his property without due process of law and cannot be held valid" (*Truax* 1921, 328). The legislative power can only be "exerted in subordination to the fundamental principles of rights and justice," which the due process guarantee is intended to preserve. Any arbitrary exercise of governmental power where a "wrongful and highly injurious invasion of property rights" occurs, such as prohibiting state courts from using restraining orders in labor disputes, is "wholly at variance with those principles" (330).

Taft interpreted the language of the Fourth Amendment literally—that it prevented the unreasonable seizure of *material* things from inside a person's residence or office. In *Olmstead v. United States* (1928), the Court addressed the issue of wiretapping, a law enforcement method that does not require actual entry onto a premises. Taft said that the language of the amendment is not to be "extended and expanded" by courts. The amendment cannot be applied to the wires, which reach "to the whole world from the defendant's house" (*Olmstead* 1928, 465). The telephone wires were not part of Olmstead's house or office "any more than are the highways along which they are stretched" (465). Furthermore, Taft pointed to history that reveals that much evidence has been admissible in criminal courts "although not obtained by conformity to the highest ethics" (468). Taft did not want to create a standard that would "make society suffer and give criminals greater immunity than has been known heretofore" (468).

Although protection of private property interests was paramount in Taft's mind, it was not altogether absolute. He also believed that the "mutual dependency" inherent in modern industrial society occasionally required that property be regulated by government in a manner "appreciative of the change of conditions and the necessity for a liberal construction of the restrictions of the Constitution" (Post 1994, 461). As a result, he could be found, albeit infrequently, joining progressive opinions such as that in *Village of Euclid v. Ambler Realty Co.* (1926), in which the Court upheld the constitutionality of municipal zoning authority. The approach Taft used to reach the conclusion that a certain governmental regulation was constitutional is reflected in *Charles Wolff Packing Co. v. Court of Industrial Relations* (1923), which distinguished between "ordinary property"—property essentially immune from governmental regulation—and property so "affected with a public interest" that it could be "subjected to extensive administrative control by the state" (461).

There was also room in Taft's jurisprudence for certain nationalist views. He saw the federal commerce power as extensive even though it might be used to regulate certain property interests. Some of Taft's most noteworthy opinions came in cases in which the federal commerce power was expanded. In *Stafford v. Wallace* (1922), for example, Taft used the "stream of commerce" concept to uphold the Packers and Stockyards Act of 1921, which was designed to regulate monopolistic influences affecting livestock and meat products moved in interstate commerce. Taft saw collusion between stockyard operators and meat packers that both arbitrarily and unduly increased the consumer price of meat products. The federal law treated stockyards as "great national public utilities" that provided a "throat" through which commerce flowed. As such, the stockyards are businesses "affected by a public use of a national character and subject to national regulation" (*Stafford* 1922, 516).

Taft's expansive view of the federal commerce power did not transfer to all commercial situations or to the federal taxing power, however. *Bailey v. Drexel Furniture Co.* (1922) reflects these contrasting positions. Congress had passed a law that imposed a tax on items produced by child labor that were subsequently shipped interstate. Taft's opinion in *Bailey* featured powerful statements on the federal-state relationship. He concluded that such regulation of child labor through the federal taxing power usurped state sovereignty. A separate question in *Bailey* was whether the Child Labor Tax Act was primarily a revenue-raising measure or the use of the taxing power in a punitive fashion against businesses that continued to use child labor. The Taft Court decided it was the latter—that the primary objective of the Child Labor Tax Act was regulatory. A court "must be blind not to see that the so-called tax is imposed to stop the employment of children" (*Bailey* 1922, 37). Its regulatory purpose and effect are "palpable." This congressional motive is widely recognized and understood, so "how can we properly shut our minds to it?" (37). If this application of the federal taxing power were allowed and such "magic" accorded the term "tax," all constitutional limits on the power of Congress would "break down and completely wipe out the sovereignty of the States" (37–38).

Labor unions were viewed with suspicion by Taft, and he believed the influence of organized labor threatened private property rights. In his labor decisions, Taft tried to distinguish between recognizing labor's right to organize (see *American Steel Foundries v. Tri-City Central Trades Council* [1921]) and restricting union tactics that seemed coercive if not lawless. Labor picketing and the secondary boycott fit in the latter category for Taft.

One of Taft's more important opinions came in *Carroll v. United States* (1925), which examined whether evidence obtained by wiretapping could be used in federal criminal trials. The Court ruled that it could. *Olmstead* was similar to other cases, such as *United States v. Lanza* (1922), in which the Taft Court supported federal enforcement of national prohibition. Taft generally supported the government in virtually all criminal rights cases.

Taft's Court also rendered important decisions about the institutional power of the presidency. In these cases the influence of Taft's service as president was evident. In *Myers v. United States* (1926), the Court upheld the president's authority to remove a postmaster without the consent of the Senate. "I never wrote an opinion that I felt to be so important in its effect," Taft said later. The previous year he had upheld the president's power to pardon a person found in contempt of court. Taft wrote for a unanimous Court in *Ex parte Grossman* (1925), which rejected the argument that sustaining such executive authority would necessarily weaken the judiciary (Mason 1995b, 1065).

Taft ranks highly when compared to other chief justices. His first three years were extraordinarily successful both inside the Court and in securing important reforms in the decision-making processes of the Court. He frequently had success in achieving a consensus if not unanimity among his colleagues on the most important issues coming before his Court. In Mason's estimation, none of Taft's predecessors, "with the possible exception of Chief Justice Marshall, entertained such an expansive view of the chief justiceship or made such effective use of it on so many different fronts" (Mason 1995b, 1067). He was a superior administrator and unmatched as a "judicial architect." Taft's chief justiceship might have been more constructive but for his "haunting fear of progressivism and progressives" (1067). Had he maintained the positions he took in commerce power cases and his minimum wage dissent in *Adkins v. Children's Hospital* (1923), he might have, "with the backing of Holmes, Brandeis, Stone and possibly Sanford, swung the Court along the line the great triumvirate was so eloquently staking out" (1067).

George Sutherland (1862–1942)

George Sutherland was the second of President Warren Harding's four Supreme Court nominees. He was nominated on 5 September 1922 and confirmed by the Sen-

George Sutherland (Harris and Ewing, Collection of the Supreme Court of the United States)

ate on the same day by voice vote. Sutherland served on the Court until his retirement on 18 January 1938. In his 15-plus years on the Court, Sutherland wrote 288 majority opinions and 23 dissenting opinions. Sutherland joined the Taft Court in its second year and participated in 87.67 percent of its cases decided with opinions in his seven and one-half years as a member of that Court. In that time, he wrote 150 (9.29 percent) Taft Court majority opinions, and he wrote or joined 39 dissenting opinions.

George Sutherland was born in Buckinghamshire, England, on 25 March 1862. He earned his law degree from the University of Michigan and was admitted to the Michigan Bar in 1883. Sutherland moved to Utah and joined one of Salt Lake City's prominent law firms. He became active in Republican politics in the state and served in the territorial legislature and as a state senator prior to his election to the U.S. House of Representatives in 1900. As Utah's only representative in the House, Sutherland was particularly sensitive to the development of Utah's economy and supported protective tariffs despite being a free-market laissez-faire proponent. After one term in Congress, Sutherland returned to Utah and in 1905 was selected by the state legislature to represent Utah in the U.S. Senate, where he served two six-year terms. During his Senate tenure, Sutherland established a national reputation for his oratorical skills and his knowledge of the Constitution. He supported most worker protection measures and women's suffrage (C. Cushman 1993, 348). In 1916 Sutherland stood for popular election to the Senate, but did not retain his seat. Sutherland chose to remain in Washington to practice law and during part of this time served as president of the American Bar Association. The election of Warren Harding as president in 1920 brought Sutherland back into public life. When Harding was nominated by the Republicans, Sutherland was one of Harding's principal advisers and was instrumental in devising the "front-porch" strategy that kept Harding off the campaign trail and out of the media spotlight. Sutherland was described as Harding's "most trusted campaign adviser in the field of thought and policy" (Burner 1995e, 1074). Following Harding's inauguration, Sutherland was appointed chair of the advisory committee of the U.S. delegation to the International Conference on the Limitation of Naval Armaments. The unexpected resignation of Justice John Clarke in September 1922 provided Harding with the opportunity to select Sutherland. He served on the Court until his retirement in January 1938. During Sutherland's tenure on the Court, there was some media discussion that he would have been well suited for the presidency, but his birth in England constitutionally disqualified him.

Sutherland was a political conservative—an ideological orientation that was evident throughout his tenure on the Court. He was an economic laissez-faire advocate, a value that was clearly reflected in the substantive due process cases of the period. He was an ardent defender of property rights and consistently voted with Chief Justice William H. Taft and Justices Willis Van Devanter and Pierce Butler on property cases. Indeed, Sutherland's use of the Fourteenth Amendment provided the foundation for the Court's conservative bloc to strike down state initiatives found to be substantively unreasonable. Sutherland was one of the "Four Horsemen," a group of four conservative justices who steadfastly opposed Roosevelt's New Deal initiatives in the 1930s. His identification as one of the Horsemen blurs the complexity of his record, however. Sutherland frequently defended First Amendment freedoms and the procedural protections of the accused.

Protection of property rights would become one of Sutherland's defining values, but during his early congressional years he supported some reform measures that did not seriously compromise property interests. During Woodrow Wilson's presidency, Sutherland's conservatism "broadened and thrust out in many directions" (Burner 1995e, 1073). In 1911 he opposed statehood for Arizona and New Mexico, for example, on the grounds that their constitutions provided for such progressive reforms as the initiative, referendum, and recall. Sutherland strongly opposed such federal initiatives as the Federal Reserve Act, the Federal Trade Commission Act, the Clayton Anti-Trust Act, and the constitutional amendment for an income tax, believing that they impermissibly encroached on property rights. Sutherland was also active in the effort to defeat the Supreme Court nomination of Louis D. Brandeis in 1916 (1073–1074).

Sutherland's property rights values were evident in his majority opinion in *Adkins v. Children's Hospital* (1923), one of the most important rulings of the Taft Court era. To support the doctrine of freedom of contract, Sutherland revisited the Court's reasoning in *Lochner v. New York* (1905), and concluded that states did not have the authority to regulate hours of work for women and children. Sutherland biographer Joel Paschal suggests that Sutherland's opinion could only be read as asserting that it was constitutionally impossible to "attempt the solution of certain modern social problems by legislation" (Paschal 1969, 123–124). Substantive due process and freedom of contract were featured concepts in Sutherland's jurisprudence until he left the Court in 1938, and he believed that legislative authority, federal or state, could only be justified under the most exceptional circumstances. Following *Adkins,* Sutherland became the leading spokesman for the conservative justices, and he "constantly reiterated the themes of limited government, dual federalism, and the separation of powers" (Burner 1995e, 1076).

Sutherland was what David Burner characterizes as a "constitutional realis[t]," a quality revealed in the companion cases of *Massachusetts v. Mellon* and *Frothingham v. Mellon* (1923). Also evident in these cases was Sutherland's commitment to the separation-of-powers concept, a doctrine Sutherland viewed as a "foundation stone of the American governmental structure" (Paschal 1969, 149). The two cases, one brought by a taxpayer and the other by a state, sought to enjoin a federal grant to the state under the Maternity Act of 1921. Sutherland disposed of the taxpayer case (*Frothingham*) by concluding the plaintiff's interest was not substantial enough to establish standing to bring the case to court. In *Massachusetts v. Mellon*, he refused to support the state's claim on the ground that to do so would "assume a position of authority over the governmental acts of another and co-equal department, an authority which plainly we do not possess" (*Mellon* 1923, 488).

Sutherland's views were shared by the majority of Taft Court justices. Even after Taft and Sanford left the Court in 1930, Sutherland was able to sustain a conservative majority into the 1930s. He often used the dual federalism doctrine to invalidate federal regulatory initiatives. Dual federalism notwithstanding, Sutherland used substantive due process to limit the capacity of the states to impose economic regulations. He did so by finding that virtually no business was so "clothed" with a public interest to justify its regulation. In *Tyson & Bros. v. Banton* (1927), for example, the Court reviewed a state law prohibiting the resale of theater tickets at a price greater than fifty cents above the face value of the ticket. Sutherland's opinion for the Court in *Tyson* concluded that the ticket brokerage business was merely an "appendage" of the theater and was in no substantial way "affected with a public interest." Similarly in *Ribnik v. McBride* (1928), Sutherland extended the *Tyson* reasoning to the point where virtually any broker was "immune from price regulation" (Paschal 1969, 129–130). Sutherland's "reinvigoration of *Lochner*" provided the conservative bloc with the "intellectual leadership needed to sustain its crusade against confiscatory, arbitrary and unreasonable social and economic legislation" (Wolf 1994, 450).

Sutherland was capable of applying Bill of Rights provisions in a protective manner. In the first Scottsboro case, *Powell v. Alabama* (1932), for example, Sutherland upheld the right of criminal defendants to have counsel provided by the state in death penalty cases. More often, Sutherland sided with the government. In *Moore v. Dempsey* (1923), he voted to affirm a murder conviction despite the "highly prejudiced atmosphere" surrounding the trial. Similarly, he joined the Court majorities in *Gitlow v. New York* (1925) and *Whitney v. California* (1927), upholding state convictions for "subversive" political expression. In *United States v. MacIntosh* (1931), Sutherland agreed that any person who refuses to bear arms in defense of the country can be denied naturalized citizenship.

The Great Depression prompted a great number of economic recovery initiatives by Congress and the states. Most of the federal measures were part of Franklin Roosevelt's New Deal program. A basic question before the Court in reviewing the components of the New Deal was whether the Court should nullify legislative judgments. Sutherland, the three other "Horsemen," Chief Justice Charles Evans Hughes, and Justice Owen Roberts frequently chose to set aside legislative initiatives. Indeed, during Roosevelt's first term, the Court struck down virtually all of the New Deal enactments and Sutherland was often the Court's spokesman. The Court narrowly interpreted the federal commerce and taxing powers and used substantive due process to forestall state economic regulations. Sutherland served on the Court nearly sixteen years, during which time the Court invalidated some eighteen acts of Congress, and he was in the majority in all but one of those decisions. During the same period, the Court ruled more than 185 state statutes or local ordinances unconstitutional, with Sutherland dissenting only nine times (C. Cushman 1993, 349).

Sutherland was ready to leave the Court in 1936, but Roosevelt's "court-packing" proposal led him to postpone his retirement—he wanted to stay on the Court as long as it was "under attack from Roosevelt and the New Dealers" (Wolf 1994, 453). The Court's "new majority" in *West Coast Hotel v. Parrish* (1937) persuaded him that the fight was over, however, and he resigned in January 1938. Some of his opinions, particularly those involving the capacity of the federal government to regulate the national economy, were overturned following the Court's doctrinal shift in 1937. A number of opinions, however, provided the basis for extending individual rights protections. Opinions such as *Powell* distinguish Sutherland from the three more reactionary Horsemen. Sutherland also left behind what David Burner calls "one of the few coherent defenses of very conservative social values" (Burner 1995e, 1080). With exclusive focus on his substantive due process opinions as well as the intransigence of the Four Horsemen, Sutherland's legacy "seems thin indeed" (Wolf 1994, 453). If attention is directed instead to the "way in which he fashioned and presented his arguments," in particular in such opinions as *Village of Euclid v. Ambler Realty Co.* (1926), *Home Building & Loan Ass'n v. Blaisdell* (1934), *Powell v. Alabama* (1932), and *United States v. Curtiss-Wright Corp.* (1936), "we cannot help but be struck by Sutherland's mastery of the judicial craft" (453). Sutherland died in July 1942.

Pierce Butler (1866–1939)

Pierce Butler was President Warren Harding's third nominee to the Court. He was nominated on 23 November 1922, and confirmed by the Senate on 21 December 1922 by a vote of sixty-one to eight. Butler left the Court on 18 November 1939 after almost seventeen years of service. During that time, Butler wrote 325 opinions of the Court, 35 dissents, and 6 concurring opinions. In just over 7 years as a member of the Taft Court, Butler participated in 84.26 percent (1,360) of cases decided with an opinion. He wrote 161 Taft Court majority opinions (9.98 percent) and wrote or joined in 25 dissenting opinions.

Butler was born in Pine Bend, Minnesota, on 18 November 1866. Butler was an ideological conservative despite a lifelong affiliation to the Democratic Party. He obtained his undergraduate degree from Carleton College in 1887 and was admitted to the bar a year later. After two years as an assistant county attorney, Butler was elected Ramsey County attorney in 1892, a position he held for four years. Butler did not seek a third term as county attorney in 1896, choosing instead to begin a private law practice. Although he served as a special prosecutor in several antitrust cases

Pierce Butler (Harris and Ewing, Collection of the Supreme Court of the United States)

during this period, his practice was almost exclusively devoted to representing railroads, rather than the government. He was highly regarded throughout Minnesota, which led to his election as president of the Minnesota State Bar in 1908. The following year, Butler was asked by Attorney General George Wickersham to handle antitrust actions against grain millers and meat packers. Wickersham was impressed with Butler's performance, prompting the attorney general to call Butler the "foremost lawyer in his part of the country" (Burner 1995a, 1083).

Chief Justice Taft played an active role in the selection of justices for his Court. He initially supported John W. Davis to replace Justice William R. Day on the Court, but when Davis withdrew, Taft personally lobbied President Harding to nominate Butler. Butler allowed Harding to represent several constituencies—Butler was a Democrat, from the Midwest, and he was a Roman Catholic. Butler's nomination to the Court was marked by controversy. His conservatism attracted influential Republicans, but progressives and organized labor vigorously opposed Butler's nomination. Beyond ideological considerations, Butler's opponents argued that he lacked judicial temperament. Organized labor's opposition was reflected by AFL head Samuel Gompers's characterization of Butler as an "impossible reactionary" (Burner 1995a, 1084).

Butler was one of the dogmatic laissez-faire ideologues on the Taft and Hughes Courts. One of the "Four Horsemen" (Justices McReynolds, Sutherland, and Van Devanter were the others), Butler opposed all of Roosevelt's New Deal proposals during the 1930s. Butler advocated using substantive due process considerations as a means of protecting property rights. In addition to his laissez-faire economic views, patriotism and morality were among the most important values for Butler. Butler not only opposed the New Deal initiatives, but as a laissez-faire advocate he also opposed state regulation of business as well. One of his last opinions for the Court came in *Morehead v. New York ex rel. Tipaldo* (1936), in which the Court struck down a state minimum wage law for women. *Morehead* was reversed less than a year later at the time the Hughes Court had its doctrinal turnaround in 1937. Once he was relegated to minority status on the Hughes Court, Butler dissented more often in his last two years of service on the Court than he had in the previous fifteen years. He was also committed to maintaining judicial precedent, believing that the Court's decisions should be both definite and permanent, a value he echoed frequently during these last two years on the Court.

Butler's decisions on the Court reflected what David Burner characterizes as "unrelenting conservatism." He influenced the definition of the phrase "'business affected with a public interest' by consistently voting to narrow the classification" (Burner 1995a, 1086). Butler wrote more than 300 majority opinions during his seventeen years on the Court, but few were particularly distinguished. Indeed, he deliberately sought to minimize the use of his opinions by editing out discussion that might become frequently quoted.

Butler was willing to protect individual rights, but rights protection was subordinate to his patriotism and morality values. In *United States v. Schwimmer* (1929), for example, Butler took the position that naturalized citizenship could be withheld from anyone refusing to bear arms in defense of the country; even a woman approaching the age of sixty. In his view, people such as Rosika Schwimmer constituted a danger because they not only failed to comply with laws themselves but encouraged others not to comply as well. Pacifists like Schwimmer, according to Butler, lacked such essential ingredients of a good citizen as a "sense of nationalism" and "ties of affection" to the United States (Danelski 1994, 83). Similarly, Butler's opinion in *United States v. MacIntosh* (1931) denied citizenship to a Canadian theologian who indicated he would refuse to participate in any war he thought morally unjustified. Butler also voted to uphold a state law making it a crime to display a red flag in public in *Stromberg v. California* (1931). According to political scientiest David Danelski, Butler voted against the individual in every nonunanimous decision involving political radicals or aliens who "refused to swear unqualified allegiance" to the United States (1964, 83).

Procedural due process issues produced a less conservative response by Butler. He occasionally supported claims of due process violations and separated himself from Taft Court majorities in doing so. In *Olmstead v. United States* (1928), for example, Butler concluded that the government ought not to be able to use wiretap evidence. In Butler's view, users of phone lines were entitled to privacy. Butler believed that during the transmission of any message, the exclusive use of phone lines belongs to the persons served by it. In *Powell v. Alabama* (1932), on the other hand, Butler dissented from a decision calling for a new trial for a number of minority defendants who had been unrepresented at their capital rape trial. He also voted to uphold a state law enabling the racially exclusive primary elections in *Nixon v. Condon* (1932).

Many Court observers are unimpressed with Butler's Court record. Indeed, his performance is rated as a "failure" by a number of academic evaluators. Attorney and legal historian Fred Rodell characterized Butler as the "least intellectually gifted of the Nine Old Men" (Rodell 1955, 220). Some of those who argued cases before the Court viewed him differently. Robert H. Jackson, for example, suggested Butler was a man of "great ability." Jackson recalled that as solicitor general he had to prepare carefully to argue cases before the Court because those arguments would have to "face the scrutiny of Justice Butler" (Danelski 1994, 83). Butler died on 16 November 1939, at the age of seventy-three, leaving Justice McReynolds as the only remaining member of the Four Horsemen on the Court. Ironically, the vacancy created by Butler's death was filled by Frank Murphy, perhaps the most liberal justice ever to sit on the Court.

Edward Terry Sanford (1865–1930)

President Harding's fourth and final nominee for the Supreme Court was Edward Terry Sanford. He filled the vacancy created by the resignation of Justice Mahlon Pitney. Sanford was nominated on 24 January 1923, and the Senate confirmed him by voice vote five days later. Sanford served on the Court until his death on 8 March 1930—a period of slightly more than seven years. He sat for 1,404 (86.99 percent) of the Taft Court cases decided with an opinion. He wrote the Court's majority opinion in 128 (7.93 percent) of those cases. He also wrote or joined twenty-three dissenting opinions and seven concurring opinions during that period.

Sanford was born in Knoxville, Tennessee, on 23 July 1865. He received his B.A. and Ph.B. from the University of Tennessee in 1883. He earned a second B.A. two years later at Harvard and following a year of study abroad, graduated from Harvard Law School in 1889. He returned to Knoxville, where he was involved with his private law practice until 1907. In 1905 Sanford was named special assistant to the U.S. attorney general to prosecute the Fertilizer Trust, which led to his appointment as assistant attorney general two years later. He returned to Tennessee in 1908 when Theodore Roosevelt appointed him to the federal district court. Sanford initially refused the nomination, but was persuaded to accept by Justice Edward Douglass White, who suggested that the district court experience might prove to be a valuable stepping stone to the Supreme Court. Indeed, it was his performance on the federal trial bench that led Chief Justice Taft to strongly recommend his elevation to the Supreme Court in 1923. Support for Sanford's nomination came from other quarters as well, including labor leaders, businessmen, and public officials of both parties from the state of Tennessee.

Sanford was generally receptive to federal and state exercises of regulatory power during his limited tenure on the Court. He voted to sustain federal regulation of grain elevators and stockyards against both substantive due process and Tenth Amendment challenges in *Chicago Board of Trade v. Olsen* (1923) and *Tagg Bros. & Moorhead v. United States* (1930). Sanford's background as an antitrust prosecutor was evident in such cases as *Maple Flooring Manufacturers Ass'n v. United States* (1925) and *Cement Manufacturers Protective Ass'n v. United States* (1925), in which he sided with the government. His record in antitrust proceedings targeting labor unions was similar. For example, he joined Taft's unanimous opinion in the second *Coronado Coal* case (1925), voting to uphold a lower court ruling against the United Mine Workers. Similarly, in *Bedford Cut Stone* (1927), he was among the majority upholding a ruling against the union for boycotting the company's store.

Sanford delivered 130 opinions of the Court during his seven-year tenure, many of them in highly technical areas as such as taxation, bankruptcy, and patent law. His opinion in the *Pocket Veto Case* (1929) resolved a long-standing dispute between the

Edward Terry Sanford (Knaff and Brakebill, Collection of the Supreme Court of the United States)

legislative and executive branches and clarified the process by which the president could exercise pocket veto powers. Sanford supported local residential zoning in *Village of Euclid v. Ambler Realty Co.* (1926), and he disagreed with the Court's invalidation of minimum wage regulation in *Adkins v. Children Hospital* (1923). Sanford had the utmost respect for judicial precedent, and he frequently deferred to prior decisions even when they resolved questions of law in ways with which he had initially disagreed.

Sanford was relatively sensitive to the rights of individuals. Sanford joined the Court in such cases as *Meyer v. Nebraska* (1923), *Pierce v. Society of Sisters* (1925), and *Farrington v. Tokushiga* (1927), three cases in which both Catholics and immigrants were protected from restrictive state laws. His record was less patterned in civil rights cases, however. He was among the majority in *Moore v. Dempsey* (1923), which reversed the convictions of minority defendants in a trial influenced by a mob, and voted to invalidate the Texas all-white Democratic primary in *Nixon v. Herndon* (1927). At the same time, he voted in support of segregated public education in *Gong Lum v. Rice* (1927) and wrote the opinion sustaining racially restrictive real estate covenants in *Corrigan v. Buckley* (1926).

Sanford is best remembered for his First Amendment opinions in two landmark cases. In *Gitlow v. New York* (1925) and *Whitney v. California* (1927), Sanford's opinions sustained state authority to punish advocacy of the violent overthrow of government. If speech tended toward incitement of unlawful actions, Sanford thought, it fell outside the amendment's protections. The state cannot reasonably be required to "measure the danger from every such utterance in the nice balance of a jeweler's scale." Government authorities might extinguish a revolutionary "spark without waiting until it has enkindled the flame or blazed into the conflagration" (*Gitlow* 1925, 669).

The "bad tendency" doctrine utilized in *Gitlow* by Sanford was not particularly protective of political expression, but the opinion provided the foundation for more protective rulings by later Courts as it explicitly determined that the free speech provisions of the First Amendment applied to state governments through the Fourteenth Amendment. Sanford's opinion in *Gitlow* was characteristic of the post–World War I decisions upholding the conviction of Socialists and others who had opposed the war, even if the individuals posed no clear and present danger. The decision modified the "clear and present danger" test with the "bad tendency" or presumptive intent approach to determining when public security was sufficiently threatened to justify governmental intervention. *Whitney* upheld criminal convictions under a California syndicalism law, which provided for both imprisonment and a fine for joining an organization that favored violence in a political cause or industrial dispute.

Sanford was not categorically opposed to recognizing the First Amendment rights of political radicals, however. He wrote the Court's opinion in *Fiske v. Kansas*

(1927), which overturned the state criminal conviction of a member of the Industrial Workers of the World. *Fiske* marked the first successful defense invoking the Fourteenth Amendment to guarantee the federal right of free speech against state statutes. Similarly, Sanford dissented from the decision to deny American citizenship to Rosika Schwimmer, a pacifist who would not promise to bear arms in the nation's defense, in *United States v. Schwimmer* (1929).

Justice Sanford died unexpectedly on 8 March 1930 at the age of sixty-four and after just seven years on the Supreme Court. Sanford's death occurred on the same day as Chief Justice Taft's. David Burner commented that Sanford had so consistently voted with Taft that it was "fitting irony for the two to die on the same day" (Burner 1995d, 1098).

The Calvin Coolidge Appointment

Harlan Fiske Stone (1872–1946)

Harlan Fiske Stone was President Calvin Coolidge's only nominee for the Supreme Court and the last justice appointed while Taft was chief justice. Stone was nominated to replace Justice Joseph McKenna, who left the Court in late 1924. Stone was nominated on 25 January 1925, and confirmed by a vote of seventy-one to six in the Senate on 5 February 1925. Stone served on the Court until his death on 22 April 1946. His last five years on the Court were as its chief justice. In his twenty-one years on the Court, Stone produced 456 majority opinions. He also wrote ninety-three dissenting and thirty-seven concurring opinions. During his five years on the Taft Court, Stone participated in just over half (835) of its decisions with an opinion (51.73 percent). Stone wrote 113 (7.0 percent) of the Taft Court's majority opinions and wrote or joined thirty-five dissents and fifteen concurring opinions during those five years.

Stone was born in Chesterfield, New Hampshire, on 11 November 1872. He took his B.A. and M.A. degrees from Amherst College before completing his law degree at Columbia University in 1898. During his youth, he was a friend of Calvin Coolidge, and the two attended Amherst together. Stone was admitted to the New York Bar and began a successful corporate law practice. During this period, Stone became a professor of law at Columbia. He later served thirteen years as Dean of the Columbia Law School before returning to private practice in 1923. During this same period, Coolidge succeeded to the presidency upon the death of Warren Harding. He brought Stone to Washington in 1924 to replace U.S. attorney general Harry Daugherty, whose tenure as head of the Justice Department was ended by corruption including the Teapot Dome scandal. Coolidge not only wanted the scandal fully investigated, but wanted someone with a "squeaky clean" reputation. Stone met these needs. Although

Harlan Fiske Stone (Harris and Ewing, Collection of the Supreme Court of the United States)

he held the position of attorney general for only a year, Stone was able to effect substantial organizational changes in the Justice Department.

Stone was the first Supreme Court nominee to actually appear before the Senate committee reviewing his nomination. Stone effectively responded to the questions posed by the committee's members, and was subsequently confirmed by the full Senate on 5 February 1925. When Taft resigned in 1930, many expected Stone to succeed him. Taft, however, fearing that Stone would be unable to "mass" the Court—persuade the justices to join a single opinion—influenced Hoover to appoint Charles Evans Hughes instead. Stone served as an associate justice until 12 June 1941, when President Franklin Roosevelt nominated him to replace Hughes as chief justice. Stone was confirmed as chief justice in the Senate by voice vote on 27 June 1941, and he served in that capacity until his death on 22 April 1946.

Stone joined the Taft Court in 1925. Chief Justice Taft and the "Four Horsemen"—Justices Pierce Butler, James McReynolds, George Sutherland, and Willis Van Devanter—constituted an unyielding conservative majority throughout the decade of the 1920s. Many expected Stone to join this group, but almost immediately Stone became the third member of the Court's moderate/liberal minority, joining Oliver Wendell Holmes and Louis Brandeis. Throughout the remaining terms of the Taft Court, Stone's positions were typically represented in the opinions of Holmes and Brandeis, and it was not until the 1930s and the Hughes Court period that Stone became a spokesman for the moderate/liberal dissenters. Comparatively speaking, the Taft Court had a low dissent rate. Stone was the third most likely member of the Taft Court to dissent, ranking behind Holmes and Brandeis.

As a member of the Hughes Court, Stone was often found with Justices Brandeis and Benjamin Cardozo on the minority side in many significant economic regulation rulings. Like Holmes and Brandeis, Stone subscribed to the judicial self-restraint view. He believed that policy matters are the exclusive domain of the legislative branch, and Stone sought not to substitute his own policy preferences for those of elected legislators.

One of Stone's most powerful opinions was his dissent in *United States v. Butler*, a case that clearly reflected his judicial philosophy of self-restraint. To Stone, the majority in *Butler* read the Constitution too narrowly. In an emergency such as the Depression, courts ought not question the means by which Congress exercises delegated powers. The judicial power is to review legislative power to enact statutes, not whether the laws establish sound policy. Further, while executive and legislative actions are subject to judicial review, such review must be limited by the Court's self-imposed restraint. Stone remained on the minority side of most split decisions until the Court's doctrinal change of 1937. As a result of this change, Stone became part of the moderate/liberal majority for the remainder of the Hughes Court period.

During the infamous court-packing controversy of 1937, Stone indicated to Roosevelt that he did not support changing the Court's size. At the same time, he understood Roosevelt's frustration with the Court and was active behind the scenes in urging the nomination of justices with the judicial philosophy of Justices Brandeis, Cardozo, and himself. After 1937 the Court essentially deferred to economic regulation initiatives both at the federal and state level. The Court's consensus on government power to regulate the economy did not generalize to all other constitutional issues, however. Cases involving civil liberties became more frequent as World War II approached, and these issues would prove to be even more divisive than economic issues. The Roosevelt appointees on the Court were more than willing to speak their minds on these matters, causing Stone to refer to justices such as Hugo Black, William Douglas, and Frank Murphy as "wild horses." Stone's relations with most of the Roosevelt-appointed justices, both before and after his elevation to chief justice, were strained at best.

During his first term as chief justice, Stone agreed with Justices Black and Douglas in only 25 and 23 percent of the Court's decisions, respectively. His highest agreement rate was 70 percent with Justice Roberts. In 1943 Stone's agreement percentage was highest with Justices Reed (78 percent) and Frankfurter (70 percent). Stone's agreement level with Roberts dropped to 49 percent and rose to above 50 percent with the liberal activist members of the Court in 1943. Justice Jackson was in Germany for the war trials during Stone's last term, and the Court functioned with only eight members. During this last term, Stone agreed most often with Justices Reed (80 percent) and Burton (78 percent). His agreement rate with the liberal activist bloc was in the 40 percent range.

One of Stone's greatest contributions to American law came in his majority opinion in *United States v. Carolene Products Co.* (1938). The most significant aspect of this opinion was Footnote 4, in which Stone suggested that the Court should subject statutes dealing with civil liberties and discrimination issues to more searching examinations than laws pertaining to economic matters. He called for a "double standard." The decision affirmed the economic self-restraint position that Stone so strongly endorsed, but paradoxically suggested that statutes that restrict individual rights should be subject to a closer scrutiny. In Stone's view, the provisions of the Bill of Rights occupy a "preferred position" and require greater judicial vigilance. The doctrine still retains analytic value when the Court considers constitutional limits on government.

Stone's 1941 opinion in *United States v. Darby Lumber Co.* examined the Fair Labor Standards Act of 1938, viewed by many as the last major piece of New Deal legislation passed by Congress. The ruling reversed *Hammer v. Dagenhart* (1918), and Stone's opinion abandoned the previously operative distinction between manufacturing and commerce. Stone concluded that the goods produced and marketed by the lumber company were part of a stream of commerce and thus could be regulated under the commerce power. The *Darby* opinion also rejected the doctrine of "dual federalism" from Tenth Amendment jurisprudence. Stone suggested that the Tenth Amendment "states but a truism that all is retained which has not been surrendered" (*Darby* 1941, 124).

One of Stone's most noteworthy civil liberties opinions was delivered in *Minersville School District v. Gobitis* (1940). The Court ruled in *Gobitis* that citizens, at least public school students, could be compelled to salute the flag. Compulsory participation in the flag salute exercise was challenged by Jehovah's Witnesses on free exercise of religion grounds. Justice Frankfurter said for the majority that "conscientious scruples" cannot relieve citizens from obedience to "general law not aimed at the promotion or restriction of religious beliefs" (*Gobitis* 1940, 594). Stone was the only member of the Court to disagree. He concluded that if First Amendment guarantees are to "have any meaning they must be deemed to withhold from the state any authority to compel belief or expression of it where that expression violates religious convictions, whatever may be the legislative view of the desirability of such compulsion" (604). The position Stone advanced in *Gobitis* was sufficiently compelling that five other justices joined him when the Court overruled *Gobitis* less than three years later in *West Virginia State Board of Education v. Barnette* (1943).

As sensitive as Stone was to civil liberties, he failed to weigh in against the egregious internment of Japanese Americans during World War II. As an associate justice, Stone was one of the most significant contributors to American law. His chief justiceship was strikingly unsuccessful by comparison. Although his appointment to head the Court was universally praised, he proved ineffective in the post. He disliked administrative work and lacked the skills necessary to unify his Court and keep differences under control. Stone's Court was the most frequently divided and openly quarrelsome in history. The conflict included personal sniping and bickering as well as substantive differences on issues. By the end of Stone's tenure, critics asserted that the divisiveness had caused a decline in the Court's dignity and authority.

In many ways, the chief justiceship was an unhappy ending to an otherwise illustrious public life. Part of Stone's difficulty as chief justice was his tolerance for disagreement. In the minds of some Court colleagues, he let conferences over pending cases and certiorari petitions continue far too long. The Stone Court did not generally observe the normal Court protocol of allowing the justices to speak in turn by ascending levels of seniority. As a result, the discussions went in many different directions. Another problem was that Stone did not have the ability or perhaps the inclination to indulge the egos of some of his colleagues. Jackson believed that Stone's problem was that he dreaded conflict and wished to avoid it even at high cost. His willingness to permit dissension to continue unintentionally abetted the already high degree of conflict that was inevitable given the positions and personalities of the "wild horses" (Johnson 1994, 433).

Stone's performance as an associate justice led most scholars to rank him as one of the great justices to sit on the Court. His performance as chief justice was certainly less than that, but ought not obscure his otherwise outstanding tenure on the Court. He was incapable of applying the type of pressure that Taft and Hughes could exert in the conferences. He either could not or would not rely on comradeship or persuasiveness or political loyalties to bind his colleagues to him. He would not even seek to create this illusion for the public. Stone was almost sixty-nine when he succeeded Hughes in the center chair and served in that capacity less than five years. Those five years proved less satisfactory, less happy than his sixteen as associate justice. Even so, the experts ranked him as one of the great justices to sit on the Court.

References and Further Reading

Baker, Liva. 1991. *The Justice of Beacon Hill: The Life and Times of Oliver Wendell Holmes.* New York: HarperCollins.

Belknap, Michal R. 1986. "Mr. Justice Pitney and Progressivism." *Seton Hall Law Review* 16: 381–425.

Burner, David. 1995a. "Pierce Butler." In *The Justices of the Supreme Court, 1789–1995.* Leon Friedman and Fred L. Israel, eds. New York: Chelsea House, 1081–1090.

———. 1995b. "John H. Clarke." In *The Justices of the Supreme Court, 1789–1995.* Leon Friedman and Fred L. Israel, eds. New York: Chelsea House, 1038–1048.

———. 1995c. "James C. McReynolds." In *The Justices of the Supreme Court, 1789–1995.* Leon Friedman and Fred L. Israel, eds. New York: Chelsea House, 1006–1017.

———. 1995d. "Edward Terry Sanford." In *The Justices of the Supreme Court, 1789–1995.* Leon Friedman and Fred L. Israel, eds. New York: Chelsea House, 1091–1098.

———. 1995e. "George Sutherland." In *The Justices of the Supreme Court, 1789–1995.* Leon Friedman and Fred L. Israel, eds. New York: Chelsea House, 1069–1080.

———. 1995f. "Willis Van Devanter." In *The Justices of the Supreme Court, 1789–1995.* Leon Friedman and Fred L. Israel, eds. New York: Chelsea House, 969–977.

Cushman, Barry. 1994. "Mahlon Pitney." In *The Supreme Court Justices: A Biographical Dictionary.* Melvin I. Urofsky, ed. New York: Garland, 355–356.

Cushman, Clare, ed. 1993. *The Supreme Court Justices: Illustrated Biographies, 1789–1995.* Washington, DC: Congressional Quarterly Press.

Danelski, David J. 1994. "Pierce Butler." In *The Supreme Court Justices: A Biographical Dictionary.* Melvin I. Urofsky, ed. New York: Garland, 81–85.

Hamm, Richard F. 1994a. "Williams Rufus Day." In *The Supreme Court Justices: A Biographical Dictionary.* Melvin I. Urofsky, ed. New York: Garland, 139–140.

———. 1994b. "Joseph McKenna." In *The Supreme Court Justices: A Biographical Dictionary.* Melvin I. Urofsky, ed. New York: Garland, 289–290.

Johnson, John W. 1994. "Harlan Fiske Stone." In *The Supreme Court Justices: A Biographical Dictionary.* Melvin I. Urofsky, ed. New York: Garland, 425–434.

Mason, Alpheus T. 1956. *Harlan Fiske Stone: Pillar of the Law.* New York: Viking.

———. 1964. *William Howard Taft: Chief Justice.* New York: Simon and Schuster.

———. 1995a. "Louis D. Brandeis." In *The Justices of the Supreme Court, 1789–1995.* Leon Friedman and Fred L. Israel, eds. New York: Chelsea House, 1018–1035.

———. 1995b. "William Howard Taft." In *The Justices of the Supreme Court, 1789–1995.* Leon Friedman and Fred L. Israel, eds. New York: Chelsea House, 1049–1068.

McDevitt, Br. Matthew. 1974. *Joseph McKenna: Associate Justice of the United States.* New York: Da Capo.

McLean, Joseph E. 1946. *William Rufus Day: Supreme Court Justice from Ohio.* Baltimore, MD: Johns Hopkins University Press.

Paschal, Joel Francis. 1969. *Mr. Justice Sutherland: A Man against the State.* New York: Greenwood Press.

Post, Robert C. 1994. "William Howard Taft." In *The Supreme Court Justices: A Biographical Dictionary.* Melvin I. Urofsky, ed. New York: Garland, 457–463.

Rodell, Fred. 1955. *Nine Men: A Political History of the Supreme Court of the United States from 1790 to 1955.* New York: Vintage Books.

Shoemaker, Rebecca Sheppard. 1994. "Willis Van Devanter." In *The Supreme Court Justices: A Biographical Dictionary.* Melvin I. Urofsky, ed. New York: Garland, 485–487.

Strum, Philippa. 1984. *Louis D. Brandeis: Justice for the People.* Cambridge, MA: Harvard University Press.

———. 1994. "Louis Dembitz Brandeis." In *The Supreme Court Justices: A Biographical Dictionary.* Melvin I. Urofsky, ed. New York: Garland, 39–48.

Warner, Hoyt Landon. 1959. *The Life of Mr. Justice Clarke: A Testament to the Power of Liberal Dissent in America.* Cleveland, OH: Western Reserve University Press.

Watts, James F., Jr. 1995. "William R. Day." In *The Justices of the Supreme Court, 1789–1995.* Leon Friedman and Fred L. Israel, eds. New York: Chelsea House, 883–901.

White, G. Edward. 1976. *The American Judicial Tradition: Profiles of Leading American Judges.* Oxford, UK: Oxford University Press.

———. 1994. "Oliver Wendell Holmes, Jr." In *The Supreme Court Justices: A Biographical Dictionary.* Melvin I. Urofsky, ed. New York: Garland, 225–234.

Wolf, Michael Allan. 1994. "George Sutherland." In *The Supreme Court Justices: A Biographical Dictionary.* Melvin I. Urofsky, ed. New York: Garland, 449–453.

3

Significant Decisions

The 1920s was a decade of economic prosperity. National income reached $80 billion by 1929—more than double that of 1915. The decade featured what presidential candidate Warren G. Harding termed a period for the country to "return to normalcy," a time free from the reform agenda of the Progressive Party and the pervasive governmental controls associated with a world war. The 1920s was the time during which women's suffrage began and the nation experimented with Prohibition. The Taft Court of the 1920s, both conservative and activist in character, largely embraced the values and priorities of this period.

The most significant Taft Court decisions fall into four broad categories. First, there were rulings that addressed the institutional authority of the three branches of national government. Issues examined in this category included presidential appointment power and the authority of Congress to conduct investigations. Second, a number of significant rulings examined the extent of federal power to regulate interstate commerce and collect and spend tax revenues, and the authority of federal courts to review congressional spending decisions. Third were cases that involved initiatives by the states to regulate property. In these cases the Taft Court frequently utilized an approach known as substantive due process to strike down state regulatory measures. Fourth were decisions that addressed the constitutional rights of individuals. The discussion that follows attempts to represent the Taft Court's most significant responses to these constitutional issues.

A brief statistical overview begins the chapter. The average number of new cases that reached the Taft Court increased substantially when compared with the previous five terms of the White Court (1916–1920). The number of new cases on the Court's docket continued to increase during the first five terms of the Hughes Court (1930–1934). The total number of cases on the Court's docket was fairly stable over this same period—the Taft Court's average total docket level was slightly larger than both the White and Hughes Courts in their last five and first five terms, respectively. These numbers are represented in Table 3.1.

Table 3.2 indicates the average number of cases disposed as well as signed opinions issued between 1916 and 1934. The Taft Court disposed of 7.07 percent fewer

Table 3.1 Average Caseload Comparisons

	New Cases	% Change	Total Docket	% Change
White Court (1916–1920 Terms)	598.6	+12.27*	1090.2	–4.08*
Taft Court (1921–1929 Terms)	756.22	+26.33	1122.56	+2.97
Hughes Court (1930–1934 Terms)	966.2	+27.77	1070.0	–4.68

*Compared to 1911–1915 Terms of the White Court
(Epstein, Segal, Spaeth, and Walker 1994, 58–59)

Table 3.2 White, Taft, and Hughes Courts: Average Cases Disposed and Signed Opinions

	Signed Opinions	Cases Disposed
White Court (1916–1920 Terms)	202.6	239
Taft Court (1921–1929 Terms)	187.11	222.11
Hughes Court (1930–1934 Terms)	159.6	193.8

(Epstein, Segal, Spaeth, and Walker 1994, 72)

cases and issued 7.65 percent fewer signed opinions than the White Court during its 1916–1920 terms. The Hughes Court's productivity as defined by case dispositions and signed opinions in its first five full terms (1930–1934) declined from the levels of the Taft Court—the Hughes Court was down 12.75 percent in total cases disposed and 14.70 percent signed opinions from the Taft Court levels. These figures reflect some of the effect of the Judiciary Act of 1925, which gave the Supreme Court greater discretion over its docket. The average number of cases disposed by the Taft Court in its six terms before the act took effect was 248.5. The average number of cases disposed in the three terms following the effective date of the act was 161.67, a decrease of 34.94 percent.

Chief Justice Taft aggressively sought to "mass" the Court—to maximize the number of unanimous decisions rendered by his Court. To achieve this end, Taft "exploited personal courtesy and charm, maximized the assignment and reassignment powers, [and] relied on the expertise of his associates" (Mason 1964, 198). To a large degree, Taft was successful in achieving this result. Table 3.3 contains the average number of unanimous and one-vote rulings from 1916 through 1934. The average number of unanimous decisions over the nine Taft Court terms was 164 or 91.4 percent of its decisions. The rate of unanimous decisions was below that of the White

Table 3.3 White, Taft, and Hughes Courts:
Average Unanimous Decisions and One-Vote Decisions

	Signed Opinions	Unanimous Rulings	Percent Unanimous	One-Vote Decisions	Percent One-Vote
White Court (1916–1920 Terms)	202.6	186.2	91.9	7.4	3.65
Taft Court (1921–1929 Terms)	187.1	164.0	91.4	1.77	.95
Hughes Court (1930–1934 Terms)	159.6	144.6	90.6	5.0	3.13

(Epstein, Segal, Spaeth, and Walker 1994, 147, 161)

Court (1916–1920 terms) and higher than the Hughes Court (1930–1934 terms), but only marginally. Although division within these three periods is comparable, the extent of division is not. Less than 1 percent of the Taft Court decisions were decided by one vote while the proportion of one-vote decisions of the adjacent White and Hughes Court periods was over three times higher.

Table 3.4 presents the voting divisions on the Taft Court on a term-by-term basis. The level of unanimous rulings ranged from a high of 92.82 percent in the 1925 Term to a low of 78.61 percent in Taft's first term as chief justice.

Table 3.5 represents the individual performance of Taft Court justices. Five justices, Chief Justice Taft and Justices Brandeis, Holmes, McReynolds, and Van Devanter, participated in virtually all of the Taft Court's cases. Chief Justice Taft wrote the highest number of majority opinions for his Court; his 252 opinions of the Court accounted for 15.61 percent of the majority opinions issued during his tenure. Justices Holmes and Brandeis produced 215 (13.32 percent) and 201 (12.45 percent) of the Taft Court majority opinions, respectively. Of the five justices sitting for the entirety of the Taft Court period, Justice Van Devanter produced only 98 of the Court's majority opinions (6.07 percent) in the nine full terms. Justice Stone, by comparison, wrote 113 (7.0 percent) of the majority opinions in only five Taft Court terms. Individual data on each justice on a term-by-term basis is provided in the Appendix.

Institutional Rulings

The most significant rulings from the Taft Court included those which examined the institutional power of the three branches of the federal government. Among the most important were decisions about congressional capacity to delegate power to the executive branch, the scope of congressional power to conduct investigations, regulate interstate commerce, tax, and spend, and whether the courts ought to intervene

Table 3.4 Taft Court Vote Summaries by Term

Year	1921	1922	1923	1924	1925	1926	1927	1928	1929	total
9-0	119	205	179	153	179	156	134	103	55	1283
% 9-0	68.79	91.11	85.43	66.52	85.64	78.39	77.46	79.84	85.94	79.49
8-0	17	3	8	53	15	11	10	3	1	121
% 8-0	9.83	1.33	3.77	23.04	7.18	5.53	5.78	2.33	1.56	7.49
7-0			1	1		1	2	1		6
% 7-0			.47	.43		.50	1.16	.78		.37
6-0						1				1
% 6-0						.50				.06
% unan	78.61	92.44	88.68	90.00	92.82	84.92	84.39	82.95	87.50	87.42
8-1	6	4	8	9	5	8	3	9	1	53
% 8-1	3.47	1.78	3.77	3.91	2.40	4.02	1.73	6.98	1.56	3.28
7-1	3			4	1					8
% 7-1	1.73			1.74	.48					.50
6-1	1					1				2
% 6-1	.57					.50				.12
7-2	8	10	6	4	4	7	7	4	2	52
% 7-2	4.62	4.44	2.83	1.74	1.91	3.52	4.05	3.10	3.13	3.22
6-2	1		5						1	7
% 6-2	.57		2.36						1.56	.37
6-3	13	2	4	3	4	9	10	7	3	55
% 6-3	7.51	.89	1.89	1.30	1.91	4.52	5.78	5.43	4.69	3.41
5-3	3	1	1	1		1		1		8
% 5-3	1.73	.44	.47	.43		.50		.78		.50
5-4	2			2	1	4	7	1	1	18
% 5-4	1.16			.87	.48	2.01	4.05	.78	1.56	1.12
Total opins	173	225	212	230	209	199	173	129	64*	1612
Total case	209	304	247	255	250	226	206	145	73*	1915

*The number of cases and signed opinions during Taft's service as chief justice. Charles Evans Hughes replaced Taft in February 1930. The Court disposed of 156 cases during the full term and issued 145 opinions.

Table 3.5 Taft Court Vote Summaries by Justice

Justice	Taft Ct Yrs	Participation	Maj Opins	Concurring	Dissents
BRANDEIS	all	1603	201	23	87
%		99.32	12.45	1.43	5.39
BUTLER	7.5	1360	161	4	25
%		84.26	9.98	.25	1.55
CLARKE	1	163	20	6	13
%		10.10	1.24	.37	.81
DAY	1	171	15	0	4
%		10.59	.93		.25
HOLMES	all	1609	215	14	68
%		99.69	13.32	.87	4.21
McKENNA	3.5	699	67	0	18
%		43.31	4.15		1.12
McREYNOLDS	all	1610	183	11	80
%		99.75	11.83	.68	4.96
PITNEY	1	166	11	2	4
%		10.29	.68	.12	.25
SANFORD	7.5	1404	128	7	23
%		86.99	7.93	.43	1.43
STONE	5	835	113	15	35
%		51.73	7.00	.93	2.17
SUTHERLAND	7.5	1415	150	3	39
%		87.67	9.29	.19	2.42
TAFT	all	1608	252	3	19
%		99.63	15.61	.19	1.18
VAN DEVANTER	all	1612	98	2	20
%		99.88	6.07	.12	1.24

on behalf of taxpayers to review federal spending measures. Several of the most important institutional power cases during the Taft Court era involved executive power—not surprising for a Court headed by an ex-president.

The power to appoint and remove federal officials has occasionally produced conflict between the president and Congress. President Andrew Johnson, for example, was nearly impeached in 1868 for his dismissal of Secretary of War Edward Stanton in violation of the federal Tenure of Office Act that required Senate consent for the removal. A decade later, Congress passed another law that provided that several classes of postmasters, appointed for four-year terms, could be removed by the president but only with the advice and consent of the Senate. The Taft Court had occasion to review this law in *Myers v. United States* (1926). President Woodrow Wilson had removed a postmaster without Senate consent before the end of the postmaster's four-year term. By a six-to-three vote, the Taft Court upheld the removal, finding that the 1876 statute requiring Senate consent was an unconstitutional interference with executive prerogative. Seeking to clarify the issue, Taft wrote an unusually lengthy (in excess of seventy pages) opinion making clear that the president's removal power was an inherent part of executive power under virtually any circumstances—that authority to remove is plenary and free from limitations that might be imposed by Congress. This was certainly a prerogative Taft would have valued during his term as chief executive.

Taft contended that had the constitutional framers wished to give the Senate advice and consent over removals, it would have expressly said so. In the absence of such constitutional language, the removal power was exclusively an executive prerogative. The framers could never have intended to leave Congress "unlimited discretion to vary fundamentally the operation of the great independent branch of government and thus most seriously to weaken it." The absence of an explicit limit placed on the removal power by the executive is a "convincing indication that none was intended" (*Myers* 1926, 127–128).

The ability to remove personnel is an essential means by which a president can exert executive control. In Taft's view, the constitutional framers were unwilling to compromise the president's authority to appoint executive officers and limited the Senate's role to assessing prospective appointees at the time of nomination only. When the Senate advises and consents on nominees, it has "full power" to reject "newly proposed" nominees. Such a check, Taft continued, "enables the Senate to prevent the filling of offices with bad or incompetent men or with those against whom there is a tenable objection." The power to prevent the removal of an officer who has already served under the president, however, is fundamentally different. A veto by the Senate on removals is a "much greater limitation upon the executive branch and a much more serious blending of the legislative with the executive than a rejection of a proposed appointment" (*Myers* 1926, 121). Presumably the Senate is well informed when reviewing the fitness of a nominee. But in the nature of things, said the former president, the "defects" of an executive officer are "facts to which the President . . . must be better informed than the Senate." These executive branch officers must be the president's "alter ego" in the matters of that department where the president is required by law to exercise authority. When the president "loses confidence in the intelligence, ability, judgment or loyalty of any one of them, he must have the power to remove him without delay" (133–134). The power to remove previously confirmed executive officers, he argued, was an element of the executive power granted the president by Article II incidental to the power of appointment.

Taft argued that the Constitution does not require the president to retain executive branch officials who contradict his orders. Article II directs the president to "take care that the law be faithfully executed." This he could do only "by the assistance of subordinates." It would be both unreasonable and undesirable to conclude that Congress could "fasten upon him, as subordinate executive officers, men who would by their insufficient service under him, by their lack of loyalty to the service, or by their different view of policy, might make it impossible to fulfill his executive obligations" (*Myers* 1926, 131). Thus, Taft concluded, a president has an unrestricted power to remove all officials nominated by him.

In separate dissents McReynolds and Brandeis argued that Senate consent was required for the removal of executive branch officers. Removal itself may be an executive act, but determining the conditions for removal is a legislative function committed to Congress under the necessary and proper clause. McReynolds argued that the Taft "theory" allowed the president to "override the declared will of the [Senate]." The Taft view goes "far beyond" practices previously followed and "conflicts with the history of the Constitution." Indeed, said McReynolds, to adopt it would be "revolutionary" (*Myers* 1926, 204). Brandeis's dissent more sharply focused the separation of powers issue. The concept was put into the Constitution "not to promote efficiency, but to preclude the exercise of arbitrary power" and the concept did not make each branch of government "completely autonomous" (291, 293). His reading of the Constitution led him to conclude that "nothing" in support of the asserted power can be inferred from the "silence of the Convention of 1787 on the subject of removal." Brandeis pointed to the many statutes that restricted unilateral presidential removal. Each of these statutes "became law with the approval of the President." He cited historical evidence that revealed a legislative practice, "established by concurrent affirmative action of Congress and the President, to make consent of the Senate a condition of removal for those offices to which a President made fixed-term appointments with such consent" (294). The presidents of the 1920s were not inclined to utilize the broad removal power identified in the *Myers* ruling. The decision raised the possibility, however, that future presidents might even remove members of independent federal commissions notwithstanding the fact that in some instances the conditions for the removal of such officers were stipulated by Congress. Nine years after *Myers*, the uncertainty was resolved. The Hughes Court distinguished in *Humphrey's Executor v. United States* (1935) between purely executive officials subject to presidential removal and those who perform quasi-legislative or quasi-judicial functions, who may not be unilaterally removed by the president.

The president has authority to reduce or rescind federal criminal penalties through the power to pardon. The pardon clause is contained in Article II, Section 2, and provides that the president shall have the power to "grant reprieves or pardons for offenses against the United States, except in cases of impeachment." A presidential pardon frees a convicted criminal from serving any uncompleted term of imprisonment and from paying any unpaid fine. The pardon power is to be used to correct a conviction or sentence that seems mistaken, harsh, or disproportionate to a crime. Loss of certain civil rights often accompanies conviction of a crime. Described by John Marshall as an "act of grace," a pardon relieves a person not only from a criminal sentence as such, but also restores any civil rights that may have been lost. Because a pardon restores these rights, one may still be sought on behalf of persons who have completed sentences.

The Taft Court considered presidential pardons in two cases, *Ex parte Grossman* (1925) and *Biddle v. Perovich* (1927). Philip Grossman operated a speakeasy in Chicago during prohibition. Federal officials obtained an injunction against Grossman enjoining further alcohol-related activity. He persisted, however, and was charged with violation of the court order. He was found guilty, fined, and sentenced to a one-year prison term. In December 1923, President Coolidge pardoned Grossman and reduced his sentence to payment of the fine. Grossman was released, but the federal trial court judge who had originally cited Grossman for contempt ordered him back to jail notwithstanding the pardon. It was the trial judge's opinion that the presidential power to pardon applied only to offenses against the United States and did not extend to sentences for contempt of court. The Taft Court unanimously upheld the pardons. Executive intervention through a pardon is intended to afford relief from "undue harshness or evident mistake in the operation or enforcement of the criminal law." The administration of justice by courts, Taft continued, is "not always wise or certainly considerate of circumstances which may properly mitigate guilt." In order to provide remedy where appropriate, it has "always been thought essential" to vest in some authority other than the courts' power to "ameliorate or avoid particular criminal judgments." It is a check given to the executive for special cases. Taft called it a "perver[sion]" to exercise the power to "destroy the deterrent effect of judicial punishments." Nonetheless, "whoever is to make it useful must have full discretion to exercise it" (*Grossman* 1925, 121–122). Taft acknowledged that courts must have the power to protect themselves by resorting to the contempt power, but that power is exercised "without the restraining effect of a jury and without many of the guaranties which the Bill of Rights offers." Is it unreasonable, Taft posed, to provide for the "possibility that the personal element may sometimes enter into a summary judgment pronounced by a judge who thinks his authority is flouted or denied?" (122). Taft's answer was no.

Two years after *Grossman*, the Taft Court examined the presidential pardon power in *Biddle v Perovich*. Vuco Perovich was convicted of murder in Alaska and sentenced to be hanged. President Taft intervened and commuted his sentence to life imprisonment. Perovich himself challenged the sentence commutation some years later because he had not consented to it. The Court, with Chief Justice Taft not participating, unanimously rejected Perovich's challenge. Justice Holmes said for the

Court that the power to pardon is "part of the constitutional scheme." When a pardon is granted it is the "determination of the ultimate authority" that the public interest would be served by "inflicting less than what the judgment fixed." Just as the original sentence was "imposed without regard to the prisoner's consent and in the teeth of his will, . . . the public welfare, not his consent, determines what shall be done" (*Perovich* 1927, 486).

An unusual separation of powers issue arose in *Springer v. Philippine Islands* (1928). The Philippine Organic Act served as the constitution for the territory and created a government for the islands based on the "separation of powers" principle. A number of government-owned corporations operated in the Philippines. The governor general of the Islands possessed exclusive power to vote the stock of these corporations. The Philippine legislature then enacted a statute providing that the presiding officers of each of the two legislative chambers would serve on the Board of Control of these corporations in addition to the governor general. The governor general challenged the law, contending that the statute impermissibly encroached on his executive authority. The Taft Court agreed in a six-to-three ruling.

Relying in part on *Myers*, Justice Sutherland's majority opinion concluded that the appointment of corporation officers was an executive function rather than a legislative one. He suggested that the legislative function was to make laws, but it was the executive function to "enforce them or appoint agents charged with the duty of such enforcement." Because the legislative branch does not have the power of appointment unless expressly granted, the legislature "cannot engraft executive duties upon a legislative office, since that would be to usurp the power of appointment by indirection." The Court determined that the legislative members serving on the Board of Control were not performing either legislative or judicial functions. As a result, there was "logical ground for concluding that they do fall within that of the remaining one of the three among which the powers of government are divided" (*Springer* 1928, 202).

Justice Holmes, in dissent, did not see the distinction between legislative and executive functions as identifiable with "mathematical precision" that would divide governmental branches into "watertight compartments." The Constitution does not establish fields of "black and white." Even the specific constitutional provisions are "found to terminate in a penumbra shading gradually from one extreme to the other" (*Springer* 1928, 210–211). Nonetheless, Holmes saw the legislature as appropriately involved in the operations of government-owned corporations. The corporations involved were "private concerns which the legislature had the power to incorporate." Although the majority contended that the functions of the Board of Control were neither legislative nor judicial, Holmes saw these duties as "no part of the executive functions of Government but rather fall into the indiscriminate residue of matters within legislative control" (212).

The "separation of powers" principle does not categorically preclude the involvement of one branch in the business or processes of another. The presidential veto is a good example. The Constitution places the president into the legislative process to the extent that the president must sign a proposed law before it goes into effect. The president is alternatively allowed to veto a proposed law, in which case Congress may, if it has enough votes, override the presidential veto. The Taft Court dealt with what is called the "pocket veto" in 1929. Article I, Section 7 provides for the conventionally understood form of presidential veto. It also says that if a president does not return a proposed bill to Congress within ten days, the proposal shall become law "in like manner as if he had signed it." The Court ruled in the *Pocket Veto Case* (1929) that the Article I reference to ten days was to ten calendar days. Article I further provides, however, that the bill shall become law if not returned within ten days to the "House in which it shall have originated unless the Congress by their adjournment prevent its return, in which case it shall not be a law." In the *Pocket Veto Case,* a case that involved monetary claims presented by a number of Indian tribes in the state of Washington, Congress had passed a proposal and presented it to President Calvin Coolidge. Before the ten days had passed and before Coolidge took any action, both houses of Congress adjourned. The primary objective of the veto language in Article I was to give the president a conditional veto power, one subject to congressional response. The ten-day requirement prevents the president from turning this conditional veto authority into an absolute one by his own inaction. Every congressional recess is not subject to this rule because a president might try to exploit every brief recess to circumvent the legislative right to override his veto. The rule from this decision applies only if Congress actually concludes its business and formally adjourns. In virtually all of the cases involving presidential power, the Taft Court resolved separation of power issues in favor of the executive.

Congress and Legislative Power

Article I vests all legislative power in a two-chamber Congress. Article I is silent on investigative power that might reside with Congress although it is believed that it is an implicit power auxiliary to the authority to legislate and appropriate. The Waite Court had narrowly defined congressional investigative power in *Kilbourn v. Thompson* (1881). The Taft Court significantly broadened the scope of congressional investigative power in *McGrain v. Daugherty* (1927). The Senate inquiry in *McGrain* arose out of the oil lease and other scandals that occurred during the Harding presidency. Harry Daugherty managed Harding's successful presidential campaign in 1920 and then became United States attorney general. Daugherty's Justice Department failed to prosecute those involved in the scandals, and Daugherty was eventually forced by

President Coolidge to resign his post in March 1924. The Senate appointed a special committee to investigate not only the scandals, but the Justice Department's shortcomings as well. Among those subpoenaed to appear before the committee was Mally Daugherty, the attorney general's brother. He failed to appear and an arrest warrant was issued. McGrain, a deputy sergeant at arms of the Senate, arrested Daugherty with the intention of bringing him before the Senate to testify. Daugherty was freed from custody by a federal district court, which concluded that the Senate had exceeded its authority by initiating the investigation and ordering Daugherty's arrest.

The Taft Court unanimously disagreed. Justice Van Devanter, speaking for the Court, acknowledged that there is no express provision vesting either house of Congress with "power to make investigations and exact testimony to the end that it may exercise its legislative function advisedly and effectively." He pointed, however, to established legislative practice, noting that the power to "secure needed information by such means has long been treated as an attribute of the power to legislate" (*McGrain* 1927, 161). Although Congress has no "general power to inquire into private affairs," investigations may be conducted into subjects on which Congress can legislate. Under this broad "proper legislative purpose" test, congressional investigations could range widely.

Van Devanter reviewed both congressional enactments such as the Compulsory Testimony Act of 1857 and previous Court decisions, and concluded that Congress has authority not only to institute inquiries and exact evidence touching subjects within its jurisdiction but also to subject "defaulting and contumacious witnesses to indictment and punishment in the courts" (*McGrain* 1927, 168). The power of inquiry, "with process to enforce it," said Van Devanter, "is an essential and appropriate auxiliary to the legislative function." A legislative body cannot effectively legislate in the absence of information about the subject of prospective legislation. It is often the case that the legislative body does not possess the information it needs, so "recourse must be had to others who do possess it." Van Devanter said that "experience has taught us that mere requests for such information often are unavailing." In addition, information that is volunteered is "not always accurate or complete." As a result, "some means of compulsion are essential to obtain what is needed" (174–175).

The lower court that had ordered Daugherty's discharge from custody believed the Senate investigation had put the former attorney general "on trial," and thus exercised a judicial authority it did not possess. When the Senate's investigation was "rightly interpreted," however, it revealed that the object of the investigation was to "obtain information for legislative purposes." Although the resolution that initiated the investigation of Teapot Dome and other scandals did not explicitly "avow that it is intended to be in aid of legislation," said Van Devanter, it showed "that the subject to be investigated was the administration of the Department of Justice." This subject was one on which "legislation could be had and would be materially aided by the information which the investigation was calculated to elicit." The only "legitimate object" the Senate could have had in ordering the investigation was to support its legislative function. The Court was satisfied that the "subject matter was such that the presumption should be indulged that this was the real object." Daugherty argued that if the power of inquiry is sustained, it may be "abusively and oppressively exerted." Van Devanter replied that even if this contention is true, it "affords no ground for denying the power" (*McGrain* 1927, 176–178). *McGrain* clearly established that Congress could use its contempt power to compel unwilling witnesses to appear. At the same time, *McGrain* recognized the rights of witnesses testifying before congressional committees—witnesses cannot be compelled to answer questions that exceed the scope of committee authority or are not pertinent to the subject under inquiry.

Two years later, the Taft Court expanded *McGrain* in *Barry v. United States ex rel. Cunningham* by sustaining the power of a committee to punish an uncooperative witness for contempt. Cunningham was subpoenaed to appear before a Senate committee investigating campaign finance irregularities in the election of Senator William Vare from Pennsylvania. Cunningham was a member of Vare's campaign organization and refused to disclose certain information to the committee. He was cited for contempt of Congress and arrested. He challenged the arrest by arguing that he had been taken into custody for the purpose of getting the sought-after information. The Court of Appeals for the District of Columbia determined that the information sought from Cunningham was not pertinent and that he was justified in refusing to answer the committee's questions. The Taft Court unanimously reversed, concluding that the committee's inquiry was within its constitutional authority. Justice Sutherland agreed that the committee's investigation appeared judicial in character because when the Senate or House exercises the power to judge elections and the qualifications of its members, it acts as a "judicial tribunal." Because the Senate is the sole authority under the Constitution to make these determinations about its members, "it may exercise . . . the incidental power of compelling the attendance of witnesses without the aid of statute" (*Barry* 1929, 616, 619).

There is a principle that generally prohibits the redelegation of authority conveyed by the Constitution. Article I assigns the lawmaking power to Congress, which it can exercise or, under certain circumstances, delegate further. The nondelegation principle seems straightforward at an abstract level, but becomes more problematic when applied to particular situations. Since the inception of our constitutional system it has been understood that some legislative power must be delegated to the executive branch. The Supreme Court has recognized this reality and allowed the limited delegation of legislative power. Chief Justice Taft said in *J.W. Hampton, Jr. & Company v. United States* that the "extent and character of permissible delegation must be fixed according to common sense and the inherent necessities of the governmental coordination" (*Hampton* 1928, 406).

The *Hampton* case provided the Taft Court with an opportunity to consider the delegation issue raised by implementation of the Tariff Act of 1922. As was evident in *Myers*, the Taft Court was clearly willing to expand executive branch authority. A tariff is a tax imposed on goods coming into the country and is intended to protect American products from unfair competition from items produced in foreign countries. The statute established tariff rates, but authorized the president to adjust those rates to effectively offset lower foreign production costs and thereby achieve the policy objectives set by Congress. The Court concluded that the delegation of power in this instance was not excessive. Rather, the law merely called upon the president to execute "an intelligible principle" laid down by Congress.

Taft said it was "clear what Congress intended" in the statute. Congress wished to "secure by law" the use of customs duties on imported products that would "equal the difference between the cost of producing in a foreign country the articles in question and laying them down for sale in the United States, and the cost of producing and selling like or similar articles in the United States." Such duties not only produce revenue, but allow domestic producers to "compete on terms of equality with foreign producers" in U.S. markets (*Hampton* 1928, 404). Taft then addressed the center of the delegation issue. He noted the difficulty in measuring the difference between domestic and foreign production costs and concluded that Congress could have reasonably doubted its own capacity to "make the adjustment accurately" (405).

It was for these reasons that Congress set forth its policy objectives and authorized the executive branch to implement that policy. This authorization included monitoring the production cost differential and adjusting the duty to achieve congressional policy objectives. If Congress were required to "fix every rate," it would be "impossible to exercise the power at all." Taft said that "common sense" requires that in fixing the duty rates, Congress may direct the executive branch to "fix those rates after hearing evidence and argument concerning them from interested parties." Although Congress may not delegate its "purely legislative power" to the executive branch, it may set forth "general rules of action" under which the executive agent shall proceed. The Court concluded the "same principle" that allows Congress to delegate rate making in interstate commerce "justifies a similar provision for fixing of customs duties on imported merchandise" (*Hampton* 1928, 407–409).

The Taft Court's rulings in cases like *McGrain* and *Hampton* substantially expanded the prerogatives of Congress. The Court's approach in legislative power cases such as these was similar to that used in *Missouri v. Holland* (1920), a case decided during the last year of the White Court era. *Missouri v. Holland* involved a treaty between the United States and Great Britain (for Canada) designed to protect migratory birds. The treaty directed both the United States and Canada to enact legislation prohibiting the "killing, capturing or selling" of migratory birds. Congress did so with the Migratory Bird Act of 1918, which established closed seasons on several species of birds migrating between Canada and the United States. The state of Missouri brought suit, attempting to bar enforcement of the federal statutory regulations. The White Court concluded that although a treaty is subject to constitutional limitations, a treaty and any statute enacted pursuant to it will prevail over Tenth Amendment claims. The theory contained in Holmes's opinion not only recognized the supremacy of treaties over state sovereignty, but was later used to assert the supremacy of executive agreements over state law.

Courts and Judicial Power

The Taft Court examined a number of issues relating to federal courts and their authority. One such issue involved the independence of the federal judiciary. Article III prohibits reducing the compensation of any federal judge for the duration of his or her judicial tenure. This was one of the ways the constitutional framers sought to secure the independence of the judicial branch. In 1920 the White Court ruled in *Evans v. Gore* that a federal judge could not be assessed income tax because it would unconstitutionally reduce his salary. Justice Van Devanter said that the "primary purpose" of the prohibition against diminishing judges' salaries was not to "benefit the judges, but, like the clause in respect to tenure, to attract good and competent men to the bench and to promote that independence of action and judgment which is essential to the maintenance of [constitutional principles]" (*Evans* 1920, 253). Except for his salary, Van Devanter continued, a federal judge "is as much within the taxing power as other men are." But for the "common good," his compensation must be protected from diminution "in any form" to further the end that federal judges are "perfectly and completely independent" (263). Holmes and Brandeis disagreed, concluding that judges were not a "privileged class, free from bearing their share of the costs of the institutions upon which their well-being if not their life depends" (265). More importantly, Holmes saw the language of the Sixteenth Amendment as conclusively resolving the issue—it gave Congress the power to collect taxes on incomes "from whatever source derived."

The Taft Court extended the *Evans* reasoning in 1925 when it held in *Miles v. Graham* that a judge appointed after the effective date of a tax was also entitled to immunity. Compensation was fixed by Congress when Graham began his official duties, and "to tax in respect of this," said Justice McReynolds, "would diminish it within the plain rule of *Evans v. Gore*" (*Miles* 1925, 509). Congress overrode *Miles* by express legislation and the Hughes Court overruled *Evans v. Gore* in *O'Malley v. Woodrough* (1939).

States have occasionally attempted to restrict the transfer of civil suits from state courts to federal courts, particularly for out-of-state corporations. The Supreme

Court historically had ruled these attempts to be unconstitutional, and the Taft Court did so as well. In *Terral v. Burke Construction Co.* (1922), for example, the Court reviewed an Arkansas law that provided that when an out-of-state corporation removed a suit to federal court, its license to do business within the state would be revoked. The Taft Court unanimously held that the law inhibited the free exercise of a constitutional right. Chief Justice Taft referred to prior decisions as prohibiting a state from imposing conditions on doing business in the state. The principle, he suggested, does not depend on the "character of the business the corporation does." Rather, the Constitution "confers upon citizens of one State the right to resort to federal courts in another," and even the sovereign power of a state in excluding out-of-state corporations is subject to the constitutional limitations (*Terral* 1922, 533–534).

Fairchild v. Hughes, also decided in 1922, involved a citizen's challenge to the process used to ratify the Nineteenth Amendment, which extended the vote to women. Fairchild sought to prevent Secretary of State Charles Evans Hughes from declaring the amendment officially ratified and putting it into effect. He claimed there were irregularities in some state ratification processes that precluded those states from being tallied as states approving the amendment. The Taft Court unanimously concluded that Fairchild's challenge did not meet the "cases or controversies" requirement of Article III. Fairchild has the right, said Justice Brandeis, only to require the government to act according to law. This general right does not entitle a private citizen to use federal courts to determine whether a "constitutional amendment about to be adopted, will be valid" (*Fairchild* 1922, 129–130).

The issue in *Keller v. Potomac Electric Power Co.* (1923) was whether Congress could confer on Article III courts the authority to revise determinations of administrative agencies. The District of Columbia Court of Appeals had set aside an order of the Public Utilities Commission, which had set the value of utility property for rate-setting purposes. The federal law that had extended jurisdiction on such matters had prohibited Supreme Court review of the appellate court's decisions. The Taft Court struck down the statute, however, because it had empowered the appellate court to review and modify the legislative judgment of the commission. As a result, the law brought the appellate court "intimately into the legislative machinery for fixing rates" (*Keller* 1923, 422). The Taft Court concluded that Congress could not impose a legislative, executive, or administrative duty on a court exercising judicial power derived from Article III. An Article III court, the Taft Court concluded, could decide only judicial cases or controversies.

Two other Taft Court rulings substantially insulated the spending decisions of Congress from challenges in federal court. The two consolidated cases were *Frothingham v. Mellon* and *Massachusetts v. Mellon* (1923). The enactment under attack in these cases was the Sheppard-Towner Maternity Act of 1921 that appropriated federal funds to those states complying with its objectives to reduce maternal and infant mortality and protect the health of mothers and infants. Frothingham, an individual taxpayer, sought an injunction against implementation of the act on the ground that she was deprived of property "under the guise of taxation." Massachusetts sought an injunction claiming federal usurpation of state authority to provide for the health and well-being of its citizenry. The Court disposed of both cases on standing grounds, without getting to the substantive taxing and spending issues as such. In a unanimous decision, the Court found that Frothingham had no interest or injury either "inflicted or threatened" to establish standing to sue. Similarly, Massachusetts was seen as presenting no "justiciable controversy" either in "its own behalf" or as a "representative of its citizens."

Justice Sutherland authored the opinion of the Court. He characterized Frothingham's interest in municipal taxing and spending as "direct and immediate." Her status as a federal taxpayer, however, was "very different." The taxpayer's interest is "shared with millions of others" and is "comparatively minute and indeterminable." Future effects on tax levels are "so remote, fluctuating, and uncertain" that there is no basis for activating the "preventive powers of a court of equity." Given the vast numbers of taxpayers involved, administration of such statutes as the Maternity Act is a "matter of public, and not of individual, concern." If single taxpayers may litigate such issues, then every other taxpayer may challenge any and all other enactments (*Frothingham* 1923, 486–487). To make the courts a continuous forum for such challenges would interfere with the apportionment of functions under the American system of government. Rather, courts are to be reserved for cases in which a party can not only demonstrate invalidity of a statute, but also can show that he or she has "sustained or is in immediate danger of sustaining some direct injury" and has not merely suffered in some "indefinite way in common with people generally" (488).

The Court held in the Massachusetts case that Article III did not automatically confer jurisdiction simply because the state was a party to an action rather than an individual. Jurisdiction extends to suits in which a state is an actual "party to proceedings of judicial cognizance." Opponents of Sheppard-Towner argued that the federal program impermissibly usurped functions properly belonging to the states and undermined state sovereignty, but the Court found the state without injury in this case. The burden of taxation falls to the state's inhabitants, and the statute did not "require the states to do or yield anything." As a result, the question presented was "political and not judicial in character," and therefore is not a matter where courts should act (480, 482). The Court also rejected the state's attempt to bring suit "as the representative of its citizens." The only way that a state may afford protection to its citizens is through "enforcement of its own criminal statutes," or by "opening its courts to the injured persons for the maintenance of civil suits or actions." Citizens must bring suits themselves. The state may not act as *parens patriae* [reference to a traditional state role as "parent of the country" or legal guardian] in a federal case because the United States, not the states, stands in that capacity. Thus, Massachusetts was determined to have no justiciable interest in this situation and could not bring suit on its own behalf (485–486).

These cases provided the Court with an opportunity to examine whether taxpayer status established standing to sue. The Court's answer in *Frothingham* was that taxpayer status in itself did not satisfy the standing requirement. To have standing, a party must demonstrate a direct injury. Frothingham's interest was simply too "minute and indeterminable" as well as "remote, fluctuating, and uncertain to warrant judicial introduction." The Court was fearful that allowing the status of taxpayers to satisfy the standing requirements would trigger judicial examination of virtually every federal enactment appropriating public funds. To a substantial degree, separation of power arguments permeated Sutherland's opinion in *Frothingham*. He reviewed the functions of each branch and said that the courts were not to "invade" the legislative domain of appropriation as a "general rule" (487–488). The law of standing is thought by many to begin with *Frothingham*, as it was the first case in which the Court focused on the nature of the plaintiff's interest. The *Frothingham* case served as an effective barrier to taxpayer suits challenging federal expenditures until the late 1960s, when the Court allowed challenge of the federal funding of certain activities in nonpublic schools in *Flast v. Cohen* (1968).

The Taft Court decided a number of cases that defined the jurisdictional boundaries of lower federal courts. Section 2 of Article III gives the federal courts jurisdiction over cases "affecting Ambassadors, other public Ministers and Consuls." The Taft Court held in *Ex parte Gruber* (1925) that this refers to diplomatic personnel of foreign countries to the United States, and not to American ambassadors representing the United States abroad. Justice Sutherland said the provision was put into Section III because of the "important and sometimes delicate nature of our relations with and intercourse with other nations." It is a privilege, he concluded, "not of the official, but of the sovereign or government he represents, . . . considerations which plainly do not apply to the United States in its own territory" (*Gruber* 1925, 303). In a closely related decision, the Taft Court held in *Ohio ex rel. Popovici v. Agler* (1930), that the Article III language extending federal judicial power to ambassadors did not exclude jurisdiction of state courts over a suit against a vice-consul for divorce and alimony. Despite the seemingly "sweeping" language of Article III, Justice Holmes said the interpretation of the jurisdictional provisions of the Article must draw on tacit assumptions about the reason certain language was chosen by the constitutional framers. It long has been understood, he argued, that the "whole subject of the domestic relations of husband and wife, parent and child, belongs to the States and not to the laws of the United States" (*Popovici* 1930, 383).

The judicial power question addressed in *Tutun v. United States* (1926) was whether a person seeking U.S. citizenship can appeal the denial of a naturalization petition to a circuit court of appeals. The Taft Court answered in the affirmative. The decision turned on whether a naturalization proceeding is a "case" meeting the "cases and controversies" requirement in Article III. Justice Brandeis said for the unanimous Court that whether a proceeding that "results in a grant is a judicial one, does not depend on the nature of the thing granted, but upon the nature of the proceeding which Congress has provided for securing the grant." Whenever the law provides a "remedy enforceable in the courts according to the regular course of legal procedure and that remedy is pursued, there arises a case within the meaning of the Constitution." A petition for naturalization, Brandeis concluded, "is clearly a proceeding of that character" (*Tutun* 1926, 576–577).

The Taft Court held in *Postum Cereal Co. v California Fig Nut Co.* (1927) that a proceeding in the Court of Appeals of the District of Columbia under terms of the Trade-Mark Registration Act of 1905 was an administrative matter and not a "case" within the meaning of Article III. The commissioner of patents had rejected a request to cancel a trademark registration and the court of appeals had refused review. The Trade-Mark Act had conferred jurisdiction on the court of appeals to review judgments of the commissioner of patents. The act was amended in 1920 without the explicit language on court of appeals jurisdiction contained in the earlier version. The court of appeals concluded that the amendment divested it of jurisdiction and refused to review the commissioner's decision in the *Postum Cereal* case. The Taft Court ruled that the court of appeals's jurisdiction had not been withdrawn by the 1920 amendment, but also that the Supreme Court could not review any Trade-Mark Act decision of the court of appeals. Chief Justice Taft said that the court of appeals's decisions in trademark cases "is not a judicial judgment," but merely an "administrative decision." It is an "instruction" to the commissioner of patents "by a court which is made part of the machinery of the Patent Office for administrative purposes." In the exercise of such administrative function "it does not enter a judgment binding parties in a case as the term case is used in the third article of the Constitution" (*Postum Cereal* 1927, 698–699).

A Kentucky law provided that parties before a general jurisdiction court of the state could petition for a declaratory judgment. Liberty Warehouse Company filed a petition seeking a declaratory judgment from a federal district court of its rights under terms of the Kentucky law. The Taft Court ruled in *Liberty Warehouse Co. v. Grannis* (1927) that the federal courts did not have jurisdiction to make such a declaration. Jurisdiction under Article III, said Justice Sanford, extends only to "cases and controversies" and does not extend to the "determination of abstract questions or issues framed for the purpose of invoking the advice of the court without real parties or a real case" even though state law permitted it for state courts (*Liberty Warehouse* 1927, 74). The Taft Court reiterated this conclusion in *Willing v. Chicago Auditorium Ass'n* the following year.

Congressional authority to create courts is not confined to provisions of Article III. Language in Article I allows Congress to "constitute tribunals inferior to the Supreme Court." Courts established on the authority of Article I are known as legislative courts, and while their function is partially judicial, such courts often perform administrative functions as well. Article I courts are those in U.S. territories and the District of Columbia, for example, where the courts were created for special geographical reasons. In *Keller* and *Postum*, the Taft Court acknowledged the authority of District of Columbia courts over local matters and that the Supreme Court could not review decisions of such courts when they disposed of administrative, nonjudicial issues. The Taft Court held in *Ex parte Bakelite Corp.* (1929) that specialized federal courts such as the Court of Claims and the Court of Customs and Patent Appeals were "neither confined in their jurisdiction nor protected in independence by Article III, but both had been created by virtue of substantive powers possessed by Congress under Article I." As a result of their Article I origin, Congress could give such courts "nonjudicial functions such as revisionary powers over grants of patents and rates fixed by the local public utility commission" (Pritchett 1984, 119).

Bakelite involved a petition to prevent the Court of Customs Appeals from reviewing the findings of the Tariff Commission. Unlike constitutional courts, jurisdiction exercised by Article I courts is "not part of that judicial power which is defined in the third article of the Constitution." Article I courts, said Justice Van Devanter, "may be clothed with the authority and charged with the duty of giving advisory opinions in proceedings which are not cases or controversies within the meaning of Article III." Article I courts are thus created "in aid of legislative or executive action, and therefore outside the admissible jurisdiction of courts established under [Article III]" (*Bakelite* 1929, 450).

Van Devanter's opinion specifically addressed the Court of Claims as well. That court was created and maintained as a special tribunal to examine and determine money claims against the United States. This is a function "which belongs primarily to Congress as an incident of its power to pay the debts of the United States"—a power over which Congress "has discretion either to exercise directly or to delegate to other agencies." On the specific question of the Court of Appeals reviewing the findings of the Tariff Commission, the Taft Court concluded it could not keep the court from "proceeding within the limits of its jurisdiction, as [it] was doing in this instance" (452, 461).

Federal Commerce Power

Congress began more frequently to exercise its authority over interstate commerce in the late 1800s than in the preceding century. Among the commerce clause-based measures Congress enacted were the Sherman and Clayton Acts, which were designed to regulate market restraints produced by industrial monopolies. The Supreme Court was typically unreceptive to these antitrust initiatives, however. In addition, the White Court began to limit the authority of some federal regulatory agencies created by Congress under the commerce power. In these cases, the Court typically distinguished between production and commerce and limited the reach of federal commerce power to the latter only.

One of the agencies subjected to Court-imposed restraints was the Federal Trade Commission (FTC). In *Federal Trade Commission v. Gratz* (1920), for example, the White Court denied the FTC the power to determine unfair methods of competition because the language of the Federal Trade Commission Act of 1914 had not sufficiently defined what constituted unlawful business practices. The act had been designed to allow the FTC some flexibility when considering new kinds of unfair practices. The White Court concluded, however, that "it is for the courts, not the Commission, ultimately to determine as a matter of law what they include" (*Gratz* 1920, 427). By doing so, the Court eroded the finality of many of the FTC's determinations.

The Taft Court maintained this approach into the 1920s. In *Federal Trade Commission v. Curtis Publishing Co.* (1923), for example, the Court unanimously set aside an FTC order against a publisher that had entered into agreements with wholesalers to prohibit the wholesalers from distributing publications of other publishers. Justice McReynolds said that the Court must "have power to examine the whole record and ascertain for itself the issues presented and whether there are material facts not reported by the Commission." When the Court did its own fact-finding, it concluded that Curtis Publishing Company's publisher's contract was "one of agency, not of sale upon condition," and found nothing in the case record to show that Curtis Publishing had acted unlawfully (*Curtis Publishing* 1923, 580–581).

The White Court had decided *United States v. L. Cohen Grocery Co.* (1921) on this same basis, although *Cohen* did not involve the FTC, but a provision of the Lever Act. The Lever Act was enacted as a war measure and made it illegal to "exact excessive prices for any necessities." The law remained in effect even after the cessation of hostilities until ratification of the peace treaty officially concluded the war. The Court found the law unconstitutional because the statute had failed to set sufficiently clear standards for determining what constituted unjust pricing. The vagueness of the statute impermissibly delegated legislative power to the courts and deprived businesses such as L. Cohen Grocery of the right to be informed of the charges brought against it. The Court concluded that the law was unconstitutional not because it attempted to regulate prices, but because it failed to clearly specify prohibited acts.

The Court did not categorically reject wartime measures that imposed price restraints. The scarcity of housing in the District of Columbia led Congress to impose rent controls and other regulations on property located in the District. Unlike the

Lever Act, Congress provided more clearly defined standards by which rental prices could be judged. Although the statute controlled prices, it also assured landlords a reasonable return on their property. The White Court upheld the law in *Block v. Hirsh* (1921). Justice Holmes spoke for the five-justice majority and referred to the severe housing shortage in the District, saying that "circumstances have clothed the letting of buildings in the District with a public interest so great as to justify regulation by law" (*Block* 1921, 155). The law had been carefully drafted, its criteria were comparatively clear, and it would be in effect for only two years. The dissenters, Chief Justice Taft, Justices McKenna, Van Devanter, and McReynolds, essentially reiterated the majority opinion from *L. Cohen Grocery.*

The District of Columbia rent control regulation upheld in *Block v. Hirsh* came before the Taft Court again in *Chastleton Corp. v. Sinclair* (1924). Although the language of the statute remained the same as in *Block,* the Taft Court reached a different conclusion. A unanimous Court ruled against the Rent Commission in *Chastleton* for several reasons, but primarily because the emergency that "justified interference with the ordinarily existing private rights in 1919 had come to an end by 1922." Although the emergency stemming from the war might continue beyond the armistice, Justice Holmes said that if "all that remains of war conditions is the increased cost of living, that is not in itself a justification of the act" (*Chastleton* 1924, 546, 548).

Throughout the Fuller Court era, federal commerce power regulations were typically found constitutionally defective. This position was large retained by the White and Taft Courts, with one notable exception—federal regulation of the "instruments" of commerce. At the time, the railroads were most vulnerable to regulation. The White Court ruled in the *Shreveport Rate Case* (*Houston, East and West Texas Railway Co. v. United States,* 1914) and other railroad rate cases that the Interstate Commerce Commission (ICC) could regulate intrastate rates that affected interstate rate structures. Congress passed the Transportation Act of 1920, which returned the railroads to management by private owners after a period of strict government control during World War I. In addition, the act expanded the authority of the ICC not only over interstate rates, but intrastate rates as well. The Taft Court unanimously upheld the act and with it the authority to revise intrastate rates in *Railroad Commission v. Chicago, Burlington & Quincy Railroad* (1922).

The ICC had established new rate structures in 1921 that in some instances overrode rate schedules established by state regulatory agencies. The Transportation Act imposed an "affirmative duty" on the ICC to "fix rates and to take other important steps to maintain an adequate railway service for the people of the United States." Although the act did not enable the ICC to deal with intrastate rates themselves, it authorized the ICC to "remove any discrimination against interstate or foreign commerce." This mandate, said Chief Justice Taft, "clearly contemplates that such discrimination, resulting from intrastate rates unduly low as compared with interstate rates . . . and tending to thwart the purpose of that section [of the Transportation Act], may be removed by the Commission." Taft suggested that if the purpose of the act was "interfered with by a disparity of intrastate rates, the Commission is authorized to end the disparity by directly removing it, because it is plainly an undue, unreasonable, or unjust discrimination against interstate or foreign commerce, within the ordinary meaning of those words" (*Railroad Commission* 1922, 585–586). The effect of this and similar rulings was to blur any distinction between inter- and intrastate rail rates and expand federal authority over a national rail system through the ICC.

The Packers and Stockyards Act of 1921 was enacted to address a number of "discriminatory and deceptive" practices in the meat packing business. The concern prompting the legislation was fear of a meat packing monopoly that would produce arbitrarily lowered prices to sellers and impose higher consumer prices. The law authorized the secretary of agriculture to supervise rates for handling livestock in the stockyards and to issue cease and desist orders, with the force of law, to halt what he considered unwarranted behavior not in the public interest. The objective to be gained through the law was the "free and unfettered flow of live stock from the ranges and farms of the West and the Southwest . . . to the feeding places and fattening farms in the Middle West or East for further preparation for the market" (*Stafford v. Wallace* 1922, 515). Over the sole dissent of Justice McReynolds, the Court upheld the act.

The Court's opinion in *Stafford* was delivered by Chief Justice Taft. Key to the Court's sustaining of the federal act was the "stream of commerce" concept, which had its origin in *Swift & Company v. United States* (1905). When products are "in stream," commerce is still in progress. Even interruption of transit short of final destination did not limit the reach of federal commerce power. In this instance, Taft said that the stockyards are "not a place of rest or final destination." Livestock continually arrives, is sold, and "moved out" to give place to the "constantly flowing traffic that presses behind." The stockyards were seen as "but a throat through which the current flows." The transactions that occur in the stockyards "are only incident to this current." These transactions "cannot be separated from the movement to which they contribute" and "necessarily take on its character." The act treats stockyards as "great national public utilities" in an attempt to promote the flow of commerce from producers in the West to consumers in the East. The act assumed that stockyards conducted business so affected with a public interest that they could be subjected to federal regulation (*Stafford* 1922, 515–516).

Taft emphasized that this interpretation of the commerce clause was the result of "natural development" of interstate commerce under "modern conditions." It was the "inevitable recognition" that the "stream of commerce" concept captured the "very essence" of commerce among the states (518–519). The stream-of-commerce approach permitted the Taft Court to sustain regulation of those stockyard practices taking place between the receipt of livestock in the yards and the subsequent shipment of that same livestock interstate. Taft and several of his colleagues were not known for deferring to legislative judgments when it came to property regulation, but Taft called for such deference in stream-of-commerce cases. Whatever activity amounts to "more or less constant practice, and threatens to obstruct or unduly burden the freedom of interstate commerce" is within the regulatory reach of Congress. Further, it is "primarily for Congress to consider and decide the fact of danger and meet it." The Court, said Taft, will "certainly not substitute its judgment" for that of Congress in these situations unless the "relation of the subject to interstate commerce and its effect upon it are clearly nonexistent" (521).

The stream-of-commerce rationale applied in cases like *Stafford* provided the most significant exception to the general predisposition of the Taft Court to limit the reach of federal commerce power. Justice Holmes's opinion in *Swift* suggested that the sale of commodities was an essential component of the interstate commerce stream. The Taft Court went even further in *Chicago Board of Trade v. Olsen* (1923) by defining the kinds of effects on streams of commerce that could be regulated through the federal commerce power. Congress had tried to regulate the sale of commodity futures in the Futures Trading Act of 1921, a measure that was based on federal taxing power. The Taft Court ruled in *Hill v. Wallace* (1922) that the dealings of boards of trade were essentially local in character and could not be brought under federal control through the taxing power. Following the Court's ruling in *Hill v. Wallace,* Congress passed the Grain Futures Act in September 1922. The measure was intended to prevent "obstructions and burdens" on the interstate trading of grain and regulate the buying and selling of grain futures. Although the regulatory objectives were similar to those in the Future Trading Act, The Taft Court upheld the Grain Futures Act as a legitimate regulation of interstate commerce in *Chicago Board of Trade v. Olsen.*

Chief Justice Taft distinguished the two statutes. The Grain Futures Act "only purports to regulate interstate commerce and sales of grain for future delivery on boards of trade" because Congress found that manipulation of grain futures had become a "constantly recurring burden and obstruction to that commerce" (*Chicago Board of Trade* 1923, 32). Taft saw the regulation of the sale of grain futures as analogous to the regulation of the activities of stockyards. Like the stockyards, the sales on the Chicago Board of Trade are "just as indispensable to the continuity of the flow of wheat from the West to the mills and distributing points of the East and Europe." Taft acknowledged differences in "form and detail" between the Grain Futures Act and the Packers and Stockyards Act at issue in *Stafford,* but concluded that the Court's conclusion "must be the same" as in *Stafford* (54). Taft noted that the "manipulations of grain futures for speculative profit . . . exert a vicious influence and produce abnormal and disturbing . . . fluctuations that are not responsive to actual supply and demand . . . [and] disturb the normal flow of actual consignments" (58–59). The Taft Court's conclusion was that the Chicago Board of Trade engaged in activities that were so closely related to the public interest that the Grain Futures Act was a permissible exercise of the commerce power.

Federal regulation of railroads was frequently upheld, even when other federal attempts to regulate privately owned business were struck down, because railroads were seen as "instruments" of interstate commerce. One of the most extreme railroad regulations came in the Adamson Act of 1916. The act was a wartime statute that, among other things, dealt with workday and compensation issues for railroad workers. The White Court sustained the Adamson Act in *Wilson v. New* (1917), seeing the law as necessary to prevent the wartime interruption of commercial flow because of labor-management disputes in the nation's railroads.

The provisions of the Transportation Act of 1924 called for the recapture of railroad earnings that exceeded a "fair return" on their property. The recaptured funds were to be distributed to less profitable railroads. The Taft Court unanimously upheld the law in *Dayton-Goose Creek Railway Co. v. United States* (1924). The reasoning from *Railroad Commission* provided the basis of Chief Justice Taft's majority opinion. Dayton-Goose Creek Railway engaged in both interstate and intrastate commerce and challenged the recapture provisions of the Transportation Act upon receiving an ICC order to create a reserve fund for so-called excess profits. The *Railroad Commission* opinion had referred to the need for an integrated national railway system. To that end, the ICC was recognized as having authority both to prevent burdens on interstate commerce as well as to raise intrastate rates if they were so low as to discriminate against interstate rates. Taft concluded that a federal commerce power that reached only the fixing of reasonable rates and prevention of discriminatory rates was "too narrow." Rather, to regulate railroads "in the sense intended" by Congress, the ICC must have the power to "foster, protect, and control the commerce with appropriate regard to the welfare of those who are immediately concerned, as well as the public at large." If the commerce clause enables Congress to build railroads, "it certainly may exert affirmative control over privately owned railroads, to see that such are equipped to perform, and do perform, the requisite public service" (*Dayton-Goose Creek Railway* 1924, 478–479).

Taft then turned to the recapture of railroad revenue exceeding a fair return. Railroads, "however strong financially, however economical its facilities, or favorably situated as to traffic, are not entitled as a constitutional right to more than a net operating income upon the value of its properties which are being devoted to transportation." The owner of a business dedicated to public service "must recognize that . . . [he] cannot expect either high or speculative dividends but that his obligation limits him to only fair or reasonable profit" (481). Although the railroads have excess returns in their possession, the so-called excess "never becomes its property and [the railroads] accept custody of the product of all the rates with this understanding." The Court found it evident that the carrier "never has title to the excess as to render the recapture of it by the Government a taking without due process" (484). The policy contained in the Transportation Act of 1924 viewed all railway lines as part of an integrated national system similar to that existing during World War I. Although some carriers might generate more income than others, the public interest required that the ICC make sure that less profitable carriers be kept operating.

The need to see the railroads as components of a national system also shaped the Court's response in *Colorado v. United States* (1926). This case involved an ICC order permitting a railroad company to abandon a branch line lying wholly within Colorado. The Taft Court concluded that the ICC had the authority to order abandonment. The branch line had become unprofitable, and the Court's judgment was that continued operation of the branch would produce deficits for the company, which, in turn, would place an undue burden on the interstate operations of the carrier. Justice Brandeis spoke for a unanimous Court and said that "excessive local expenditures may so weaken the financial condition of the carrier" that it might have to increase interstate rates to offset losses resulting from the continued operation of the branch (*Colorado* 1926, 163). Such a result would unduly burden interstate commerce. The Court concluded that the federal commerce power enables Congress to determine the extent to which intrastate service must be subordinated to ensure that interstate service is adequately provided.

Three years after the *Stafford v. Wallace* ruling, the Taft Court unanimously sustained the National Motor Vehicle Theft Act of 1919 in *Brooks v. United States* (1925). The statute prohibited the interstate movement of stolen automobiles and was an obvious attempt by Congress to use the federal commerce power for police power ends. The measure was not unlike the failed congressional attempt to regulate child labor, which had been struck down by the White Court in *Hammer v. Dagenhart* (1918). The Child Labor (Keating-Owen) Act of 1916 prohibited the interstate movement of items produced by child labor. *Hammer* severely limited the use of federal authority over interstate commerce as a means for pursuing police power (governmental authority to regulate for health, safety, morals, and general welfare) objectives. The White Court concluded that the Child Labor Act usurped authority reserved to the states by the Tenth Amendment. In doing so, the White Court distinguished the child labor measure from previously upheld uses of the federal commerce power. The children involved in the challenge to Keating-Owen worked in a North Carolina cotton mill. The Court found that the items produced by the mill were themselves "harmless." Although Congress could ban the flow of lottery tickets, impure food, intoxicating liquor, and prostitutes in interstate commerce, it could not use the commerce power to ban interstate transportation of harmless goods simply to reach the evil of child labor.

Chief Justice Taft wrote in *Brooks* that established doctrine allowed Congress to exercise "the police power . . . within the field of interstate commerce" to prevent the "use of such commerce as an agency to promote immorality, dishonesty or the spread of any evil or harm to the people of other states from the state of origin" (*Brooks* 1925, 436–437). Interstate commerce facilitated theft by "help[ing] to conceal the trail of the thieves," which was deemed a sufficient reason to use the commerce power to combat car theft. It was generally understood, Taft argued, that the automobile "radical[ly] change[d] the transportation of persons and goods." The speed with which automobiles move and the "ease with which evil-minded persons can avoid capture have greatly encouraged and increased crimes," and Congress was reasonably prompted to respond. "Congress may properly punish such interstate transportation," Taft continued, "because of its harmful result and its defeat of the property rights of those whose machines against their will are taken into other jurisdictions" (438–439).

When the White Court upheld federal bans on interstate transportation of such things as lottery tickets and liquor, it had suggested that these federal initiatives were consistent with existing state policy and acted to further the effect of state law. This was not true with respect to child labor. Many states had not regulated child labor, and restrictions based on the federal commerce power would, in the Court's view, effectively "control the States in their exercise of the police power over local trade and manufacture." The Court was much more willing to sustain federal measures that reinforced state policies than those that did not. Unlike the child labor law, the National Motor Vehicle Theft Act was compatible with state law.

The Taft Court's ruling in *Brooks* did not generalize. More often, the production-commerce distinction was used to limit federal commerce power. In *Oliver Iron Mining Co. v. Lord* (1923) and several other consolidated cases, the Court considered state taxes on iron mining and concluded that mining itself was not interstate commerce. Like manufacturing, the mining of iron ore was seen as a "local business subject to local regulation and taxation." Justice Van Devanter said that "its character in this regard is intrinsic, is not affected by the intended use or disposal of the product, . . . and persists even though the business be conducted in close connection with interstate commerce" (*Oliver Iron Mining* 1923, 178–179).

Sherman Act

The Sherman Anti-Trust Act of 1890 was intended to protect commerce from unlawful restraints on trade—from economic damage resulting from monopolies. The objectives of the statute were not achieved because the Supreme Court, particularly under Chief Justice Melville Fuller, restricted its application in such rulings as *United States v. E.C. Knight Co.* (1895). In *Knight* the Court distinguished monopolies of production or manufacture from monopolies that involved actual transport, an action that occurs only after production is completed. Monopolies of production were determined to be outside the reach of the Sherman Act. The White Court then followed with its "rule of reason," which diminished even further the effectiveness of the Sherman Act. In cases such as *Standard Oil Co. v. United States* and *United States v. American Tobacco Co.* (1911), the White Court ruled that the Sherman Act could regulate only those business practices that unduly restrained trade. Use of the so-called rule of reason allowed the Court to exempt a number of practices from antitrust regulation because they were not "unreasonable" despite their monopolistic character. As important as the restrictions the Court placed on the Sherman Act were, states evidenced no inclination to take action against production monopolies on their own, leaving many businesses virtually free from any kind of regulation as a result.

Following World War I, the White Court indicated that it was not receptive to governmental attempts to restrict business practices alleged to be destructive of open competition. Prior to the war, United States Steel, the country's largest corporation, was charged with using its dominant position to eliminate competition within the industry. Ten years later, the White Court dismissed the suit in a four-to-three decision, with Justices Brandeis and McReynolds not participating. Brandeis chose not to participate because he had been publicly critical of the corporation prior to joining the Court. McReynolds recused himself because he had led the antitrust prosecution of U.S. Steel during his tenure as attorney general. Chief Justice White and Justices McKenna, Holmes, and Van Devanter put an end to the government's efforts by applying the rule of reason. It was their view that corporate size by itself did not inevitably result in Sherman Act violations. Even if an industrial combination is created with the expectation of becoming a monopoly, that in itself is insufficient to make it an actual monopoly for Sherman Act purposes. Corporations like U.S. Steel could only be held accountable for deliberate attempts to exploit their monopoly status.

Many of the Taft Court's antitrust rulings reaffirmed the doctrines of the previous three decades. In 1922 the Court concluded in *Federal Baseball Club of Baltimore, Inc. v. National League* that professional baseball was entitled to an exemption from the Sherman Act. Although teams constantly traveled from one state to another, the Court ruled that baseball was not a subject of commerce. The business of presenting exhibitions of baseball is "purely a state affair," and movement of players across state lines "is not enough to change the character of the business." Transport, said Justice Holmes, "is a mere incident, not the essential thing" (*Federal Baseball Club* 1922, 208–209).

The Taft Court used the distinction between production and commerce—the latter commencing only after the former is concluded—to free the mining industry from the Sherman Act as well. In *United Mine Workers v. Coronado Coal Co.* (1922), the Court concluded that coal mining is not interstate commerce. As a result, conspiracy to obstruct mining at a particular site, through a labor strike for example, may not be a restraint of interstate commerce even though it "may prevent coal from going into interstate commerce." It can become enough of a restraint on commerce, Chief Justice Taft suggested, only if it is "intended to restrain commerce . . . or has necessarily such a direct, material and substantial effect to restrain it that the intent reasonably must be inferred" (*United Mine Workers* 1922, 410).

The Harding-Coolidge Commerce Department, headed by Secretary Herbert Hoover, supported the development of trade associations as a means of stabilizing economic conditions. Such coordinated action by businesses arguably impaired competition in violation of federal antitrust laws. The Taft Court, however, gave this cooperative business technique limited immunity from antitrust laws. In *Maple Flooring Manufacturers Ass'n v. United States* (1925), the Court found no evidence that the trade association had a "necessary tendency to cause direct and undue restraint of competition" prohibited by the Sherman Act (*Maple Flooring Manufacturers* 1925, 578). Trade associations "openly and fairly gather and disseminate information" about their products and their costs. Competition, said Justice Stone, "does not become less free merely because the conduct of commercial operations becomes more intelligent through the distribution of knowledge of all the essential factors entering into the commercial transaction." Although knowledge that there is a surplus of a market commodity, Stone continued, "would undoubtedly tend to diminish production, the dissemination of that information cannot itself be said to be restraint upon commerce in any legal sense." Restraint on free competition begins when "improper use is made of that information through any concerted action which operates to restrain the freedom of action of those who buy and sell" (583).

The Court held that the Sherman Act was neither intended to "inhibit the intelligent conduct of business operations nor . . . suppress such influences as might affect operations of interstate commerce through the application of the individual intelligence of those engaged in commerce." Persons who cooperate in gathering and disseminating information, Justice Stone concluded, "are not engaged in unlawful conspiracies in restraint of trade merely because the ultimate result of their efforts may be to stabilize prices or limit production" (583–584).

As in earlier Court eras, the principal deviation from the Taft Court's practice of restricting application of antitrust laws occurred in railroad cases. In these cases the Court dealt with interstate carriers as the means by which interstate commerce took place. Anything that impaired their capacity to deliver interstate transportation was seen as subject to federal legislation. These rulings closely resembled the "stream" or "flow of commerce" rulings in such cases as *Stafford v. Wallace*. In *United States v. Southern Pacific Co.* (1922), for example, the Court concluded that one system of railroad transportation cannot acquire control of another when the effect of such acquisition is to "suppress or materially reduce the free and normal flow of competition in the channels of interstate trade" (*Southern Pacific* 1922, 230).

Labor and Antitrust

Near the end of the nineteenth century, businesses successfully sought court orders to protect their interests against labor unions. The Sherman Act frequently provided the basis for judicial intervention because certain activities, such as strikes, were seen as resulting in unlawful restraint of trade. Use of the Sherman Act against unions in such cases as the *Danbury Hatters Case* (*Loewe v. Lawlor* 1908), prompted Congress to exempt unions from injunctions in the Clayton Act of 1914. The act provided that labor was neither a commodity nor an article of commerce and that antitrust regulations should not be applied to prevent unions from pursuing lawful objectives. Section 20 of the Clayton Act expressly prohibited federal courts from issuing injunctions or restraining orders in labor disputes "unless necessary to prevent irreparable injury to property, or to a property right." Section 20 also forbade injunctions against peaceful picketing or primary boycotts. Although union leaders regarded these provisions as creating absolute immunity from judicial intervention in labor-management disputes, the courts interpreted the Clayton Act otherwise.

The Supreme Court did not rule on the Clayton Act provisions until *Duplex Printing Co. v. Deering* (1921) and substantially limited their utility for unions by finding that most labor actions had direct effects on commerce. *Duplex Printing* involved a secondary boycott of a manufacturer's products in New York in support of a strike in Michigan. A boycott is the practice of abstaining from dealing with someone, most often a business or merchant. A boycott is usually undertaken in response to a dispute between a party and the business. A secondary boycott involves an attempt by the initiating party to persuade other customers of the business to similarly withdraw patronage. The White Court concluded that the Clayton Act had neither legitimized secondary boycotts nor provided unions with a blanket exemption from the antitrust laws. Rather, the law protected unions only when they pursued legitimate objectives in lawful ways. The Court further concluded that a secondary boycott could be enjoined because the Clayton Act limits on judicial intervention applied only to the immediate parties in a dispute. Because the union engaged in the secondary boycott was not an immediate party, its illegal conduct was subject to a restraining order. In other words, the White Court determined that any combination and conspiracy to restrain interstate commerce was subject to injunction under the Sherman Act, even as amended by the Clayton Act. The Court's decision in *Duplex Printing*, coming less than two months after Warren Harding's election as president, suggested that the injunction was again available to businesses for use against organized labor notwithstanding the seemingly clear directives of the Clayton Act.

The Taft Court examined the effect of labor union actions on interstate commerce in several cases, one of which was *United Mine Workers v. Coronado Coal Co.* (1922). The Court ruled that national unions such as the United Mine Workers could not be held liable for damage occurring during local strikes without substantial evidence of the national union's participation or ratification of the destructive actions of union members. At the same time, the Court held that unions at both the national and local level were subject to federal suit under the Sherman Act to recover damages for destruction of property committed in strikes if it could be shown that the union conspired to restrain interstate commerce.

A second case involving Coronado Coal, *Coronado Coal Co. v. United Mine Workers* (1925), had an even more damaging effect on organized labor. The case grew out of the United Mine Workers efforts to unionize southern coal mines in order to protect wage levels for union miners in other parts of the country. The company's owners sought to change its labor force from union to nonunion miners and shut down its mines in preparation for reopening on an open-shop basis. Once the mines resumed operations union members appeared at one of the mines, overwhelmed guards who had been hired by the company, and stopped all mining operations. Management then obtained an injunction against the union leadership and its members.

United States marshals were placed on site to enforce the injunction. When mining operations began again, a "large force of union members and their sympathizers" armed with guns furnished by the union local, appeared at the mine site. The union members attacked the replacement workers and proceeded to destroy the property and equipment. The Taft Court found that the violence on the part of union members was aimed at stopping the interstate shipment of nonunion coal and fell within the reach of the Sherman Act. When unlawful activities are intended to "restrain or control the supply entering and moving in interstate commerce . . . their action is a direct violation of the Anti-trust Act" (*Coronado Coal* 1925, 310). The actions of the union and its members in this case were, in the Taft Court's view, intended to stop production of nonunion coal and prevent its shipment to markets in other states.

The Taft Court extended the *Coronado Coal* ruling to boycotts in *Bedford Cut Stone Co. v. Journeyman Stone Cutters' Ass'n* (1927). A number of union stonecutters refused to work on limestone cut by workers employed by Bedford Cut Stone, a nonunion company. Bedford Cut Stone obtained an injunction against the striking stonecutters on the basis that the Sherman Act prohibited secondary boycotts. The Taft Court concluded that even though this particular strike appeared to have limited effect because of its local character, it nonetheless unduly burdened the stream of interstate commerce. Justice Sutherland acknowledged that the "ultimate end" of the strike was to unionize cutters and carvers at the Bedford Cut Stone Co., but inquired "how was that end to be effected?" The evidence, Sutherland suggested, "shows indubitably that it was an attack upon the use of the product in other states to which it had been and was being shipped." The strike was directed against the use of Bedford Cut Stone's products in other states with the "plain design of suppressing or narrowing the interstate market" over and above the attempt to bring about a "change of conduct on the part of [Bedford Cut Stone] in respect of the employment of union members in Indiana" (*Bedford Cut Stone* 1927, 47). There was obvious incongruity between the narrow view of interstate commerce taken in cases such as *E.C. Knight* and *Hammer v. Dagenhart* and the Taft Court's opinion in *Bedford* where no distinction between local and national effects on commerce was noted. Many trade restrictions resulting from industry action "would be tolerated by the Court under the rule of reason." At the same time, the Court would disregard its rule of reason "when asked to apply it to the clearly reasonable activities of a labor union" (Urofsky and Finkelman 2002, 636–637). Minimal local activity thus became interstate commerce when the Court felt the need to immunize a manufacturer from interference by a labor union. Justices Brandeis and Holmes disagreed. They saw neither an attempt by the union to boycott Bedford Cut Stone nor a broader "class struggle." Rather, it was simply a struggle between "particular employers and their employees" (*Bedford Cut Stone* 1927, 60).

Federal Taxing Power

The Sixteenth Amendment provides that Congress "shall have the power to lay and collect taxes on incomes from whatever source derived, without apportionment among the several states, and without regard to any census or enumeration." The Supreme Court has regarded federal authority to tax incomes as subject to certain limitations, however. In *Eisner v. Macomber* (1920), for example, the White Court held that stock dividends could not be treated as taxable income; stock dividends were viewed as capital and not income. Nonetheless, the Court recognized in cases such as *McCray v. United States* (1904) and *United States v. Doremus* (1919) that the federal taxing power could be used to achieve regulatory objectives. In *Doremus* Congress was allowed to use a tax to compel persons engaged in the production or distribution of narcotics to register with the government. *Doremus* was a five-to-four decision with four justices dissenting on the ground that the statute was an attempt to exercise police power reserved to the states. The views of the *Doremus* dissenters won control of the Taft Court three years later in *Bailey v. Drexel Furniture Co.* (1922), also known as the *Child Labor Tax Case*. The *Bailey* decision invalidated the Federal Child Labor Tax Act of 1919. The tax was enacted by Congress in an effort to regulate child labor after an earlier commerce power-based law, the Child Labor

(Keating-Owen) Act, was struck down by the White Court in *Hammer v. Dagenhart* (1918). The clumsily drafted law levied a tax on the annual profits of businesses that employed children. The Taft Court, while denying it had the authority to review congressional motives, concluded that the tax was not a revenue measure, but rather an attempt to regulate child labor; the regulatory motives of Congress were transparent in this instance.

The Child Labor Tax Act imposed a tax on, among other things, mills and factories employing children under the age of sixteen. The tax amounted to 10 percent of the mill's or factory's net profits. Drexel Furniture was found to have employed a fourteen-year-old and was assessed the tax. The company paid the tax, but brought suit to recover the amount paid. Chief Justice Taft delivered the opinion of the Court and spoke for all but Justice Clarke. The critical question was whether the measure was a tax with incidental regulatory effects or a regulation that imposed a tax as a penalty. The Court decided it was the latter. The act did more than simply impose a tax; it provided a "heavy exaction for the departure from a detailed and specified course of conduct." In addition, the tax was insensitive to either the extent or frequency of the violations; the tax of one-tenth of the annual net business income was the same for the employment of one child for one day or any number of children for any length of time. Finally, the act excused from the tax any employer who unknowingly utilized an underage worker. The Court suggested that a violation contingent on prior knowledge was not usually a component of taxes, but more characteristic of criminal law. The Taft Court concluded that "in light of the features of the act, a court must be blind not to see that the so-called tax is imposed to stop the employment of children." The regulatory purpose and effect of the statute was called "palpable" (*Bailey* 1922, 36–37).

Taft allowed that tax legislation was typically presumed valid, but occasionally a law is reviewed in which "proof of the contrary is found on the very face of its provisions." Considerations of federalism weighed heavily in this case. To find the enactment to be principally a regulation rather than a tax was crucial because regulation of child labor was not seen as a matter "entrusted to Congress." Rather, it was a subject committed by the Constitution "to the control of the states." Taft said that the Court's duty was to strike down federal laws that exceed the limits of congressional authority even if the "legislation is designed to promote the highest good." The word "tax" could not be used indiscriminately by Congress as a way of breaking down "constitutional limitations of the powers of Congress" or as a means to "completely wipe out the sovereignty of the States." Taxes retain their identity as taxes even when accompanied by some other motive. But "there comes a time in the extension of the penalizing features of the so-called tax when it loses its character as such, and becomes a mere penalty with the characteristics of regulation and punishment" (*Bailey* 1922, 39).

Bailey held that laws imposing a penalty by means of a tax may lose their character as revenue measures, making them subject to other limitations on the exercise of federal legislative power. In Taft's view, were the Court to uphold the child labor tax, it would give license to indirectly pursue through the taxing power what could not be directly accomplished through congressional authority to regulate interstate commerce. The Court concluded that the law at issue in *Bailey* could not be distinguished from that in *Hammer v. Dagenhart*. The "so-called tax" in *Bailey*, Taft concluded, is a "penalty to coerce people of a State to act as Congress wishes them to act in respect of a matter completely the business of the state government" (*Bailey* 1922, 39).

Hill v. Wallace was decided on the same day as *Bailey* and essentially reached the same result. The Future Trading Act imposed a tax of twenty cents per bushel on all contracts for the sale of grain for future delivery. The tax did not apply to sales on boards of trade designated as contract markets by the secretary of agriculture, provided those boards complied with requirements set forth in the law. The constitutionality of the act was challenged by several members of the Chicago Board of Trade. The "manifest purpose" of the law, said Chief Justice Taft, was to "compel Boards of Trade to comply with regulations, many of which have no relevancy to the collection of the tax at all." The Court concluded that the regulation of boards of trade could not be justified on interstate commerce grounds either, and that Congress resorted to the taxing power to attempt to accomplish regulation not otherwise possible. As a result, said Taft, the decision in *Bailey* "completely covers this case" (*Hill* 1922, 66–67).

In *Florida v. Mellon* (1927), the Court reviewed a petition from the state of Florida seeking to prevent collection of federal inheritance taxes in the state. The case focused on the uniformity requirement found in Article I that whatever is taxed must be taxed at the same rate throughout the United States. The Taft Court unanimously upheld the federal estate tax provisions of the Revenue Act of 1926 and concluded that it must prevail over conflicting provisions of Florida law on supremacy grounds. The act allowed deduction of state inheritance taxes in computing the federal tax. Florida contended that the federal tax was not uniform because some states impose inheritance taxes while Florida does not. The Court rejected this contention. Justice Sutherland said that Congress "cannot accommodate its legislation to the conflicting or dissimilar laws of the several states nor control the diverse conditions to be found in the various states which necessarily work unlike results from the enforcement of the same tax" (*Florida v. Mellon* 1927, 17).

State Taxation, Rate Making, and Commerce

From the turn of the twentieth century, the Supreme Court had allowed states to regulate businesses, at least those "clothed with a public interest." At the same time, the Court concluded that businesses had a right to a fair return on their property. The Court's rulings directed that state rate-making commissions base their decisions on the current value of property, an approach that maximized property values. The Taft Court saw no reason to depart from this practice. In *Southwestern Bell Telephone Co. v. Public Service Commission* (1923), for example, the Court ruled that state rate-making bodies must allow businesses, including public utilities, to earn a fair return on the value of their property dedicated to public service. The Taft Court ruled in *Southwestern Bell* that Missouri's Public Service Commission had not allowed the telephone utility sufficient opportunity for a fair return on its capital investments because it had improperly assessed the current value of Southwestern Bell's property.

Justice McReynolds spoke for seven justices in his majority opinion, and he focused squarely on the fair return issue. It is impossible to determine what a fair return is on privately owned property that is devoted to the public interest, he said, "without giving consideration to the cost of labor, supplies, etc.," at the time the assessment is made. An "honest and intelligent forecast of probable future values made upon a view of all the relevant circumstances is essential." If the critically important component of present costs is "wholly disregarded such a forecast becomes impossible" (*Southwestern Bell* 1923, 287–288). McReynolds concluded by saying that "it must never be forgotten that while the State may regulate with a view to enforcing reasonable rates and charges, it is not the owner of the property of public utility companies and is not clothed with the general power of management incident to ownership" (289).

The Court also limited the states' capacity to tax certain property. For example, property cannot be subjected to state taxation while it is in interstate transit. When interstate transport has come to an end, however, the goods can be taxed by the states. The Taft Court applied this principle in *Sonneborn Bros. v. Cureton* (1923). Texas levied an occupation tax on wholesale oil dealers based on the gross amount of their in-state sales. Sonneborn Brothers, a New York–based company engaged in selling petroleum products, had opened an office in Texas and maintained a rented warehouse in the state. Sonneborn Brothers challenged the tax, contending that it imposed a burden on interstate commerce when applied to local sales of oil previously shipped into the state and stored by dealers as inventory. A unanimous Taft Court disagreed.

Chief Justice Taft's opinion rested on the "original package" doctrine, a construct fashioned by Chief Justice John Marshall in *Brown v. Maryland* (1827) almost a century earlier. Imports from outside the country and goods transported across state lines must be immune to state taxation, but Marshall realized that such immunity could not be perpetual. The problem was determining when interstate transport ended. If an import has entered a state from which it will not exit, commercial transport has concluded—the items of commerce "become assimilated into the general mass of property in a state and subject to state taxation" (*Brown* 1827, 441). Marshall suggested that immunity from state taxation lasts as long as transported imports remain in the form or package in which they came into the state. When the importer mixes the import into his other property—breaks down the original package—the import has lost its defining character.

Sonneborn transported oil from outside Texas to its warehouse in Texas for sale in its original packages within the state. The Taft Court concluded that volume of sales was a reasonable basis for the occupation tax levied against Sonneborn Brothers, as long as the tax applied to all wholesale oil dealers making sales and deliveries in Texas. Taft saw the tax as neither a regulation of nor burden upon interstate commerce. The oil had "come to rest" in the Texas warehouse and "become part of the [Sonneborn Brothers'] stock with which they proposed to do business as wholesale dealers in the state." The interstate transportation had ended, making the "state tax upon the oil as property or upon its sale in the State" a permissible action by Texas (*Sonneborn Brothers* 1923, 508–509).

Intergovernmental Tax Immunity

Chief Justice John Marshall introduced an intergovernmental tax immunity doctrine in *McCulloch v. Maryland* (1819) to protect federal entities from taxation by the states. The doctrine was later applied as a limit on federal taxing power—state governments, state property, and state functions could not be subjected to federal taxation. In the words of political scientist C. Herman Pritchett, the Taft Court "carried the immunity doctrine to ridiculous extremes" (Pritchett 1984, 208). Several examples that follow support his conclusion.

Oklahoma taxed the net income "arising from all sources" of every person in the state. Gillespie had income derived from sales of his share of oil taken under terms of a lease from restricted Native American lands. The Taft Court ruled in *Gillespie v. Oklahoma* (1922) that Gillespie had become an instrumentality of the United States used to carry out "federal duties to the Indians." Justice Holmes suggested that a certain amount of state "interference with interstate commerce cannot be avoided if the States are to exist and make laws." The rule covering federal instrumentalities, however, is "absolute in form and at least stricter in substance." A tax on the leases, Holmes continued, "is a tax upon the power to make them, and could be used to destroy the power to make them." Regardless of whether this property could be subject to any other kind of tax, the Court concluded that "it cannot be reached as profits or income from leases such as those before us" (*Gillespie* 1922, 505–506).

Six years later, the Taft Court decided *Panhandle Oil Co. v. Mississippi* and *Long v. Rockwood* (1928). *Panhandle Oil* involved a state excise tax of one cent per gallon on distributors or retail dealers of gasoline. The state attempted to recover the tax from a Coast Guard station and a Veterans' Administration hospital located in the state. In a five-to-four decision, Justice Butler said for the Court that states could not "burden or interfere with the exertion of national power or make it a source of revenue or take funds raised or tax the means used for the performance of federal functions" (*Panhandle Oil* 1928, 221).

Long v. Rockwood was decided the same day as *Panhandle Oil* and was perhaps the most extreme of these three decisions. Massachusetts attempted to collect a tax on income received as royalties for the use of patents issued by the United States. In another five-to-four decision, the Taft Court held that it was unconstitutional for a state to tax royalties from federal patents because that would interfere with federal efforts to promote the "progress of science and useful arts." The patent, said Justice McReynolds, "is the instrument by which that end is to be accomplished" (*Long* 1928, 147).

Finally, in *Macallen Co. v. Massachusetts* (1929), the Taft Court held that states could not tax interest income derived from federal bonds and securities. Justice Sutherland spoke for the six-justice majority and said that a state tax, however small, on interest generated by federal bonds and securities "interferes or tends to interfere with the constitutional power of the general government to borrow money on the credit of the United States." Such a tax imposes a "burden upon the operations of government, and carried far enough would prove destructive" (*MaCallen Co.* 1929, 624). Sutherland extended the ruling by concluding that neither county nor municipal bonds could be taxed either.

State Economic Regulation: Substantive Due Process

Substantive due process is a judicial doctrine under which every type of state policy is subject to close scrutiny by the Supreme Court. The doctrine calls for the Court to examine the reasonableness of legislative enactments to ensure that the policies are substantively "fair and reasonable." In the words of C. Herman Pritchett, "transformation of the due process class from a guarantee of fair procedures into an activist judicial warrant for passing judgment on the substantive policies of legislative regulations must rate as one of the Supreme Court's most significant creative efforts" (Pritchett 1984, 292). Substantive due process enabled the laissez-faire conservatives on the Supreme Court to free private property from most state regulations from the late nineteenth century until the mid-1930s.

One of the Taft Court's first substantive due process rulings was in *Pennsylvania Coal Company v. Mahon* (1922). A Pennsylvania law prohibited mining operations that could cause private residential property, public streets, and public buildings to settle or sink. Pennsylvania Coal Company owned the subsurface rights under a number of private and public properties including that belonging to Mahon. The company's mining operations threatened the destruction of Mahon's home. The law, on the other hand, prevented the company from reaching valuable coal deposits under Mahon's and others' property. Over the single dissent of Justice Brandeis, the Taft Court held that the statute took the company's property without compensation, thus depriving the company of its property without due process.

The coal company conveyed surface property to various owners, but expressly reserved the right to remove all coal from under these properties. Mahon argued that the Pennsylvania statute rescinded the subsurface mining rights. Justice Holmes understood that government "could hardly go on if to some extent values incident to property could not be diminished without paying for every such change in the general law." It was established in previous cases that some property values "enjoyed under an implied limitation . . . must yield to the police power." At the same time, any implied limitation "must have its limits, or the contract and due process clauses are gone." The key is the extent to which property values are diminished. When the diminished value reaches a certain magnitude, there must be in most situations an "exercise of eminent domain and compensation to sustain the act" (*Mahon* 1922, 412–413). The question depends on the factual particulars of each case.

The *Mahon* case involved a single private residence. Although Holmes did not doubt that "there is a public interest even in this," the law could not be sustained as an exercise of the police power so far as it affects the "mining of coal under streets or cities in places where the right to mine coal has been reserved." The right to coal, Holmes observed, "consists in the right to mine it." What makes this right valuable is that "it can be exercised with profit." If the mining of coal is made commercially impracticable, the right has been "appropriat[ed] or destroy[ed] for constitutional purposes" (413–414).

Holmes distinguished the Pennsylvania law from instances in which the rights of the public in a street have been purchased or acquired through eminent domain. In either instance, those are public rights that the public has purchased. On the other hand, when public officials have been so "short sighted" as to acquire only surface rights, "we see no more authority for supplying [beneath surface rights] without compensation than there was for taking the right of way in the first place and refusing to pay for it because the public wanted it very much." The property protection afforded by the Fifth Amendment assumes that the property is wanted for public use, but that it "shall not be taken for such use without compensation." If this seemingly absolute protection is qualified by the police power, the "natural tendency of human nature is to extend the qualification more and more until at last private property disappears." A strong public desire to improve the general welfare is not enough to justify achievement of that objective "by a shorter cut than the constitutional way of paying for the change." When communities take the risk of acquiring only surface rights, Holmes concluded, "we cannot see that the fact that their risk has become a danger warrants the giving to them greater rights than they bought" (415–416).

The sole dissenter was Justice Brandeis. He saw every restriction on the use of private property as depriving the owner of "some right theretofore enjoyed." Restrictions imposed to protect the public health or safety from threatened dangers, however, did not constitute an unlawful taking in his view. The restriction in this case was "merely the prohibition of a noxious use." The private property in this case remained the possession of the owner, and the state did not attempt to make any use of that property. The state "merely prevents the owner from making a use which interferes with the paramount rights of the public." A restriction is permissible if it is an "appropriate means to the public end." To keep the coal in place under Mahon's house is "surely an appropriate means of preventing subsidence of the surface; and ordinarily it is the only available means." A restriction on property use is not unconstitutional simply because it "deprives the owner of the only use to which the property can then be profitably put" (417–418).

Perhaps the classic substantive due process ruling was *Lochner v. New York* (1905). In *Lochner*, the Fuller Court struck down a state law limiting the hours of work of bakers, and did so on liberty-of-contract grounds. Three years later, however, the same Court upheld a maximum hours of work law for women employees in *Muller v. Oregon* (1908). When a maximum hours of work law for both men and women employees was upheld in *Bunting v. Oregon* (1917), *Lochner v. New York* was not even mentioned in Justice McKenna's majority opinion. Many believed the Court had abandoned the *Lochner* doctrine, but the Taft Court was to prove them mistaken in *Adkins v. Children's Hospital* (1923).

The *Adkins* ruling struck down the Minimum Wage Act of 1918. The act established a minimum wage board for the District of Columbia. The regulatory board had authority to examine wages paid to women and minors and to establish binding minimum levels of compensation where appropriate. Children's Hospital employed a number of women, including Adkins, whom it laid off rather than pay the minimum wage established by the board. Satisfied with their wages and working conditions prior to the imposition of the minimum wage order, Adkins and others brought suit seeking to forestall implementation of the act. They argued that they were constitutionally entitled to take whatever job at whatever pay they wished. The Supreme Court agreed in a five-to-three decision and invalidated the act. Brandeis did not participate in *Adkins* for two reasons. First, the Minimum Wage Act closely resembled the state law at issue in *Muller v. Oregon* (1908), in which Brandeis had represented Oregon in defense of its state law. Second, his daughter was a member the District of Columbia Minimum Wage Board that had ordered the minimum wage adjustments in *Adkins*.

The opinion of the Court was delivered by Justice Sutherland. Key for the majority was whether the statute impermissibly interfered with the liberty of contract. The

Taft Court felt strongly that the freedom to "contract about one's affairs" was a fundamental constitutional liberty. Although this freedom is not quite absolute, "freedom of contract is, nevertheless, the general rule and restraint the exception" (*Adkins* 1923, 545–546). Sutherland suggested that the gender difference that was so crucial in the *Muller* ruling had diminished in relevance and he rejected the contention that restrictions on women's liberty of contract could be upheld when similar restraints on men would not. Sutherland called the statute a "price-fixing law" imposed upon women "who are as legally capable of contracting themselves as men" (554).

The Court viewed the minimum wage policy as a misguided attempt to protect the health and welfare of women. Sutherland argued that there was no relation between morals and what women earn. More important, the law was defective because it considered only the needs of the employee. The law forced the employer to pay a certain wage regardless of the employee's capability of earning it or whether the business could sustain the burden of the imposed wage schedule. The act exacted an "arbitrary payment for a purpose and upon a basis having no causal connection with his business." The basis of the wage was not the value of the service rendered by the employee, but the "extraneous circumstance that the employee needs to get a prescribed sum of money to insure her subsistence, health, and morals." Sutherland said the law ignored the relationship of payment and service, and it placed employers in the position of bearing the costs of raising the employee out of poverty. The employer has "neither caused nor contributed" to that poverty (557–558). Sutherland concluded by saying that a law that prescribes wage payments based solely on "circumstances apart from the contract of employment, the business affected by it, and the work done under it, is so clearly the product of a naked, arbitrary exercise of power, that it cannot be allowed to stand" (559). The rationale from *Adkins* would survive into the late 1930s.

Chief Justice Taft, joined by Justice Sanford, dissented. He noted that employers and employees, particularly women employees, do not have "equality of choice" with their employers and suggested women's "necessitous circumstances" make them "prone to accept pretty much anything that is offered." They are "peculiarly subject" to the "overreaching of harsh and greedy employers." The "evils of the sweating system" were well known, he continued, and Congress had the authority to address those problems. Taft admitted it was debatable in the field of political economy how effective a maximum hours or minimum wage statute might be in combating these evils. But it is not the function of the courts, he argued, to nullify congressional acts simply because they are "passed to carry out economic views which the court believes to be unwise or unsound" (562). Furthermore, Taft could not accept the majority's use of *Lochner* as the basis for the *Adkins* ruling. He said he "could not reconcile *Lochner* with *Muller* or *Bunting* and that he thought that *Lochner* had been overruled *sub silentio*" (564).

Justice Holmes also dissented. He developed many of the same points as Taft, but also suggested that the majority had transformed the Due Process Clause into the "dogma, Liberty of Contract," a concept not explicitly mentioned in the Fourteenth Amendment. The end of removing conditions "leading to ill health, immorality, and the deterioration of the race . . . no one would deny to be within the scope of constitutional legislation" (567). Holmes concluded by indicating he thought *Muller* was "still as good law today as it was in 1908," and that legislatures could still take gender into account in fashioning social and economic legislation. Indeed, Holmes said that it would take "more than the Nineteenth Amendment to convince me that there are no differences between men and women," or that legislation cannot act on those differences (567, 569).

Two months after *Adkins*, the Court announced its decision in *Charles Wolff Packing Co. v. Court of Industrial Relations*. This ruling revealed how narrowly the Taft Court would apply the "affected with a public interest" concept as it reviewed state regulatory measures. The Court of Industrial Relations Act was enacted in Kansas in 1920. The statute provided that food, clothing, fuel, and transportation industries were "affected with a public interest," and attempted to subject them to compulsory arbitration and wage fixing through an industrial relations court. The objective of the statute was to maintain continuity of supplying food, clothing, and fuel to state residents. The statute was challenged by Wolff Packing, and the Taft Court unanimously ruled that the statute interfered with freedom of contract and violated the due process provision of the Fourteenth Amendment.

Chief Justice Taft said mere legislative declaration that a business is affected with a public interest is "not conclusive of the question whether its attempted regulation on that ground is justified." The public is "concerned about all lawful businesses because they contribute to the prosperity and well-being of the people." The public may be adversely affected by high prices or labor disputes, but the expression "clothed with a public interest . . . means more than that the public welfare is affected by continuity or the price at which a commodity is sold or a service rendered." The circumstances that "clothe" businesses with a public interest must create a particularly close relation between the public and those engaged in the business, and raise "implications of an affirmative obligation on their part to be reasonable in dealing with the public" (*Charles Wolff Packing* 1923, 536). Taft suggested that one does not devote one's business or property "to the public use or clothe it with a public interest merely because one makes commodities for, and sells to, the public." The food preparation industry had never been subject to wage or price regulation merely because monopoly was possible. Rather, Taft contended that the threat of monopoly was remote in the food preparation industry because the prices charged for prepared food products are "fixed by competition throughout the country at large" (537–538). Under this narrow view of public interest the Taft Court would subsequently strike down a number of state property regulations. In doing so, the Taft Court reversed almost fifty years of doctrine beginning with *Munn v. Illinois* (1877) and put nearly all businesses outside the reach of state police power. The Taft Court returned to the Kansas Court of Industrial Relations Act a year after *Charles Wolff Packing* in *Dorchy v. Kansas* (1924). Using the same reasoning as in *Charles Wolff Packing,* the Court found the compulsory arbitration for the state's coal mining industry deficient as well.

On the same day *Dorchy* was decided, the Taft Court unanimously upheld in *Radice v. New York* (1924) a New York statute prohibiting the nighttime (10:00 P.M. through 6:00 A.M.) employment of women in restaurants located in the state's larger cities. The regulation was challenged on the grounds that it deprived both the employer and employee of their liberty of contract, and that it was an unreasonable and arbitrary classification in violation of the equal protection clause. The Taft Court was unpersuaded and unanimously returned to the paternalistic stance taken in previous decisions involving women in the workplace.

Justice Sutherland referred to a "mass of information" that had prompted the New York legislature to conclude that night work was particularly detrimental to the health of women. The Court concluded that it was not in a position to second-guess the legislative judgment in this instance. Sutherland suggested that the loss of a "restful night's sleep" was not easily made up by daytime sleep in busy cities. The legislature had judged that the injurious consequences of nighttime employment bore more heavily against women than men. "Considering their more delicate organism," said Sutherland, "there would seem to be good reason for thinking so" (*Radice* 1924, 294). Such deference by the Taft Court to legislative judgment was atypical and occurred only with laws protective of women workers.

Those challenging the statute argued that the *Adkins* precedent applied. The Court, however, saw *Adkins* as presenting an "entirely different" question than *Radice.* The statute at issue in *Adkins* was a "wage-fixing law pure and simple," and had "nothing to do with working conditions." The Court rejected equal protection claims as well. Sutherland said there was no substance to the contention that excluding restaurant employees working in smaller communities rendered the law "obnoxious" to the Constitution. An impermissible action under the Equal Protection Clause must be "actually and palpably unreasonable and arbitrary" (*Radice* 1924, 295–296).

The Taft Court exhibited its more typical substantive due process position in *Jay Burns Baking Co. v. Bryan* (1924). A Nebraska statute established a maximum weight for loaves of bread, and established penalties for making or selling bread in other weights. Nebraska argued the statute was necessary to protect consumers from unscrupulous bakers selling smaller loaves than shown on the package label. In a seven-to-two decision, the Court struck down the statute on due process grounds. Justice Butler said for the majority that a state may not, "under the guise of protecting the public, arbitrarily interfere with private business or prohibit lawful occupations or impose unreasonable and unnecessary restrictions on them" (*Jay Burns Baking* 1924, 513). Butler suggested that a number of things produce "unavoidable variations" in the weight of bread, including evaporation of moisture. There was consumer demand for unwrapped bread, but unwrapped bread was prone to evaporation of some ingredients. As a result, the bread would weigh less. It would be unreasonable, Butler said, to "prevent unwrapped bread being furnished to those who want it in order technically to comply with a weight regulation" (516). Justice Brandeis, joined by Justice Holmes, dissented. In their view, Nebraska could attempt to protect consumers from "short weights" and honest bakers from unfair competition. A more compelling conclusion was legislative deference—the Court ought not concern itself with the "wisdom of the legislation." Brandeis argued that for the Court to reject the fact basis for the statute was an "exercise of the powers of a super-Legislature not the performance of the constitutional function of judicial review" (534).

In a similar manner, the Taft Court struck down a Connecticut law that prohibited the use of certain materials in the production of quilt or quilt-like bedding. Justice Butler spoke for a six-justice majority in *Weaver v. Palmer Bros. Co.* (1926) and recognized that legislative determinations are "entitled to great weight." At the same time, Butler indicated that attempts to show that a legislature has "transgressed the limits of its power" is always an option for those affected by regulations (*Weaver* 1926, 410). The Court saw no reason for a ban on certain materials as they could all be inexpensively sterilized and made safe for consumer use. Aside from posing no danger to the public health, bedding made from materials banned under the act were in demand by the public. Finally, Butler pointed out that because every article of bedding had a tag showing the materials contained, the statute could not be sustained as a means of protecting the public from deception by manufacturers such as Palmer Brothers Company. Justices Holmes, Brandeis, and Stone dissented. Holmes reiterated the self-restraint argument Brandeis had offered in *Jay Burns Baking.* If the legislature concluded, on the basis of factual evidence, that bedding containing certain materials posed a danger to the public despite the inspection and tagging regulations, it could absolutely prohibit the use of those materials in the manufacture of bedding and upholstery (415).

One of the most important Taft Court state police power decisions came in the zoning ordinance case of *Village of Euclid v. Ambler Realty Co.* (1926). Zoning ordinances typically classify land within a local political unit on the basis of the use, for example, residential, industrial, commercial, etc. All land and any buildings within a zone must comply with any restrictions established for the zone. In *Ambler Realty* the Court reviewed a village ordinance that designated certain lands for exclusively residential use. Ambler Realty held property within the village limits and intended to use it for industrial development rather than residential use. The Euclid ordinance also regulated apartments and other multiple-family dwellings, lot sizes, and building heights, among other things. Ambler Realty was able to obtain an injunction against enforcement of the ordinance, but the Taft Court upheld the local zoning ordinance against Ambler Realty's claim that it was deprived of property without due process.

The opinion of the Court was delivered by Justice Sutherland, who disagreed with the other three "Horsemen" (Justices Van Devanter, McReynolds, and Butler) for one of the few times during the Taft Court era. Zoning regulations such as those contained in the Euclid ordinance were developed as urban areas increased in population and urban life became more complex. Sutherland speculated that continued or even additional regulation was likely with the transition from rural to urban life in the United States. As times change, so does the "wisdom, necessity and validity" of regulation. Even regulations that had been rejected previously as too intrusive could be sustained with evolving conditions. Sutherland said the Court must take an adaptive approach when reviewing such regulations. Although the "meaning of constitutional guarantees never varies, the scope of the application must expand or contract to meet the new and different conditions which are constantly coming within the field of their operation." An ordinance like the one involved in this case must "find justification in some aspect of the police power, asserted for the public welfare." The line between the regulation that is legitimate and that which is not is "not capable of precise delineation." Rather, it varies with "circumstances and conditions"—it is situational. Sutherland indicated that some matters cannot be resolved by giving "abstract consideration" to the effects of the regulation, but only by examining the "circumstances" and "locality" (*Euclid* 1926, 387).

The Court considered the categorical character of the regulation—that every nonresidential use was banned within the zone. Sutherland suggested that the legislative objectives the village was seeking were sufficient to justify the "general rule of the ordinance" even though some industries of an "innocent character might fall within the proscribed class." The ordinance, in the Court's view, did not pass the "bounds of reason" and take on the "character of a merely arbitrary fiat." Sutherland enumerated specific benefits to be derived from the zoning regulation. Citing such factors as traffic control and fire protection, Sutherland had little difficulty distinguishing industrial and residential land use. The Court found that restrictions on multiple-resident dwellings could be justified as well. Sutherland noted that as one apartment "is followed by others," interference with the "free circulation of air" and "monopolizing the rays of the sun" would occur. Increased traffic and parking problems, more neighborhood noise, and a possible deprivation of "quiet and open places" for children to play threatened as well. In short, the Court saw Euclid's reasons for enacting its zoning regulations as "sufficiently cogent" to preclude finding the provisions "arbitrary and unreasonable, having no substantial relation to the public health, safety, morals, or general welfare" (394–395). Justices Van Devanter, Butler, and McReynolds disagreed without issuing a dissenting opinion.

Several months after *Village of Euclid v. Ambler Realty Co.*, Sutherland rejoined his conservative brethren in *Tyson & Bros. v. Banton* (1927) as the Court struck down a New York statute that forbade the resale of theater tickets at more than a fifty-cent markup over the face value ticket price. Sutherland again provided the Court's rationale, this time for a five-justice majority. His opinion limited the "clothed with a public interest" doctrine to utilities and a small number of comparable industries, thus making *Tyson* a particularly significant substantive due process ruling. This turned the doctrine into a device through which the laissez-faire adherents could remove previously regulated property from continued public control. The ticket brokers were seen as the "mere appendage of the theater," which prompted Sutherland to reshape the question. The "real inquiry is whether every public exhibition, game, contest or performance . . . is clothed with a public interest" sufficient to permit rate fixing by a state legislature (*Tyson* 1927, 249). The Court concluded they were not.

A business is not affected or clothed with a public interest, Sutherland argued, simply because the public may have a "feeling or concern in respect of its maintenance." Nor can a public interest stem from the mere fact that the public "derives benefit, accommodation, ease, or enjoyment from the existence or operation of the business." Legislative declaration that a particular kind of business or property is affected with a public interest, Sutherland continued, is not itself conclusive on the validity of a regulation. Invoking the typical substantive due process view, Sutherland suggested that the matter of reasonable regulation is "one which is always open to judicial inquiry" (431). Pertaining to government price control initiatives, Sutherland said review of such regulations should turn on "the existence of conditions, peculiar to the business under consideration, which [bear] a substantial and definite relation to the public interest as to justify an indulgence of the legal fiction of a grant by the owner to the public of an interest in the use" (438).

Applying these factors to the price regulation at issue in *Tyson*, the Court distinguished a privately owned place of entertainment from, for example, a grain elevator, which stands at the gateway of commerce. Sales of theater tickets bear "no relation" to the country's commerce. A theater is "in no legal sense a utility," and its activities are unrelated to any emergency condition. Instead, entertainment has an interest that is analogous, but not equivalent, to grocery stores or rental homes. Legislatures do not possess power to fix prices of food, shelter, or clothing "in the absence of some controlling emergency." Accordingly, the Court was unable to perceive any "dissimilarities of such quality or degree as to justify a different rule in respect of amusements and entertainments" (440–441).

New York argued that the regulation of ticket brokers was intended to prevent fraud, extortion, and "collusive arrangements" between the management of theaters and ticket brokers. Sutherland acknowledged that such practices occur, but suggested that legislatures may not respond through regulatory schemes that impermissibly interfere with essential rights of private property. The New York statute applied irrespective of the existence of the evils the law was intended to suppress by fixing resale prices whether or not the undesirable practices actually occurred. State legislatures are constitutionally barred from enacting laws, Sutherland concluded, which spread an "all-inclusive net for the feet of everybody upon the chance that, while the innocent will surely be entangled in its meshes, some wrongdoers also may be caught" (442–443).

Holmes, Sanford, and Stone each dissented, and Justice Brandeis concurred with the dissents of Holmes and Stone. Each of the dissenters argued that state legislatures have the authority to gauge that which affects the public interest enough to warrant government regulation. Holmes suggested it was not his function to determine whether the law was "wise and rational." If residents of New York, speaking through their legislature, indicated that they wanted such a law, Holmes saw "nothing in the Constitution . . . to prevent their having their will" (447). In Stone's view, the New York law was like the attempt by Illinois to regulate the rates charged by proprietors of grain elevators, a regulatory scheme upheld by the Court in *Munn v. Illinois* (1877). In both instances, regulations were designed to "protect a large class of consumers from exorbitant prices made possible by the strategic position of a group of intermediaries in the distribution of a product from producer to consumer" (449–450). Self-interest, Stone argued, "is not permitted to invoke constitutional protection at the expense of the public interest." Stone rejected the contention that the exercise of regulatory power becomes less reasonable "because the interests protected are in some degree less essential to life than some others." Laws aimed at the "evils of monopoly" are not unreasonable merely because they apply to other than the "bare necessities of life" (452–453).

Late in the 1927 Term the Taft Court struck down in *Ribnik v. McBride* a New Jersey law that attempted to regulate the fees charged by employment agencies. Justice Sutherland grounded his majority opinion on *Tyson & Brothers v. Banton.* Even though the regulation was intended to protect job seekers, the Court again used a narrowly defined "affected with a public interest" concept to conclude that regulation of employment agencies could not be justified. Such businesses as employment agencies, said Sutherland, are "essentially private." Although these agencies deal with the public, so do the "druggist, the butcher, the baker, the grocer, the apartment or tenement house owner and the broker who acts as an intermediary between such owners and his tenants." The Court did not see the public interest in the matter of employment as different in any respect from its interest in the other businesses enumerated by Sutherland. In none of them is the public interest sufficient to warrant legislative price control (*Ribnik* 1927, 357). Sutherland thus saw the business of securing jobs for the unemployed as no different from that of the ticket broker in *Tyson.*

The only justice to vote differently in *Ribnik* than in *Tyson* was Sanford, who joined the majority on the basis that *Tyson* was now the controlling precedent even though he had disagreed with that decision. Justice Stone, joined by Justices Holmes and Brandeis, dissented. Stone noted that the problem of unemployment is of "grave public concern," and that the practices of employment agencies "affect vitally the lives of great numbers of the population." Furthermore, employment agencies deal with persons in need of work—a "necessitous class" who are often not free to "move from place to place" and often under "exceptional economic compulsion to accept such terms as the agencies offer." Persons who are in such a position are "particularly the prey of the unscrupulous and designing" (361). It was the dissenters' view that the New Jersey regulation was reasonable.

The Taft Court decided *Di Santo v. Pennsylvania* (1927) in much the same way it decided *Ribnik*. Pennsylvania required sellers of steamship tickets for international travel to be licensed. The license was obtained upon the filing of a bond and demonstration that the person selling was a bona fide agent of the steamship companies. The law was intended to lessen the possibility of fraud on the traveling public, but the Taft Court majority struck it down as a regulation of foreign commerce—a function that was exclusively federal. Three years earlier, the Taft Court had disallowed a municipal license tax in *Texas Transport & Terminal Co. v. New Orleans* (1924). The Court concluded that a tax on agents of steamship companies whose vessels were engaged in interstate and foreign commerce was the exclusive domain of the federal government. Justice Butler drew on *Texas Transport* in his *Di Santo* opinion and reiterated that Congress has "complete and paramount authority to regulate foreign commerce" and the Pennsylvania regulation imposed a "direct burden on that commerce" (*Di Santo* 1927, 37). Justices Brandeis, Holmes, and Stone disagreed that the state law attempted to regulate foreign commerce. In their view, the "transaction regulated is wholly intrastate" and affected commerce only incidentally. Although Congress could engage in the kind of regulation Pennsylvania was attempting, Brandeis noted that it had not done so, thus there could be "no contention that Congress had occupied the field" (38–39). The laissez-faire views expressed by Justice Butler prompted C. Herman Pritchett to say that it was "fairly clear that the decision did not register an intent to protect commerce, but simply a distaste for all business regulation" (Pritchett 1984, 249).

The freedom of contract concept was again decisive in *Fairmont Creamery Co. v. Minnesota* (1927). A Minnesota law prohibited creameries from purchasing cream at higher prices in one locality than another. The state legislature determined that the payment of excessive prices by large-volume buyers of cream threatened competition and sought to prevent such a possibility by requiring every buyer "to adhere to a uniform price fixed by a single transaction." Because the statute applied "irrespective of [buyer] motive," Justice McReynolds said, there was an "obvious attempt to destroy [the buyer's] liberty to enter into normal contracts long regarded not only as essential to the freedom of trade and commerce but also beneficial to the public." Enforcement of the statute would amount to fixing the price for cream purchases "since one purchase would establish this for all points without regard to ordinary trade conditions" (*Fairmont Creamery* 1927, 8–9).

In *Miller v. Schoene* (1928), the Taft Court unanimously upheld a Virginia statute that required the destruction of ornamental cedar trees infected with a disease damaging to nearby apple orchards. Schoene, the state entomologist, ordered a large number of cedars on Miller's property cut down as a means of preventing the communication of the disease to apple orchards in the vicinity. In doing so, the Court returned to the diminution-of-value question present in such cases as *Pennsylvania Coal Co. v. Mahon* (1922). Justice Stone considered the comparative value of cedars and apple trees. The red cedar, indigenous to Virginia, was not "cultivated or dealt in commercially on any substantial scale," and beyond its ornamental use had only "occasional use and value as lumber." Apple growing, on the other hand, was one of the "principal agricultural pursuits in Virginia." Investment in apple growing was substantial, and the industry furnished employment for a "large portion of the population." It was thus necessary for the state to choose between the "preservation of one class of property and that of the other wherever both existed in dangerous proximity." When compelled to make such a choice, the state does not "exceed its constitutional powers by deciding upon the destruction of one class of property in order to save another. . . ." Stone concluded by saying that where the public interest is involved "preferment of that interest over the property interest of the individual, to the extent even of its destruction, is one of the distinguishing characteristics of every exercise of police power which affects property" (*Miller* 1928, 280–281).

The Court used the equal protection clause in *Quaker City Cab Co. v. Pennsylvania* (1928) to invalidate a Pennsylvania tax that applied only to receipts of cab companies operated by corporations. Justice Butler spoke for a six-justice majority, saying that the equal protection clause "does not detract from the right of the State justly to exert its taxing power and prevent it from adjusting its legislation to differences in situation or forbid classification in that connection." The clause does require, however, that a classification not be arbitrary but based on "real and substantial difference having a reasonable relation to the subject of the particular legislation." Pennsylvania created two classes of cabs—those owned by incorporated operators and those owned by "natural persons." The "character of the owner is the sole fact on which the distinction and discrimination are made to depend" (*Quaker City Cab* 1928, 400, 402).

Justices Holmes, Brandeis, and Stone disagreed. Holmes observed that if there was an "important difference" of degree between business done by corporations and that done by individuals, there was "no reason why the larger businesses may not be taxed and the small ones disregarded" (403). In Brandeis's mind, the equal protection clause, "does not forbid a State to classify for purposes of taxation." The clause only requires that a "classification shall be reasonable." He saw the difference between business carried on in corporate form and the same business carried on by "natural persons" to be both real and important. As to Pennsylvania's motive in imposing a heavier tax on corporations, the Court "has no occasion to enquire" (406, 409).

The following year, however, in *White River Lumber Co. v. Arkansas ex rel. Applegate*, the Taft Court concluded that it was permissible for a state to reassess corporate property undervalued for tax purposes without providing comparable recovery in the instance of individually owned property. Justice Sanford distinguished *Quaker City Cab* from this case by saying that it contained no back-tax issue. A policy does not violate the equal protection clause, Sanford said, "merely because it is not all-embracing." The statute must be presumed to target "an evil where experience shows it to be most felt, and to be deemed by the legislature coextensive with the practical need." Such a law is not to be invalidated "merely because other instances may be suggested to which also it might have been applied," and the classification is not open to objection unless it is "so lacking in any adequate or reasonable basis as to preclude the assumption that it was made in the exercise of legislative judgment and discretion" (*White River Lumber* 1929, 696–697). Justice Butler, joined by Chief Justice Taft and Justice Van Devanter, could not distinguish the case from *Quaker City Cab*. They concluded that the discrimination was deliberate. The procedure Pennsylvania chose to correct underassessments and collect back taxes "is not affected by the character of the owner." Land owned by individuals, the dissenters concluded, is "as likely to be erroneously undervalued as . . . [property] belonging to corporations" (701, 703).

Even at the height of its substantive due process jurisprudence, the Taft Court occasionally presumed the validity of state laws aimed at furthering public health, and accepted the regulation of professions closely related to public health. A case in which it did not was *Liggett Co. v. Baldridge* (1928), in which the Taft Court struck down a Pennsylvania law requiring all stockholders of any corporation owning drugstores to be licensed pharmacists. The controlling question for the seven-justice majority was "what is the effect of mere ownership of a drug store in respect of the public health?" Under Pennsylvania law, the owner of a drug store, whether a licensed pharmacist or not, can neither prescribe medications nor dispense impure medicines. The Court concluded that "ample safeguards existed to prevent injury to the public health by pharmacy owners in the buying, compounding, or selling drugs and medicines." Justice Sutherland said, "mere stock ownership" in a corporation owning a drug store "can have no real or substantial relation to the public health." Accordingly, the Pennsylvania law was seen as an "unreasonable and unnecessary restriction upon private business" (*Liggett Co.* 1928, 112–113). In dissent, Justice

Holmes suggested corporate ownership often causes businesses "to be owned by people who do not know anything about [the particular business]." Holmes was convinced that a "divorce between the power of control and knowledge is an evil." He said the selling of drugs "calls for knowledge in a high degree," and notwithstanding other safeguards in place, Pennsylvania had determined that the separation of control and knowledge was undesirable. The Constitution does not require that "preventive legislation . . . work a perfect cure," said Holmes, only that it has a "manifest tendency to cure or at least to make the evil less" (113–115).

A ruling from late in the Taft Court era reflects the dominant property rights values of most of the Court's justices. In *Williams v. Standard Oil Co.* (1929), the Taft Court struck down a Tennessee price-fixing statute for gasoline sold in the state. Justice Sutherland's opinion reiterated the rationale from such earlier Taft Court rulings as *Charles Wolff Packing*, *Tyson & Bros.*, and *Ribnik*. Unless a business is vested or affected with a public interest, a state has no power to engage in price fixing, no matter how many people might be adversely affected without the regulation. Tennessee sought to justify the regulation by pointing to the "widespread use" of gasoline and its "indispensab[ility] in carrying on commercial and other activities within the state." Sutherland said that the Court was "concerned with the character of the business, not with its size or the extent to which the commodity is used." He suggested that gasoline was "one of the ordinary commodities of trade differing . . . in no essential respect from a great variety of other articles commonly bought and sold by merchants and private dealers in the country." Businesses selling such common commodities, regardless of sales volume, do not come within the phrase "affected with a public interest" (*Williams* 1929, 240). A majority of the Taft Court justices consistently minimized the number of business endeavors affected with a sufficient public interest to justify governmental regulation.

Protection of property rights was a primary value for the Taft Court during the 1920s. Its jurisprudence in this respect was not unique, however. The use of substantive due process as the principal means for protecting private property from governmental regulation had begun with the Fuller Court in the late 1880s. Thus, the Taft Court has been characterized as a maintaining Court on this dominant issue.

National Prohibition

The most extensive exercise of federal authority during the decade of the 1920s was national prohibition. Long on the agenda of social reformers, a number of states had enacted statewide prohibition laws by 1915, and most of the other states had adopted legislation that enabled local governments to do so within their respective jurisdictions. The first congressional enactment was the Webb-Kenyon Act in 1913. The measure made state prohibition laws more effective by barring the interstate shipment of liquor to states where its use or sale was already prohibited. In 1917 the White Court upheld Webb-Kenyon in *Clark Distilling Co. v. Western Maryland Railway.* A number of states, however, chose not to adopt prohibition, prompting advocates to pursue a constitutional amendment that would outlaw alcoholic beverages nationally. Nineteen seventeen proved to be the pivotal year. Congress took an intermediate step in the draft law of that year when it banned the sale of liquor to servicemen. Soon after, Congress passed the Lever Act, which authorized the president to forbid, as a wartime food-control measure, the use of any foodstuffs in the production of alcoholic beverages. In December 1917 Congress submitted the Eighteenth Amendment to the states. The proposed amendment prohibited the "manufacture, sale or transportation of intoxicating liquors within, the importation thereof into, or the exportation thereof from the United States." In addition, President Wilson issued a series of executive orders during the war that established virtual prohibition. Shortly after the Armistice in 1918, Congress passed the Wartime Prohibition Act, which prohibited the manufacture or distribution of liquors until war demobilization had been concluded. In *Hamilton v. Kentucky Distilleries* (1919), the White Court sustained the statute over the objection of distillers, who argued that the government could not utilize war powers once the hostilities had actually ended. The Court deferred to congressional judgment that a state of wartime emergency still existed and allowed the war power-based control to remain operative.

The Eighteenth Amendment, proposed in December 1917, was ratified in January 1919 and went into effect one calendar year later. The amendment gave Congress and the states concurrent powers of enforcement. In late 1919 just before the Eighteenth Amendment would take effect, Congress passed the Volstead Act, which set forth particulars for the enforcement of National Prohibition. The act, among other things, defined any beverage containing at least 0.5 percent alcohol by volume to be intoxicating. Despite the fact that almost every state ratified the Eighteenth Amendment, anti-Prohibition sentiment prompted legal challenges to both the Volstead Act and the amendment itself. In *Jacob Ruppert, Inc. v. Caffey* (1920), the White Court upheld the Volstead Act's definition of intoxication. Justice Brandeis spoke for the Court, offering a self-restraintist rationale. He argued that the Court must not "second-guess" congressional judgment that 0.5 percent would constitute an intoxicating level of alcohol.

The *National Prohibition Cases*, decided by the White Court in 1920, marked the first time the Court reviewed a challenge to the constitutionality of an amendment. Rhode Island, one of two nonratifying states, based its challenge on state sovereignty grounds as well as contending that the amendment had accomplished a legislative end that exceeded the scope of the constitutional amending power. If the amending power could be used to regulate alcohol, the challengers argued, state police power would be diminished. The Court sustained the Eighteenth Amendment, concluding that it had not impermissibly changed the balance of federal-state authority and pointing out that congressional interstate commerce power could reach into the states as well.

The Taft Court was similarly supportive as it dealt with issues resulting directly from the Prohibition Amendment—it upheld every effort to give full effect to the provisions of the amendment. The first case was *Vigliotti v. Pennsylvania* (1922), in which the Court held that a state law that predated both the Eighteenth Amendment and the Volstead Act was not superseded by them. The Pennsylvania statute prohibited the sale of liquor without a license and was regarded as an "additional instrument which the State supplies in the effort to make prohibition effective." If the law had been adopted by Pennsylvania the day after the ratification of the Eighteenth Amendment, Justice Brandeis suggested, it would have obviously been "appropriate legislation" under the amendment's terms calling for concurrent federal-state enforcement of Prohibition. He concluded the Pennsylvania law was "not less so because it was already in existence" when the amendment was adopted (*Vigliotti* 1922, 408–409).

A month after *Vigliotti*, the Taft Court ruled in *Grogan v. Hiram Walker & Sons* (1922) that the transport of whiskey from Canada to the United States for shipment to another country was forbidden by the Eighteenth Amendment. In a companion case, *Anchor Lines v. Aldridge*, the Court held that whiskey could not be transferred from one British ship to another while the ships were in an American port. Justice Holmes said that the Eighteenth Amendment "meant a great revolution in the policy of this country, and presumably and obviously meant to upset a good many things on as well as off the statute book." It is "obvious," Holmes continued, that those whose views were embodied in the amendment "meant to stop the whole business." They did not want "intoxicating liquor in the United States and reasonably may have thought that if they let it in some of it was likely to stay" (*Grogan* 1922, 89–90). Justice McKenna, joined by Justices Day and Clarke, said in dissent that the Court had assigned "prevailing force to the Eighteenth Amendment and the Volstead Act" over treaty and statutory provisions in existence prior to the ratification of the amendment (91).

In much the same way, the Taft Court disposed of suits brought by a number of steamship companies seeking to prevent U.S. officials from seizing liquors carried into American territorial waters. The Court concluded that the Volstead Act was "intended to apply to all merchant vessels, whether foreign or domestic, when within those waters" (*Cunard Steamship Co. v. Mellon* 1923, 129). Justice Van Devanter suggested that the situation was analogous to that of the innkeeper "whose accustomed privilege of selling liquor to his guests is taken away, or that of the dining car proprietor who is prevented from serving liquor to those who use the car which he operates." He found it immaterial that the liquor on the ships was carried as sea stores;

"being sea stores does not make them liquors any the less nor does it change the incidents of their use as beverages" (129–130). Justices Sutherland and McReynolds agreed that the Volstead Act covered domestic ships, but disagreed that it applied to "foreign ships coming into our ports under the circumstances here disclosed" (132).

The Treasury Department developed regulations pursuant to the Volstead Act that permitted physicians to prescribe certain distilled spirits, wines, and other alcoholic medicinal preparations. Soon thereafter, Congress enacted a Supplemental Prohibition Act, which reversed the Treasury regulations and categorically prohibited physicians from prescribing intoxicating malt liquors even for medicinal purposes. The Taft Court upheld the ban in the companion cases of *James Everard's Breweries v. Day* and *Burke, Ltd. v. Blair* (1924). The breweries argued, among other things, that the Eighteenth Amendment gave Congress the authority only to prohibit traffic in intoxicating liquors intended for beverage purposes. They contended that control of liquor for any nonbeverage purposes was exclusively reserved to the states. The Court concluded, however, that the purpose of the Eighteenth Amendment was to "suppress the entire traffic in intoxicating liquor." As a result, Congress could adopt any appropriate means to make that prohibition effective (*James Everard's Breweries* 1924, 558). The opportunity to manufacture, sell, and prescribe intoxicating liquors for "medicinal purposes, opens many doors to clandestine traffic in them as beverages under the guise of medicines; facilitates many frauds, subterfuges and artifices; aids evasion; and, thereby and to that extent, hampers and obstructs the enforcement of the Eighteenth Amendment" (560–561). Although states were given concurrent enforcement authority, Justice Sanford suggested that provisions of federal law adopted pursuant to the Eighteenth Amendment did not need state approval before taking effect.

Congress amended the Volstead Act in 1921 and provided, among other things, that a physician could not prescribe more than a pint of "spirituous liquor" for medicinal purposes within a ten-day period and that no prescription could be filled more than once. The Court upheld the regulation in *Lambert v. Yellowley* (1926) using the reasoning from *James Everard's Breweries*, concluding that the restriction was a permissible measure for "enforcing the prohibition ordained by the Eighteenth Amendment." Justice Brandeis said that Lambert's belief in the medicinal value of liquor "is not of controlling significance; it merely places him in what was shown to Congress to be the minor fraction of his profession." In addition, Brandeis said that there is no right to practice medicine that is "not subordinate" to the appropriate exercise of governmental authority (*Lambert* 1926, 595–596).

In 1925 Meyer Selzman challenged his conviction under the Volstead Act for selling denatured alcohol. He argued that the Eighteenth Amendment did not extend to denatured alcohol and thus the Volstead Act could not criminalize its sale. The Taft Court disagreed in *Selzman v. United States* (1925). Chief Justice Taft said for a unanimous Court that "denaturing in order to render the making and sale of industrial alcohol compatible with the enforcement of prohibition of alcohol for beverage purposes is not always effective." The "ignorance of some, the craving and the hardihood of others, and the fraud and cupidity of still others, often tend to defeat its object." It furthers the primary purpose of the Eighteenth Amendment, therefore, to "hedge about the making and disposition of the denatured article every reasonable precaution and penalty to prevent the proper industrial use of it from being perverted to drinking it" (*Selzman* 1925, 468–469).

Ratification of the Eighteenth Amendment involved the federal government in criminal law enforcement to an unprecedented degree. The Taft Court examined a number of constitutional issues stemming from enforcement of Prohibition, and in virtually all of these cases, the Court sustained government over individual rights claims. Particularly notable were the search and seizure rulings. The more important of these decisions are discussed in greater detail in the individual rights section that follows, but several examples are helpful here. In *Hester v. United States* (1924), the Court used the "open fields" doctrine to permit introduction of evidence seized by federal agents without a warrant. The following year, the Court held in *Carroll v. United States* (1925) that a vehicle could be searched without a warrant if enforcement agents believed it contained liquor. In *United States v. Lee* (1927), the Court extended *Carroll* to ships and boats and further determined that shining a spotlight on a boat did not constitute a search for Fourth Amendment purposes. Similarly, the Taft Court ruled in *Olmstead v. United States* (1928) that the interception of conversations by means of wiretapping did not fall within the reach of the Fourth Amendment either. Finally, the Taft Court used the doctrine of dual sovereignty in *United States v. Lanza* (1925) to reject the claim that successive federal and state prosecutions for violation of both federal and state prohibition laws constituted double jeopardy. National Prohibition was repealed by the Twenty-first Amendment in 1933, although each state was allowed to maintain prohibition if it wished to do so.

Individual Rights

The Taft Court record on civil liberties was mixed at best. By comparison, however, the Taft Court was more receptive to claimed constitutional rights violations than it was to federal and state economic regulation and social legislation. Indeed, it was the Taft Court that began the transition to a modern jurisprudence of civil liberties, which would reach full development half a century later during the Warren Court era. Ratification of the Fourteenth Amendment, intended or not, enabled the Supreme Court to protect property and economic rights from both federal and state regulation from the late nineteenth century into the early 1930s. Ironically, it was the Taft Court's preoccupation with protecting property interests that led it to make more protective rulings on civil liberties issues. Once the "pattern of intervention on behalf of property rights was established, it was but a short step to national protection of civil liberties against state infringement" (Kelly, Harbison, and Belz 1991, 509).

The Incorporation Question

The incorporation question asks whether federal Bill of Rights provisions apply to actions of state governments. Prior to the addition of the Fourteenth Amendment to the Constitution, there was no connection between state governments and federal Bill of Rights provisions. Chief Justice Marshall said in *Barron v. Baltimore* (1833) that the Bill of Rights "constrained only the government created by the document," the federal government, not the "distinct governments," the states (*Barron* 1833, 247). In other words, states would be prevented from violating individual rights by terms of state law only. *Barron* was the controlling decision on this issue until ratification of the Fourteenth Amendment following the Civil War. The Fourteenth Amendment reopened the question because its language was clearly directed at the states. The Fourteenth Amendment provides in part that states cannot "deprive any person of life, liberty, or property, without due process of law." Several schools of thought developed on this issue, but the Supreme Court in the late nineteenth century was unwilling to find that the Fourteenth Amendment connected particular Bill of Rights provisions to the states. The Supreme Court eventually settled on a "selective" approach to incorporation, which extended to the states those rights that, in the words of Justice Benjamin Cardozo, are "of the very essence of a scheme of ordered liberty" (*Palko v. Connecticut* 1937, 325). This approach was not fully defined until the Taft Court era had concluded, but the Taft Court contributed to the debate on nationalizing Bill of Rights protections nonetheless.

Conflicts over individual rights during World War I brought a number of cases stemming from various First Amendment challenges to federal law. At the state and local level, however, a substantial network of regulations aimed at political radical and nonmainstream religious practices were already in place. Substantive First Amendment doctrine is discussed in more detail below, but the Taft Court contributed to a broadening of the scope of the Fourteenth Amendment, particularly in relation to the First Amendment.

In December 1920 the White Court upheld a state law criminalizing speech aimed at discouraging enlistment in the armed forces of the United States in *Gilbert v. Minnesota*. *Gilbert* was the first case since the Fourteenth Amendment was added to the Constitution in which the Court reviewed a state sedition law. The Court, through Justice Joseph McKenna, said that while states could not raise or direct armies, they could "restrain the exertion of baleful influences against the promptings of patriotic duty to the detriment of the welfare of the Nation and State." For a state to do so does "not usurp a National power" because a state is not "inhibited from making the national purposes its own purposes to the extent of exerting its police power to prevent its own citizens from obstructing the accomplishment of such purposes" (*Gilbert* 1920, 331).

Justice Brandeis, in his *Gilbert* dissent, concluded that the Minnesota law impermissibly interfered with the right of a citizen to discuss such federal functions as the war power. Brandeis said that he had difficulty in believing that the liberty guaranteed by the Constitution did not "include liberty to teach . . . the doctrine of pacifism," at least until Congress determines that the nation's security requires such a limitation of expression. He concluded by saying that he was not persuaded that the "liberty guaranteed by the Fourteenth Amendment includes only liberty to acquire and to enjoy property" (343). Extension of federal Bill of Rights provisions to the states began during the Taft Court era and rested in large part on Brandeis's dissent in *Gilbert*.

The Taft Court reached the conclusion that the free speech provision of the First Amendment applied to the states through the Fourteenth Amendment in *Gitlow v. New York* (1925) although it did so in an almost offhand manner. Gitlow had been convicted under a state criminal anarchy law for publishing a radical newspaper and other allegedly subversive materials. Although the Court upheld Gitlow's conviction, Justice Sanford said in his majority opinion: "For present purposes, we may and do assume that freedom of speech and of the press—which are protected by the First Amendment from abridgment by Congress—are among the fundamental personal rights and liberties protected by the due process clause of the Fourteenth Amendment from impairment by the state" (*Gitlow* 1925, 666). Thus in *Gitlow*, the Taft Court took the first step toward incorporating or nationalizing the First Amendment. In doing so, the Taft Court's position was derived from its property protection, substantive due process jurisprudence.

The Due Process Clause of the Fourteenth Amendment

Gitlow followed two other Taft Court rulings, *Meyer v. Nebraska* (1923) and *Pierce v. Society of Sisters* (1925), which broadened the reach of the Fourteenth Amendment. Unlike *Gitlow*, neither *Meyer* nor *Pierce* were grounded on the Fourteenth Amendment rather than the First Amendment. From the early 1870s, the Court had used the due process language of the Fourteenth Amendment to insulate private property and most commercial activities from government regulation. The Court had not hesitated to strike down state legislation on what came to be known as substantive due process grounds. In *Meyer v. Nebraska*, the Court reviewed a case in which property rights and government censorship were intertwined. Nebraska enacted a law that forbade any person, "individually or as a teacher," from "teach[ing] any subject to any person in any language other than the English language" in any "private, denominational, parochial or public school" within the state until a student had completed eighth grade (*Meyer* 1923, 397). The law was similar to those passed in a number of states during World War I. The Supreme Court saw the statute as incompatible with the Fourteenth Amendment, however. Meyer, a teacher at Zion Parochial School, was convicted of unlawfully teaching the subject of reading in the German language to a ten-year-old child.

Although the Taft Court did not subscribe to the emerging libertarian views evident in the postwar period, the justices' laissez-faire orientation toward government regulation of economic matters was fully evident in *Meyer*. The obvious purpose of the statute, said Justice McReynolds, "was that the English language should be and become the mother tongue of all children reared in [Nebraska]" and to "foster a homogenous people with American ideals . . . (397, 402). As well-meaning as Nebraska's objectives may have been, the Court concluded that the state had attempted "materially to interfere with the calling of modern language teachers, with the opportunities of pupils to acquire knowledge, and with the power of parents to control the education of their own" (401). McReynolds observed that knowledge of the German language could not be regarded as harmful. Indeed, such knowledge was "commonly looked on as helpful and desirable" (400). The Court set aside Meyer's conviction, concluding that the due process language of the Fourteenth Amendment protected a teacher's right to teach and parents' rights to hire him to do so. The inclusion of the right to educate one's children was something of a stretch because Meyer lacked standing to assert such a claim. His own right to teach, on the other hand, was an economic liberty of the type that had long been protected. The Court chose, nonetheless, to include the parents' right as part of the ruling. Although recognizing the legitimacy of the end sought by Nebraska, the Court found that the means chosen to attain these ends were too extreme and a less intrusive approach could have pursued the same goals at less cost to personal liberty. A state cannot use coercive methods that conflict with the Constitution—even a "desirable end cannot be promoted by prohibited means" (401). In addition, the Court was troubled by the selective character of the state policy. The statute "undertakes to interfere only with teaching which involves a modern language leaving complete freedom as to other matters." McReynolds said the Fourteenth Amendment protected the right to "generally enjoy privileges essential to the orderly pursuit of happiness by free men" (399). *Meyer* marked the beginning of a different kind of substantive due process, one that provided foundation for the Warren Court's recognition of a constitutional right to privacy several decades later.

Two years after *Meyer*, the Court invalidated an Oregon law that required parents or guardians of children between the ages of eight and sixteen to send them to a public school. Failure to comply with the law was a misdemeanor. The Taft Court upheld the right of children to attend nonpublic schools where religious education could be provided and struck down the law as an interference with the "business and property" of private and parochial schools. The Ku Klux Klan had pushed the law through the Oregon legislature with the clear intent of driving the Catholic schools out of existence. Proponents of the measure argued that increasing juvenile crime in Oregon was the result of too many students not being educated in the public schools. It was also argued that compulsory public education was necessary to encourage the patriotism and ensure the loyalty of citizens in the future.

Justice McReynolds again spoke for the Court and again focused on the property dimension. The Court found "no peculiar circumstances or present emergencies" to justify such an extraordinary measure. Enforcement of the statute, McReynolds continued, "would seriously impair, perhaps destroy, the profitable features of the society's business and greatly diminish the value of their property" (*Pierce* 1925, 531). Indeed, the "inevitable practical result" of enforcing the law "would be the destruction of the [Society's] primary schools" (534).

McReynolds said that states possessed the authority to reasonably regulate all schools—to oversee and monitor teacher and pupil performance, compel school attendance, make sure that all teachers "be of good moral character and patriotic disposition," that subjects "essential to good citizenship" be taught, and that nothing be taught "which is manifestly inimical to the public welfare" (534). The Oregon law interfered with both personal and property rights, however. "The child is not the mere creature of the State," McReynolds wrote; "those who nurture him and direct his destiny have the right, coupled with the high duty, to prepare him for future obligations." The "fundamental theory of liberty upon which all governments in the Union repose," McReynolds concluded, "excludes any general power of the State to standardize its children by forcing them to accept instruction from public teachers only" (535). Like *Meyer*, *Pierce* influenced civil liberties jurisprudence by recognizing an implicit fundamental right to privacy as well as some degree of parental autonomy to raise their children free from unreasonable government interference.

Another significant case decided on due process grounds was *Buck v. Bell* (1927). Unlike the outcomes in *Meyer* and *Pierce*, however, the Taft Court upheld the challenged state policy in *Buck*. A Virginia law provided that persons affected with hereditary insanity, idiocy, imbecility, feeblemindedness, or epilepsy could be subjected to compulsory sexual sterilization. Sterilization was limited to inmates of state institutions and the law contained provisions requiring proper notice, hearing, and judicial review before such operations were performed. This case involved a seventeen-year-old "feebleminded" female named Carrie Buck, an inmate of a state institution. Previous to her admission to the institution, Carrie had given birth to an allegedly mentally defective child. In the judicial proceedings held to authorize the sterilization, evidence was presented concerning the mental capacity of Carrie Buck. There was also testimony offered in support of the statute by eugenicists who argued that mental defects such as those suffered by Carrie Buck were both hereditary and incurable. In fact, her mother was a "feebleminded" inmate of the same institution. At the conclusion of the hearing, a Virginia court ordered Buck's sterilization, and that order was upheld through the appellate process in the state. The Supreme Court reviewed the case to consider whether the Virginia law authorizing the sterilization judgment violated the due process and equal protection provisions of the Fourteenth Amendment. The equal protection claim was based on the contention that there was different treatment accorded institutional inmates as well as those outside public institutions.

Justice Holmes spoke for the Court. He dismissed the procedural claims by saying that Buck's rights were "most carefully considered," and as "every step in this case was taken in scrupulous compliance with the statute and after months of observation, there is no doubt that in this respect [Buck] has had due process of law" (*Buck v. Bell* 1927, 207). Holmes then turned to the substantive considerations—whether under any circumstances a law such as this could be constitutionally justified. He indicated that as a matter of law sufficient grounds for the sterilization policy might exist, "and if they exist they justify the result." As the public welfare might occasionally "call upon the best citizens for their lives," presumably referring to military service during wartime, Holmes suggested it would be "strange if it could not call upon those who already sap the strength of the State for these lesser sacrifices, often not felt to be such by those concerned, in order to prevent our being swamped with incompetence." Holmes concluded by saying that it is "better for all the world, if instead of waiting to execute degenerate offspring for crime, or to let them starve for their imbecility, society can prevent those who are manifestly unfit from continuing their kind." The principle that sustains compulsory vaccination, he continued, "is broad enough to cover cutting the Fallopian tubes." Certainly in this case, Holmes said, "three generations of imbeciles are enough" (207).

The Court also rejected the equal protection argument. It was contended that the justification for Buck's sterilization becomes insufficient when it was applied only to the small number of persons confined to state mental institutions and not applied to the many persons not so confined. Holmes responded that the law does "all that is needed when it does all that it can, indicates a policy, applies it to all within the lines, and seeks to bring within the lines all similarly situated so far and so fast as its means allow" (208).

Holmes's opinion in *Buck v. Bell* reflected his predisposition to defer to legislative judgments. Indeed, Holmes biographer Liva Baker suggests that his "commitment to legislative power reached its apogee" in *Buck v. Bell*. During this period, the American public was "caught up in a eugenics craze . . . that selective breeding could vastly improve the composition of the human race" (Baker 1991, 599–600). *Buck v. Bell*, unlike most of Holmes's opinions, was not a case "where he exhibited indifference toward the social policy embodied in the statute he was sustaining." He was, in fact, an "enthusiast for eugenics," the movement that had precipitated the Virginia statute applied in *Buck v. Bell* (White 1994, 230). Holmes's opinion "disappointed admirers" and "threatened to tarnish the growing Holmes legend." Such reactions were "of no consequence to him." Nonetheless, Holmes took "pleasure" at writing the Court's opinion in a case in which he could "combine support for legislative authority with personal approval of the social measure at issue" (Baker 1991, 599–600).

Selected First Amendment Rulings

Cases involving the First Amendment were infrequently entertained by the Supreme Court prior to World War I. Because there was so little case law on First Amendment issues, the limits of constitutionally protected expression, among other First Amendment issues, lacked any meaningful definition. The situation was aggravated because the Marshall Court had held in *Barron v. Baltimore* (1833) that liberties guaranteed by the federal Bill of Rights did not apply to the states. The Taft Court would address this matter in the mid-1920s, but in the interim, socialists, anarchists, and other radical critics of American society were extensively restricted during the Progressive Era and World War I. Federal and state laws put political radicals and aliens on the defensive, to say the least. American entry into World War I raised serious questions about constitutional rights during wartime, and the White Court responded more extensively than any previous Court. Most of the federal cases involved two statutes, the Espionage Act of 1917 and the Sedition Act of 1918. The White Court's decisions in these cases significantly shaped the thinking of the Taft Court on free speech issues. Following the war federal, state, and local officials, led by U.S. Attorney General A. Mitchell Palmer, arrested and prosecuted large number of labor leaders, socialists, and communists. These arrests produced additional opportunity for the Taft Court to consider free speech issues.

The Espionage Act, among other things, penalized circulation of statements intended to interfere with the military, including obstructing recruitment, attempting to impede its operations, and causing disloyalty within the ranks. The act also had postal censorship provisions that prohibited using the mails to distribute materials regarded as seditious or treasonous. Challenge to the provisions of the Espionage Act first came before the White Court in the case of *Schenck v. United States* (1919), a ruling that established some basic standards for freedom of expression issues.

Charles Schenck, head of the Socialist Party in Philadelphia, and others printed and circulated materials to men called for military service. Using "impassioned language," Schenck and the Socialists "intimated that conscription was despotism in its worst form and a monstrous wrong against humanity in the interest of Wall Street's chosen few" (*Schenck* 1919, 51). The government alleged that these materials were intended to persuade men not to enlist for military service or submit to the military draft, in violation of the Espionage Act. These defendants were also indicted for unlawful use of the mails for the transmission of their materials. The defendants were convicted of these charges and appealed on First Amendment grounds. A unanimous White Court upheld the convictions.

Justice Holmes spoke for the Court in *Schenck*. He said the right of expression does not absolutely protect all speech. Rather, free speech is a conditional right with boundaries set by the circumstances under which the expression is undertaken. He offered his frequently quoted observation that even the most stringent protection of free speech "would not protect a man in falsely shouting fire in a crowded theater and causing a panic" (52). Having established a situational context for evaluating expression, Holmes then fashioned a "clear and present danger" standard by which expression can be examined. The issue in every free speech case is "whether the words used are used in such circumstances and are of such a nature as to create a clear and present danger that they will bring about the substantive evil that Congress has a right to prevent" (52). If speech is linked closely enough to illegal action, it can be restricted. It is a question of "proximity and degree," Holmes suggested. Schenck's expression was intended to have effect on military recruitment, a point conceded by Schenck. Under peacetime circumstances, Schenck's expression would have been neither clearly nor presently dangerous enough to warrant regulation. Schenck's words were offered while the country was at war, however, and posed both recognizable and immediate dangers in the Court's view. Holmes observed that "when a nation is at war many things that might be said in time of peace are such a hindrance to its efforts that their utterance will not be endured so long as men fight" (52). The *Schenck* ruling and the "clear and present danger" test provided a basic rubric by which the Taft Court's free speech cases would be reviewed.

Several cases followed *Schenck* in rapid succession. The *Schenck* ruling indicated that the White Court was favorably disposed to the government's national security initiatives during the war. A similar response came soon after *Schenck* in *Frohwerk v. United States* and *Debs v. United States* (1919), Espionage Act cases decided a week after *Schenck*. In both cases, the White Court upheld convictions stemming from speeches and publications critical of the war. Jacob Frohwerk, editor of a German-language newspaper, was convicted for publishing a series of articles characterizing American participation in World War I as "imperialistic." Eugene Debs, head of the Socialist Party in the United States, was convicted for his advocacy of socialism and his praise for the political revolution in Russia. Holmes accepted the trial court finding that Debs had intended to interfere with war mobilization in his militant antiwar speech. He was prosecuted under the Espionage Act for attempting to incite insubordination. Holmes again wrote for the White Court and focused on the speakers' intent and probable effect of their expression on the government's military efforts. He suggested that the First Amendment was "obviously not intended to give immunity for every possible use of language" (*Frohwerk* 1919, 206).

Congress amended the Espionage Act in 1918, and the amended act became known as the Sedition Act. The act was more general, but also more comprehensive than the initial act. The law made it a crime to utter or publish words intended to bring into "contempt or disrepute" the government of the United States or its Constitution, flag, or military. The act also made it a crime to incite resistance to the American government or promote the causes of its enemies. Jacob Abrams and several other political radicals published and circulated pamphlets attacking the Wilson administration's decision to send American troops into Russia in the summer of 1918. The group also called for a general strike of American workers in protest of the policy. The defendants were all convicted of Sedition Act charges. Unlike the earlier cases, both Holmes and Brandeis broke from their fellow justices and voted instead to overturn the convictions in *Abrams v. United States* (1919). The Court divided over the question of expression standards. Applying the "clear and present danger" test, the two dissenters were unconvinced of a danger that was imminent enough to sustain the convictions. The majority opinion, written by Justice John Clarke, upheld both the Sedition Act and the convictions of Abrams and the other defendants. In doing so, Clarke moved the Court away from the "clear and present danger" standard to a test that was grounded in the defendants' intentions. The purpose of the pamphlet, Clarke said, was to "excite, at the supreme crisis of the war, disaffection, sedition, riots, and . . . revolution, in this country for the purpose of embarrassing and if possible defeating the military plans of the Government in Europe" (*Abrams* 1919, 623). The defendants, Clarke continued, "must be held to have intended, and be accountable for, the effects which their acts were likely to produce" (621). No such objective could be protected by the First Amendment. Justice Holmes, joined by Justice Brandeis, dissented from the majority on the ground that the pamphlet simply had no immediate effect upon the government's war effort. Congress cannot prohibit "all effort to change the mind of the country." Nobody can suppose, he continued, "that the surreptitious publishing of a silly leaflet by an unknown man, without more, would present any immediate danger that its opinions would hinder the success of the government arms or have appreciable tendency to do so" (628). The White Court, except for Holmes and Brandeis, turned away from the "clear and present danger" test in *Abrams* using a "bad tendency" standard in its place. This doctrinal change would remain throughout the Taft Court era.

Four months after *Abrams*, the Court announced its decision in *Schaefer v. United States* (1920). Five defendants including Schaefer published a German-language newspaper in Philadelphia. They were accused of publishing articles critical of the United States and its allies. McKenna spoke for the majority and grounded his opinion on the less protective "bad tendency" test. Under the bad tendency test, the issue was whether expression intended to prompt a particular and presumably dangerous action. Accordingly, the convictions were upheld. Brandeis and Holmes again registered dissents. Brandeis had joined Holmes's dissent in *Abrams*, but in *Schaefer* it was Brandeis who voiced his disagreement with the Court's ruling and the standard used in reaching its conclusion. He attempted to reestablish the rigor of the "clear and present danger" test for free speech cases, and thereby more extensively to protect expression from government interference. Brandeis's dissent argued that free speech was essential in a democratic society and that while free speech protections might be abused, the benefits far outweighed any possible abuse. He referred to the "clear and present danger" test as a "rule of reason." If applied properly, the clear and present danger standard "will preserve the right of free speech from both suppression by tyrannous, well-meaning majorities, and from abuse by irresponsible, fanatical minorities" (*Schaefer* 1920, 482). He argued that even during the stress associated with wartime, free expression must be maintained. An intolerant majority, he declared, "swayed by passion or fear, may be prone in the future, as it has often been in the past, to stamp as disloyal opinions with which it disagrees." Convictions such as that of Abrams, besides abridging freedom of speech, "threaten freedom of thought and of belief" (495). He and Holmes would adhere to the views expressed in *Schaefer* through the Taft Court era, but they would remain a minority of two. The last of the leading Espionage Act cases, *Pierce v. United States* (1920) would repeat the themes developed in *Schaefer*.

By the end of the 1920 Term, Brandeis had become the Court's leading proponent of free speech. His passion and eloquence on the subject were evident in *Gilbert v. Minnesota* (1920) as the Court upheld a state sedition conviction for unlawful advocacy. The Nonpartisan League (NPL), an organization that operated in such farm states as Minnesota, advocated a number of "radical" political proposals. The NPL encountered strong opposition from politicians who were using wartime loyalty issues to discredit proposed political reforms. Joseph Gilbert and other NPL leaders were arrested and prosecuted for violating Minnesota's state sedition law. Gilbert was charged for remarks made in a speech in August 1917 advocating that men should not enlist and that persons should not support the war effort. The jury was instructed that it could convict Gilbert if the "natural and reasonable effect" of his words might "threaten certain governmental functions or the public safety." The jury convicted Gilbert, and he appealed to the Minnesota Supreme Court, contending that he had not intended to interfere with the war effort.

The White Court decided the *Gilbert* case in December 1920. It marked the first time that the Court reviewed a conviction under a state sedition law. Seven members of the Court concluded that Minnesota's attempt to preserve the peace of the state was a reasonable exercise of the state's police power. Justice Joseph McKenna's majority opinion argued that the World War I cases prosecuted under the federal Espionage and Sedition Acts had clearly established that the right to free speech was not absolute and was subject to "restriction and limitation" especially during wartime. The Minnesota law was a "local police measure, aimed to suppress a species of seditious speech which the legislature had found objectionable" (*Gilbert* 1920, 331). The First Amendment, McKenna continued, was not "intended to give immunity for every possible use of language." The nation was at war, and military forces necessarily were being recruited. Gilbert's words were intended as a "discouragement" of that objective (332–333).

Justice Brandeis disagreed and developed two important themes in his dissent. First, he argued that federal Bill of Rights provisions reached state as well as federal actions. The nationalization or incorporation of the Bill of Rights through the Fourteenth Amendment was developed more fully in the decades that followed, and the views Brandeis set forth in his *Gilbert* dissent provided much of the underlying reasoning. Second, Brandeis urged far greater protection of expression than the majority would entertain. He concluded that the Minnesota law was constitutionally defective because it not only interfered with federal functions, but with the right of citizens to discuss those functions and public policy as well. Brandeis rejected the contention that the Minnesota law was a wartime measure. The law's provisions were not limited to wartime, but instead abridged free speech "not in a particular emergency, in order to avert a clear and present danger, but under all circumstances." The restriction imposed by the law "relates to the teaching of the doctrine of pacifism and the legislature in effect proscribes it for all time" (334). The prohibition imposed by the law has "no relation to existing needs or desires" of the federal government. It applies even when recruitment of persons into military service is "neither in process nor in contemplation." As a result, the law was aimed at preventing "not acts but beliefs" (335). Brandeis pointed out that the law made it punishable for any person to teach any other person that a citizen "should not aid in carrying on war" regardless of the relationship of the two persons. Thus, the statute could be applied to a parent and child, which Brandeis saw as an unlawful "inva[sion] of privacy and freedom of the home"; a father and mother may not "follow the promptings of religious belief or conscious conviction, and teach son or daughter the doctrine of pacifism. If they do any police officer may summarily arrest them" (335–336).

Post Office control of second-class mailing privileges was one of the approaches used during World War I to censor the press. The postmaster general received power under several federal statutes such as the Trading with the Enemy

Act of 1917 to ban foreign-language and other publications from the mails. Similarly, the Sedition Act prohibited "uttering, printing, writing, or publishing any disloyal, profane, scurrilous or abusive language." A section of the act was specifically aimed at use of the mails for publications containing subversive content. The act provided that newspapers published in violation of any provisions of the act could not be distributed through the mails. In one of its last First Amendment rulings, the White Court upheld the action in a case against Victor Berger's *Milwaukee Leader*, a socialist newspaper. The government charged the *Leader* with hindering military operations, interfering with recruitment of military personnel, and aiding the enemy. President Wilson deferred the task of dealing with political subversives to others in his administration including Postmaster General Albert Burleson, a political conservative who considered any criticism of the government unpatriotic and dangerous.

Justice Clarke spoke for the Court in *United States ex rel. Milwaukee Social Democratic Publishing Co. v. Burleson* (1921). In doing so, he rejected the defense claim that the free press rights of the *Leader* had been violated. Clarke pointed to articles that, among other things, asserted that the war was "unjustifiable, dishonorable, and capitalistic," and was "forced upon the people by a class, to serve its selfish ends" (*Burleson* 1921, 413). The Constitution, Clarke declared, was adopted to "preserve our Government, not to serve as a protecting screen for those who, while claiming its privileges, seek to destroy it" (414).

Holmes and Brandeis again dissented, contending that the federal statutes did not categorically confer upon the postmaster general the authority to refuse second-class privileges to all issues of a newspaper of which some issues contained "non-mailable" materials. Justice Brandeis protested that the power to regulate use of the mails is, like any other power, subject to "the limitations of the Bill of Rights." Congress may not through its postal police power "put limitations upon the freedom of the press which if directly attempted would be unconstitutional" (430). Delivering newspapers at a sixth of the regular mailing rate and denying that service to only one paper "because to the Postmaster General views contained therein expressed in the past seem illegal, would prove an effective censorship and abridge seriously freedom of expression" (431). Justice Holmes argued separately that the United States may choose to end postal service at any time, but while it continues the service, "use of the mails is almost as much a part of free speech as the right to use our tongues, and it would take very strong language to convince me that Congress ever intended to give such a practically despotic power to any one man" (437).

The First Amendment jurisprudence developed late in the White Court era was fully maintained by the Taft Court. An early indication came in *American Steel Foundries v. Tri-City Central Trades Council* (1921). American Steel Foundries obtained an injunction barring the Trades Council from utilizing picketing accompanied by threats, intimidation, and violence that targeted persons employed or seeking employment at the foundry. The Trades Council claimed that the picketing was peaceful, and therefore, protected by the Clayton Act, but the Taft Court ruled that an injunction was not barred by the law.

Chief Justice Taft spoke for the Court and grounded his opinion, at least in part, on the property rights of the business. When employees or would-be employees are intercepted near the place of business, the action obstructs and interferes with the employer's property right of access. Attempted discussion and argument "in such proximity is certain to attract attention and congregation of the curious . . . thus increas[ing] the obstruction as well as the aspect of intimidation which the situation quickly assumes" (*American Steel Foundries* 1921, 204). All information, argument, or persuasion used in such circumstances was intimidating by definition. Taft considered it "idle" to talk of peaceful communication in such a place and under such conditions. The picketing constituted intimidation, and the "name 'picket' indicated a militant purpose, inconsistent with peaceful persuasion." The crowds drawn by the picketing made the passage of employees to and from work one of "running the gauntlet." Persuasion or communication attempted in such a presence and under such conditions was "anything but peaceful and lawful" (205). Only Justice Clarke dissented from the Court's ruling in this case.

In *Gitlow v. New York* (1925) the Taft Court incorporated the free speech provisions of the First Amendment through the Due Process Clause of the Fourteenth Amendment. It did so notwithstanding its ruling in *Prudential Insurance Co. v. Cheek* (1923) that state infringement of civil liberties remained outside the reach of the federal Constitution. Cheek had sued his former employer, demanding a letter from his former supervisor describing the quality of his work. Even if state law might try to address such situations, Justice Day suggested that the relations between a corporation and its employees and former employees were a matter of "wholly private concern." Neither the Fourteenth Amendment nor any other federal constitutional provision imposes on the states any restrictions about "freedom of speech or liberty of silence" (*Prudential Insurance* 1923, 543).

The Fuller and White Courts had used the Fourteenth Amendment to insulate private property from state regulation. The due process language of the Fourteenth Amendment provided the basis for judicial examination of the reasonableness of regulatory measures enacted by the state. In *Gitlow v. New York* (1925) the Court used the Due Process Clause of the Fourteenth Amendment to consider whether state laws impermissibly encroached on the free speech rights of individuals notwithstanding the ruling in *Prudential Insurance.* Benjamin Gitlow, a former Socialist assemblyman and participant in the founding of the American Communist Party, was convicted for violating New York's Criminal Anarchy Act. Because federal statutes such as the Sedition Act had lost their effect when World War I ended, states became the principal prosecutors of political radicals. By 1920 almost three-quarters of the states had enacted sedition or antisyndicalism laws of their own. The New York law was not enacted after the war, but rather was passed in 1902 shortly after the assassination of President William McKinley. The specific charge against Gitlow and several other Communist Party members was that they had violated the state law by publishing such "subversive" pieces as the *Revolutionary Age* and *The Left Wing Manifesto.*

Gitlow's defense was lead by Clarence Darrow, a highly renowned trial attorney. From the outset, Gitlow admitted he was a Communist and that he was responsible for the publication and circulation of the materials, and he did not contest that his primary objective in distributing these materials was the "destruction, conquest and the annihilation of the government of the United States." He denied, however, that these materials amounted to an actual call for violent revolution or that his writings came within the scope of the New York law. At trial, Darrow argued that while the Communists might be wrong and badly misguided, they were entitled to a chance to make their views known. The real danger, Darrow contended, was not in the ideas or publications of the defendants, but in the government's attempt to limit their expression.

The trial judge limited these contentions by instructing the jury that the free speech aspects of the statute were not in question. The jury took the judge at his word and convicted Gitlow and the others after less than three hours of deliberation. Gitlow was then sentenced to a minimum of five years in prison. Gitlow and the others sentenced under the New York law all gained their freedom before serving the minimum term by having their convictions overturned in the New York appellate courts or by receiving a pardon from Governor Alfred E. Smith. Governor Smith postponed his pardon of Gitlow to enable the appeal of his case to the Supreme Court. In June 1925 the Supreme Court found New York's anarchy statute constitutional and upheld Gitlow's conviction by a seven-to-two vote. Gitlow returned to jail for a time after the Court upheld his conviction, but he was soon pardoned by Governor Smith and resumed active participation in the Communist Party.

The Court's opinion was written by Justice Edward Sanford. He acknowledged that "there was no was evidence of any effect resulting from the publication and circulation" of the *Manifesto,* but suggested that this was not the decisive factor in the Court's view (*Gitlow* 1925, 656). The statute was constitutional because it "did not penalize the utterance or publication of abstract 'doctrine' or academic discussion having no quality of incitement to any concrete action." The law was neither directed at "mere historical or philosophical essays" nor did it "restrain the advocacy of changes in the form of government by constitutional and lawful means" (664). Rather, the law prohibited advocacy of government overthrow by unlawful means. The Court concluded that the *Manifesto* was not the statement of abstract doctrine or the "mere prediction that industrial disturbances and revolutionary mass strikes will result spontaneously in an inevitable process of evolution in the economic system." Instead, it "advocates and urges in fervent language mass action . . . [and] concludes with a call to action" (665). The means advocated by the *Manifesto* for bringing about the overthrow of the government "necessarily imply the use of force and violence and in their nature are inherently unlawful in a constitutional government of law and order." It was apparent to the Court that the jury was warranted in concluding that the *Manifesto* "advocated not merely the abstract doctrine of overthrowing organized government by force, violence and unlawful means" (666).

The Constitution does not confer an "absolute right to speak or publish, without responsibility, whatever one may choose, or an unrestricted and unbridled license that gives immunity for every possible use of language and prevents the punishment of those who abuse this freedom." Reasonably limited, the freedom of expression is an "inestimable privilege in a free government, [but] without such limitation, it might become the scourge of the republic" (666–667). There was no question, in the Court's view, that a state may exercise its police power to "punish those who abuse this freedom by utterances inimical to the public welfare"; utterances that "endanger the foundations of organized government and threatening its overthrow by unlawful means." Such utterances "imperil its own existence as a constitutional State." The First Amendment, Sanford suggested, does not deprive a state of the "primary and essential right of self preservation" (667–668).

The Criminal Anarchy Act reflected the New York legislature's determination that expression advocating government overthrow by unlawful means represented a sufficient danger of "substantive evil" that such expression may be prohibited. The state legislature's determination, said Sanford, "must be given great weight," and the Court must entertain "every presumption . . . in favor of the validity of the statute" (668). The danger to which the state responds is no less real and substantial because the "effect of a given utterance cannot be accurately foreseen." A state cannot be required to measure the danger of utterances "in the nice balance of a jeweler's scale" (669).

Advocacy of the objectives contained in the *Manifesto* may provide the "spark" that causes a "smoldering fire" to "burst into a sweeping and destructive conflagration." A state does not act arbitrarily or unreasonably if it seeks to "extinguish the spark without waiting until it has enkindled the flame." A state cannot be required to postpone adoption of protective measures until the revolutionary utterances lead to "imminent or immediate danger." If a state were required to wait until the danger becomes certain, Sanford continued, then its right to protect itself "would come into being simultaneously with the overthrow of the government, when there would be neither prosecuting officers nor courts for the enforcement of the law." In other words, a state may "suppress the threatened danger in its incipiency" (669–670). Sanford's reference to anticipated danger prompted the characterization of the Court's ruling in *Gitlow* as enabling the "killing of the serpent in the egg."

Justice Holmes, writing for Justice Brandeis and himself, sharply disagreed that the *Manifesto* was an unlawful incitement. "Every idea," he countered, "is an incitement." Had the "clear and present danger" test been properly applied in this case, there was no present danger of an attempt to overthrow the government by force on the part of the admittedly small minority who shared Gitlow's views. The only difference between expression of an opinion and an incitement is the "speaker's enthusiasm for the result." Eloquence "may set fire to reason," but "whatever may be thought of the redundant discourse before us it had no chance of starting a present conflagration" (673).

The basic question in *Gitlow* thus was whether the legislative prohibition of incitement to violent overthrow of the government was reasonable, or whether the statute should have been limited to those incitements that produced a measurable clear and present danger of harm. Holmes had suggested in *Schenck* that the mere probability of harm would not suffice to make speech punishable. The Taft Court majority in *Gitlow* diverged from this view, however, by concluding that a tendency toward an unlawful result could be suppressed. As a result of this change in the standard, history has not dealt favorably with *Gitlow* and the incitement test fashioned by Sanford in *Gitlow*.

Two years after *Gitlow*, the Taft Court returned to a First Amendment standard that more closely approximated Holmes's "clear and present danger" formulation in *Schenck*. The case was *Whitney v. California*, a case that focused on the issues of political expression and the right of association. Between 1919 and 1924, California arrested a number of political radicals and prosecuted more than 250 persons for alleged violation of the law. Anita Charlotte Whitney, a niece of Supreme Court Justice Stephen J. Field, was a political activist. Hers was the first and most publicized prosecution conducted under the California Criminal Syndicalism Act of 1919. On 9 November 1919, Whitney and others held a convention in Oakland to organize a California branch of the Communist Labor Party (CLP). Whitney was an active participant in the convention proceedings. As she left the convention site, she was arrested and charged with violation of the statute. The charge was based on her attendance at the CLP convention. At trial, Whitney was the only defense witness, and she attempted to minimize her role in the CLP by suggesting that the convention majority had actually voted down her position on political action. She did not deny her affiliation with the CLP, however, and was convicted for her membership in the party. She was sentenced to fourteen years for her CLP activity. In her appeals to higher California courts, Whitney argued that her actions were insufficient to constitute a public offense and that there was insufficient evidence to demonstrate that the activities of the CLP were actually covered by the syndicalism statute. In response, California relied on World War I precedents involving the federal Espionage Act of 1917 and Sedition Act of 1918 prosecutions.

Whitney was an even weaker case than *Gitlow*. As in *Gitlow*, the Court said it could not examine the defendant's actual behavior, deferring instead to the jury finding. The question of whether Whitney had knowledge of the Communist Labor Party's unlawful character and purpose was, in Sanford's words, "foreclosed by the verdict of the jury"; it was a question of fact "which is not open to review in this Court" (*Whitney* 1927, 367). Before addressing the First Amendment issues, Sanford said that California's syndicalism act did not violate the Due Process Clause by reason of vagueness and uncertainty of definition—the act clearly and specifically defined criminal syndicalism. Similarly, the act did not violate the equal protection clause because its penalties were "confined to those who advocate a resort to violent and unlawful methods as a means of changing industrial and political conditions." Sanford said that the equal protection clause "does not take from a State the power to classify in the adoption of police laws." A statute is not impermissible "class legislation" merely because it is "not all-embracing" (368–370).

Enactment of California's syndicalism law was seen by the Taft Court as a declaration by the state legislature that affiliation with an association that advocates violent overthrow of the government "involves such danger to the public peace and the security of the State, that these acts should be penalized in the exercise of its police power." Such a determination by a state "must be given great weight [and] every presumption is to be indulged in favor of the validity of the statute" (371). Combining with others in an association for the accomplishment of the desired objectives through the advocacy and use of criminal and unlawful methods "partakes of the nature of a criminal conspiracy." Such "united action" involves even greater danger to public security than "isolated utterances and acts of individuals." As a result, the Court could not conclude, Sanford said, that the law was an "unreasonable or arbitrary exercise" of state police power that "unwarrantably infring[ed] any right of free speech, assembly or association" (372).

Joined by Holmes, Brandeis eloquently enlarged upon the former's explanation of the purposes of the First Amendment and reaffirmed that the danger of harm must be both immediate and serious. Brandeis suggested that Sanford's opinion was based on faulty premises. Sanford had, for example, measured the limits of free speech against property interests and ignored the benefits that free exchange of ideas provided a society. Those who won the country's independence, Brandeis countered, "valued liberty as both an end and as a means." They believed that freedom to "think as you will and speak as you think are means indispensable to the discovery and spread of political truth." Without free speech and assembly, "discussion would be futile," and with them "discussion affords ordinarily adequate protection against the dissemination of noxious doctrine" (375). Suppression of free speech can only be justified, Brandeis concluded, if there is "reasonable ground to fear that serious evil will result if free speech is practiced." Even "imminent danger" cannot justify restriction of free expression "unless the evil apprehended is relatively serious." The fact that speech may result in "some violence or in destruction of property is not enough to justify its suppression." Instead, there must be the "probability of serious injury to the State" (377–378). A few months after the Court's decision, California Governor C. C. Young pardoned Whitney, and his accompanying statement resembled Brandeis's reasoning. The *Whitney* ruling diminished radical political left-wing activity, or at least drove it underground. More than four decades later, the Supreme Court overturned the *Whitney* precedent in a unanimous decision in *Brandenburg v. Ohio* (1969).

On the same day *Whitney* was decided, the Court reversed a Kansas criminal syndicalism conviction in *Fiske v. Kansas.* Fiske had been attempting to recruit new members for the Industrial Workers of the World, a labor organization viewed as "radical" by many. The Court did not strike down the Kansas law, but overturned Fiske's conviction, concluding that his prosecution violated his right to expression. The statute at issue in *Fiske* was much the same as those upheld in *Gitlow* and *Whitney,* but while the Court refused to review the facts in *Whitney,* it did just the opposite in *Fiske.* Fiske had circulated pamphlets and other materials advocating "criminal syndicalism and sabotage" as he sought to recruit members for the union. After examining the constitution of the organization, the Court concluded that "no substantial inference" could be drawn by a jury from its language of the "sinister meaning attributed to it by the state." Thus, the Court saw the language of the organization's materials as "essentially different from that of the [*Manifesto*] involved in *Gitlow,* and lack[ing] the essential elements which brought the [*Manifesto*] under the condemnation of the law." In contrast to *Gitlow* and *Whitney,* there was neither charge nor evidence that the organization for which Fiske sought members "advocated any crime, violence or other unlawful acts as a means of effecting industrial or political change or revolution." Applied in this way, the Court concluded that Fiske's conviction constituted an "arbitrary and unreasonable exercise of the [State's] police power" (*Fiske* 1927, 386). The Court's view in *Fiske* was atypical for the period, but would reflect the Warren Court's thinking in the 1950s and 1960s as it decided a number of cases involving so-called subversives.

The Taft Court dealt with a difficult associational rights issue in *New York ex rel. Bryant v. Zimmerman.* A New York law mandated that every "membership corporation and . . . unincorporated association" that required an oath as a condition of membership, and had a membership of twenty or more persons must file with the state a copy of its constitution, bylaws, membership oath, and membership roster. The New York law was enforced against organizations such as the Ku Klux Klan, even though other private organizations such as labor unions, and in some cases secret organizations like the Masons, Odd Fellows, and Knights of Columbus were exempted. Bryant, a member of the Klan, was charged with violating the statute. He challenged the law on both right-of-association and equal protection grounds. The Court upheld the law over the single dissent of Justice McReynolds. The Court ruled that a state may require associations having a membership oath to comply with any reasonable regulation calculated to ensure that the purposes and activities of such associations remain "within limits which are consistent with the rights of others and the public welfare" (*Bryant* 1928, 72). Obtaining the information required under the law was seen by the Court as better protecting the public well-being than if such disclosure was not required.

Claims of unlawful discrimination against particular groups was a more difficult issue to resolve. Justice Van Devanter stressed that the nature of Klan activities, specifically including intimidation and violence, was distinguishable from the nature of the activities of exempted groups. A state may classify "with reference to the evil to be prevented," and may differentiate among groups if it is found "that the danger is characteristic of the class named"; a "lack of abstract symmetry does not matter." A state is free to recognize "degrees of harm," and it may confine restrictions to those classes for which the need is most evident. The equal protection clause does not prevent a state from "adjusting its legislation to differences in situation or forbid classification in that connection" (73, 75).

The superpatriotism of the postwar period manifested itself in cases denying citizenship to any alien who refused to bear arms in defense of the country. The leading Taft Court ruling is *United States v. Schwimmer* (1929). Rosika Schwimmer, a forty-nine-year-old Quaker from Hungary was refused naturalization by a federal district court because of her pacifist beliefs. The Taft Court upheld the decision to withhold citizenship in a six-to-three decision. Justice Butler wrote for the majority and observed that except for eligibility to serve as president, naturalized citizens stand on the "same footing as do native born citizens." As a consequence, "all alike owe allegiance to the Government, and the Government owes to them the duty of protection. These are reciprocal obligations" (*Schwimmer* 1929, 649). Butler said it was a "fundamental principle of the Constitution that citizens have a duty to defend our government by force of arms against all enemies whenever the necessity arises" (650). Whatever tends to "lessen the willingness of citizens to discharge their duty to bear arms in the country's defense detracts from the strength and safety of the Government." The opinions and beliefs of citizens, as well as their behavior, Butler continued, indicate "a disposition to hinder in the performance of that duty." These opinions and beliefs are of "vital importance, for if all or a large number of citizens oppose such defense the 'good order and happiness' of the United States can not long endure" (650–651).

Butler took direct aim at Schwimmer's pacifism. Although the word is used to describe someone who "seeks to maintain peace and to abolish war," it is also used and understood to mean one who "refuses or is unwilling for any purpose to bear arms because of conscientious considerations and who is disposed to encourage others in such refusal." Laws governing naturalization appropriately require such commitment because "one who is without any sense of nationalism is not well bound or held by the ties of affection to any nation or government." Butler described Schwimmer's attitude toward constitutional principles as "vague and ambiguous." The burden was on Schwimmer to show that her "pacifism and lack of nationalistic sense" did not oppose the principle that it is a "duty of citizenship by force of arms when necessary to defend the country against all enemies," and that her opinions and beliefs would not "prevent or impair the true faith and allegiance" required by federal law governing naturalization. In Butler's view, Schwimmer "failed to do so" (652–653).

The *Schwimmer* case drew one of Justice Holmes's most eloquent dissents, a dissent joined by Justices Brandeis and Sanford. He referred to Schwimmer as a woman of "superior character and intelligence." He also noted the irrelevance of her statement that she would not bear arms—"inasmuch as she is a woman over fifty years of age, [she] would not be allowed to bear arms if she wanted to" (653). Furthermore, she held none of the "now-dreaded creeds but believes in organized government" and prefers that of the United States to any other in the world. Surely, Holmes concluded, "it cannot show a lack of attachment to the principles of the Constitution that she thinks that it can be improved." Some of Schwimmer's statements might "excite popular prejudice," but if there is any principle of the Constitution that more "imperatively calls for attachment than any other it is the principle of free thought." He suggested that the Quakers "have done their share to make this country what it is," and it was not "supposed hitherto that we regretted our inability to expel [pacifists] because they believe more than some of us do in the teachings of the Sermon on the Mount" (654–655). Two years after *Schwimmer*, two Canadian pacifists were denied citizenship because of their refusal to bear arms. A majority of the Hughes Court relied on the nation's "right to survive" argument to sustain the Immigration Service decision to deny citizenship in *United States v. Macintosh* and *United States v. Bland* (1931). These rulings were overruled fifteen years later by the Stone Court in *Girouard v. United States* (1946).

The Supreme Court's first full examination of the establishment of religion clause did not occur until the *Everson v. Board of Education* (1947) ruling. The Court had an opportunity to do so seventeen years earlier in *Cochran v. Louisiana State Board of Education* (1930), a case that was decided several weeks after Taft's death. Louisiana supplied free textbooks to students in parochial as well as public schools. The constitutional challenge was based on a due process objection of taking property for private use. The unanimous Court ruled, however, that the appropriation of tax funds was for a public purpose. The new Chief Justice Charles Evans Hughes introduced what later would be called the "child benefit" concept in rationalizing the Louisiana policy. The appropriations were made for the specific purpose of purchasing books for the use of the state's school children. The students and not the schools are beneficiaries of these appropriations. The schools "obtain nothing from them, nor are they relieved of a single obligation, because of them." Looking at the Louisiana statute as having the "effect

. . . attributed to it," Hughes concluded, "we cannot doubt that the taxing power of the State is exerted for a public purpose" (*Cochran* 1930, 375).

Rights of the Accused

The Taft Court preferred to leave criminal justice issues to the states. The process of nationalizing the Bill of Rights to the states had not reached the rights of the accused provisions by the 1920s, and the Taft Court chose to maintain the status quo. As a result, the Taft Court's criminal justice rulings were limited in number and largely confined to federal cases. There were a number of significant rulings nonetheless, including several important cases with origins in the federal government's enforcement of national prohibition.

The Taft Court retreated from the Fourth Amendment position taken by the White Court in its last term. One such White Court case was *Silverthorne Lumber Co. v. United States* (1920), which involved two persons who had been indicted by a federal grand jury and taken into custody. While the persons were detained, federal officials raided their offices and seized papers and documents found there. The federal government expressed regret over the illegal seizure of the materials, but it also sought to "avail itself of the knowledge obtained by that means which otherwise it would not have had." The government contended that evidence gained even in violation of the Fourth Amendment could be used in a criminal prosecution. Justice Holmes, speaking for a seven-justice majority, characterized the government's action an "outrage." He strongly condemned the tactics of the federal agents and said that seized material could not be used in any way. Holmes said that "knowledge gained by the Government's own wrong cannot be used by it." For the government to gain advantage of material obtained in this way would "reduce the Fourth Amendment to a form of words." Even the rights of a corporation "against unlawful search and seizure are to be protected even if the same result might have been achieved in a lawful way" (*Silverthorne* 1920, 391–392). The *Silverthorne* opinion contributed to the development of the exclusionary rule, a rule designed to ensure that the federal government could not benefit from illegally secured evidence.

Similarly, the White Court ruled in *Gouled v. United States* (1921) that the Fourth Amendment could be violated by stealthy intrusions into a constitutionally protected area. The Court considered the admissibility of evidence surreptitiously removed from Gouled's office by a business acquaintance acting under the direction of army intelligence officers. The Court unanimously held this an unconstitutional search and seizure. Justice Clarke suggested that the Fourth Amendment prohibits unreasonable searches and seizures "by force or by illegal threat or show of force, amounting to coercion." It would be "impossible to successfully contend that a like search and seizure would be a reasonable one if only admission were obtained by stealth instead of coercion" (*Gouled* 1921, 305).

Perhaps the most important search and seizure decisions of the Taft Court stemmed from enforcement of Prohibition. The first Prohibition search case came to the Taft Court in *Hester v. United States* (1924). The Court departed from the reasoning in both *Silverthorne* and *Gouled* as it held that "open fields" surrounding a house were not protected by the Fourth Amendment. The evidence objected to in *Hester* was obtained by revenue agents who accessed Hester's father's property without permission. The officers saw Hester give a bottle to a second man. As officers approached, Hester went to his car, grabbed a gallon jug, and, along with the second man, attempted to flee. During the pursuit of Hester and the other man, a officer fired his gun. Hester dropped the jug and the second man threw away his bottle. The jug and the bottle both contained "moonshine"—illicitly distilled whiskey. This evidence was not obtained by entering Hester's father's house. The "only shadow of a ground" suggesting a Fourth Amendment violation was that examination of the jug and bottle took place on Hester's father's land. Holmes disposed of the Fourth Amendment issue in just two sentences—"the special protection accorded by the Fourth Amendment to the people in their 'persons, houses, papers and effects,' is not extended to the open fields. The distinction between the latter and the house is as old as the common law" (*Hester* 1924, 59).

The most significant and long-lasting of the Taft Court's Fourth Amendment rulings came in *Carroll v. United States* (1925). The ruling sustained Prohibition officers' seizure of liquor concealed in an automobile against a claim that it violated the Fourth Amendment. Carroll and a companion were convicted for transporting liquor in violation of the National Prohibition Act. At trial, evidence in the form of sixty-eight quarts of whiskey and gin, seized without warrant from the car, was introduced. Carroll contended that the evidence was inadmissible because its seizure was unlawful. By the time of Carroll's trial federal courts had been applying the exclusionary rule in instances of Fourth Amendment violations by federal agents. The central question before the Court in *Carroll* was whether the search was lawful or not. The Court said it was and that the evidence was admissible.

The National Prohibition Act was amended in late 1921. Supplemental language made it a misdemeanor for any federal officer to search a building without a warrant, but Congress clearly distinguished homes and offices from automobiles. The question in *Carroll* was whether the legislative distinction could pass Fourth Amendment muster. The Court concluded that it could—the Fourth Amendment "does not denounce all searches and seizures, but only such as are unreasonable" (*Carroll* 1925, 147). Taft related a history going back as far as 1790 when such places as dwellings were distinguished from things that are mobile. Since the beginning of our constitutional history, Taft said, the Fourth Amendment has been interpreted in a way that "recognize[s] a necessary difference between a search of a store, dwelling house or other structure . . . and a search of a ship, motor boat, wagon or automobile" where it is not "practicable to secure a warrant because the vehicle can be quickly moved out of the locality or jurisdiction in which the warrant must be sought" (153).

Once the exigency of mobility was established, Taft examined the circumstances under which a warrantless vehicle search could occur. For those persons lawfully within the country and entitled to use the public highways, there is a right to uninterrupted free passage "unless there is known to a competent official authorized to search, probable cause for believing that their vehicles are carrying contraband or illegal merchandise." In cases in which the securing of a warrant is "reasonably practicable, it must be used" (153–156). Thus, the Court fashioned a warrant exception for vehicles although the exception was a conditional one. Justices McReynolds and Sutherland, not known for great sensitivity to the rights of criminal defendants, dissented, saying that the "damnable character of the bootlegger's business should not close our eyes to the mischief which will surely follow any attempt to destroy it by unwarranted methods" (163).

The Fourth Amendment claims reviewed in *Carroll* were analyzed with an eye to enforcement of National Prohibition, and the Taft Court's response reflected an emerging judicial realism. Because illegal bootleg liquor was not going to be left easily accessible for seizure by prohibition agents, the Court relaxed the constitutional barrier and permitted search and seizure, without warrant, of automobiles used for its illegal transport. The long-term impact of *Carroll* extended well beyond the Prohibition context. Because of the exigency resulting from the mobility of vehicles, the warrant exception established in *Carroll* remains in effect into the twenty-first century, long after the abandonment of Prohibition.

Several weeks after the *Carroll* decision, the Taft Court considered another warrant exception in *Agnello v. United States.* Agnello and a number of others were arrested for violating the Harrison Act by conspiring to sell cocaine without having first paid the federal regulatory tax on the drug. The arrests took place at the home of Stephen Alba, one of the conspirators. While some police officers were taking Agnello and the others to the police station, other officers entered Agnello's home without a warrant and seized a can of cocaine. The Court acknowledged that police could, without a warrant, search the place where an arrest occurs in order to seize evidence related to criminal conduct or weapons with which the arrested person might effect an escape. In this case, however, Agnello's residence was several blocks from Alba's house. When Agnello's residence was entered and searched, said Justice Butler, the "conspiracy was ended and the defendants were under arrest and in custody elsewhere." As a result, the search could not be sustained as an incident of the arrests. The search of a private dwelling without a warrant "is in itself unreasonable and abhorrent to our laws" (*Agnello* 1925, 30–32).

The Taft Court combined the themes from *Hester*, *Carroll*, and *Agnello* as it reviewed another search issue stemming from the Prohibition Act in *United States v. Lee* (1927). Lee and two others were arrested by Coast Guard officers on a boat registered to Lee. The arrest occurred at a place known as Rum Row, a location some twenty-four miles from land. In addition to arresting the three persons aboard the boat, authorities seized the boat and seventy-one cases of grain alcohol found aboard it. The court of appeals set aside Lee's conviction, concluding that the Coast Guard is not permitted to stop and search American vessels on the high seas more than twelve miles from the coast. The Taft Court disagreed. There was probable cause to believe that federal law was being violated, thus the Coast Guard made a lawful seizure on the high seas notwithstanding the twelve-mile limit. The Court concluded the warrantless seizure of Lee's boat was comparable to the warrantless search and seizure of an automobile upheld in *Carroll*. In addition, because Lee and the others were lawfully taken into custody, a search incident to their arrest could be conducted. Finally, the cases of liquor were on deck rather than concealed elsewhere on the boat, thus the "search" was really discovery of something out in the open as in *Hester*. Even a subsequent trespass by Coast Guard officers, had it occurred, would not have rendered inadmissible anything legally obtained up to that point.

Technology also gave the government new means to wage its fight against crime, including the ability to pry into the private affairs of a suspect without actually entering the premises. By a five-to-four majority, the Taft Court gave its blessing to wiretapping in *Olmstead v. United States* (1928). Olmstead ran a bootlegging business that, according to federal agents, operated from three different locations in Seattle, Washington, employed a large number of people, and used a number of vehicles and ships to illicitly transport liquor throughout the state of Washington and western Canada. Federal agents found out about his bootlegging operations, described as being of "amazing magnitude," by wiretapping the telephone lines to one of his offices as well as telephone lines into the homes of several of his employees. On the basis of the wiretap evidence, Olmstead and upwards of seventy-five people were indicted for violating National Prohibition.

The case raised two major issues. One was the extent to which the Court would interpret the Fourth Amendment's search and seizure clause in light of technological developments—would the amendment be held to prohibit wiretapping, a government action that those writing the amendment could not have anticipated? The second issue was whether the Court would employ the exclusionary rule to suppress the use of wiretap evidence in federal courtrooms.

Chief Justice Taft, writing for himself and four other justices, upheld the convictions. In their view, the wiretap evidence had not been obtained illegally. Applying the Fourth Amendment literally, the Court concluded that neither a search nor seizure had occurred. Federal agents did not enter the houses or offices of the defendants. It was reasonable to assume, said Taft, that "one who installs in his house a telephone instrument with connecting wire intends to project his voice to those quite outside," and that the wires beyond his house and the messages passing through them are not protected by the Fourth Amendment. The language of the amendment, Taft continued, cannot be "extended and expanded" to include telephone wires "reaching to the whole world from the house or office." The intervening wires are "not part of his house or office, any more than are the highways along which they are stretched" (*Olmstead* 1928, 465–466).

The Court concluded that a seizure had not occurred either. The agents took nothing tangible into their possession. A search is to be of "material things—the person, the house, his papers, or his effects. The description of the warrant necessary to make the proceeding lawful is that it must specify the place to be searched and the persons or *things* to be seized" (464). The agents merely intercepted words. Olmstead also pressed a self-incrimination claim, but that was rejected as well. The Fifth Amendment's privilege against self-incrimination had not been violated in this case because no one had made the defendants talk on the telephone or coerced them to make incriminating disclosures in any other way. Taft indicated that there is "no room in the present case for applying the Fifth Amendment unless the Fourth is first violated" (462).

Taft's formalistic treatment of wiretapping certainly minimized the spirit of the Fourth Amendment. At a more pragmatic level, Taft expressed reluctance to demand only "nice ethical conduct by government officials." To do so "would make society suffer and give criminals greater immunity than has been known heretofore." He expressed great reluctance to adapt, modernize, or expand upon provisions of the Constitution. Congress, of course, could pass a statute prohibiting wiretapping and make evidence derived from wiretaps inadmissible in federal criminal trials, but the courts had no authority to add such "an enlarged and unusual meaning" to the Fourth Amendment (468).

Taft's opinion elicited dissents from Justices Holmes, Brandeis, and Butler. Approaching the discussion historically, the generally conservative Butler rejected Taft's literal and therefore narrow interpretation of the Fourth Amendment. Holmes condemned wiretapping as a "dirty business" and suggested that it was a "less[er] evil that some criminals should escape than that the Government should play an ignoble part" (470). Justice Stone joined both of their dissents.

The most extended and impressive dissenting opinion came from Brandeis. He reminded the Court that its own decisions had sanctioned an adaptive approach to interpreting governmental authority conferred by the Constitution to meet modern conditions. Brandeis argued that the same approach must be used to interpret and apply clauses "guaranteeing to the individual protection against specific abuses of power" (472). The privacy that the Fourth Amendment was designed to protect could now be invaded by "subtler and more far-reaching means"—subtler because no physical intrusion was needed to tap a phone line, and more far-reaching because wiretapping invaded the privacy of all persons involved in the intercepted conversations. Brandeis added that "[d]iscovery and invention have made it possible for the Government . . . to obtain disclosure in court of what is whispered in the closet. . . ." This was of major concern to Brandeis, who viewed wiretaps as a threat not only to those accused of crime, but to the democratic process as well. "The greatest dangers to liberty," Brandeis argued, "lurk in insidious encroachment by men of zeal, well-meaning but without understanding" (479). Our government is the "potent, omnipresent teacher. For good or ill, it teaches the whole people by its example. . . . If the government becomes a lawbreaker, it breeds contempt for law; it invites every man to become a law unto himself; it invites anarchy." In Brandeis's view, admission of wiretap evidence in court was tantamount to a declaration by the Court that "the end justifies the means" (485). Justice Stone concurred with Brandeis's dissent as well.

One of the consequences of our federal form of government is that persons are expected to comply with the criminal prohibitions of both state and national law. The extent to which federal and state governments can make the same act a criminal offense is limited, but there is some overlap. This overlap presents an interesting double jeopardy issue, an issue the Taft Court addressed in *United States v. Lanza* (1922). Once again, enforcement of the Prohibition Amendment provided the occasion. Lanza had been convicted for violating a state's prohibition statute. Federal prosecutors then obtained an indictment against Lanza for violation of the Volstead Act, the federal prohibition statute. The Court held that successive federal-state prosecutions are permissible on dual sovereignty grounds. This occurs because our government system has "two sovereignties, deriving power from different sources, capable of dealing with the same subject matter within the same territory." It follows, said Chief Justice Taft, that an "act denounced as a crime by both national and state sovereignties is an offense against the peace and dignity of both, and may be punished by each" (*Lanza* 1922, 382). Taft said that Congress could direct that federal prosecutions not take place if a defendant is first convicted of the same offense at the state level, but because Congress had not done so, Lanza was lawfully subject to prosecution by both levels of government.

The Taft Court ruled in *Moore v. Dempsey* (1923) that a trial conducted in an atmosphere of racial conflict and mob violence is inherently unfair. Moore was one of five African Americans convicted in an Arkansas court of killing a white man and was sentenced to death. The Supreme Court ordered a new trial, concluding that the neighborhood was "thronged with an adverse crowd that threatened the most dangerous consequences to anyone interfering with the desired result" (*Moore* 1923, 89). Although acknowledging that "mere mistakes of law" may not warrant setting aside the results of the first trial, Justice Holmes went on to say that if the "whole proceeding is a mask—that counsel, jury and judge were swept to the fatal end by an irresistible wave of public passion," the Supreme Court must provide relief if state courts "do not correct the wrong" (91). In dissent, Justice McReynolds expressed concern that if any defendant convicted in a state trial could offer allegations "tending to impeach his trial" and obtain further review of his case, then "another way has been added to a list already unfortunately long to prevent prompt punishment" (93).

Congress passed a law in 1920 intended to expedite the deportation of aliens who had been charged with violation of wartime statutes. Chief Justice Taft rejected the contention that such a measure was invalid as an ex post facto law in *Mahler v. Eby* (1924). A law cannot be held to be ex post facto unless it imposes punishment for past acts. A deportation law authorizing expulsion of aliens for criminal acts committed before its passage was held not ex post facto. The Court did not consider deportation a punishment, but rather a discretionary exercise of sovereign power (Pritchett 1984, 177). Deportation, said Chief Justice Taft for a unanimous Court, while "burdensome and severe for the alien, is not a punishment." The right to expel aliens is a "sovereign power necessary to the safety of the country and only limited by treaty obligations" (*Mahler* 1924, 38).

Criminal statutes must be sufficiently clear and specific to define and give adequate notice of the kind of conduct that they forbid. In the absence of such clarity and specificity, statutes must be voided for vagueness. In *Connally v. General Construction Co.* (1926) the Taft Court struck down an Oklahoma statute that made it a crime to pay wages below the local prevailing wage. The applicable "void for vagueness" defect was framed by Justice Sutherland—that if the statutory provisions of the Oklahoma law were enforced, General Construction Co., its officers, agents, and representatives would be deprived of its liberty and property without due process because the law contains "no ascertainable standard of guilt." In this instance it cannot be determined with certainty "what sum constitutes a current wage in any locality," and the term "locality itself is fatally vague and uncertain" (*Connally* 1926, 390).

In *Byars v. United States* and *Gambino v. United States*, both decided in 1927 and involving illicit liquor, the Taft Court considered what came to be known as the "silver platter" doctrine. The doctrine directs that when evidence is taken by unlawful means, it would still be admissible in a federal court provided that federal agents were not involved in obtaining it. The doctrine brought dangers with it, however. State agents could violate reasonable search and seizure requirements and then turn the evidence over to federal officers, on the so-called silver platter. The federal officers were then able to use the evidence in federal proceedings. Justice Sutherland said that the Court did not "question the right of the federal government to avail itself of evidence improperly seized by state officers operating entirely upon their own account." The doctrine does not extend to situations in which federal agents "officially participate in the wrongful search" (*Byars* 1927, 33). The Court concluded that the evidence obtained in *Byars* had been seized through a joint operation of federal and state agents and was, therefore, inadmissible. Similarly, in *Gambino*, the Court ruled that if it appears that state officers were "acting solely on behalf" of the United States, evidence thus obtained is inadmissible.

Despite the Taft Court's reluctance to extend Bill of Rights criminal rights provisions to the states, it became more watchful of state procedures that might not meet fundamental fairness requirements. In *Tumey v. Ohio* (1927), the Court reversed the conviction of a bootlegger who had been tried before the mayor of a small town. The Ohio law allowed mayors to keep fines and court costs as payment for judicial work. No costs were collected if the defendant were acquitted. Tumey was found guilty of unlawfully possessing liquor by the mayor qua judge, fined $100, and held in custody until the fine and court costs were paid. In determining what fundamental fairness requires, Chief Justice Taft pointed to "those settled usages and modes of proceeding" found in common law and English statutes. Applying these standards, the Taft Court concluded it was a denial of due process to "subject his liberty or property to the judgment of a court, the judge of which has a direct, personal, substantial pecuniary interest in reaching a conclusion against him in his case" (*Tumey* 1927, 523). It was argued that because the amounts were minimal, any due process problems with this process were mitigated if not eliminated altogether. The Taft Court thought otherwise, saying it could not regard the possible receipt or loss of these costs as "minute, remote, trifling, or insignificant." It was certainly not fair to defendants brought before these justices of the peace for determination of guilt or innocence "that the prospect of such a loss by the Mayor should weigh against his acquittal" (532).

Just after Taft's death, the Court ruled in *Patton v. United States* (1930) that before a criminal defendant can forego a jury trial, the "consent of government counsel and the sanction of the court must be had, in addition to the express and intelligent consent of the defendant" (*Patton* 1930, 312). The Court made clear that the right to a jury trial means the traditional common law jury of twelve citizens rendering a unanimous verdict. Patton had agreed to continue his trial with eleven jurors after illness prevented the continued participation of one of them. The Court viewed the loss of a single juror as comparable to trial by a judge. A constitutional jury, said Justice Sutherland, "means twelve men . . . and when reduced to eleven it ceases to be such a jury quite as effectively as though the number had been reduced to a single person." To uphold the voluntary reduction of a jury from twelve to eleven "is only a slight reduction, is not to interpret that instrument but to disregard it." It is not our province, Sutherland continued, "to measure the extent to which the Constitution has been contravened and ignore the violation, if in our opinion, it is not, relatively, as bad as it might have been" (292). It would be a "highly dangerous innovation, in reference to criminal cases, upon the ancient and invaluable institution of trial by jury . . . , for the court to allow any number short of a full panel of twelve jurors" (303).

Equal Protection of the Law and Voting Rights

The authority of the Constitution and Congress over primary elections was thrown into serious doubt by the White Court's ruling in *Newberry v. United States* (1921). Provisions of the Corrupt Practices Act of 1910 restricted campaign expenditures in both primary and general elections. Truman Newberry was convicted in 1918 of violating this statute in his successful campaign for one of Michigan's U.S. Senate seats. The question contained in Newberry's appeal was whether Congress's authority to regulate congressional elections conferred by Article I, Section 4, extended to nominating processes such as primary elections. The Court set aside his conviction with five justices holding that when the Constitution referred to an election it meant the "final choice of an officer by duly qualified electors," and that the primary was "in no real sense part of the manner of holding the election." Congress was not given "indefinite" or "undefined" power over every practice remotely connected to elections. At the time the Constitution was written, said Justice McReynolds, "primaries were . . . unknown." Primaries are "in no sense elections for an office, but merely methods by which party adherents agree upon candidates whom they intend to offer and support for ultimate choice by all qualified electors" (*Newberry* 1921, 249–250). Congress apparently accepted the limitation on its statutory authority and explicitly excluded primaries in the Corrupt Practices Act passed in 1925. The *Newberry* ruling was seen in some parts of the country as enabling them to openly discriminate against black voters in primaries. Within two years, Texas explicitly prohibited African Americans from voting in the state's Democratic primaries. The Taft Court responded to that policy in *Nixon v. Herndon* (1927), which is discussed later.

The Taft Court was aware that state legislatures frequently used classifying schemes in exercising the police power—that distinguishing between or among groups or business enterprises was an effective way to impose regulations or distribute benefits. By the 1920s it was well established that courts should presume legislative classifications to be lawful and not interfere with them unless they were clearly arbitrary or capricious. In *Crescent Cotton Oil Co. v. Mississippi* (1921), the Taft Court examined a state law that prohibited any corporation engaged in the manufacture of cotton-seed oil from owning or operating cotton gins in the state, except those of a governmentally prescribed capacity and in the city or town where their oil plants were located. The law was aimed at foreign (nonresident) corporations, and it was challenged by Crescent Cotton Oil, a Tennessee corporation. Crescent Cotton Oil was prohibited from doing local business in Mississippi because of its failure to comply with the law and enjoined from operating cotton gins in the state. In addition to interstate commerce issues, Crescent Cotton Oil challenged the law on equal protection grounds because the law was applied only to corporations and not individuals. The Court did not see the cotton gins as instrumentalities of interstate commerce, so the prohibition on their use by nonresident corporations did not violate the commerce clause. Justice Clarke, speaking for a unanimous Court, said that a state has discretion to impose conditions on nonresident corporations doing business in the state, even to the extent of excluding them altogether. The "inherent differences" between persons and corporations were seen as "sufficient to sustain a classification making restrictions applicable to corporations only." Any reasonable classification, said Clarke, "will be sustained against equal protection challenge." Furthermore, every "state of facts sufficient to sustain such classification which can be reasonably conceived of as having existed when the law was enacted will be assumed" (*Crescent Cotton Oil* 1921, 137).

The Taft Court struck down a state anti-injunction statute in *Truax v. Corrigan* in December 1921. An Arizona restaurant owner sought an injunction in state court against his striking, unionized employees who were peacefully picketing his business. He claimed the state law that denied him injunctive relief had deprived him of his property rights without due process of law. A five-justice majority agreed and declared the law unconstitutional as an arbitrary and capricious exercise of state police power, and an injurious invasion of property rights. A business is a property right, said Chief Justice Taft, and "free access for employees, owner and customers to his place of business is incident to such right." Taft noted that would-be customers were subjected to conduct that constituted "moral coercion by illegal annoyance and obstruction." In his view, "violence could not have been more effective" (*Truax* 1921, 327–328).

Justices Holmes, Brandeis, and Pitney each issued dissents. Holmes suggested that business activity was not itself a "sacred" property right and that the state had the power to act on a perceived evil in the misuse of injunctions. He reiterated his customary self-restraintist argument that courts had no business second-guessing the legislature in determining social policy and engaging in social experimentation, even though such experiments "may seem futile or even noxious" (344). Justice Pitney, joined by Justice Clarke, sounded the same theme in his dissent. He argued that the states had considerable latitude to determine "each for itself, their respective conditions of law and order, and what kind of civilization they shall have as a result." The use of injunction to prevent business disturbances is "in the essential sense a measure of police regulation." States have broad discretion in establishing such regulations, but they also "have discretion, equally broad, about modifying and relaxing them" (348–349). Further, Pitney said the equal protection guarantee does not require that laws are "complete" or "perfectly symmetrical." Rather, it entitles persons to "treatment not less favorable than that given to others similarly circumstanced" (351). The Arizona statute did that in Pitney's view. Brandeis agreed with both Holmes and Pitney in his own dissent, but also said that the Arizona law constituted a positive good that could be justified in terms of the social needs that had prompted the legislation in the first place.

The Taft Court was essentially unwilling to invoke the equal protection clause on behalf of aliens. In 1870 Congress amended immigration policy to African Americans eligible for citizenship. Previously, only "free white persons" were eligible. Excluded were various nationality groups from Asia. Unless specifically exempted by Congress, non-Caucasians could be made ineligible for naturalization rights. The Taft Court unanimously interpreted the 1870 immigration act as amended to exclude those of Japanese ancestry in *Ozawa v. United States* (1922). Speaking through Justice Sutherland, a unanimous Court in *Ozawa* recognized congressional power to restrict citizenship as it wished. Having taken the step in *Ozawa*, the Court excluded East Indians on similar grounds in *United States v. Bhagat Singh Thind* (1923).

Congress enacted legislation in 1919 that allowed persons of foreign birth who served in the American military during World War I to become eligible for naturalization. The Taft Court held in *Toyota v United States* (1925) that the 1919 statute did not enlarge the class of eligible foreign-born persons to include those of Japanese ancestry who served in the military during the war—that the law was intended to modify the previous distinctions based on color or race. The Court then distinguished between Japanese and Filipinos. Like the Japanese, Filipinos were not eligible for citizenship under the original terms of the law. The military service policy affected Filipinos differently from other Asian nationality groups, however, because the Philippine Islands had become an American territory following the Spanish-American War. Consequently, the citizens of the Philippines were thereafter not regarded as aliens—they owed "no allegiance to any foreign government" (*Toyota* 1925, 411).

On a related issue, the Taft Court upheld a number of state laws, primarily found in Western states, prohibiting land ownership by aliens who had not declared their intention to become citizens. In *Terrace v. Thompson* (1923), the Court found no equal protection or due process problems with the state of Washington's Alien Land Law. The law disqualified aliens who had not declared an intention to become a citizen from "taking or holding interests in land in the state for farming or other purposes." Because Asians were ineligible for citizenship anyway, they could not satisfy the requirements of the Washington statute. Justice Butler spoke for the six-justice majority that although Congress had exclusive control over immigration, states retained full power to deny aliens economic rights within their borders in the absence of federal law to the contrary. Butler pointed out that the rights, privileges, and duties of aliens "differ widely from those of citizens, and those of aliens [declaring an intention to seek citizenship] differ substantially from those of nondeclarants" (*Terrace* 1923, 218). The Court concluded that it is "clearly within the power of the State to include nondeclarant eligible aliens and ineligible aliens in the same prohibited class." The reasons for "supporting discrimination against aliens who may but who will not naturalize," said Butler, "are obvious" (221). A similar California Alien Land Law was upheld by the Taft Court in *Porterfield v. Webb* (1923).

The White Court ruled in *Buchanan v. Warley* (1917) that a Louisville, Kentucky, ordinance prohibiting African Americans from moving into residential blocks where the occupants were primarily whites, was an undue interference with the property rights of the residential owners and thus constituted a denial of due process. Agreements among individuals establishing racially exclusive residential zones, known as restrictive covenants, became common following *Buchanan* as large numbers of communities had such "covenants running with the land." The first restrictive covenant case to reach the Taft Court was in *Corrigan v. Buckley* (1926). Buckley, a property owner and a signatory to such a covenant, attempted to enjoin Corrigan, another signatory, from breaching the covenant. The essence of the Court's unanimous ruling was that constitutional limits only proscribe actions of government and are not directed at individual actions. The opinion by Justice Sanford was extremely narrow, however. The Court concluded that neither constitutional nor statutory questions relied on as grounds for Corrigan's appeal had any "substantial quality or color of merit, or afford any jurisdictional basis for the appeal" (*Corrigan* 1926, 331). The following year, in *Harmon v. Tyler* (1927), the Taft Court invalidated similar provisions of Louisiana law on the basis of *Buchanan*. Attempts to circumvent the *Buchanan* decision were defeated in both federal and state courts, and by 1930 the unconstitutionality of municipal segregation ordinances was firmly established and remained so following the Vinson Court's ruling in *Shelley v. Kraemer* (1948).

A year after *Corrigan*, the Taft Court decided *Nixon v. Herndon*, which struck down a Texas law excluding African Americans from voting in the Democratic Party primary. The Texas law was challenged on Fifteenth Amendment voting rights grounds, but the Court framed its decision around the equal protection clause of the Fourteenth Amendment. Speaking for a unanimous Court, Justice Holmes suggested the question raised in *Herndon* was "not open to a doubt." Indeed, the Court did not even entertain the Fifteenth Amendment issue because it seemed "hard to imagine a more direct and obvious infringement of the Fourteenth." Holmes pointed to "special intent" of the Fourteenth Amendment—to "protect blacks from discrimination against them." The amendment almost categorically denied to any state the power to "withhold from them the equal protection of the laws" (*Herndon* 1927, 540–541).

Nixon v. Herndon had limited, short-term impact as the Texas legislature came back with another law authorizing political parties in the state, through their executive committees, to prescribe the qualifications for voting in their primaries. The Texas Democratic Party's executive committee then excluded African Americans from primary elections, but the Hughes Court held in *Nixon v. Condon* (1932) that the party had been delegated a role in the election process by the state, which made the action indistinguishable from actions by the state itself. The Court did not question in either *Herndon* or *Condon* the principle from *Newberry* that party primaries were outside the protection of the Constitution. Given this opening, the Texas Democratic Party convention adopted a resolution confining party membership to white citizens. It ostensibly did so on its own authority and without any official state mandate. By unanimous vote of the Hughes Court in *Grovey v. Townsend* (1935), this practice was allowed because it was an action of the political party as a private entity. The importance of the primary to the overall electoral process was made clear in *United States v. Classic* (1941), and from there the Stone Court ruled in *Smith v. Allwright* (1944) that political parties were not private actors in the election process, bringing to an end the so-called white primary.

Closely akin to the issues of discriminatory practices and voting rights was racial segregation in education. The Taft Court's only ruling involving segregated public education was in *Gong Lum v. Rice* (1927), where it maintained established practice under the "separate but equal" doctrine. *Gong Lum* concerned a child of Chinese descent who was required to attend a black school under a state of Mississippi constitutional mandate that separate schools be maintained for children of the "white and colored races." In an opinion by Chief Justice Taft representing all nine justices, it was the Court's view that there was a "white race, on the one hand, and the brown, yellow and black races on the other." As a member of the "Mongolian or yellow race," Martha Lum "could not insist on being classed with the whites under this constitutional division" (*Gong Lum* 1927, 82).

References and Further Reading

Baker, Liva. 1991. *The Justice of Beacon Hill: The Life and Times of Oliver Wendell Holmes.* New York: HarperCollins.

Currie, David P. 1990. *The Constitution in the Supreme Court: The Second Century, 1888–1986.* Chicago: University of Chicago Press.

Epstein, Lee, Jeffrey A. Segal, Harold J. Spaeth, and Thomas Walker. 1994. *The Supreme Court Compendium: Data, Decisions, and Developments.* Washington, DC: Congressional Quarterly Press.

Kelly, Alfred H., Winfred A. Harbison, and Herman Belz. 1991. *The American Constitution: Its Origins and Developments.* Vol. 2. 7th ed. New York: W. W. Norton.

Mason, Alphius T. 1964. *William Howard Taft: Chief Justice.* New York: Simon and Schuster.

Morison, Samuel Eliot, Henry Steele Commager, and William E. Leuchtenburg. 1980. *The Growth of the American Republic.* Vol. 2. New York: Oxford University Press.

Murphy, Paul L. 1972. *The Constitution in Times of Crisis, 1918–1969.* New York: Harper & Row.

Pritchett, C. Herman. 1984. *Constitutional Law of the Federal System.* Englewood Cliffs, NJ: Prentice-Hall.

Schlesinger, Arthur M., Jr. 1957. *The Crisis of the Old Order, 1919–1933.* Boston: Houghton Mifflin.

Swindler, William F. 1974. *Court and Constitution in the Twentieth Century: The Old Legality, 1889–1932.* Indianapolis, IN: Bobbs-Merrill.

Urofsky, Melvin I., and Paul Finkelman. 2002. *A March of Liberty: A Constitutional History of the United States.* Vol. 2. 2d ed. New York: Oxford University Press.

White, G. Edward. 1994. "Oliver Wendell Holmes, Jr." In *The Supreme Court Justices: A Biographical Dictionary.* Melvin I. Urofsky, ed. New York: Garland, 225–234.

4

Legacy and Impact

The Taft Court was a conservative Court in a conservative time. It embraced the ascendant national priorities reflected in the Republican administrations of Presidents Warren G. Harding, Calvin Coolidge, and Herbert C. Hoover. The Taft Court's principal legacy was its continuation and revitalization of the laissez-faire jurisprudence of the Fuller and White Courts that preceded it. The Taft Court was, first and foremost, a maintaining Court—a tribunal that sustained the entrenched laissez-faire oriented, probusiness priorities that had been in place since the late 1880s. In addition, the Taft Court utilized judicial activism to a then unprecedented extent in its attempt to protect private property from both federal and state regulation.

Despite the presence of Justices Holmes, Brandeis, and Clarke, in the early 1920s the Court was already a conservative tribunal. The appointment of Taft as chief justice in 1921 reinforced this conservatism. The prevailing mood of the country was the prevailing mood of the justices—the Taft Court wholeheartedly reflected the Republican priorities of the 1920s. Accordingly, the Court insulated corporate America from regulatory schemes pursued by federal or state politicians. Indeed, many believed that the prospect for unregulated enterprise had never been greater.

A discussion of the Taft Court legacy must begin with William Howard Taft, because understanding him is key to understanding the Supreme Court of the 1920s. In 1921 the conservative Republicans were safely in control of the executive and legislative branches of the federal government. Only the Court represented a potential problem. Taft was particularly concerned about the possibly disruptive influence of Holmes and Brandeis, but his concerns abated as Pierce Butler, George Sutherland, and Edward Sanford joined the Court. His Court now had an insurmountable conservative majority and could safeguard private property rights and fend off political radicals. The addition of these justices had the effect of marginalizing Holmes and Brandeis in cases in which the Court was not unanimous—they would not be among the majority in split-vote decisions. For Taft it was time to move away from progressive expansionism and restore the country to its traditional constitutional bases. This was Taft's own version of "normalcy," and it required his Court to set a tone for the

American legal system based on long-standing natural law principles and a Constitution whose meaning is unchanging.

Taft dominated his Court for most of the decade. This was true even though Justices Holmes and Brandeis served throughout his tenure and were justices of remarkable intellect and powerful personalities and were often at odds with Taft's legal philosophy. Despite their philosophical differences, both Holmes and Brandeis respected Taft and their interactions were both congenial and productive. This suggests that Taft was right in thinking the Supreme Court was his natural milieu. His effectiveness as chief justice was, in large part, the product of his previous experience in the political arena, and therein lies something of an irony—without the hands-on political experience Taft gained after 1900, his performance as chief justice might have been less impressive. It was the combination of Taft's legal knowledge, judicial temperament, and political-administrative skills that made him a distinctive chief justice.

Taft had long believed that the federal courts were in great need of reform. He was particularly concerned about the capacity of the federal judiciary to handle its caseload. The caseload difficulties were aggravated by the great volume of litigation stemming from World War I and the Eighteenth Amendment. Large numbers of civil and criminal cases involving such matters as espionage, civil liberties, and wartime contracts crowded federal dockets, but nothing contributed to the growing caseload as much as the effort to enforce National Prohibition. Cases stemming from Prohibition alone produced a 10 percent increase in federal cases. Taft used his congressional connections to secure reorganization of the federal judiciary in 1922, which brought badly needed reforms in the administration and productivity of the federal courts. Taft took a more significant step in strengthening the Supreme Court when he obtained congressional approval for the Judiciary Act in 1925. The Court's workload had increased to such an extent that it took nearly two years between the initial filing of a case and its disposition. The Judiciary Act gave the Court greater discretionary power over its own docket. From 1925 on, the Court would only take cases that raised significant constitutional issues and cases that could be decided in a more timely fashion. As a further result of Taft's work, the significance of the cases decided by the Court increased substantially. More importantly, Taft's Judiciary Act marked the beginning of the modern Supreme Court era. The act allowed the Court to play a more prominent role in the U.S. governmental system and defines the Court's authority and practices to this day.

Taft had been politically inept as president, but he proved himself one of the most politically astute chief justices. Taft "completely refashioned the role of chief justice and at the same time modernized the structure of the federal court system" (Urofsky and Finkelman 2002, 627). Taft saw the judicial system as a fully coordinated branch of the federal government, but it required effective management. He saw the chief justice as the person who could provide that administrative leadership.

For the first time the "country had a man willing and able to carry out both constitutionally assigned roles—the chief justice of the United States as well as the chief justice of the Supreme Court" (627).

There is no best training ground for a Supreme Court justice, much less a chief justice. Some, like Chief Justice Earl Warren, have backgrounds in practical politics. Others, such as Felix Frankfurter and Harlan Fiske Stone, come from academe. Still others have extended service in the lower courts. History suggests that all these types of experiences have value, but Taft had all three—he brought unique qualifications to the chief justiceship. Moreover, he had been a dedicated student of the Supreme Court, and held definite views on its place in the American government framework. For Taft, as for Alexander Hamilton, judicial review was the hallmark of the American system of free government. The greatest advantage of our plan of government over every other, Taft wrote, "is the character of the judicial power vested in the Supreme Court" (Mason 1979, 46–47).

Before becoming chief justice, Taft had expressed the view that courts must look beyond the law to meet existing social and economic conditions. He had considered it both proper and necessary for judges to adapt the law to new social conditions. During his tenure as chief justice, he became more convinced that the Supreme Court must protect the institutions of property and contract from political radicals who threatened to restrict or regulate them. He referred to those who sought to depart from "sound legal" views as "sentimentalists," "socialists," "progressives," and "bolshevists." Under Taft's leadership the Court's majority saw itself as the vanguard of national progress. Judicial preeminence, assuming that the justices were properly committed to the dogma of laissez-faire, was society's best hope for the future, in Taft's view (Mason 1979, 66–67).

Taft believed that judges should exercise political discretion, a view that is consistent with his desire to keep the Court insulated from popular whim. The most important political function the Court performs is to "soften the impact of popular passions to restrain the impulsive desires of the majority." Taft believed that individual liberty, which to him meant economic liberty, was the foundation of our constitutional system. In his view, the Constitution rested on personal liberty and the right of property with the latter including the right of contract and the right of labor. His conception of a free man was one who could spend what he earns for his comfort or pleasure; "personal liberty and the right of property were indispensable to any possible useful progress of society" (Mason 1979, 49). Stability in society and in judicial decisions was the primary priority for Taft. Unlike some of his colleagues, he did not try to conceal the Court's important policy-making function by suggesting that judicial decisions were mechanically produced through the application of neutral legal principles.

Taft believed that the Court needed to perform a critical function in sustaining the constitutional system. In order to perform this function, there had to be consensus on the Court. Taft was able to facilitate the development of consensus during his tenure as chief justice. He was able to encourage consensus through the power of persuasion, but also by influencing the selection of some of his colleagues. Warren Harding was president for less than three years, but named four justices to the Court. Taft used his influence with Harding to secure not only his own nomination, but also the nominations of Butler, Sutherland, and Sanford, three unyielding conservatives. These appointments, coupled with the conservative justices who carried over from the White Court, gave Taft the fail-safe majority he needed. In order to preserve that unity, "Taft often found himself voting for positions far more reactionary than he would otherwise have adopted." In the early part of Taft's tenure, only Holmes and Brandeis "opposed the general trend of the Court." Brandeis would occasionally dissent because of his "belief in the need to restrain business and to allow the states to use their powers to protect the less fortunate members of society" and Holmes because of his "skepticism and his advocacy of judicial restraint" (Urofsky and Finkelman 2002, 626).

Taft displayed an unusual political flair in an office some think should remain remote from the political arena. He brought an enthusiasm to the role of chief justice that he carried to extraordinary lengths as head of the Court. He responded so positively to the work because it suited him well and he was able to pass along his enthusiasm to his colleagues. At least through the 1927 Term, Taft was a singularly successful chief justice. After 1927 the Court was more divided in its constitutional outlook and its decisions were based on divergent assessments of the law. Only in his last year in office, which was also the last year of his life, did Taft's pace slacken.

Taft's dedication to and affection for the Court were without parallel. Few justices worked as hard as he did. During his nine-year tenure he wrote almost 20 percent of his Court's opinions. Taft "worshiped the institution and its functions"; its personnel had become "his," even if Holmes, Brandeis, and Stone—"all of whom respected and liked the Big Chief"—would occasionally dissent from the otherwise intractable Taft majority. Taft provided "administrative and technical leadership second to none." His orchestration of consensus, of "massing the Court into a majority, was often spectacular." He proved to be a "superb judicial leader and architect," even in the face of occasional division (Abraham 1999, 141).

Taft had two opportunities to affect the composition of the Court. The first came during his tenure as president, when he named six justices to the Court. The second came with the election of Warren Harding. Taft was unrelenting in his pursuit of the chief justiceship and was eventually able to convince Harding to nominate him. His selection allowed him to realize his long-held ambition to preside over a Court that could be counted on to quell any "socialistic raids on property rights" (Mason 1979, 52). Once he assumed the center chair, Taft then counseled Harding on all subsequent judicial nominations. Taft was responsible for the nomination of three of the

Four Horsemen (McReynolds was the exception), whose ultraconservatism would dominate the Court until the late 1930s. Not only was Taft in a position of unparalleled prominence in the appointments process during those years, he "actively intervened, as no chief justice has before or since, to promote candidacies of his friends and to block those of others" (White 1976, 179). Taft knew what qualities he wanted in a Supreme Court justice and "labored hard from 1909 on to find men who possessed them" (180). His highest priority was prospective nominees with "sound" social views.

Taft's own jurisprudence closely resembled that of Justice Stephen J. Field, a Lincoln appointee who sat on the Court from 1863 until 1897. Field was the classic defender of property rights and a most enthusiastic advocate of laissez-faire economics. He believed that the Constitution had absolutely secured property rights against governmental interference, a sentiment shared by Taft. Taft saw the appellate courts as protectors of the Constitution against "encroachment by the uneducated masses and their misguided spokesmen." Once he was certain of the "soundness, political savvy, and also the integrity of a given candidate, he sought to satisfy himself as to the individual's ability to meet the demands of the Court's workload" (White 1976, 180–181).

Some of the justices already on the Court when Taft became chief justice presented difficult challenges to his teamwork concept. Justice James McReynolds, for example, was lazy and unwilling to pull his weight. More significantly, McReynolds had a highly disagreeable manner. Taft described him as "selfish to the last degree . . . fuller of prejudice than any man I have ever known . . . one who delights in making others uncomfortable . . . a continual grouch . . . [who] really seems to have less of a loyal spirit to the Court than anybody" (Mason 1964, 215–216). In addition, Justice Joseph McKenna had suffered such mental deterioration he could not be assigned cases. Taft spent a great deal of time attempting to convince McKenna to resign from the Court, which he did in 1925 (Mason 1964, 215). Also plaguing Taft were the liberals of the Court—Brandeis, Holmes, Clarke, and later Stone. During the last two years of Taft's tenure, his own health declined and division on the Court increased. He was the only justice with a good personal relationship with every other member of the Court.

The Taft Court was comfortable engaging in judicial activism. An activist Court is one that does not automatically defer to legislative judgments. Rather, it sees its role as closely scrutinizing legislative actions and nullifying those legislative actions it deems unreasonable. Under Taft's leadership his Court often took on the role of a "superlegislature" by substituting its judgment for that of elected legislators. During the decade of the 1920s, the Taft Court invalidated twelve federal laws and 131 state statutes. Table 4.1 puts these numbers in historical perspective. Not until the Warren and Burger eras, both of which were longer than the Taft era, were more federal and state laws invalidated by a single Court. The chief justice carried his Court to such

Table 4.1 Decisions Overruling Previous Court Decisions or Striking Down Federal or State Laws and Municipal Ordinances

Period	Supreme Court Decisions Overruled	Acts of Congress Overturned	State Laws Overturned	Ordinances Overturned
1889–1910 (Fuller)	4	14	73	15
1910–1921 (White)	5	12	107	18
1921–1930 (Taft)	6	12	131	12
1931–1940 (Hughes)	21	14	78	5
1941–1946 (Stone)	15	2	25	7
1947–1952 (Vinson)	13	1	38	7
1953–1969 (Warren)	45	25	150	16
1969–1986 (Burger)	52	34	192	15
1986–1996 (Rehnquist)	26	11	58	16

Adapted from Lawrence Baum, *The Supreme Court*, 7th ed. (Washington, DC: Congressional Quarterly Press, 2001, 197, 199)

"dizzying heights" in our politics that Holmes was prompted to say that he saw virtually no limit to the Court's use of the Fourteenth Amendment to nullify state regulatory schemes. The labels of liberal and conservative mask the underlying cleavage. All the justices were conservatives including Holmes and Brandeis, at least on a number of issues. Instead, in the view of Alpheus T. Mason, the division among them was "rooted in fundamental differences as to the nature of the judicial function" (Mason 1979, 71). Unlike the Taft Court majority, Holmes and Brandeis preferred to let elected officials make policy judgments.

Under Taft's guidance, the majority of his Court stayed focused on its conservative doctrinal priorities. Just as Harding and Coolidge called for a "return to traditional values, so the conservative majority intended to reaffirm the natural law/vested interests interpretation of the Constitution." It relied primarily on the liberty-of-contract concept, substantive due process, and dual federalism as the principal means through which it could accomplish its jurisprudential ends. These constructs allowed the Court to create a broad zone in which neither federal nor state government could act against property. The Tenth Amendment was an effective barrier to federal intervention in matters traditionally reserved to the states. The Tenth Amendment was a convenient approach because it allowed the laissez-faire and states' rights enthusiasts to coalesce against federal initiatives. The states' rightists could tolerate state regulation but would join the laissez-faire ideologues in opposing federal regulation, not because they categorically opposed regulation but because of the source of the regulation. Even in areas where the Constitution specifically granted authority to the national government, federal initiatives did not automatically prevail over state autonomy. At the same time, the Taft Court conservatives were not averse to striking down state initiatives on either substantive due process or national supremacy grounds. Overall, the Taft Court "preferred as little governmental interference with economic liberty or property rights as possible; it showed no similar desire to rein in state restrictions on labor, radicals, or other groups that criticized the status quo" (Urofsky and Finkelman 2002, 626–627).

An "uncompromising defense of property rights and commitment to maintaining the jurisprudential status quo were the dominant objectives of the Taft Court" (Urofsky and Finkelman 2002, 625). These priorities, however, obscured another important dimension of the Taft Court legacy. History often suggests that the Taft Court preoccupation with property rights made it indifferent to civil rights and civil liberties. However, unlike prior Courts, the Taft Court revealed a sympathy, albeit tentative and restrained, toward individual rights. The Taft Court era began in the wake of prosecutions of war dissenters and political radicals and its First Amendment decisions were influenced if not defined by these cases. In addition, many of the Taft Court's criminal rights rulings were developed during National Prohibition and almost invariably favored the interests of law enforcement over the interests of the accused. Nonetheless, it was the Taft Court that "took the first steps in formulating the modern view of the Bill of Rights" (644).

Taft brought to the Court a clear image of the office and prerogatives of the chief justiceship. Much of his tenure was driven by a passion for "teamwork" and doctrinal consensus that alone could give "weight and solidarity to judicial decisions." Indeed, he was preoccupied by a desire to "mass" his Court—he pressed very hard for unanimity. To this end, he "persuaded by example, frowned on dissents, exploited personal courtesy and charm, maximized the assignment and reassignment powers, and relied on the expertise of his associates" (Mason 1964, 198). Divisions on the Court were masked not only by Taft's own efforts, but also by his colleagues' interest in furthering consensus. It was not unusual for justices to write on the back of circulated draft opinions "I shall acquiesce in silence unless someone else dissents"; or "I do not agree, but shall submit" (Mason 1979, 60–61). Like Chief Justice Edward White before him, Taft was an effective social leader of his Court. He established and maintained a positive working environment for his fellow justices. He "never let his differences on social and intellectual issues override his desire for harmonious personal relations" (White 1976, 179). Unlike White, Taft recognized his own limitations. As a consequence Taft shared the intellectual and task leadership with Justice Willis Van Devanter—Van Devanter was often the actual task leader of the Court's conferences (179–180).

Taft hated dissenting opinions, wrote very few himself, and made every effort to dissuade others from writing them. He was successful, at least to a degree, in developing doctrinal consensus on his Court. The Taft Court rendered unanimous rulings in more than 91 percent of its cases. This figure was very similar to the unanimity rates of the last five terms of the White Court and the first five terms of the Hughes Court (see Table 3.3 in the preceding chapter). Table 4.2 contains measures of disagreement across all nine terms of the Taft Court. Additional data organized by term is contained in the Appendix. The extent to which Taft was successful in fostering consensus can best be appreciated by comparing his Court to those later in the twentieth century. The Warren Court, for example, rendered unanimous rulings in less than 28 percent of its decisions in the 1959 Term. The Burger Court was unanimous in only 25 percent of its rulings during the 1979 Term.

Although Taft's efforts to "mass" his Court did not produce distinctive unanimity rates in comparison to the White and Hughes Courts, seldom did his Court make rulings decided by a single vote. Indeed, less than 1 percent of the Taft Court's rulings were single-vote decisions. The White and Hughes Courts, so similar to the Taft Court in unanimity rates, had more than three times as many one-vote decisions. Comparison with more recent Courts reveals how unusually low the Taft Court's single-vote decision rate was. For example, almost one-third (31.6 percent) of the Rehnquist Court's rulings in the 2000–2001 Term were five-to-four decisions. As Table 4.2 shows, justices of the Taft Court were not inclined to dissent frequently. When there were dissents, they were most often registered by Justices Brandeis and Holmes. Table 4.3 presents the individual dissent rates of Taft Court justices by term.

Doctrinal Legacy: Short and Long Term

Taft interpreted the 1920 election as a "call for returning the control of the nation to the hands of private leadership" (Mason 1964, 289). Among other things, this meant protecting against the use of law as an agent of social change. Instead, judicial activism became the Taft Court's principal way of both preventing government-mandated change and recreating the laissez-faire policies of the 1890s. Taft was pushed to more conservative positions than he might have taken otherwise by the ultraconservative majority that resulted from the additions of George Sutherland and Pierce Butler to the Court. Along with Willis Van Devanter and James McReynolds, these justices, known as the "Four Horsemen," were "committed to the protection of a social order uniquely explained and justified by the tenets of John Locke, Adam Smith, the Manchester economists, Blackstone, Cooley and Spencer" (Currie 1990, 134–135).

The Taft Court aggressively used substantive due process to nullify social or "protective" legislative initiatives. It also applied Fourteenth Amendment and prop-

TABLE 4.2 Disagreement on the Taft Court, 1921–1929 Terms

		Non-Unanimous Opinions		Dissenting Votes		5-4
Term	Total Opinions	Number	Percent	Number	Per Opinion	Votes
1921	173	37	21.39	84	.486	2
1922	225	17	7.55	33	.147	0
1923	212	24	11.32	45	.212	0
1924	230	23	10.00	41	.178	2
1925	209	15	7.17	30	.144	1
1926	199	31	15.57	69	.347	4
1927	173	27	15.60	75	.434	7
1928	129	22	17.05	45	.349	1
1929	134	12	8.96	21	.157	1
Total	1684	208	12.89	443	.274	18

TABLE 4.3 Individual Justice Dissent Rates (in percent), 1921–1929 Terms

	1921	1922	1923	1924	1925	1926	1927	1928	1929
Brandeis	8.1	2.7	5.2	2.6	2.9	7.0	9.8	6.2	7.8
Butler	xx	0	1.4	1.3	.5	4.5	2.3	3.9	0
Clarke	7.5	xx	xx	xx	xx	xx	xx	xx	xx
Day	2.3	xx	xx	xx	xx	xx	xx	xx	xx
Holmes	5.2	2.7	3.3	.9	1.4	5.5	9.8	5.4	9.4
McKenna	6.4	.9	1.9	.4	xx	xx	xx	xx	xx
McReynolds	6.9	2.7	6.1	4.8	3.8	5.0	5.2	7.8	1.6
Pitney	2.3	xx	xx	xx	xx	xx	xx	xx	xx
Sanford	xx	.4	.9	1.3	1.4	1.5	4.1	3.1	0
Stone	xx	xx	xx	0	1.9	4.5	8.0	3.9	4.7
Sutherland	xx	3.1	.9	3.0	1.9	4.0	4.1	2.3	1.6
Taft	3.5	1.3	.5	2.2	0	1.0	0	1.6	0
Van Devanter	4.6	0	.9	.9	.5	1.0	0	2.3	3.1

erty rights concepts to new fields. It used a property rights approach to prevent a state from banning the teaching of foreign languages in elementary schools and a prohibition on students attending anything but public schools at least through the eighth grade. On issues involving the division of federal and state governmental authority, the Taft Court made decisions that went both ways. The Taft Court supported broad congressional authority to enforce the Prohibition Amendment and regulate such instruments of interstate commerce as railroads and stockyards. It also recognized a limited federal police power by upholding the ban on interstate transportation of stolen cars. At the same time, the Taft Court used the Tenth Amendment to substantially restrict the reach of federal authority.

The sociopolitical environment of the 1920s strongly favored business, prompting President Calvin Coolidge to say, “the business of America is business.” Industrial productivity expanded significantly after World War I and brought with it a dramatic rise in the American standard of living. These factors prompted presidential candidate Herbert Hoover to predict that poverty would soon become a condition of the past in the United States. Given the conservative composition of the Taft Court, its strongly probusiness predisposition was hardly surprising. Taft strongly believed in the sanctity of property rights and thought that the Court should play the decisive role in maintaining a constitutional system to safeguard those rights. Taft found strong allies in the Four Horsemen as well as justices Mahlon Pitney and Edward Sanford. Together these justices constituted a comfortable majority that struck down both federal and state legislative attempts to regulate business and property. Only Justices Oliver Wendell Holmes, Louis Brandeis, and Harlan Fiske Stone challenged the majority view. The remainder of this chapter describes the legacy of the Taft Court and the rulings that best represent this legacy. The place to start is with the Taft Court's defense of property rights.

Substantive Due Process—Safeguarding Private Property Interests

The Fourteenth Amendment was ratified in 1868 and provided, in part, that no state “shall make or enforce any law, which shall abridge the privileges or immunities of citizens of the United States” nor “deprive any person of life, liberty or property without due process of law.” For the states' rightist majorities of the Chase and Waite Courts, this language posed the potential problem of enabling federal courts to drastically limit state police power. The Court's initial decisions indicated that the Fourteenth Amendment had only marginally changed the constitutional landscape. The best example of such a ruling is the Chase Court's ruling in the *Slaughterhouse Cases* (1873). Louisiana had passed a law establishing a butchering monopoly for the city of New Orleans. It was argued by those challenging the law that the Fourteenth Amendment was intended, at least in part, to protect the property rights of individuals. The challengers contended that a monopoly franchise such as the one established by the Louisiana legislature violated both the privileges and immunities and due process provisions of the Fourteenth Amendment. The Chase Court concluded that the Louisiana statute did neither. Four years later, the Waite Court again refused to use the Fourteenth Amendment to invalidate a state property regulation in *Munn v. Illinois* (1877). Illinois had sought to set rate ceilings for the storage of grain in privately owned warehouses and elevators. The Court approved the rate-fixing law by recognizing a category of businesses so "affected with a public interest" that they could be subjected to reasonable regulation. The Court further concluded that determination of which businesses fit the category was a legislative judgment not subject to judicial second-guessing.

Following *Munn*, the Court was gradually infused with a new outlook as laissez-faire capitalists joined the Court. Concern for corporate rights by these justices was clearly evident in *Santa Clara County v. Southern Pacific Railroad* (1886), in which corporations were determined to be "persons" for Fourteenth Amendment purposes. Eleven years after *Santa Clara*, the Fuller Court explicitly held that the Fourteenth Amendment's Due Process Clause protected a substantive, but implicit "liberty of contract." In *Allgeyer v. Louisiana* (1897), the Court unanimously invalidated a Louisiana law restricting the issuance of insurance policies and imposing a $1,000 fine on anyone having an illegal policy. Justice Horace Peckham suggested that the liberty protected by the Fourteenth Amendment included the right to earn a lawful livelihood and enter any and all contracts necessary to do so. *Allgeyer* ushered in what became known as the *Lochner* era of substantive due process.

The *Lochner* case involved a New York law that limited bakery workers to ten hours of work per day and sixty hours per week. Justice Peckham again spoke for the Fuller Court, although this time for only five justices. He declared that the law imposed an absolute prohibition on both employer and employee to work more than the number of hours specified in the law. It was the classic liberty-of-contract reasoning. The right to purchase or sell labor was part of the liberty protected by the Fourteenth Amendment and the New York statute impermissibly interfered with the right to contract between the employer and the employee. Interference with the right to contract was beyond the reach of state police power except for compelling reasons. No such reason was present in *Lochner*.

Substantive due process, with its emphasis on judicial scrutiny of the reasonableness of regulatory measures, occasionally led the Court to uphold regulatory legislation. Several years prior to *Lochner*, the Court used *Lochner*-like reasoning in *Holden v. Hardy* (1898) to approve a state law limiting the industrial workday to ten hours for women. The difference between these decisions was that in *Lochner* the Court saw no justification for the protection of workers in a nondangerous business. A ruling similar to *Holden* came ten years later in *Muller v. Oregon* (1908) after the Court was inundated by socioeconomic evidence offered by Louis Brandeis in defense of the state law. In *Muller*, the Court upheld a state law limiting the workday of female workers. Nine years later, in *Bunting v. Oregon* (1917), the Court extended the *Muller* decision to male as well as female workers. More importantly, the Court approved a mandatory overtime pay provision, a kind of wage regulation the Court had steadfastly resisted previously. The *Muller* and *Bunting* decisions seemed to suggest that substantive due process might have run its course. The Taft Court would prove otherwise.

Soon after the *Bunting* decision, the Court decided the first of two federal child labor cases, *Hammer v. Dagenhart* (1918). The federal law at issue in *Hammer*, the Keating-Owen Child Labor Law, prohibited goods produced by child labor from being shipped interstate. The White Court struck down the law, however, concluding that federal control of child labor impermissibly entered the domain reserved for the states. The second federal child labor initiative, this time based on federal taxing power, was also struck down by the Taft Court on state sovereignty grounds in *Bailey v. Drexel Furniture Co.* (1922). These decisions were unexpected because it seemed that after *Muller* and *Bunting* the Court had recognized a role for federal government regulation of certain business practices—albeit a limited role. *Hammer* and *Bailey* postponed that possibility, at least for the short term. As for state regulations, it seemed that *Muller* and *Bunting* had overruled *Lochner* and that the Court was ready to allow state police power to be used for protective purposes, at least for particularly vulnerable people. Instead, *Adkins v. Children's Hospital* (1923), decided the year after *Drexel Furniture*, restored *Lochner* as the controlling precedent.

One decision that epitomized the probusiness orientation of the Taft Court was *Adkins v. Children's Hospital* (1923). *Adkins* led even the conservative Taft to protest. As the Fuller Court had done in *Lochner*, the Taft Court chose a social welfare measure to make its stand. As in the earlier substantive due process decisions, the underlying notion in *Adkins* was that courts must decide important questions about the economy and controls imposed on it. In striking down a District of Columbia minimum-wage statute for women, Justice Sutherland reiterated the supremacy of contractual liberty in economic matters. By this time many believed that the states and the federal government could protect women workers. Sutherland, however, held that the Nineteenth Amendment giving women the vote had more generally emancipated women and that they no longer needed legislative protection. *Adkins* was one of the Court's most striking laissez-faire decisions. The intended purpose of the law under review was the protection of women's health and morals from poor living conditions caused by inadequate wages.

Justice Sutherland, who was now becoming the intellectual leader of the more conservative justices, offered the classic liberty-of-contract rationale in *Adkins*. Wages, Sutherland said, were basic to the employment contract and must be determined by the marketplace, not government fiat. The District of Columbia forbade two parties to freely contract with one another with respect to the price for which one shall offer labor to the other. This was a purely private arrangement to which both parties must be willing to agree. Freedom of contract was the general rule for the Taft Court, restraint the exception, and the economic inequality of women did not create such an exception. In any case, Sutherland said, it would be unfair to place a remedial burden that belongs to society at large on the shoulders of employers. Sutherland ignored the fact that higher minimum wage costs could in most cases be passed on to society as part of product price. Many, including Taft and several other justices, had thought rulings like *Muller* and *Bunting* had overruled *Lochner*, at least implicitly. *Adkins* resurrected *Lochner* as the controlling precedent in state economic regulation cases, however. By revitalizing the liberty-of-contract doctrine, *Adkins* dampened reform well into the 1930s. It became one of the most cited of the Court's decisions until it was overruled in *West Coast Hotel v. Parrish* in 1937, a case that signaled the beginning of the end of the Court's conflict with the New Deal. The effect of *Adkins* was particularly severe on states trying to pursue regulatory objectives. Many of the almost 140 state laws found unconstitutional by the Taft Court after *Adkins* were struck down as violating liberty of contract.

In *Adkins*, Sutherland had suggested circumstances under which restraints on contractual freedom might occur. One such circumstance was for work on public projects. Another was for rates charged by businesses "affected with the public interest." Some political reformers and progressives had hoped that an expanded view of "affected with a public interest" would allow some experimentation by the states. They soon learned differently. In late 1923 the conservative majority in *Charles Wolff Packing Co.* adopted a narrow definition of business affected with a public interest. Kansas had passed the Court of Industrial Relations Act following a costly coal strike. The law required compulsory arbitration of all labor disputes in the food, clothing, fuel, and certain other industries that the state legislature found to be "affected with the public interest." The innovative enactment, unpopular with business and labor, set up a special court to hear the disputes and gave it power to restrict strikes and employer lockouts and, if needed, to set wages and work conditions. The Supreme Court unanimously found the scheme to violate liberty of contract.

In *Charles Wolff Packing* Taft declared that merely because a state declared a business affected with a public interest did not necessarily make it so. Taft confined the public interest doctrine to common carriers, utilities, and other publicly created monopolies, and to a handful of other businesses such as inns, historically thought to be affected with the public interest. The class of included businesses could not be expanded by legislative assertion. Though the decision appeared reasonable enough on the surface, the Court again paid little attention to the complex, integrated nature of the nation's economy. Applying standards better suited to an earlier day, it ignored a principle many observers thought commonplace after the war experience: that all basic economic activity affected the public interest. For those who favored governmental regulation of business, the only check in the absence of an explicit constitutional limit lay in politics rather than in a rigidly applied substantive doctrine read into the Constitution by the Court. Chief Justice Taft countered that economic liberty was a "preferred freedom" that required the Court's utmost vigilance.

The practical effect of *Charles Wolff Packing* was that very few businesses would fit into Taft's classification of a business clothed with a public interest. This conclusion was reiterated in numerous Taft Court decisions. In *Tyson & Bros. v. Banton* (1927), for example, the Court struck down a New York law limiting the markup on the resale of theater tickets. The Taft Court concluded that theaters were neither public utilities nor clothed with a public interest. Similarly, in *Ribnik v. McBride* (1928), the Taft Court invalidated a New Jersey law that sought to regulate fees charged by employment agencies. The Court saw these businesses as private and thus as immune from rate-fixing regulations as food or housing prices. It is hardly surprising that the National Association of Manufacturers passed resolutions praising the Supreme Court as the "indispensable interpreter of our written Constitution" and the protector of property from the "babel voices of the mob." So long as the nation continued to be prosperous it appeared that business could do no wrong and the Court, despite powerful protests from Justices Holmes and Brandeis, made sure that government did not interfere with business.

The property rights preoccupation of the Taft Court was also evident in rulings that did not involve substantive due process. The case of *Truax v. Corrigan* (1921), for example, provided a different slant on the property rights issue. In *Truax*, the Court struck down an Arizona statute forbidding state courts to grant injunctions against picketers. Under terms of the law, Arizona courts could not intervene in a labor dispute. Taft concluded that the employers' right to injunctive relief in a labor dispute is "fundamental." The limit Arizona placed on the use of injunctions in labor disputes was a denial of a fundamental principle of liberty that inheres in the very idea of free government and is the inalienable right of a citizen of such government. The Court could have sustained the statute, but it would have required a "latitudinarian" interpretation of the Constitution. Taft deplored such an approach to constitutional interpretation, however, and would not accord such regulatory latitude to the states. In no other case decided during Taft's chief justiceship was the conservative property rights view more sharply contrasted with the Holmes and Brandeis position and their deference to legislative experimentation than in *Truax*. The effect of the Court's decision in *Truax* was to affirm that property owners were entitled to use injunctions in labor disputes, a practice begun in the late 1880s.

The Taft Court Takings Clause and Zoning

Urbanization and the congestion it produced in American cities generated new constitutional issues about the public regulation of real property. Occasionally these cases involved ownership interests of two private parties. The case of *Pennsylvania Coal Co. v. Mahon* (1922) is illustrative. Coal companies often sold surface rights to private parties, but would retain the right to continue mining operations below the surface. As streets and buildings were built, surface owners, fearing collapse if mining continued, got the state to limit extraction of coal under the improved areas. In *Mahon*, a coal company challenged a Pennsylvania law that prohibited mining in such a way that would damage residences or streets. The Fifth Amendment prohibits the "taking of private property for public use without just compensation." The coal company challenged the Pennsylvania regulation claiming that it was a "taking" within the meaning of the Fifth Amendment.

The Taft Court agreed. Justice Holmes wrote for the Court and suggested that the shield of the Fifth Amendment takings clause was not limited to physical intrusion or seizure by eminent domain. In addition to direct appropriation, the clause protects against loss of an owner's right to use property as he or she wishes, or against an owner incurring higher costs for the property's use. Loss of property value or income that can be derived from property requires just compensation as though the property were actually confiscated for public use. The purpose of the takings clause, Holmes explained, was to keep the financial burdens imposed by public action from falling on an individual property owner. After the *Mahon* ruling, the takings clause declined in significance as a constitutional method for protecting private property. The Taft Court's position on the takings clause has been revitalized, however, by the Rehnquist Court and once again is a constitutional provision with substantial contemporary significance for property owners. Holmes suggested in *Mahon* that if private property was to be effectively protected through the takings clause, the Constitution must limit governmental power to redefine the interests attaching to property ownership. This view has become the hallmark of Rehnquist Court takings clause jurisprudence.

A case that reflected the Taft Court's occasional departure from its more typical takings clause position was *Village of Euclid v. Ambler Realty Co.* (1926), which involved local land use restrictions. Many communities turned to zoning regulations as a means of controlling industrial and residential development. The difficulty, of course, was that if a city or town could regulate private property through zoning ordinances, the distinction between and public and private becomes less clear. In other words, if private property can be regulated because it is "clothed" or "affected with a public interest," few limits remain on what the government can regulate. The zoning regulation upheld in *Ambler Realty* was designed to protect health, safety, and morals of community residents and thus was not viewed as a "taking." To the contrary, the Taft Court believed that such laws could actually increase property values by classifying property uses and assigning those uses to different geographic areas in a community. In the final analysis, the Court did not view such restrictions as hostile to property rights, although Sutherland's opinion focused on the long-recognized authority of state and local governments to combat nuisances. The constitutionality of zoning ordinances has been maintained since the Taft era and has been expanded to include objectives such as aesthetics as legitimate public ends to pursue through such regulation.

Federal Institutional Authority

One of the most interesting aspects of the Taft Court legacy is evident in a number of decisions examining the authority of the institutions of the federal government. The Taft Court era was not one in which the justices deliberately expanded federal authority. Indeed, the Taft Court was typically reluctant to recognize more extensive federal authority and certainly not at the expense of property rights or the police power of the states. At the same time, the Taft Court redefined the boundaries of institutional authority of the legislative and executive branches of the federal government, particularly in relation to each other. Issues involving federal judicial power were also examined in several cases. The judicial power cases focused on such subjects as the case-or-controversy limitation and declaratory judgments. Together, all these rulings were significant because they considered institutional boundary issues not examined by the Court. The landmark case of *Myers v. United States*, for example, resolved a long-standing controversy about a president's power to unilaterally remove an executive branch subordinate. Rulings such as *Springer v. Philippine Islands* and *J.W. Hampton, Jr. & Co. v. United States* enhanced executive authority to appoint officers of government corporations and allowed Congress to delegate extensive discretion to the executive, respectively. In addition, the *Pocket Veto Case* gave a liberal interpretation of the president's power to prevent congressional override of a veto.

It is not surprising that decisions favorable to the executive branch came from the Court headed by a former president. The most pervasive executive power ruling came in *Myers*. The case originated with a first-class postmaster who had been removed from his post before the end of his four-year term. Had the *Myers* decision been confined to the removal of executive officials, it would not have been as noteworthy a decision. But Taft seized the opportunity to expand the *Myers* holding to even quasi-judicial officers. His opinion was contrary to the statutory mandates contained in the legislation creating such agencies as the Interstate Commerce Commission and Federal Trade Commission. The implications of such broad removal power raised fundamental questions about the independence of quasi-judicial agencies and the statutory language that limited removals to situations of malfeasance in office. The dictum offered by Taft in the *Myers* case was narrowed by the Hughes Court in *Humphrey's Executor v. United States* (1935).

The Taft Court also enhanced executive power in *Springer v. Philippine Islands* (1928) and the *Pocket Veto Case* (1929). *Springer* involved the selection of directors for public corporations. Relying on the reasoning in *Myers*, the Court concluded that the appointment of any nonlegislative official was an exclusively executive function; the legislative branch was not to be involved. On the veto issue, a president can allow a bill to become law without signing it by failing to return it with his or her signature within a ten-day period. There are political reasons a president may choose to take this course. The Taft Court added another dimension to this practice in the *Pocket Veto Case.* The Court ruled that if Congress is not in session for the full ten days after sending a bill to the president, the bill does not become law if the president does not sign it and is instead conclusively vetoed because Congress cannot attempt to repass the unsigned bill.

In *J.W. Hampton, Jr. & Co. v. United States* (1928) the Taft Court upheld a federal law providing for a variable tariff. The issue was whether the executive branch could be given authority by Congress to adjust the tariff rates within a legislatively set range—whether such legislative power could be delegated to the executive branch. The decision in *Hampton* not only provided Congress with increased flexibility in the selection of tax or tariff policies, but also recognized the value of executive discretion in implementing such policies. The Court's ruling in *Hampton* reflected a pragmatism that was not evident in cases in which conservative dogma influenced decisions. The constitutional view underlying *Hampton* continues to inform the Court's thinking in delegation of legislative power cases.

At the federal level, the Court moved on the one hand from a permissive interpretation of federal authority on nonproperty matters to contraction of federal power in areas that might adversely affect business on the other. Despite the diverse outcomes in the cases involving legislative power, there was a net gain of legislative authority for Congress. In *Missouri v. Holland* (1920), the White Court, through the opinion of Justice Holmes, broadly interpreted the treaty-making power. The Court held that once a treaty is ratified it can be implemented through legislation that would have been invalid in the absence of the treaty. This was true even in areas previously reserved for the states. If the subject matter was sufficiently related to the general welfare, was in the national interest, and the national interest could only be advanced by federal action in concert with another power, the treaty-making power could be used to extend the reach of Congress. Although Congress does not frequently legislate in support of treaties, *Missouri v. Holland* raised the prospect that the Court might further extend federal legislative power in ways that carved into the previously exclusive domain of the states.

The federal taxing power received a similar boost in *Massachusetts v. Mellon* and *Frothingham v. Mellon* (1923) when the Taft Court held that the appropriations of money from revenues raised by the federal taxing power would not be reviewed by federal courts in suits brought by taxpayers. The Court ruled that taxpayers had not suffered sufficient injury to establish standing to bring suit in federal courts. More importantly, the ruling freed congressional expenditures from endless judicial review and acknowledged broad legislative discretion with grant-in-aid programs. In other words, these cases established that federal spending could be used to pursue economic and social purposes that were ostensibly reserved to the states. The Court's deferential position on Congress's authority to tax and spend was exactly opposite from that taken with respect to federal regulatory agencies where the Court reserved judicial scrutiny of all agency findings of fact. The former would become vitally important in the 1930s with the extensive social spending initiatives of the Roosevelt administration.

Congress's power was also expanded in connection with investigations to obtain information necessary for prospective legislation. The Court in *McGrain v. Daugherty* (1927) ruled that Congress could subpoena witnesses under threat of contempt if they failed to appear. Prior to *McGrain*, congressional investigations were limited to matters over which Congress held the power and interest to legislate. *McGrain* dramatically extended those boundaries by broadening the definition of what constituted a permissible legislative objective. As importantly, *McGrain* suggested that courts should presume that congressional inquiries are within Congress's authority and reflect its intention to legislate. Congressional power to investigate remains as extensive as the Taft Court viewed it with the exception that First Amendment limits on the investigative power were recognized by the Warren Court in the 1950s. The *McGrain* holding was expanded in *Barry v. United States ex rel. Cunningham* (1929) to permit punishment for a witness who refused to answer questions.

Congressional Authority over Interstate Commerce

Congress had done very little with its power to regulate interstate commerce prior to the late nineteenth century. It was at that time that Congress had begun to exercise the commerce power by passing such federal laws as the Interstate Commerce Act and the Sherman Anti-Trust Act. In *United States v. E.C. Knight Co.* (1895), however, the Fuller Court ruled that the Sherman Act could not be applied to a monopoly in the sugar industry. The principal reason was that the sugar trust was a monopoly of the manufacture of refined sugar—the refining process and not the subsequent shipping. Commerce was seen as a discrete act, one that commenced only after manufacture had ended. Federal commerce power could not be applied to manufacture. Using the reasoning from *Knight*, it was easy to conclude, for example, that Congress could not regulate child labor. Not only was child labor limited to the production stage, the welfare of children was a matter reserved exclusively to the states. The Fuller, White, and Taft Courts were unwilling to turn the federal commerce power into something like the state police power. A few federal initiatives such as the Mann Act, which barred prostitutes from interstate commerce, and the Pure Food and Drug Act, which barred adulterated food were upheld by the Court, but these were clearly departures from the norm. The Court was concerned that if Congress could exclude from interstate commerce any article it wished, even those items that might be harmful to public morals, then Congress could also control production for businesses dependent upon interstate commerce. The Taft Court maintained the production-commerce distinction and its limiting of the federal commerce power, a distinction that would remain in effect until 1937.

The Taft Court, under certain circumstances, attempted to attenuate the negative commerce power doctrines stemming from *Knight* and other similar rulings. It is significant that these changes, however limited, were created not to replace the more negative doctrines, but to coexist with them as alternative formulations. The primary modification in commerce clause jurisprudence involved the nation's railroads. The Court's willingness to support federal railroad regulation often shocked laissez-faire capitalists and was most difficult if not impossible to reconcile with the dogmatic stance in *Knight.*

The Transportation Act of 1920 restored the railroads to private management after wartime measures had placed them under government control. The act also expanded the authority of the Interstate Commerce Commission by adding authority over intrastate in addition to interstate rail rates. In the Court's view, the law imposed an "affirmative duty to fix rates and take other important steps to maintain an adequate railway service for the people of the United States." The Taft Court's ruling in *Railroad Commission v. Chicago, Burlington & Quincy Railroad* went well beyond the White Court's decision in the *Shreveport Rate Case* (1914), ruling by eliminating any meaningful distinction between intra- and interstate rates. By sustaining the ICC's intrastate rate order, the Court not only acted in the interests of higher rates for the railroads, but the decision also recognized the country's need to have a functioning national transportation system (Urofsky 1994, 630–631).

Perhaps the high point of the Taft Court's recognition of ICC regulatory authority was reached in *Dayton-Goose Creek Railway Co. v. United States* (1924). *Dayton-Goose Creek* upheld provisions of the Transportation Act, which required railroads that earned more than a certain fixed "fair return" to turn over one-half of the excess to the ICC and to hold the rest in a reserve fund to be used as the ICC directed. Even more problematic, the requirement applied to income earned on wholly intrastate business. Nonetheless, the Taft Court supported these provisions. Taft's construction of the commerce clauses was influenced by Holmes's landmark opinion in *Swift & Company v. United States* (1905). As Holmes did in *Swift,* Taft held that the commerce clause must be applied to the "real and practical essence of modern business growth." Whatever regular or constant practices threaten to obstruct or unduly to burden the freedom of interstate commerce are within the regulatory reach of Congress under the commerce clause. The Taft Court did not substitute its judgment for that of Congress where the pathways of commerce were involved unless the "relation of the subject to interstate commerce and its effects upon it are clearly nonexistent." On the basis of this "stream of commerce" doctrine, the Taft Court sustained the Grain Futures Act and Motor Vehicle Theft Act (Mason 1979, 57–58). In *Stafford v. Wallace*

(1922), Taft expanded on the doctrine to uphold the Packers and Stockyards Act of 1921. Although most commercial activity was still outside the reach of federal regulatory authority, those businesses such as railroads that affected the actual flow of interstate commerce could be regulated. Indeed, they must be regulated in the national interest, but also in the interests of those businesses that used these instruments of interstate commerce; the Court insisted that the federal government not only could but must remove burdens to the free flow of commerce. As long as the "essential categories of substantive due process jurisprudence as well as the critical differentiation between public and private remained intact, the stream of commerce doctrine posed no threat to the dual federalism established by the Court" (Urofsky 1994, 631–632).

Other federal regulatory agencies did not fare as well before the Taft Court as the ICC. Even before Taft became chief justice, the White Court's negative attitude toward federal regulatory agencies was clear. The principal target of the Court's hostility was the Federal Trade Commission. The Court began its attack on the Federal Trade Commission in *Federal Trade Commission v. Gratz* (1920), in which the Court held that the agency could not determine "unfair methods of competition" because the authorizing statute had not been sufficiently clear on what this phrase meant. Just as the Court had earlier limited the authority of the ICC by making the determination of the fairness of rates a judicial issue, judges would also decide what constituted unfair competition. In other cases involving the FTC, the Court extended the *Gratz* holding. The consequence was that the FTC was put in the same position as the ICC had been before 1906. Hostile courts gave FTC investigations little credence and frequently dismissed their factual findings if they did not agree with the results. Companies could appeal to the courts for review not only of the legal issues but of the findings of fact as well. The resulting "impotence of the FTC and other regulatory agencies can only partially be blamed on the Court"; the Harding and Coolidge administrations nominated commissioners completely sympathetic to the business interests their agencies were to oversee (Urofsky 1994, 629). This negative predisposition toward federal regulatory agencies would persist until the late 1930s.

Labor and the Taft Court

The Court's probusiness activism had its counterpart in a strong antilabor bias. In *Truax v. Corrigan* (1921), the Taft Court struck down an Arizona law that barred state courts from issuing injunctions to stop peaceful picketing. A union had picketed a restaurant, causing its business to decline. By removing the legal remedy of injunction, Taft said, the law was a capricious exercise of power and deprived the business owner of a property right to which he was entitled. By singling out disputes between employer and employees, it also violated equal protection of the laws.

With passage of the Clayton Act in 1914, labor leaders thought they had won protection from having the Sherman Act, intended to break up trusts, applied to unions. Section 6 of the act declared that labor was not an article of commerce and that antitrust laws should not be used to prevent unions from pursuing lawful objectives. Section 20 of the Clayton Act was a response to the widespread use of restraining orders against unions and barred federal courts from issuing injunctions against union picketing unless needed to prevent what the statute termed "irreparable injury to property." Organized labor did not anticipate that the White and Taft Courts would give the protective language of the act the narrowest possible reading. In *Duplex Printing Co. v. Deering* (1921), in which several New York unions had boycotted products of a Michigan company whose workers were on strike, the Court held that the Clayton Act's anti-injunction provision protected only immediate parties to a suit, not those in secondary boycotts. The Court concluded that the law did not exempt secondary boycotts and ruled that injunctions could thus be issued not only against the immediate parties but also against anyone trying to help the unions. Similarly, in *American Steel Foundries v. Tri-City Central Trades Council* (1921), decided the same year, the Court held that even peaceful picketing could be sufficiently intimidating to justify its being enjoined. The effect of these rulings was to preclude both state and federal restrictions on injunctions. As a result, both state and federal courts continued to issue injunctions in labor disputes notwithstanding explicit language to the contrary in the Clayton Act. This issue was not resolved until Congress passed the Norris-LaGuardia Anti-Injunction Act of 1932, when the Depression had eroded the influence of business interests.

Labor's supposed protection under the Clayton Act eroded further in the two *Coronado Coal Company* cases in 1925. The Court concluded that a strike could have such a direct and injurious effect on commerce to justify Sherman Act proceedings against the United Mine Workers. Two years later, the Court again demonstrated how it would interpret statutory definitions to restrict organized labor—it turned a small, local strike by local stonecutters into a secondary boycott. The boycott sufficiently burdened interstate commerce and was thus subject to a judicial restraining order. The holding in *Bedford Cut Stone Co. v. Journeymen Stone Cutters Ass'n* (1927) departed from the theory dating to the *Sugar Trust* case that production was always local and thus not part of interstate commerce. It was not until the Norris-LaGuardia Act that Congress removed from the courts power to enjoin peaceful strikes, picketing, and secondary boycotts.

Civil Liberties and Civil Rights

The Taft Court was so overwhelmingly probusiness and antilabor that one would have expected it to be unreceptive to civil rights and civil liberties. There are certainly many decisions that support this view, such as the infamous *Buck v. Bell*

(1927), in which the Court upheld a state compulsory sterilization law. The Taft Court showed little concern for freedom of speech in the postwar years and by the end of the 1920s upheld government wiretaps against bootleggers. But this is only part of the Taft Court record. The clash between traditional and more contemporary values was reflected by the Taft Court's response to individual rights issues. Although the Court was generally grounded in the traditional values of the 1920s, it was during this period that it took its first steps toward a modern jurisprudence of civil rights and liberties. In some ways, the Taft Court's civil liberties rulings must be seen as one of the more notable aspects of its record.

The 1920s were not a particularly likely time for the development of a protective civil liberties jurisprudence. The decade began with the Palmer Raids on political dissidents and continued through the Roaring Twenties with the revitalization of the Ku Klux Klan, persecution of aliens and radicals, open hostility to organized labor, the Sacco and Vanzetti prosecutions, and the trial of a teacher for teaching evolution. In the political fundamentalism of the period, "middle America condemned any and all efforts at social change as unpatriotic" (Urofsky and Finkelman 2002, 650). Those who feared foreigners were able to secure passage of the highly restrictive National Origins Act of 1924. The assault on civil liberties represented by these events "reflected the tension in the country between the forces of modernism and tradition" (650). Not surprisingly, "these same forces operated on the Supreme Court" (650). As a result, some of the Taft Court's rulings demonstrated a "casual indifference to those liberties of ideas and expression that we now have guaranteed by the First Amendment" (650). At the same time, the Court's decisions did not reflect a "cohesive pattern of repression" (650). Instead, the justices seemed to display a "keener perception of constitutional liberties" and the Court "slowly began to establish the modern interpretation of the Bill of Rights" (650).

Brandeis and Holmes provided much of the impetus for the Taft Court's departure from previous thinking on civil liberties issues. They were the foundation of the civil liberties consciousness that emerged as Taft assumed the center chair in 1921. They gained a dependable ally when Harlan Fiske Stone joined the Court in 1925. Holmes, Brandeis, and Stone were a bloc that was two votes short of a majority, however. Interestingly and perhaps unexpectedly, civil liberties issues occasionally prompted support from the ranks of the Court's conservatives. Reacting in libertarian fashion, one or more of the conservatives occasionally objected to governmental excesses as did the more liberal justices. Justice Butler, for example, vigorously argued that the Fourth Amendment prohibited the government from gaining evidence by means of wiretapping. Justice McReynolds, the most conservative of all the Taft Court justices, broke new ground for civil liberties by using the Fourteenth Amendment to safeguard the right to teach a language other than English in public elementary schools as well as the right of parents to send their children to parochial schools.

Similarly, Justice Sanford joined Holmes and Brandeis in several cases, including the defense of an alien denied naturalization because of her advocacy of pacifism. Thus, a "rather strange assortment of radicals and conservatives, socialists and social workers, professors and judges, lawyers and ministers, set out to preserve and protect American civil liberties in the 1920s" (Urofsky and Finkelman 2002, 648).

Nationalization of the Bill of Rights: Origins

The Marshall Court decided in *Barron v. Baltimore* (1833) that the Bill of Rights guarantees contained in the U.S. Constitution applied only against the federal government and not the states. Even after the ratification of the Fourteenth Amendment in 1868 and its due process language directed at the states, the Courts of the late nineteenth century were reluctant to rethink the question. There were some such as Justice John M. Harlan (I) who argued that the due process language of the Fourteenth Amendment extended all the Bill of Rights provisions to the states, but he persuaded few of his colleagues. As a result, limits on state governments remained the exclusive domain of state law.

Nationalizing federal Bill of Rights guarantees began soon after World War I and Justice Brandeis provided much of the impetus. He argued in *Gilbert v. Minnesota* (1920), a state free speech case, that it was time to reject the view that the liberty guaranteed by the Fourteenth Amendment included only liberty to acquire and enjoy property. Brandeis believed that the guarantees of the federal Bill of Rights should all apply to the states. His remained the minority view for a period after *Gilbert* as was evident in *Prudential Insurance Co. v. Cheek* (1922). In *Cheek*, the Court chose to affirm the position that state infringement of civil liberties should remain outside the reach of the U.S. Constitution or the federal courts. Indeed, Justice Pitney said in *Cheek* that "neither the Fourteenth Amendment nor any other provision of the Constitution of the United States imposes upon the states any restrictions about freedom of speech." It appeared as though the status quo on this point would be maintained indefinitely, but that was not to be the case.

The arguments from Brandeis's *Gilbert* opinion began to gain traction the same year as *Cheek*, although Brandeis was not explicitly credited. Surprisingly, the spokesperson for the Court was the ultraconservative Justice James McReynolds. In *Meyer v. Nebraska*, McReynolds applied the substantive due process doctrine from *Lochner v. New York* (1905), a classic property rights decision, to invalidate a Nebraska law that prohibited the teaching of any language except English to any student not yet having completed the eighth grade. McReynolds focused exclusively on the property rights issue in his *Meyer* opinion. The Nebraska law was found unconstitutional because it "materially interfered" with the "calling of modern language teachers." McReynolds could find no justification for the state's restraints on teachers' capacity to earn a living by teaching a foreign language. The Due Process Clause of the Fourteenth Amendment, McReynolds declared, went beyond freedom from bodily restraint to include "those privileges long recognized [in] common law as essential to the orderly pursuit of happiness by free men." Without using the words themselves, McReynolds concluded the state was not sufficiently endangered by the teaching of foreign languages to warrant its prohibition. As importantly, McReynolds also noted that parents who paid for this type of education had the right to have their children educated without state interference. Because the children were essentially their property, this was interfering with the way they wanted that property treated. The ruling suggested parental immunity from state interference when making decisions about the well-being of their children.

Two years later, McReynolds spoke for a unanimous Court in *Pierce v. Society of Sisters* (1925). Oregon had required that all school students in the state attend public schools through eighth grade. McReynolds had alluded to the constitutional right to parochial education in *Meyer*, but explicitly established such a right in *Pierce*. McReynolds found the justification for both *Meyer* and *Pierce* wholly within the Due Process Clause of the Fourteenth Amendment. The Oregon statute, he argued, destroyed the property rights of private schools as well as the freedom of parents to utilize educational programs of their choice. He used the *Lochner* doctrine, but intimated that more than property rights might be protected by the clause as well. Attorneys for the American Civil Liberties Union were encouraged by McReynolds's two school opinions as well as Brandeis's dissent in *Gilbert* and decided to challenge directly the traditional doctrine that even selected provisions of the Bill of Rights did not apply to the states. Their opportunity came in 1925 in *Gitlow v. New York* (Urofsky and Finkelman 2002, 650–651).

Benjamin Gitlow was one of the leaders of the American Community Party. He was convicted under provisions of New York's Criminal Anarchy Act for his advocacy of the "overthrow of the government by force, violence and unlawful means." Gitlow's criminal advocacy stemmed from two of his political publications, *The Left Wing Manifesto* and *The Revolutionary Age*. Seven members of the Taft Court upheld the New York statute against Gitlow's First Amendment challenge and affirmed his conviction. Justice Sanford noted, however, that "for present purposes we may and do assume that freedom of speech and the press—which are protected by the First Amendment from abridgement by Congress—are among the fundamental personal rights protected by the due process clause of the Fourteenth Amendment from impairment by the States." Justice Sanford's statement opened the door to a new era in the constitutional law of civil liberties. Other cases followed, confirming the new association between due process and the guarantees of the Fourteenth Amendment. By 1931 both freedom of speech and press had been incorporated against state interference.

The immediate impact of the *Gitlow* ruling was muted because the Court upheld his conviction. It would be several years before the holding would result in any major doctrinal change regarding the extent to which the Fourteenth Amendment incorporated other rights. The next step was the Hughes Court's ruling incorporating the free press provision of the First Amendment in *Near v. Minnesota* (1931). Six years later, the selective incorporation doctrine was fashioned by Justice Benjamin Cardozo in *Palko v. Connecticut* (1937) whereby some, but not necessarily all, Bill of Rights provisions would be extended to the states on a selective or piecemeal basis. The Warren Court would eventually use the selective incorporation doctrine to conclude that almost the entire Bill of Rights must apply to the states. It was the Taft Court that started this process, although unenthusiastically. The Taft Court's ruling in *Gitlow* was confined to the First Amendment. Incorporating Bill of Rights criminal process rights would take longer because criminal justice was viewed as the exclusive domain of the states for at least another two decades. At the same time, the Taft Court ruled in *Moore v. Dempsey* (1923) that a federal court should review the convictions of five African American defendants convicted on first-degree murder charges by an Arkansas state court where the constant threat of mob violence had tainted the proceedings. *Moore v. Dempsey* did not consider the incorporation issue as such, but the reasoning from that case was subsequently applied in incorporation cases dealing with criminal rights.

Free Speech

The Court's first real involvement with free speech cases had its origin in the Espionage and Sedition Acts enacted near the end of World War I. In *Schenck v. United States* (1919), a unanimous White Court upheld the convictions of Schenck and others for attempting to obstruct the recruiting of men for military service. The defendants had mailed leaflets to men eligible for the draft, attempting to persuade them not to submit to conscription. The Court concluded that the defendants' expression created a "clear and present danger" and thus could be restricted. It was the Court's first authoritative interpretation of the free speech clause. Although the *Schenck* ruling was not particularly protective of expression during wartime, Justice Holmes's clear and present danger test required the government to demonstrate a relationship between speech and criminal conduct—that relationship must be clear and immediate, not remote and indirect. The free speech cases that followed *Schenck*, including *Gitlow*, became less protective of expression during the 1920s. Although *Gitlow* was a positive ruling on the incorporation question, it devolved from "clear and present danger" to allow the government to restrict speech that might remotely tend to bring about unlawful ends. Although Holmes, Brandeis, and Stone disagreed, the Taft Court never returned to the "clear and present danger" standard.

The free speech cases gave Holmes an opportunity to discuss the incompatible objectives of legislative deference and the need to insulate most speech from legislative reach. In most areas Holmes believed it was necessary to defer to legislative judgments, but in the case of expression the predisposition to defer to elected legislators was trumped by the free speech value. Holmes's concept of free speech found its fullest expression in his *Abrams v. United States* (1919) dissent. Holmes stressed the need for truth to prevail in the marketplace of ideas. His "clear and present danger" standard from *Schenck* was a conditional protection for expression—a test that focused on the proximity and degree between speech and the dangers that legislatures were able to prevent. Holmes's thinking endured longer than the Taft Court's "bad tendency" standard contained in *Gitlow,* finally reemerging in the 1950s during the Warren Court era.

Another important Taft Court free speech decision is *Whitney v. California* (1927), in which the Court upheld a state syndicalism conviction of a local Communist. Although the Court ruled against Whitney, the case provided Justice Brandeis with the last opportunity during the Taft era to resuscitate the "clear and present danger" test. His concurring opinion provided a compelling defense of intellectual freedom "unmatched for its powerful reasoning in the annals of the Court" (Urofsky and Finkelman 2002, 653). Holmes had rested his First Amendment views on the "marketplace of ideas" concept. Holmes saw nothing inherently good or bad in free speech "other than the forum it allowed for intellectual competition." Brandeis, on the other hand, saw free speech as "an essential aspect of citizenship" (653–654). One consequence of the *Whitney* decision was that it seemed to endorse guilt by association—Whitney was guilty of criminal advocacy simply because of her membership in a Marxist political party. The Hughes Court would not accept the holding in *Whitney* and fashioned its own stance on associational rights. The thoughts contained in Brandeis's opinion, however, would be used by the Warren Court to expressly overrule *Whitney* in *Brandenburg v. Ohio* (1969).

Criminal Rights—The Impact of Prohibition

None of the federal Bill of Rights provisions were viewed as applicable to the states going into the 1920s. This was certainly true of the constitutional rights accorded those accused of crimes. Rather, administration of justice matters were viewed as entirely in the hands of the states. Whatever protections existed for criminal defendants came from state law. Under extreme circumstances—in the instance of violations of fundamental rules of fairness—the Court intervened using the due process language of the Fourteenth Amendment. Otherwise, the Court typically permitted states to operate with no federal constitutional constraints. For that matter, the Taft Court allowed federal agents to operate with only minimal constitutional restrictions as well.

The Taft Court had inherited relatively enlightened Fourth Amendment thinking from the White Court's *Silverthorne Lumber* decision. In *Silverthorne*, the Court held that to allow the government to reclaim by subpoena evidence that had been unlawfully seized would greatly devalue the Fourth Amendment. A federal agent had, "without a shadow of authority," seized books and papers of two suspects who were being detained at the time. The ruling insisted that the knowledge gained by the government's own wrong cannot be used as evidence in criminal trials. In the wave of cases stemming from efforts to enforce Prohibition, the Taft Court backed away from the view contained in *Silverthorne*. For example, in *Byars v. United States* and *Gambino v. United States*, both decided in 1927, the Court developed the so-called silver platter practice. Because federal agents were at least theoretically restrained by the Fourth Amendment, evidence illegally seized by them was inadmissible in criminal trials. If the evidence was illegally seized by state agents and turned over to federal authorities on the "silver platter," it could be used in federal criminal trials. The "silver platter" doctrine was an end-run around the Fourth Amendment and invited abuses by law enforcement agents. This permissive doctrine remained in place for more than thirty years until the Warren Court eliminated it in *Elkins v. United States* (1960).

Prohibition prompted two other significant Fourth Amendment issues on which the Taft Court had significant and long-term impact. First, the Court gave its blessing to wiretapping in *Olmstead v. United States* (1928). Taft's literalistic view of wiretapping ignored the protective intent of the Fourth Amendment. There had been no actual entry into Olmstead's office because federal agents had intercepted conversations from outside the premises. To prohibit the overhearing of conversations such as these would, in Taft's words, "pay too much attention to nice ethical conduct by government officials [and] would make society suffer and give criminals greater immunity than has been known heretofore." In subsequent years, wiretapping and other forms of electronic surveillance were repeatedly challenged, but it was not until the Warren Court's rulings in *Katz v. United States* and *Berger v. New York* (1967) that the Warren Court concluded that these practices were subject to Fourth Amendment limits. Taft's opinion elicited a short dissent from Holmes, who called wiretapping a "dirty business," and a longer, well-reasoned dissent from the conservative Justice Butler. The most significant dissent, however, came from Justice Brandeis who focused on the issue of privacy. It was his view that the Constitution protected personal privacy even though it did not do so expressly. His dissent would provide the foundation for the Warren Court's determination in *Griswold v. Connecticut* (1965) that there was a constitutionally protected right of privacy.

Second, the Taft Court created the most enduring exception to the Fourth Amendment warrant requirement. Ideally, police arrests or searches are conducted under authority of a warrant. Warrantless searches are permitted when exigent circumstances make it impractical for police to obtain a warrant before making an arrest or conducting a search. In *Carroll v. United States* (1925), the Taft Court created what is known as the vehicle exception to the warrant requirement. Carroll and the others in the car were all known bootleggers and were on a highway frequently used to deliver alcohol. The Court found stopping the vehicle and subjecting it to a search in *Carroll* was reasonable because federal agents had probable cause to stop the car. The mobility of the car made it impossible, the Court reasoned, for police to secure a search warrant before stopping the vehicle. The vehicle warrant exception has come back to the Court many times since 1925, but the basic doctrine fashioned by the Taft Court in *Carroll* has remained in effect for almost eighty years (Urofsky and Finkelman 2002, 656).

Race and Alienage

Although the Taft Court preferred to leave criminal matters to the states, it occasionally reviewed state criminal cases. One case, *Moore v. Dempsey* (1923), was particularly notable because it also affected race relations, a constitutional field that the Taft Court entered with great reluctance. *Moore v. Dempsey* was an exception to this predisposition. The case was decided after the House of Representatives passed a law in 1921 that made lynching a federal crime. Lynching and other violent acts offended the Taft Court as nonviolent forms of discrimination did not. Justice Holmes said in *Moore v. Dempsey*, a case that involved threats of violence (if not lynching as such), that a federal court should hear the appeal of five black men convicted of first-degree murder by an Arkansas state court because the constant threat of mob violence had dominated the proceedings. *Moore v. Dempsey* was a signal to Congress that it may, under unusual circumstances, enter a domain previously reserved to the states.

Notwithstanding the Court's ruling in *Moore v. Dempsey*, the Taft Court generally showed very little concern over issues of racial prejudice. *Corrigan v. Buckley* (1926) was more typical of its decision making on the issue of race discrimination. In *Corrigan*, the Taft Court unanimously upheld a restrictive racial covenant that prevented those signing the covenant to convey property to racial minorities. The Taft Court concluded that the restrictive covenant did not violate the Fourteenth Amendment because the agreement was signed by private persons and no state action was involved. It was not until the 1940s that the Court adopted a more expansive view of state action and outlawed, among other discriminatory practices, restrictive housing covenants (Urofsky and Finkelman 2002, 656–657).

The year after *Corrigan*, the Taft Court struck down a Texas law in *Nixon v. Herndon* (1927) that excluded blacks from voting in the Democratic primary election. Justice Holmes speaking for a unanimous Court said that Texas could not, by statute, exclude blacks from the Democratic primary because such a law constitutes state-sponsored discrimination. *Nixon v. Herndon* had little lasting impact, however, because political party leaders in Texas soon developed informal but effective ways to exclude racial minorities from participating in the electoral process. The Hughes Court allowed the so-called white primary to continue, concluding that the discriminatory practice was undertaken by private persons and not the state. The "white primary" was eventually eliminated by the Stone Court in *Smith v. Allwright* (1944).

The Taft Court, including its more liberal justices, showed no great concern for other racial minorities or aliens. In *Ozawa v. United States* (1923), the Court unanimously interpreted provisions of the Immigration Act of 1921 to exclude Japanese from citizenship eligibility and extended the ban to East Indians in *United States v. Bhagat Singh Thind* (1923). In addition, the Court had no problem upholding various western state laws prohibiting land ownership by aliens who had not declared their intention to become citizens. In fact, these laws were specifically aimed at Asians who were ineligible for naturalization. Aliens also did not enjoy procedural rights comparable to those of citizens. Under federal law aliens were deported if convicted of violations of the Espionage or Selective Service Acts. Many of those subject to deportation had been charged for conduct that occurred before these federal laws were enacted. It was contended that this violated the Article I prohibition against ex post facto laws. In *Mahler v. Eby* (1924), the Taft Court concluded that the federal government had complete authority to deport an alien for actions that may have been legal when they were committed. The Court saw deportation as a severe sanction, but it was "not a criminal sanction and therefore did not come under the Article I, Section 10 ban on ex post facto laws" (Urofsky and Finkelman 2002, 657–658).

The superpatriotism of the decade manifested itself in the Court's denial of citizenship to aliens who, despite many exemplary qualities, happened to be pacifists. The indifference to the lack of fair procedure for aliens reflected both the Taft Court's general attitude toward civil liberties and the growing public animus toward aliens and things foreign. One Taft Court ruling that particularly "shocks the modern conscience and displays in full the Taft Court's indifference to individual liberties" dealt not with people of color or aliens or pacifists, but with a white Southern girl, Carrie Buck. Under Virginia law, Buck was scheduled for involuntary sterilization as a result of the feeblemindedness of her mother and daughter as well as her own. Justice Holmes spoke for eight members of the Taft Court (Justice Butler dissented without opinion) and upheld the Virginia law. He suggested that "three generations of imbeciles is enough" and that society ought to be able to prevent those who are "manifestly unfit from continuing their kind." Although Holmes became the "darling of the eugenics movement" as a result of his opinion in *Buck v. Bell* (1927), that movement "faded with the rise of Nazism in the 1930s, and the case has had a bad odor about it ever since" (Urofsky and Finkelman 2002, 659–660). Although the Taft Court's record on race and alienage issues left much to be desired, some of its decisions set precedent for several decades.

Conclusion

For many Americans the 1920s were good times. The nation was prosperous and untroubled by either domestic or foreign crises. Under these circumstances, it is not surprising that the Taft Court breathed new life into the laissez-faire activism of the late nineteenth century. Its rulings on property rights and the national economy would persist into the 1930s until the Hughes Court abandoned them in the wake of the Great Depression. The Taft Court maintained an almost simplistic approach to constitutional interpretation that featured the view that a highly decentralized and limited government characteristic of the mid-nineteenth century was sufficient public authority for the United States in the 1920s. In rationalizing protection of large and powerful corporate interests, many justices responded as though they were ruling on the property rights of private citizens. They embraced a judicial activism that revealed a lack of trust in the judgment of elected officials and the efficacy of political corrections available to the electorate.

There was no doubt that Taft was the leader of his Court. He wrote more opinions in constitutional cases than any other justice of the period and he kept for himself the majority opinions in such landmark decisions as *Myers v. United States, Bailey v. Drexel Furniture, Carroll v. United States, Brooks v. United States, Olmstead v. United States,* and *Stafford v. Wallace.* In these cases, Taft "set the tone for the period." Although he wrote relatively little in the field of substantive due process, Taft defined the tone here as well in such opinions as *Truax v. Corrigan* and by silently concurring with the great due process rulings of his Court (although it must be noted that he wrote his only dissent in a constitutional case in *Adkins v. Children's Hospital,* in which he protested the invalidation of minimum wage law for female employees). Taft "truly appeared to embody the spirit of the Court over which he presided" (Currie 1990, 199).

Besides Taft, the principal spokesmen for the conservative majority, especially in the substantive due process cases, were Justices Sutherland, Butler, and McReynolds. Each wrote powerful opinions that stalled both federal and state regulatory initiatives. McReynolds's judicial activism was particularly emphatic and led him to write his noteworthy liberal-sounding opinions in support of academic freedom in *Meyer* and *Pierce.* His activism also led him to "dissent more frequently in constitutional cases than anyone but Holmes and Brandeis, usually because the Court had upheld some state or federal regulation" (Currie 1990, 200). Van Devanter and Sanford contributed relatively little in the way of opinions although Sanford was responsible for the restrictive free speech rulings in *Gitlow v. New York* and *Whitney v. California.* Justices Holmes, Brandeis, and Stone were "fundamentally out of sympathy with prevailing judicial philosophy" of the Taft Court and "made their names during the 1920s very largely in dissent" (Currie 1990, 200). Judicial restraint was the "dominant theme of the numerous dissents of all three Justices, especially in substantive due process and equal protection cases" (201). In any event, it was Taft's Court and "activism in support of traditional values was the order of the day" (200–201).

Like the Fuller and White Courts before it, the Taft Court neither appreciated the qualitative changes brought about by the industrial revolution nor did it comprehend what was required from government to respond to them. As a result, the Taft Court held too tightly to the constitutional doctrines of the past. The Taft Court was not reactionary, but it was not particularly insightful either. Its constitutional policies certainly did not bring about the Great Depression, but its decisions did little to enable the government to avoid it. Instead, its jurisprudence made resistance to Roosevelt's reform efforts of the New Deal easier. It is not surprising that the business community saw the Taft Court as its indispensable ally as the preeminent protector of private property. But the Taft Court legacy is not quite so clear-cut. Although the Taft Court struck down most regulatory initiatives, it did not invalidate them all. The Taft Court blurred the public-private distinction found at the center of classical legal thought, and its interstate commerce decisions seemed to suggest that most aspects of such commerce were within federal regulatory reach. The Court consistently withheld support from labor unions and found most "protective" legislation unconstitutional. At bottom, the legacy of the Taft Court is mixed, leading some observers of the 1920s to find it difficult to characterize its jurisprudence.

The 1920s was a period that had an almost artificial or surreal quality. Government officials as well as much of the public was interested in returning to "normalcy," in restoring a bygone era. This included the Taft Court. Taft's Court attempted to revitalize and restore a constitutional order of an earlier era. In doing so, the Taft Court was insensitive to some of the pressing socioeconomic needs of the post–World War I period. Its rulings helped postpone the transition to a government, particularly at the national level, that could engage in effective economic regulation and the direct delivery of services to individual citizens. The Taft Court was a Court better suited for the late nineteenth century. Like the conservative Republican government of the 1920s, the Taft Court wished to return to a bygone era; it was a Court whose time had come and gone.

References and Further Reading

Abraham, Henry J. 1999. *Justices, Presidents, and Senators: A History of the U.S. Supreme Court Appointments from Washington to Clinton.* Rev. ed. Lanham, MD: Rowman & Littlefield.

Currie, David P. 1990. *The Constitution in the Supreme Court: The Second Century, 1886–1986.* Chicago: University of Chicago Press.

Danelski, David J. 1964. *A Supreme Court Justice Is Appointed.* New York: Random House.

Goldberg, David J. 1999. *Discontented America: The United States in the 1920s.* Baltimore, MD: Johns Hopkins University Press.

Goldman, Sheldon. *Constitutional Law: Cases and Essays.* 2d edition.

Kelly, Alfred H., Winfred A. Harbison, and Herman Belz. 1991. *The American Constitution: Its Origins and Developments.* Vol. 2. 7th ed. New York: W. W. Norton.

Mason, Alpheus T. 1964. *William Howard Taft: Chief Justice.* New York: Simon and Schuster.

———. 1979. *The Supreme Court from Taft to Burger.* 3d ed. Baton Rouge, LA: Louisiana State University Press.

Morison, Samuel Eliot, Henry Steele Commager, and William E. Leuchtenburg. 1980. *The Growth of the American Republic.* Vol. 2. New York: Oxford University Press.

Murphy, Paul L. 1972. *The Constitution in Times of Crisis, 1918–1969.* New York: Harper & Row.

Parrish, Michael E. 1992. *Anxious Decades: America in Prosperity and Depression, 1920–1941.* New York: W. W. Norton.

Pritchett, C. Herman. 1984. *Constitutional Law of the Federal System.* Englewood Cliffs, NJ: Prentice-Hall.

Schlesinger, Arthur M., Jr. 1957. *The Crisis of the Old Order, 1919–1933.* Boston, MA: Houghton Mifflin.

Urofsky, Melvin I., ed. 1994. *The Supreme Court Justices: A Biographical Dictionary.* New York: Garland.

Urofsky, Melvin I., and Paul Finkelman. 2002. *A March of Liberty: A Constitutional History of the United States.* Vol. 2. 2d ed. New York: Oxford University Press.

White, G. Edward. 1976. *The American Judicial Tradition: Profiles of Leading American Judges.* Oxford, UK: Oxford University Press.

PART TWO

Reference Materials

Key People, Laws, and Events

Agricultural Marketing Act of 1929

American agriculture suffered serious economic problems during the 1920s despite the so-called decade of prosperity. President Herbert Hoover called for government intervention even before the Great Depression began. Congress enacted the Agricultural Marketing Act in June 1929. It sought to support farm prices through largely voluntary production guidelines. The law also set up a Federal Farm Board and authorized the agency to lend funds to marketing associations and state commodity stabilization agencies, which would purchase and store surplus agricultural commodities. The objective of the program closely resembled the earlier McNary-Haugen proposal, which President Calvin Coolidge vetoed. The principal difference in the Agricultural Marketing Act was the voluntary production reductions preferred by Hoover. Within a year it became apparent that economic recovery for American agriculture could occur only through more aggressive and involuntary government regulation (Parrish 1992, 245–246).

Borah, William E. (1865–1940)

William Borah was an isolationist from Idaho. He was admitted to the Kansas Bar in 1887, but after practicing law for three years he moved west, eventually taking up residence in Boise, Idaho. In 1892 he was named chair of the Republican State Central Committee. His political visibility increased dramatically when the Populist crusade and the "free silver" issue reshaped then-existing party lines in the mid-1890s with the Populists calling for the issuing of currency based on silver as well as gold. Borah joined the so-called Silver Republicans in 1896 and supported William Jennings Bryan's unsuccessful presidential bid. In that same year, Borah lost in his bid for election to the U.S. House of Representatives. In 1902 Borah returned to the Republican Party and sought nomination for the U.S. Senate, but his candidacy was blocked by party leaders who remembered his Bryan defection in 1896. In early 1907, however, he was elected to the U.S. Senate, where he served for thirty-four years. His Senate influence increased substantially when he became chairman of the Committee on Foreign Relations in 1924. Borah was strongly nationalistic and fully supported the declaration of war against Germany. Following the end of World War I, he was one of the Senate "Irreconcilables"—senators who rejected any version of the League of Nations and U.S. participation in the World Court. Borah fully supported the Kellogg-Briand Pact in 1928 and, as a result, opposed American intervention in Latin America and the Far East. Borah supported mandatory neutrality legislation and helped block President Franklin Roosevelt's lend-lease initiatives. He also used his position on the Senate Judiciary Committee to help defeat Roosevelt's attempt to "pack" the Supreme Court. Nonetheless, his Senate influence diminished during the 1930s, and he failed in an effort to become president in 1936. Borah died in Washington in 1940.

Bryan, William Jennings (1860–1925)

Bryan was a three-time Democratic presidential nominee. He graduated valedictorian from Illinois College in 1881 and completed his law studies at Union College in 1883. He established a law practice in central Illinois before moving to Lincoln, Nebraska, in 1887. Bryan quickly became active in Democratic politics and was elected to the U.S. House of Representatives in 1890. His campaign embraced a number of Populist positions, and three years later, he played the decisive role in convincing the Nebraska legislature to elect a Populist to the U.S. Senate. In Congress, Bryan achieved national visibility by supporting, among other reforms, a proposed income tax. Instead of seeking a third term in Congress in 1894, Bryan ran in a nonbinding election for the U.S. Senate. Although he won more votes than any candidate, he was not selected by the Republican-controlled legislature.

The following year, Bryan traveled the country as a "silver advocate"—someone who supported issuing currency based on silver as well as gold. This made Bryan the front-runner for the presidential nomination at the 1896 Democratic nominating convention. He sealed his nomination with his famous "Cross of Gold" speech at the convention. The "Boy Orator of the Platte," as Bryan was often called, faced William McKinley in the general election in 1896, and while Bryan conducted an aggressive campaign, he lost by about 600,000 votes nationally. Bryan sought the presidency a second time in 1900. The campaign was largely defined by the Spanish-American War and domestic economic issues. McKinley argued that Bryan's election would endanger economic prosperity. McKinley also defended U.S. acquisition of several territories as a consequence of the war while Bryan considered the territorial acquisition imperialistic. McKinley won the election by almost a million votes. Although a twice-defeated presidential candidate, Bryan nonetheless retained substantial influence with the Democratic Party. Bryan undertook a third presidential campaign in 1908, but was soundly defeated by William Howard Taft.

Bryan supported James B. Clark for the Democratic presidential nomination in 1912, but was instrumental in swinging the deadlocked Democratic convention to Woodrow Wilson. He campaigned extensively for Wilson who, following his election, named Bryan secretary of state. Bryan hoped to make a major contribution to world peace from that position, but he was prevented from doing so by events leading to World War I. He resigned from the Cabinet in protest of Wilson's belligerent response to the sinking of the *Lusitania*. Notwithstanding his resignation from the Wilson administration, Bryan campaigned for Wilson in 1916. He strongly supported American entry in the League of Nations following the war and worked to secure American participation in the League. Once he resigned as secretary of state, Bryan turned his attention to social issues and strongly advocated women's suffrage and prohibition. Most observers of the period believed that Bryan was a major force in the ratification of the Prohibition (Eighteenth) Amendment. During the last years of his life, Bryan took on the issue of evolution, which he believed was incompatible with Christian principles. This led him to assist in the prosecution of John Scopes for violating Tennessee's ban on the teaching of evolution in public schools. Bryan prevailed at trial as Scopes was convicted by a jury, but the verdict was subsequently reversed by the Tennessee Supreme Court.

Cardozo, Benjamin Nathan (1870–1938)

Benjamin Cardozo was nominated in 1914 by the newly formed anti–Tammany Hall party as a candidate for judge of a New York trial court. He was elected by the narrowest of margins, and a month after joining the court he was appointed to the New York Court of Appeals, the state's highest tribunal, where he remained until his appointment to the U.S. Supreme Court in 1932. Cardozo achieved national visibility as chief justice of the state court, and when Justice Oliver Wendell Holmes Jr. left the U.S. Supreme Court, President Herbert Hoover nominated Cardozo as his successor. He was quickly and unanimously confirmed by the Senate. He joined Justices Brandeis and Stone in support of Franklin Roosevelt's New Deal measures and in urging deference to congressional policy choices in opposition to the conservative laissez-faire majority on the Court. The Cardozo bloc gained majority status when the Court made its famous doctrinal shift in 1937 following Roosevelt's failed "court-packing" initiative. As part of the new majority, Cardozo delivered important majority opinions in *Steward Machine Co. v. Davis* (1937) and *Helvering v. Davis* (1937), in which the Court upheld provisions of the Social Security Act as constitutional uses of congressional taxing and spending power. Another of Cardozo's more notable opinions came in *Palko v. Connecticut* (1937), in which he defined a process of "selective incorporation" for determining which Bill of Rights provisions apply to the actions of state governments. Cardozo was an ideological liberal but he believed in judicial self-restraint, which typically led him to defer to legislative judgments. He supported the expansion of federal power, and voted to uphold virtually all of Roosevelt's New Deal proposals. He died in Port Chester, New York, in July 1938 after serving only seven years on the Supreme Court.

Child Labor Tax Act of 1919

The Child Labor Tax Act levied a 10 percent tax on the net profits of any business employing child labor. The Supreme Court declared the law unconstitutional in *Bailey v. Drexel Furniture Co.* (1922) on the grounds that it usurped powers reserved to the states. Chief Justice Taft's majority opinion suggested that while the tax raised revenue, its real purpose was to enforce the child labor restriction. *Bailey* was the Court's second ruling on congressional efforts to regulate child labor. Congress had enacted the Keating-Owen Child Labor Law in 1916, which prohibited the interstate shipment of goods produced by child labor. The Court declared Keating-Owen unconstitutional in *Hammer v. Dagenhart* (1918), concluding that the act exceeded the limits of the federal interstate commerce power and that it encroached on the sovereign power of the states. Less than nine months after the *Dagenhart* decision, Congress passed the Child Labor Tax Act, using its taxing power instead of the commerce power. The Court concluded in *Bailey* that Congress could not achieve through the taxing power an objective that could not be reached with federal commerce power.

Clayton Anti-Trust Act of 1914

Antitrust laws are designed to protect competition and prohibit price fixing and other collusion among businesses to control the price or supply of a product or service. In 1914 Congress passed the Clayton Act to reinforce provisions of the first antitrust law, the Sherman Anti-Trust Act of 1890, to "plug the loopholes" in the initial antitrust statute. The Sherman Act had been weakened by the Supreme Court's use of the "rule of reason," which limited application of antitrust law to only "unreasonable" combinations in restraint of trade. The Clayton Act specifically outlawed price discrimination and forbade agreements through which manufacturers could sell only to dealers who agreed not to handle the products of a rival manufacturer. The Clayton Act banned interlocking directorates among banks, railroads, and large corporations so that, in Woodrow Wilson's words, "those who borrow and those who lend would no longer be one in the same" (Clements 1992, 47–48). Further, the Clayton Act prohibited certain mergers and other practices that might decrease competition. Labor unions and nonprofit agricultural organizations were exempted from the provisions of the act.

Clear and Present Danger Test

The "clear and present danger" test is a standard used to determine if particular expressive content is protected by the First Amendment. The test was first articulated by Justice Oliver Wendell Holmes Jr. in *Schenck v. United States* (1919), a case involving an Espionage Act prosecution for obstruction of the military draft during World War I. The Supreme Court upheld an Espionage Act conviction against free speech challenge by concluding that expression is a conditional freedom that must be evaluated in a situational context. According to Holmes, each situation must be reviewed to determine whether expression occurs in such a way and is of "such a nature as to create a clear and present danger that it will bring about the substantive evils which Congress has a right to prevent" (*Schenck* 1919, 47). If speech is linked closely enough to illegal acts, it may be restricted. The "clear and present danger" test presumes that free speech is not an absolute right. The test was designed to protect expression by limiting governmental interference with speech only when the government can demonstrate that particular speech creates both a substantial and immediate danger and essentially remains in use today.

Coolidge, Calvin (1872–1933)

Coolidge was the thirtieth president of the United States. He was born in Plymouth Notch, Vermont, on 4 July 1872. After graduating from Amherst College in 1895, he read law and was admitted to the Massachusetts Bar in 1897. He practiced law in Northampton, Massachusetts, and held a variety of public offices between 1898 and 1914—Northampton city council, city solicitor, clerk of the county courts, state representative, and Massachusetts senator. Coolidge was elected lieutenant governor of Massachusetts in 1915 and governor in 1918. He gained national prominence the following year by supporting the city of Boston's decision to fire striking police officers. He took the position that the officers had no right to strike against the public safety, a view that contributed to his overwhelming reelection as governor. Coolidge sought the Republican presidential nomination in 1920, but the convention chose Warren G. Harding of Ohio instead. Harding then selected Coolidge as his running mate and the ticket was elected convincingly. Harding died in 1923 and Coolidge succeeded to the presidency. Dubbed "Silent Cal" by the media, Coolidge was effective because of his direct and straightforward style. Coolidge easily defeated Democrat John Davis and Progressive Robert La Follette in the 1924 presidential election. Coolidge's policy priorities were similar to Harding's—he supported a modest expansion of federal programs, but only if they did not jeopardize lowering taxes and reducing the government's debt. The biggest issues during his presidency involved federal purchase of surplus agricultural commodities and additional benefits for World War I veterans. There was major conflict between Coolidge and Congress on legislation dealing with farm surpluses and Coolidge twice vetoed the McNary-Haugen bills. He was also able to block adoption of a soldiers' bonus proposal and costly flood control legislation. Most important to Coolidge, he succeeded in protecting his economic program—tax cuts, reduction of the federal debt, and containment of inflation.

Coolidge's foreign policy achievements were modest. In 1926 the Senate ratified, at Coolidge's request, American membership on the Permanent Court of International Justice. Coolidge supported the Kellogg-Briand Pact in 1928, in which fifteen nations renounced war as an instrument of national policy. Coolidge generally supported policies intended to promote American exports and enhance investment opportunities abroad. Coolidge was a popular president, but chose not to seek reelection in 1928. He left the White House and returned to Northampton, where he wrote newspaper and magazine articles. His health declined, and he died on 5 January 1933.

Cox, James M. (1870–1957)

Cox was a newspaper publisher, politician, and presidential candidates born in Jacksonville, Ohio, in 1870. He served as assistant to Congressman Paul Sorg in early 1894, and with Sorg's help purchased the *Dayton Daily News.* As Cox became more successful in his publishing ventures, he also became interested in Ohio politics. He was elected to Congress in 1908, where he served two terms. In 1912 he was elected to the first of his three terms as governor of Ohio. While governor, Cox brought about extensive reforms in the state. For example, at his initiative Ohio established an Industrial Relations Commission and a "no fault" workers' compensation program. Critics of the Cox-initiated reforms were able to defeat Cox in 1914, but he regained the office two years later and won reelection to an unprecedented third term in 1918. The 1920 Democratic nominating convention deadlocked over its choice of a presidential candidate and eventually selected Cox on the forty-fourth ballot. He waged an energetic campaign, but was overwhelmed by the Republican candidate, Warren G. Harding. Although Cox never ran for public office after 1920, he was instrumental in brokering the compromise nomination of John W. Davis in 1924. Cox opposed the nomination of Franklin Roosevelt in 1932, but following Roosevelt's nomination, Cox campaigned for the Democratic ticket and the New Deal agenda. During the period between the world wars, Cox expanded his newspaper business, acquiring the *Miami Daily News*, the *Canton Daily News*, and two Atlanta newspapers. By the beginning of World War II, the Cox communications empire had grown to national stature. Cox died in 1957 at the age of eighty-seven.

Cummins, Albert B. (1850–1926)

Cummins was governor of Iowa and a U.S. senator. He was admitted to the Illinois Bar in 1875 and practiced law in Chicago for three years before relocating to Des Moines, Iowa. His law practice specialized in railroad and patent law, but Cummins also established a reputation as a "people's advocate" by representing the Iowa Farmers' Protective Association. Cummins became active in Republican politics both at the state and national levels, and eventually became a leader of the progressive faction of the state party. He failed in bids for the U.S. Senate in 1894 and 1900, but was elected Iowa governor in 1901 and served three consecutive terms. In 1908 he was chosen to represent Iowa in the U.S. Senate. Cummins was instrumental in the formation of the National Progressive Republican League, which was intended to provide an alternative to Taft in 1912. Cummins later switched his support to Theodore Roosevelt. Even though Cummins supported Roosevelt in 1912, he remained a member of the Republican Party, at least nominally. Cummins supported a number of the components of President Woodrow Wilson's "New Freedom" platform and took part in writing the Clayton Anti-Trust Act. As an isolationist, Cummins differed with Wilson on most foreign policy issues, however. He opposed Wilson's efforts to arm merchant ships, and he was one of the Senate "Irreconcilables" who opposed U.S. membership in the League of Nations. He was a close friend of President Warren G. Harding, and he generally supported the Republican platform in the early 1920s. As he became more conservative, Cummins lost support in Iowa and he was defeated by a progressive in the 1926 primary. Cummins died in Des Moines later that year.

Daugherty, Harry M. (1860–1941)

Daugherty graduated from the University of Michigan Law School in 1881 and began a private legal practice in Ohio. He soon became prominent as an attorney and in Republican politics. After serving as a city councilman and county prosecuting attorney, Daugherty was elected to the U.S. House of Representatives where he served two terms. His career in the House was cut short by allegations that he accepted money in exchange for a particular vote—a charge that was never proven. Daugherty remained active in Ohio politics and chaired President William Howard Taft's 1912 campaign organization in the state. Among the Ohio politicians who sought his counsel was Warren G. Harding. Daugherty was instrumental in securing the 1920 presidential nomination for Harding and served as manager of Harding's successful presidential campaign. Following Harding's election, Daugherty was named attorney general. His performance as attorney general was undistinguished at best. He appointed a large number of Republican "cronies" to positions within the department and many proved to be either inept or corrupt. Daugherty did political damage to the

Harding presidency by taking a hard line against railroad workers in a 1922 strike, and he also proved unable to successfully prosecute high-profile antitrust cases. Daugherty is probably best known for the failure of his department to investigate and prosecute the oil-leasing scandals that eventually overwhelmed the Harding administration. Harding died in 1923 just as the Teapot Dome oil-leasing scandal was breaking, and his successor, Calvin Coolidge, concluded that Daugherty was a major political liability to his administration and demanded his resignation in April 1924. Daugherty contended that he was not guilty of any wrongdoing and he was twice acquitted on federal corruption charges. Daugherty returned to Ohio following the criminal trials, resumed his law practice and completed his memoirs, which were an attempt to exonerate himself from the scandals. Daugherty died in Columbus, Ohio, in October 1941.

Davis, John W. (1873–1955)

Davis was a politician and presidential candidate born in Clarksburg, West Virginia, in 1873. Davis earned both his B.A. and LL.B. degrees from Washington and Lee University, and after remaining there a year, joined his father's law practice in Clarksburg. Davis demonstrated sufficient skills as an attorney to attract a number of important corporate clients. In 1910 he won election to the U.S. House of Representatives as a Democrat and although he was an economic conservative and typically probusiness, he wrote the language in the Clayton Act that limited the use of court injunctions in labor disputes. Davis was appointed solicitor general by President Woodrow Wilson in 1913 and represented the administration in the most important cases presented to the Supreme Court during the period. Davis was named ambassador to Great Britain in 1918 and participated in fashioning post–World War I policy. In 1920 Davis was in the running for the Democratic presidential nomination, but James M. Cox emerged as the nominee on the forty-fourth ballot. Davis resumed his law practice as head of a prominent Wall Street firm, but secured the Democratic presidential nomination four years later after more than 100 ballots at the party convention. His chances were diminished, however, because the public associated the economic prosperity of the period with the Republican administration. Davis's candidacy was further damaged by his unwillingness to embrace even a portion of the progressive agenda. This decision prompted Senator Robert M. La Follette to enter the race as the nominee of the Progressive Party, which drew votes away from Davis. Following his loss to President Calvin Coolidge, Davis returned to his legal practice but remained active in partisan politics. He supported the presidential candidacy of Al Smith of New York in 1928, but did not support Franklin Roosevelt and his domestic policy objectives in 1932. Soon after Roosevelt's inauguration, Davis joined other conservative Democrats in forming the New Deal Liberty League, which sought to challenge some New Deal initiatives in court. He argued many cases before the Supreme Court, including the landmark steel seizure case *Youngstown Sheet & Tube Co. v. Sawyer* (1952) before his death in 1955.

Dawes, Charles G. (1865–1951)

Vice president of the United States from 1925 through 1929, Dawes was born in Marietta, Ohio, in 1865. He earned his B.A. and M.A. degrees from Marietta College and his LL.B. from the Cincinnati Law School in 1886. He moved from Ohio to Nebraska and established a successful law practice. He was active in McKinley's successful campaign for the presidency in 1896 and was named comptroller of the currency in the McKinley administration. He resigned the position several years later to undertake a bid for the Republican U.S. Senate nomination. When he failed to get the nomination, he left the electoral arena to become president of a trust company in Illinois. In 1921 Dawes accepted appointment as the first director of the Bureau of the Budget. When Germany was unable to meet its war reparations obligations, Dawes chaired an Allied Reparations Commission that assisted Germany in stabilizing its economy and developing a realistic plan for reparation payments. The commission's recommendations were known as the "Dawes Plan," and for this work he awarded the 1925 Nobel Peace Prize. Dawes was selected as President Calvin Coolidge's running mate for the 1924 election and traveled extensively throughout the country on behalf of the successful Republican ticket. He was an active vice president who had considerable influence in getting proposals through Congress. When Coolidge indicated that he would not seek reelection in 1928, Dawes was seen as the logical choice, but he refused to allow his nomination. Herbert Hoover became the Republican nominee and upon his election selected Dawes to become ambassador to Great Britain. In 1932 Dawes gave up the ambassadorship to head the Reconstruction Finance Corporation, an agency created by Hoover to meet the demands of the Great Depression emergency. After several months, Dawes returned to manage his own bank and never returned to national public life. He died in Chicago in 1951.

Debs, Eugene V. (1855–1926)

Debs was a labor organizer and a five-time presidential nominee of the Socialist Party. He left his hometown of Terre Haute, Indiana, before finishing high school to work on the railroad. He was laid off, however, and despite great effort, was unable to find work and so returned to Terre Haute where he worked at a grocery store. When the Brotherhood of Locomotive Firemen (BLF) organized in the area, Debs joined and soon became an elected officer of the union. Despite his union leadership position, he had serious misgivings about a proposed railroad strike and did not support the action. At the time, he believed that strikes threatened public order, preferring instead less confrontational approaches to labor-management problems. His position on the strike was well known and well received in Terre Haute and contributed to his successful candidacy for the position of city clerk. He won reelection as clerk before his election to the Indiana legislature in 1884. Within two years, however, Debs began to rethink his position on how worker interests should be represented. He concluded that employers and workers were inherently economic adversaries. He resigned his position in the BLF to help create the American Railway Union (ARU), a broad industrial union. The Pullman strike of 1894 was the first major test for the ARU. The Pullman Company was able to convince President Grover Cleveland to order military intervention to end the strike. Debs and other ARU leaders were arrested, charged, and convicted of criminal conspiracy and contempt of court. During his six-month incarceration Debs first read Karl Marx's *Das Kapital*, and within two years had become a Marxist. Beginning in 1900, Debs was the presidential candidate of the Socialist Party of America. In 1912 he received almost one million votes or about 6 percent of the votes cast nationally. Debs developed serious health problems and chose not to mount another presidential campaign in 1916. Within two years, however, he had recovered sufficiently to deliver a number of speeches critical of American involvement in World War I. This activity prompted his arrest in 1918 for impeding the war effort in violation of the Espionage Act. Following his conviction on the Espionage Act charges, he was sentenced to ten years imprisonment. In 1920 he conducted his fifth presidential campaign while incarcerated at a federal prison and won 3 percent of the vote. In December 1921 President Warren G. Harding ordered his release. Debs died five years later.

Denby, Edwin L. (1870–1929)

Edwin Denby was educated in China and served in the Chinese Maritime Customs Service until 1894. On his return to the United States, he studied law at the University of Michigan and was admitted to the Michigan Bar in 1896. He served in the U.S. Navy during the Spanish-American War and then returned to his law practice. He was elected to the Michigan House of Representatives in 1902 and to Congress two years later. He became active in banking and the automotive business after he was defeated in a bid for a fourth term in the U.S. House in 1910. Denby left his law practice and business interests to reenlist in the military in 1917. He remained in the reserves following the war and achieved the rank of lieutenant colonel. On 4 March 1921 Denby became President Warren G. Harding's secretary of the navy. Denby's political career ended as a result of the Teapot Dome scandal. His part in Teapot Dome involved the transfer of the naval oil reserves to the Department of the Interior. Interior Secretary Albert Fall, in turn, leased the federal oil lands in Teapot Dome, Wyoming, and Elk

Hills, California, to petroleum magnates Harry F. Sinclair and Edward Doheny in exchange for a payment of nearly $400,000. Congressional investigations of the leasing arrangement eventually led to a Senate resolution requesting Denby's resignation. In late February 1927 the Supreme Court concluded that Denby was not a participant in the transfer negotiations with the oil companies, a conclusion also reached by the Senate investigating committee chaired by Senator Thomas Walsh.

Doheny, Edward L. (1856–1935)

A Wisconsin-born oil developer who became involved in the Teapot Dome scandal, Doheny engaged in a variety of mining-related endeavors before he and a partner began drilling for oil near Los Angeles, California. By 1886 Doheny was one of the largest fuel oil producers in the country. The following year he began developing oil lands for the Santa Fe Railroad and opened several new oil fields in California. Doheny enhanced his reputation in the industry when he expanded his exploration efforts in Mexico. His Mexican Oil Company was the first to produce large quantities of oil from Mexican oil fields, and production from his Huasteca Petroleum Company made him the world's largest crude oil producer. Doheny was a Democrat and a large contributor to Woodrow Wilson's successful presidential campaigns in 1912 and 1916. During World War I, Doheny was a member of the National Petroleum War Services Committee, which coordinated the nation's oil resources during the war. During the period of the Harding administration, Doheny was placed in the national spotlight as a result of the Teapot Dome scandal. The scandal involved oilmen such as Doheny and Henry Sinclair securing leases on federal oil lands in Wyoming and California from Interior Secretary Albert Fall, who received nearly $400,000 from the oil producers. Doheny's leases were eventually voided by a federal judge as a result of his relationship with Fall. He was acquitted of having conspired to defraud the government, but his legal problems persisted, and he sold all of his Mexican oil lands and much of his California property by 1927. Though Fall was convicted of taking a bribe from Doheny, Doheny was acquitted of offering a bribe. Despite his acquittal, Doheny's reputation was irreparably damaged by the oil lease scandal.

Dual Federalism

Dual federalism is a concept that views the federal and state levels of government as coequals. It is based on the Tenth Amendment, which "reserves" to the states all powers not assigned to the national government. The doctrine of dual federalism evolved under Chief Justice Roger B. Taney, a strong advocate of states' rights. Proponents of the dual federalism doctrine saw the delegated powers of the national government in the narrowest terms. They viewed the reserve clause of the Tenth Amendment as a source of power for the states through which national authority may be substantially limited. The doctrine of dual federalism was a response to the national supremacy orientation of the Supreme Court under John Marshall. The doctrine gained dominance in the 1840s and remained an often-decisive factor in cases for almost a century. From the outset, it limited the exercise of national power when areas reserved to the states were affected. The Supreme Court integrated federalism arguments with laissez-faire economic thought around the turn of the century to effectively bar government regulation of private property. An example of the Court's use of this approach is *Hammer v. Dagenhart* (1918), in which the Court struck down a federal law prohibiting the shipment in interstate commerce of any goods produced by child labor. The Court said that even the exercise of the explicitly delegated commerce power was "not intended to destroy the local power always existing and carefully reserved to the states." The struggle over the New Deal initiatives ultimately led to the abandonment of the doctrine, at least as originally advanced by Taney.

Esch-Cummins Transportation Act of 1920

Esch-Cummins was a federal statute that returned the nation's railroads to private management following World War I and reaffirmed the regulatory authority of the Interstate Commerce Commission (ICC) to initiate, modify, and adjust rates so that railroads would earn a "fair return" for their services. The act contained provisions enabling the ICC to recover a portion of railroad profits in excess of 6 percent and redistribute those funds to railroads whose profits fell below 4.5 percent. In what was probably the most important feature of the act, the ICC was directed to work toward the consolidation of the railroads into a limited number of national systems. The ICC did not achieve that result. Instead, the ICC allowed the railroads broad latitude in setting financial polices and let the railroads control establishment of a national railway system (Kelly, Harbison, and Belz 1991, 458–461).

Fall, Albert B. (1861–1944)

President Warren G. Harding's secretary of the interior who was forced to resign following the Teapot Dome oil-lease scandal. Fall read law and began a law practice in the New Mexico Territory. Fall became involved in mining endeavors, where he met Edward L. Doheny, who would later achieve prominence in the oil industry. In 1887 Fall moved to Las Cruces, New Mexico, where he practiced law. Initially a Democrat, Fall served in several capacities in the New Mexico Territory—in its legislature and on its supreme court, as solicitor general and as a delegate to the constitutional convention of 1910. When New Mexico achieved statehood, he served as one of its first U.S. senators. During this period, Fall changed his partisan affiliation and actively supported Theodore Roosevelt's presidential bid in 1904. A decade later, Fall was one of the Senate's most outspoken critics of President Woodrow Wilson's foreign policy. He strongly supported U.S. intervention in Mexico and, following World War I, opposed ratification of the Treaty of Versailles and American membership in the proposed League of Nations. When President Warren G. Harding invited him to head the Department of the Interior, Fall accepted, although he had seriously considered leaving public service. His two years in the Cabinet were conflict filled; he battled not only other administration officials but outside groups, especially conservationists, as well. Fall persuaded Harding to transfer the naval oil reserve lands from the Navy Department to the Interior Department. Transfer of these lands to Fall's control allowed him to lease the Teapot Dome (Wyoming) and Elk Hills (California) reserves to petroleum magnates Harry F. Sinclair and Edward Doheny in exchange for nearly $400,000. Fall resigned from the Cabinet in March 1923 in the wake of the Senate investigation of the leases to private oil producers. Doheny and Sinclair were subsequently required to return the naval oil lands to the government, and Fall was convicted of bribery in 1929 for accepting money from Doheny. The conviction of Fall was the only successful prosecution in the various criminal cases stemming from the oil-lease scandal. Fall spent nine months in jail in 1931–1932, having the dubious distinction of being the first U.S. Cabinet member imprisoned for a felony committed in office.

Federalism

A political system in which a number of political units are joined into a larger political unit that has authority to act on behalf of the whole describes federalism. A federal system or federation preserves the political integrity or sovereignty of all the entities in the federation. Common usage equates the term *federal* with the central or national government, even though the term *federal government* technically includes both levels of government. In a federalist system authority is divided such that the national level of government retains ultimate power on at least some policy issues. Similarly, the constituent units (or states or provinces) must retain ultimate authority over at least one issue. If one level is completely without any authority, federalism cannot exist. Authority may be shared by the two levels and exercised concurrently, but the supremacy clause of Article VI of the U.S. Constitution requires that conflicts arising from the exercise of federal and state power are resolved in favor of the central government. Powers not assigned to the central government are "reserved" for the states by the Tenth Amendment.

Federalism is one structural device the framers of the Constitution utilized to minimize concentration of governmental power. The separation of powers principle assigns government functions to three branches of government: legislative, executive, and judicial. Federalism overlays the functional separation of powers with a territorial division of power. Among the consequences of federalism is that laws and policies may differ from state to state. Federalism invites the possibility of diverse or nonuniform policies at the state level as each exercises its sovereign power as it sees fit.

Four Horsemen

This nickname was used to describe the four ultraconservative Supreme Court justices who sat on the Taft and Hughes Courts. The first of the Four Horsemen, Willis Van Devanter, was appointed to the Court by President William Howard Taft in 1910. A nominee of President Woodrow Wilson, James McReynolds joined the Court in 1914. The third and fourth Horsemen were George Sutherland and Pierce Butler, both of whom were put on the Court in 1922 by President Warren G. Harding. The Horsemen were known as unyielding advocates of substantive due process, and they categorically rejected the economic and social initiatives of the New Deal.

Fuller, Melville W. (1833–1910)

Fuller was Supreme Court chief justice from 1888–1910. Born in Augusta, Maine, Fuller graduated from Bowdoin College and read law in his uncle's office prior to attending Harvard Law School for six months. Fuller was admitted to the Maine Bar in 1855. The following year, Fuller moved to Chicago where he remained until his appointment to the Supreme Court in 1888. Shortly after moving to Chicago, Fuller became involved in Democratic politics in Illinois and actively supported Stephen Douglas's U.S. Senate campaign against Abraham Lincoln. Two years later, Fuller was involved in Douglas's unsuccessful bid for the presidency. In 1862 Fuller served as a delegate to the Illinois constitutional convention and was elected to the Illinois House of Representatives the following year.

Fuller's law practice prospered and by the mid-1880s Fuller was a highly sought-after attorney in the Chicago area. When Chief Justice Morrison R. Waite died in March 1888, President Grover Cleveland nominated Fuller to be the next chief justice. Fuller was the first person to be formally commissioned "Chief Justice of the United States." Fuller never claimed intellectual leadership of the Court, but was an extraordinary administrator. Central to Fuller's jurisprudence was a commitment to states' rights. In his view, the Fourteenth Amendment had made "no revolutionary change" in American federalism and he rejected the argument that the Fourteenth Amendment made Bill of Rights guarantees binding on the states. Fuller also supported the "separate-but-equal" doctrine in *Plessy v. Ferguson* (1896). Fuller subscribed to the doctrine of substantive due process as a limit on both federal and state government power to regulate the economy and he was part of the Court's majority in cases such as *Lochner v. New York*

(1905). Fuller wrote the Court's opinion in *United States v. E.C. Knight Co.* (1895), in which the Court distinguished between production and commerce and concluded that the Sugar Trust was not subject to the Sherman Anti-Trust Act because it was a production monopoly. In *Loewe v. Lawlor* (1908), however, Fuller offered the rationale for the Court's conclusion that labor unions were subject to the Sherman Anti-Trust Act provisions. Fuller also authored the Court's opinion in *Pollock v. Farmers' Loan & Trust Co.* (1895), holding a federal income tax invalid as a prohibited direct tax.

Gitlow, Benjamin (1891–1965)

Gitlow was one of the founders of the Communist Party in the United States. Gitlow grew up in poverty in New York City. He was a member of the Socialist Party in 1909 and, for a time, headed the Retail Clerks Union of New York. He was nominated by the Socialist Party to run for the state assembly in 1917 and was one of several Socialists elected to office that year. The Russian Revolution in late 1917 prompted Gitlow to join the more militant faction of the Socialist Party. Within two years, Gitlow participated in the formation of the Communist Labor Party. As a result of his work with the Party's publication, *Revolutionary Age*, Gitlow was arrested for advocating communism and indicted under New York's Criminal Anarchy Act. His conviction was upheld by the Supreme Court in November 1925. After a trip to Moscow in 1929, Gitlow and others left the American Communist Party to organize the Communist Party, U.S.A. Gitlow unsuccessfully attempted to coalesce the various factions of communist organizations and subsequently decided to rejoin the Socialist Party. Gitlow gradually moved away from the militant political left and eventually retired from the political stage altogether. He published an autobiography before his death in 1965 that substantially repudiated the communist movement.

Gompers, Samuel (1850–1924)

Gompers was cofounder and president of the American Federation of Labor. He was born in a working-class neighborhood of London and immigrated to the United States with his family in 1863, where he and his father found work rolling cigars in New York City. He achieved "skilled" worker status and remained employed in the industry for almost twenty years. Gompers initially showed little interest in the labor movement, but was eventually introduced to a number of political economists such as Karl Marx. Gompers joined a small group of skilled workers from different trades who regularly discussed the interests of workers and the idea of trade unionism, which led him to active membership in the Cigarmakers International Union. Gompers thought political action was premature and counterproductive until workers gained greater consciousness of their group identity. Accordingly, he refused to engage unions in political campaigns of candidates for public office. By the early 1880s, Gompers had established a national reputation as a labor leader. In 1881 he helped establish the Federation of Organized Trades and Labor Unions, which subsequently became the American Federation of Labor (AFL). Gompers was elected president of the AFL in 1886, a position he held until his death in 1924. In the early 1890s he actively sought to bring the railroad unions and some of their more visible leaders such as Eugene V. Debs into the AFL. Labor achieved some notable political successes during the administration of Woodrow Wilson, including the appointment of a former union official to lead the Department of Labor. In addition, Congress enacted a number of federal laws such as the Clayton Anti-Trust Act, which protected unions from regulation under the Sherman Act. During this period AFL membership grew dramatically, and American involvement in World War I prompted more growth and enhanced organized labor's relationship with the federal government. The influence of organized labor on the federal government diminished greatly once the Republicans won the White House in 1920. Gompers rejected the candidacies of both major parties' tickets in 1924 and supported Senator Robert La Follette and the Progressive Party. Gompers died about a month after the 1924 election.

Great Depression

A depression is an economic slump that typically occurs when production facilities and credit have been overextended. The United States has suffered several depressions, but none worse than the Great Depression of the 1930s. Most mark the beginning of the Great Depression with the crash of the stock market in October 1929. Once started, the Great Depression impacted the entire country and produced such catastrophic consequences as lost savings, bankruptcies, failed banks, rising debt, declining purchases, diminished production, job layoffs, and diminished real estate values. The Hoover administration initially underestimated the seriousness of the Depression and, as a result, was largely ineffective in responding to it. The Great Depression brought about the realignment of political party affiliation, which, in turn, resulted in the election of Franklin Roosevelt and a Democratic majority in Congress in 1932. In the first 100 days of Roosevelt's administration, the Congress enacted several far-reaching economic regulatory initiatives, components of Roosevelt's New Deal program. Despite the extensive governmental activity, the Great Depression did not fully end until the American economy geared up for World War II.

Hand, Learned (1872–1961)

Hand was a distinguished federal judge who graduated from Harvard Law School in 1896. He pursued a private practice in Albany, New York, before moving to New York

City in 1902. He found the practice of law largely unrewarding, but regularly contributed articles to law journals. These efforts established Hand as a recognized legal scholar and prompted him to pursue a judicial career. In 1909 President William Howard Taft nominated Hand for a federal district court judgeship. In his early years as a judge Hand retained his political interests, and was an enthusiastic supporter of Theodore Roosevelt's presidential candidacy in 1912. He was also involved in founding the *New Republic* magazine and frequently contributed articles to it. In the succeeding years, Hand concluded that such activities were inappropriate and he ended his participation in discussion of controversial public policy issues. Hand was elevated to the Court of Appeals for the Second Circuit by President Calvin Coolidge in 1924. Hand became the Second Circuit's chief judge in 1939 and served in that capacity until he retired in 1951. He was considered several times for elevation to the Supreme Court, but despite his strong credentials, was never nominated. Hand wrote the Court of Appeals's opinion that provided the foundation for the Supreme Court's ruling in *Dennis v. United States* (1951), which upheld the Smith Act convictions of twelve leaders of the Communist Party of the United States.

Harding, Warren G. (1865–1923)

Harding was the twenty-ninth president of the United States. He was born in Blooming Grove, Ohio, in 1865. He became owner-editor of the *Marion Star* in 1884, and was prominently involved in local political and civic activities and closely affiliated with the conservative faction of the Ohio Republican Party. He was elected to the state senate in 1899 and served two terms. During his second term in the state senate, Harding sought the Republican nomination for governor, but instead accepted the nomination for lieutenant governor. He was the nominee for governor of the badly divided Republican Party in 1910, but was defeated. Harding nominated President William Howard Taft at the Republican National Convention in 1912, and two years later Harding was elected to the U.S. Senate. While the United States participated in World War I, Harding generally supported Wilson's war-related initiatives. At the end of the war, however, he became a leading critic of Wilson and such postwar proposals as the League of Nations. He favored women's suffrage, national prohibition, and federal legislation returning the railroads to private management.

Harding was not a leading contender for the presidential nomination at the Republican convention of 1920, but a deadlock allowed Harding to emerge as the compromise nominee. He conducted the 1920 campaign from his home in Marion, Ohio (his "front porch" campaign), and called for an end to the regulations adopted during the war and abandonment of the progressive agenda carried over from the Wilson presidency. Instead, Harding called for a return to "normalcy." He was elected president in November 1920 by a wide margin. As he organized his administration,

Harding selected both highly qualified people as well as cronies from the "Ohio gang." In the former category were Treasury Secretary Andrew W. Mellon, Commerce Secretary Herbert Hoover, and Secretary of State Charles Evans Hughes. Included in the latter group was Attorney General Harry Daugherty, who became a central figure in the oil-lease scandals during Harding's presidency. Historians generally regard the Harding presidency as a "failure" not only because of the scandals, but because of personal characteristics that revealed Harding's inability to cope with the demands of presidential leadership. Harding died on August 2, 1923, as he concluded a trip to the West Coast. He was succeeded by Vice President Calvin Coolidge.

Hoover, Herbert Clark (1874–1964)

Herbert Hoover was the thirtieth president of the United States. Hoover's first public service came as he directed the nation's rationing program during World War I. He was sought by both major parties as a presidential nominee in 1920, but he chose not to run. Instead, Hoover served as secretary of commerce during the administrations of Warren G. Harding and Calvin Coolidge. When President Coolidge declined renomination in 1928, Hoover became the GOP standard-bearer and defeated Alfred Smith in the general election. The overriding problem Hoover faced during his presidency was the catastrophic Depression that began near the end of his first year in office. Hoover did not accurately gauge the severity of the economic emergency and his initial response called for largely local and voluntary remedies. When it became clear that this strategy was insufficient, Hoover turned to federally mandated programs. The Democratic Congress enacted the Federal Economic Stabilization Act of 1931, a measure Hoover supported, albeit reluctantly. The act created a board with the authority to distribute federal money through public-works jobs. The Emergency and Relief Construction Act of 1932 also financed public-works projects but directed federal funds to state programs designed to address the effects of the Depression. Hoover's principal recovery initiative was the Reconstruction Finance Corporation headed by Charles Dawes. Economic conditions made it impossible for Hoover to win reelection in 1932 and he was decisively beaten by Franklin Roosevelt. Hoover did not seek public office again and spent the remainder of his life advocating policies that would not require sending American troops abroad. He opposed American membership in the NATO alliance, American participation in the Korean War, and American Cold War policy. His last public activity was to head a commission known as the Hoover Commission, which examined options for reorganization of the executive branch of the Federal Government.

Hughes, Charles Evans (1862–1948)

Hughes was a Supreme Court chief justice, governor of New York, and a presidential candidate. Hughes graduated first in his class at Columbia Law School and set a record high score on the New York Bar exam. He was admitted to the New York Bar in 1884 at the age of twenty-two. He had a highly successful private practice that specialized in corporate law. At the same time, he developed a reputation for "busting" monopolies. His high profile and his independence led to his election as governor of New York in 1906. Four years later, Hughes was nominated to the Supreme Court by President William H. Taft. Hughes resigned from the Court in 1916 to run against President Woodrow Wilson. Following his unsuccessful presidential campaign, Hughes returned to his law practice, but continued his public life as well. He served as secretary of state under Presidents Warren Harding and Calvin Coolidge until 1925 and strongly supported American participation in the League of Nations and the International Court of Justice. President Hoover nominated Hughes to succeed William Howard Taft as chief justice in 1930. His nomination was vigorously opposed by progressives and twenty-six senators ultimately opposed his confirmation, while another eighteen abstained. Hughes initially aligned himself with the conservative bloc in striking down both federal and state economic recovery measures. When President Franklin Roosevelt proposed "packing" the Court in 1937 by adding new justices, Hughes communicated his disapproval of the proposal to the Senate Judiciary Committee, an action that contributed to the proposal's defeat. Hughes changed his voting behavior following the "court-packing" episode and, with Justice Owen Roberts, became more receptive to an expanded governmental role in the national economy. Hughes was inclined to support social legislation enacted by states and he recognized broad congressional authority to regulate interstate commerce, at least after 1937. Most regard Hughes's judicial career as distinguished. His opinions remain highly regarded and he displayed extraordinary administrative abilities as chief justice. He left the Court in 1941 and died seven years later in Cape Cod, Massachusetts.

International Court of Justice

Often called the World Court, the International Court of Justice is the highest judicial agency of the United Nations and provides a means of resolving international legal disputes. It has jurisdiction over cases brought by nations or organizations and its decisions are based on established principles of international law. The Court hears relatively few cases and no nation can be compelled to appear before it. Nonetheless, a large number of nations, including the United States, have agreed generally to accept the Court's jurisdiction. The United Nations General Assembly and Security Council elect the fifteen members of the Court who may serve for a term of nine years. It currently has headquarters at The Hague in the Netherlands. The League of Nations established the Permanent Court of International Justice in December 1920, which was reorganized and renamed the International Court of Justice by the United Nations Charter in 1945.

Isolationism

Isolationism is a foreign policy based on the view that the United States ought not to be involved in the affairs of other nations. The United States pursued such a policy from the mid-1800s into the early twentieth century. Isolationism defined American foreign policy and was designed to keep the United States out of European power struggles. This outlook prompted the American public's belief that the United States should maintain neutrality during the early stages of both World War I and World War II and not join the League of Nations. The isolationist influence was evident in the 1930s as Congress passed a series of federal laws requiring American neutrality. The Neutrality Act of 1935, for example, required an embargo on most war-related items and banned the arming of U.S. merchant ships. After the German invasion of Poland in September 1939, an arms embargo was imposed on U.S. allies as well as the Axis powers. The Lend-Lease Act of 1941 repealed much of the Neutrality Act's provisions and authorized President Franklin Roosevelt to supply any materials necessary to the defense of any nation determined to be essential to U.S. security. Following World War II, the United States moved away from an isolationism-based foreign policy and did not return to it for the remainder of the twentieth century.

Johnson, Hiram (1866–1945)

Johnson was a U.S. senator born in Sacramento, California, in 1866. Johnson entered the University of California at Berkeley in 1884 and, after studying law in his father's office, was admitted to the bar in 1888. He moved to San Francisco, where he became a prominent trial attorney. In 1906 and 1907 he served as assistant district attorney in several political corruption cases that attracted the attention of progressive Republicans who convinced Johnson to run for governor in 1910. He was elected and immediately pursued a reform agenda that included regulation of railroads and other public utilities, stringent conservation of natural resources, and women's suffrage. Johnson was a supporter of Theodore Roosevelt in 1912, and left the Republican Party when Roosevelt failed to capture the party's presidential nomination. He helped establish the Progressive Party, which nominated Roosevelt for the presidency and selected Johnson as his running mate. He returned to the Republican Party for his successful U.S. Senate run in 1916. Johnson voted to declare war on Germany, but was otherwise critical of Wilson's foreign policy priorities. Following the war, Johnson was one of the "Irreconcilables"—a group of senators who categorically opposed American entry into the League of Nations. He was located to the political left of most members of Congress and favored, among other things, government ownership of the railroads and graduated income taxes. Johnson sought the Republican presidential nomination in 1920, but his persistent criticism of party conservatives prevented his nomination. Throughout the 1920s Johnson continued to oppose the League of Nations and American participation in the World Court. He voted against confirming both William Howard Taft and Charles Evans Hughes as chief justice. He won reelection to the Senate in 1922, but his unyielding commitment to isolationism eroded some of his support. Harding's death prompted Johnson to again seek the Republican presidential nomination in 1924, but he was unsuccessful. He supported neither Republican Calvin Coolidge nor Progressive Robert La Follette in the general election. His major political opponent in California was Herbert Hoover, and his criticism of Hoover continued after Hoover was elected president in 1928. Johnson was urged by both Republicans and Progressives to seek the Republican nomination in 1932, but he refused and eventually supported Franklin Roosevelt. He declined Roosevelt's invitation to head the Interior Department, preferring to stay in the Senate. He generally supported Roosevelt's New Deal program, and Roosevelt found him a valuable adviser. Roosevelt endorsed his Senate reelection bid in 1934, and Johnson became the nominee of both the Republicans and Democrats. The following year, Johnson led the successful fight against the administration's proposal to join the World Court and, along with other isolationists, supported legislation aimed at maintaining American neutrality. Despite failing health, Johnson sought reelection to the Senate in 1940 and was again the nominee of both major parties. He opposed Roosevelt seeking a third term and although he had some policy disagreements with the Republican presidential nominee Wendell Willkie, Johnson campaigned on Willkie's behalf. Declining health limited his activities thereafter and he cast his final Senate vote against American participation in the United Nations in 1945.

Johnson-Reed Immigration Act of 1924

The United States began to restrict immigration in 1921 by establishing a ceiling on annual immigration from any European country. President Calvin Coolidge and Congress shared the view that "America must be kept American," and Congress made the restrictions permanent in the Johnson-Reed Immigration Act of 1924. Congressman Albert Johnson developed support for the law by appealing to anti-Japanese sentiments particularly. He chaired the House Committee on Immigration and hired two eugenicists as consultants to the committee. These consultants believed that the purpose of immigration laws was to preserve racial purity. Acting on this view, the initial proposal called for an outright ban on Japanese immigration. Historians have regarded the exclusion of the Japanese as "turn[ing] the Japanese government toward aggression and resulted in the 1941 attack on Pearl Harbor" (Ferrell 1998, 115). The bill as initially proposed by Johnson was too discriminatory for the Senate to adopt and it chose instead to pass a proposal written by Senator David Reed that established a ceiling of 150,000 on all transatlantic immigration and apportioned this figure according to the "national origins" of the present white population. Although the national dynamics that prompted the Johnson-Reed Act had existed for a long period of time, passage of the act reflected serious reservations about the nation's capacity to absorb a steady stream of people from diverse ethnic, religious, and cultural backgrounds (Parrish 1992, 112–113).

Judicial Conference and Transfer Act

This act, passed in 1922, created the Judicial Conference of the United States, a body originally known as the Conference of Senior Circuit Judges. The Conference was the first significant attempt to centralize authority in the federal judicial system. Chaired by the chief justice, the Judicial Conference consists of the chief judges of the courts of appeals, a district judge from each circuit except the Federal Circuit, and the chief judge of the Court of International Trade. The Judicial Conference was created to be the chief administrative policy maker for the federal judiciary, although it turned out to be only a first step toward a more integrated administrative system. The position of the chief justice was strengthened because the many committees operating within the Conference report to him or her. The extensive use of committee made the Conference essentially a ratifying body for policies recommended by the committees. Such policies covered a wide variety of matters, including rules of evidence and procedure for the federal courts, the transfer of judges, and the need for additional federal judges. The Conference also produced recommendations for legislation to be submitted to Congress. The Judicial Conference remains a significant influence on the administration of the federal judiciary.

Judiciary Act (also called the "Judges" Bill) of 1925

The Judiciary Act of 1925 expanded the Supreme Court's discretionary jurisdiction by requiring that the bulk of the Court's docket come to the Court as petitions for writs of certiorari, which the Court could reject without reaching any decision on the merits (Baum 2001, 124). The passage of the Judges Bill, legislation advocated by Chief Justice William H. Taft, culminated a "calculated effort" by Congress to transform the Supreme Court from an appellate tribunal to a court with a policy-making role. The act gave the Supreme Court the power to determine its docket. Certiorari review takes place on the affirmative vote of four justices, a number chosen by Congress to assure that the Court would not become too restrictive as it utilized greater control over its docket (Pritchett 1984, 115).

Kellogg, Frank B. (1856–1937)

Kellogg was a U.S. senator and secretary of state born in Potsdam, New York, in 1856. His family moved to Olmstead County, Minnesota, where he was admitted to the bar in 1877. During his successful private law practice, Kellogg engaged extensively in litigation involving railroads and the iron-mining industry, and he came to know such prominent business figures as the Rockefellers, Andrew Carnegie, and railroad builder James J. Hill. He also developed a friendship with Theodore Roosevelt, and when Roosevelt became president, Kellogg had ready access to the White House. He was appointed special assistant attorney general and successfully took on the paper trust. He subsequently led Sherman Anti-Trust Act actions against the Union Pacific Railroad and Standard Oil Company. In 1912 he became president of the American Bar Association and four years later entered the political arena with his successful candidacy for the U.S. Senate seat from Minnesota. Kellogg served only one term in the Senate, but made his mark by supporting the Treaty of Versailles despite the opposition of fellow Republicans known as the "Irreconcilables." Kellogg was a friend of President Calvin Coolidge, who first appointed him ambassador to London in 1923 and then secretary of state in March 1925. Kellogg's principal achievement as secretary of state was the Kellogg-Briand Pact of 1928, for which he was awarded the 1929 Nobel Peace Prize.

Kellogg-Briand Pact

The Kellog-Briand Pact was a treaty concluded in 1928 that sought to outlaw war as an instrument of foreign policy. Officially titled the General Treaty for the Renunciation of War, the pact was originally proposed by French foreign minister Aristide Briand as a treaty between France and the United States. U.S. Secretary of State Frank B. Kellogg enlarged the plan to include all nations. The pact, also known as the Pact of Paris, was signed by fifteen nations in Paris, France, on 27 August 1928. By 1934 sixty-four nations had signed the pact. The pact provided that the signatories "condemn recourse to war for the solution to international controversies, and renounce it as an instrument of national policy in their relations with one another." In addition, the pact provided that the "settlement or solution of all disputes or conflicts, of whatever nature or of whatever origin . . . shall never be sought except by pacific means." The pact was an attempt to work within the peacekeeping system of the League of Nations, and it gave the United States, which had refused to join the League, an opportunity generally to condemn war. Among the pact's defects were its failure to distinguish wars of aggression from wars of national defense and to provide no method to enforce its provisions. The pact's failure to provide enforcement measures seriously compromised its objective of preventing war. Although the pact technically remains in effect, it has never made a significant contribution to maintaining international peace.

La Follette, Robert M. (1855–1925)

La Follette was a Wisconsin governor, U.S. senator, and Progressive Party presidential candidate. He graduated from the University of Wisconsin in 1879 and was admitted to the Wisconsin Bar a year later. La Follette was the successful Republican candidate for district attorney of Dane County, Wisconsin, in 1880. Four years later he was elected to the U.S. House of Representatives, where he served on the Ways and Means Committee chaired by William McKinley. A Democratic landslide in 1890 resulted in his losing his House seat. He returned to Madison, Wisconsin, and established a successful law practice. During the economic depression of the mid-1890s, La Follette's political ideology underwent significant change. Drawing from the objectives of the reform movement, he assembled a political coalition of farmers, laborers, and small businessmen and become a leading advocate of the progressive reform movement. He unsuccessfully sought the Republican nomination for governor in 1896 and 1898, but won the governorship in 1900. He stimulated a grassroots movement to elect a more progressive legislature and to support his own reelection in 1902 and 1904. With the support of the state legislature, La Follette was able to secure such progressive priorities as the direct primary, tax reform, and consumer protection. After La Follette won an unprecedented third election as governor in 1904, the state legislature elected him U.S. senator in 1905. One of his first senatorial battles involved a proposal designed to give the Interstate Commerce Commission power to regulate railroad rates. La Follette opposed the measure because he felt it was too weak. President Theodore Roosevelt strongly supported the proposal and their disagreement was the beginning of an intense personal rivalry. La Follette assumed leadership over the insurgent Republican bloc in the Senate in early 1909 and two years later was instrumental in the founding of the National Progressive Republican League. The League became the vehicle for La Follette's unsuccessful quest for the Republican presidential nomination in 1912. La Follette voted against American entry into the First World War, opposed conscription, and was highly critical of wartime restrictions on free expression. He joined Senator Henry Cabot Lodge and other Republicans to defeat the Treaty of Versailles and American entry into the League of Nations. La Follette ran for president as the nominee of the Progressive Party in 1924 against the Republican incumbent Calvin Coolidge and the Democrat John Davis. He won almost five million votes, but carried only his home state of Wisconsin. As a result of his Progressive Party candidacy, he lost the chairmanship of his Senate committee in 1925. He died later that year. In 1957 La Follette was selected as one of the five most significant members to serve in the U.S. Senate.

Laissez-faire

Laissez-faire, a French term for "allow to do," refers to an economic theory that underlies the basic principles of capitalism. Laissez-faire rejects state-imposed economic controls, calling instead for a market-driven economy with natural economic laws guiding the production and consumption of goods. Tariffs and other trade restrictions are rejected in favor of a worldwide system of free trade. The economic system becomes self-regulatory in nature and each individual's pursuit of self-interest contributes to the well-being of all. The theory was widely accepted in the Western world during the eighteenth and nineteenth centuries. Laissez-faire was, at least in part, a reaction to governmental imposition of extensive production and trade restrictions. Laissez-faire was abandoned as the basis of national economics in the United States in the 1930s and the government's role in economic affairs has expanded since then.

League of Nations

An international organization established at the end of the First World War to preserve peace and security and to promote economic and social cooperation among its members. A covenant included in the Treaty of Versailles served as the foundation for the organization. The League Covenant set forth principles intended to guide the actions of League members. The covenant also provided for the establishment of a decision-making process and established the procedures under which preservation of international peace and cooperation might be achieved. President Woodrow Wilson provided the leadership in developing the League and chaired the committee that wrote the Covenant, but was unable to persuade the isolationist majority in the U.S. Senate to ratify the treaty and with it membership in the League. A Council and Assembly, resembling the Security Council and General Assembly of the current United Nations, were the major components of the League's structure. The League's covenant tried to make war illegal under most circumstances, but the organization failed to take collective action following acts of aggression by Germany, Italy, Japan, and the Soviet Union in the 1930s. The League experience was valuable in fashioning the United Nations, which formally replaced the League in 1946.

Lever Act of 1917

The Lever Act was a war power measure that gave the federal government authority to deal with food and fuel supplies and prices during World War I. The food and fuel industries were determined to be so essential to the national interest that they must be subjected to federal regulation. The Lever Act, which took effect on 10 August 1917, made it unlawful to "waste, monopolize, fix prices, or limit production of foodstuffs." The executive branch was authorized to license the manufacture and distribution of food and to regulate markets where food was bought and sold. The president was authorized to impose price controls on any industry to meet "extreme emergencies." The Lever Act was designed primarily to control food and fuel production, but its terms were "so broad as to subject virtually the entire economic life of the nation to whatever regulation the president thought necessary for victory in World War I" (Kelly, Harbison, and Belz 1991, 433–434).

Liberty of Contract

A legal doctrine used to free private agreements from governmental regulation. The doctrine of liberty or freedom of contract was a central element of substantive due process in which the judiciary closely scrutinized the reasonableness of legislative enactments. The doctrine suggests that individuals have a right to enter into contracts about such matters as hours and working conditions and the wages paid for such work. The doctrine was used by the Supreme Court to invalidate minimum wage and maximum hours laws as impermissible interference with employers' and employees' right to contract. The liberty-of-contract doctrine was drawn from the Court's interpretation of the Due Process Clause of the Fourteenth Amendment and derived from laissez-faire economics. It was extensively used by the Supreme Court to strike down regulatory state legislation. In *Lochner v. New York* (1905), for example, the Court struck down a maximum hours-of-work law. The Court ruled that the hour limit interfered with the employer's right to "make contracts in relation to his own business," while the employee lost his right to sell his labor through an agreement with his employer. The doctrine was largely abandoned with the demise of substantive due process in the 1930s.

Lodge, Henry Cabot (1850–1924)

Lodge was a Republican U.S. senator from Massachusetts. He graduated from Harvard College in 1871 and received his law degree two years later. In 1876 he earned his Ph.D. in history. At the urging of his academic mentor, Lodge became involved in politics. Lodge was elected to the lower house of the Massachusetts General Court in

1880. After failing to win a U.S. House of Representatives seat in 1884, he ran successfully two years later and served there until his election to the U.S. Senate in 1893. Lodge was basically conservative on domestic issues during his Senate tenure, but was more interested in foreign affairs. He fully supported American involvement in the Spanish-American War and the subsequent annexation of Puerto Rico and the Philippines. He supported most of President Theodore Roosevelt's progressive domestic initiatives, but opposed proposals calling for such reforms as the direct election of senators. Lodge was a leading supporter of Roosevelt's foreign policy objectives, such as maintaining an "Open Door" policy in China and the construction of a canal across Central America. When World War I broke out, Lodge thought the United States should remain neutral. When President Woodrow Wilson asked Congress to declare war in April 1917, however, Lodge voted to do so and subsequently supported most of the Wilson administration's war policies. Lodge generally agreed with the results achieved at the Paris Peace Conference following World War I. He strongly objected, however, to the provisions about the proposed League of Nations. When the Versailles Treaty came to the Senate, Lodge, who was chair of the Senate Foreign Relations Committee, offered a number of "reservations" to the League provisions. The treaty was subsequently rejected in November 1919 and again in March 1920. His role in the defeat of the League almost cost him his Senate seat, but he won reelection to the Senate by 7,000 votes. Lodge's last significant public service was as a delegate to the Washington Disarmament Conference called by President Warren G. Harding in 1922. He died less than two years later.

McKinley, William (1843–1901)

The twenty-fifth president of the United States was born in Niles, Ohio, in 1843. He studied briefly at Allegheny College, but illness and financial problems forced him to leave school in less than a year. McKinley was a member of the Ohio Infantry during the Civil War and studied law until his admission to the Ohio Bar in 1867. He practiced law in Canton, Ohio, and became active in Republican politics. He was elected prosecuting attorney in 1869 and was elected to Congress in 1876. He became a leader of the economic nationalists that advocated protective tariffs. As chairman of the Ways and Means Committee, he was responsible for drafting what became known as the McKinley Tariff of 1890. The tariff proved unpopular, however, and resulted in extensive Republican losses in Congress in the 1890 elections. Indeed, McKinley himself was one of the casualties. A year later, McKinley was elected governor of Ohio. In 1894 he made numerous appearances for Republican congressional candidates across the country and emerged as the Republican presidential nominee in 1896. McKinley conducted a successful "front porch" campaign from his Canton home and defeated William Jennings Bryan by about 600,000 votes nationally. He proved to be a forceful executive, traveling extensively on behalf of his policy agenda. The most important foreign policy issue McKinley faced was the rebellion against Spanish rule in Cuba. The explosion of the battleship USS *Maine* in the Havana harbor in 1898 led to the Spanish-American War. During the brief conflict, McKinley proved to be an effective commander in chief. The United States was victorious in the war, and the treaty ending the engagement included the ceding of the Philippines, Puerto Rico, and Guam to the United States. A McKinley priority was a canal across Central America, which was achieved under terms of the Hay-Pauncefote Treaty of 1901. Another of McKinley's foreign policy successes was the "Open Door" policy with China. The resurgence of the national economy and McKinley's foreign policy record led to his reelection in 1900. McKinley intended to push for stronger antitrust regulations and secure a number of reciprocal trade treaties during his second term, but he was assassinated in September 1901 while in Buffalo, New York.

McNary-Haugen Act

The McNary-Haugen Act called for subsidies to be paid to the growers of certain staple crops by a Federal Farm Board. The board was empowered to use federal money to buy and sell agricultural products and make crop loans to farm cooperatives. The act was passed by Congress in February 1927 as a result of persistent pressure from agricultural interests. President Calvin Coolidge vetoed the bill on several grounds: that its price-fixing provisions for commodities exceeded the scope of the federal commerce power; that it unlawfully put the federal government into the buying and selling of agricultural commodities; and that it failed to set operating guidelines for the Farm Board. In Coolidge's view, this kind of approach "jeopardized the agricultural industry by subjecting it to the tyranny of bureaucratic regulation and control." Further, by permitting farmers to determine when controls should be put into effect, the bill unconstitutionally delegated legislative authority to private individuals (Kelly, Harbison, and Belz 1991, 461–462).

Mellon, Andrew W. (1855–1937)

Mellon was a financier and secretary of the treasury in the Harding, Coolidge, and Hoover administrations. While a student at the Western University of Pennsylvania, he became acquainted with a number of influential Republican politicians in the state. Mellon left college before graduation to begin his business career as president of the family bank. Mellon expanded the bank and invested in a number of other businesses. By 1884 he had become president of Pittsburgh's Union Trust Company. Mellon helped found the Gulf Oil Corporation in 1901, and the following year the family bank became Mellon National Bank and evolved into an enormous holding company.

By 1910 Mellon had become the leading fundraiser for the Pennsylvania Republican Party. He contributed to Charles Evans Hughes's presidential campaign against Woodrow Wilson in 1916. After World War I Mellon helped finance the campaign that opposed U.S. participation in the League of Nations. When Warren G. Harding became president in 1921, he made Mellon his secretary of the treasury, a position Mellon retained in the Coolidge and Hoover administrations. His economic views defined Republican policies of the 1920s, but may also have led to investment speculation and inflation that contributed at least indirectly to the stock market crash of 1929. He served briefly as ambassador to Great Britain, but left the position while the subject of a conflict-of-interest investigation and resumed his duties as head of the Mellon Bank. In 1934 it was alleged that he had falsified information on his federal income tax returns, and the IRS sought more than $3 million in taxes and penalties. Mellon settled the claims against him by becoming the principal sponsor of the National Gallery of Art in Washington.

New Deal

The term used to refer to the legislative program of President Franklin Roosevelt designed to achieve national economic recovery following the Great Depression. The term "New Deal" was coined by Raymond Moley and first used by Roosevelt when he accepted the Democratic Party's nomination for president in 1932. The nation's economic problems in the early 1930s were extensive. The stock market crash of 1929 was only the beginning. Banks and businesses failed, farm property was foreclosed, and workers lost their jobs. Roosevelt viewed the economic crisis as a war. Using the wartime analogy, Roosevelt created an emergency or crisis-driven government through unilateral executive actions and executive leadership of Congress. Shortly after his inauguration, Roosevelt called Congress into special session, and what followed was a period of extraordinary legislative action that became known as the Hundred Days. The New Deal legislation contained a variety of measures initiated by Roosevelt, his political and economic advisers, and Congress itself. The first priority was stabilization of the banking industry. The Emergency Banking Act was passed on 9 March 1933, subjecting banks to federal regulation. In addition, the Federal Reserve Board was given authority to regulate lending practices and the Federal Deposit Insurance Corporation was created to insure bank deposits. The Securities Act imposed full disclosure requirements on the securities industry and the Securities and Exchange Commission was created to oversee the sale of securities.

The New Deal included measures impacting various sectors of the American economy and the needs of the unemployed. The Agricultural Adjustment Act was aimed at stabilizing commodity prices by regulating production. The National Industrial Recovery Act created the National Recovery Administration, which implemented "codes of practice" across a number of economic sectors. Included in the codes were minimum wage provisions and provisions supporting the right of workers to join labor unions. Relief for the unemployed was provided through several agencies, such as the Civilian Conservation Corps, Federal Relief Administration, and Public Works Administration. The hundred-day period ended in mid-June 1933. Many of the programs created by Congress during this period were subsequently struck down by the Hughes Court.

Normalcy

Warren G. Harding's 1920 presidential campaign promised an abandonment of the activism and idealism that characterized the presidencies of Theodore Roosevelt and Woodrow Wilson. Instead, Harding proposed that the country return "not to heroism but healing, not nostrums but normalcy." Among the components of Harding's "normalcy" was a categorical probusiness bias, an orientation that defined the 1920s and the presidencies of Harding, Calvin Coolidge, and Herbert Hoover (Trani and Wilson 1977, 101). The Republican platform of the 1920s was intended to take advantage of the national exhaustion with the war, the discord prominent at the end of Wilson's presidency, and the protracted battles over the League of Nations and political radicals. Harding's presidential candidacy seemed to "represent virtues dear to the American heart: simplicity, friendliness, generosity. He was a thoroughly commonplace person, without intellectual or social pretensions" (Morison, Commager, and Leuchtenburg 1980, 416).

Norris, George W. (1861–1947)

Norris was a U.S. representative and senator from Nebraska. Born in Sandusky County, Ohio, in 1861, Norris moved to Nebraska in 1885 after finishing law school to begin a law practice. His move to Nebraska took place when farmers throughout the country were experiencing very hard times and militant agrarian protests took place across the Midwest. Indeed, William Jennings Bryan, also from Nebraska, defined his populist political career on the agrarian discontent of the period. Although Norris would become a leading insurgent and progressive, in the 1880s he was a Republican who did not share Bryan's views or party affiliation. Norris became increasingly active politically and was elected prosecuting attorney and district judge in the 1890s. In 1902 he was elected to the U.S. House of Representatives, a position he held for five terms. In 1912 he was elected U.S. senator from Nebraska, and he served in that capacity for thirty years. Norris did not identify with the progressive movement at the outset of his congressional tenure, but gradually became more progressive in his outlook. His inordinate impact in the Congress stemmed from the committees on which he served, his understanding of the legislative process, and his extraordinary parliamentary skills. Norris was best know for his advocacy on domestic issues, but he also gained notoriety for his foreign policy positions. In April 1917, for example, he was one of only six senators who voted against declaration of war on Germany. Following the war, he voted against the Versailles Treaty and American membership in the League of Nations.

Senator Norris increasingly opposed the conservative Republican policies of the 1920s, and he ultimately supported the presidential candidacy of Democrat Al Smith in 1928. He strongly supported the McNary-Haugen farm bills vetoed by President Calvin Coolidge and opposed the Hoover administration's Agricultural Marketing Act of 1929. He also led the efforts for the federal government to move into the electric power business, which brought him into conflict with private utility companies and the Republican presidents of the 1920s. Although his efforts on behalf of public power were initially unsuccessful, his objectives were realized when Congress established the Tennessee Valley Authority in 1933 to produce public power in the following decade. Although Norris remained a Republican during this period, he endorsed Franklin Roosevelt's presidential candidacy in 1932. Throughout his years in the White House, Roosevelt frequently consulted with Norris on domestic policies. Norris voted for most of the New Deal legislation proposed by the Roosevelt administration and, unlike a number of the 1920s progressives, generally identified with the New Deal liberalism. He retained his isolationist views throughout this period but eventually supported a more significant American presence in world affairs. Although he opposed extension of the draft until the United States formally declared war, he supported Roosevelt's proposals for extending American aid to the European countries threatened by Axis aggression. Norris ran for a fifth term in 1936 as an Independent Progressive and reluctantly ran for a sixth term in 1942. In this final race, Norris did not actively campaign and was defeated. In a poll conducted in 1957, historians and political scientists across the country ranked Norris as the greatest senator in American history to that time.

Packers and Stockyards Act of 1921

This federal act placed interstate meat packers and stockyards under federal control. The act was adopted following congressional inquiry into the conditions in the meat industry. The act prohibited packers to engage in unfair, discriminatory, or deceptive market practices, and required all rates charged for handling livestock in the stockyards to be reasonable and fair. The secretary of agriculture was given authority to "enforce the law through cease-and-desist orders, subject to appeal to the courts." Congress later expanded federal regulation by authorizing the formation of agricultural producer associations and exempted them from the reach of federal antitrust laws (Kelly, Harbison, and Belz 1991, 459).

Palmer, A. Mitchell (1872–1936)

Palmer was a Pennsylvania congressman who later served as President Woodrow Wilson's attorney general. Palmer practiced law in Stroudsburg, Pennsylvania, where his family was active in Democratic politics. Palmer was elected to Congress in 1908 and became part of the Democratic leadership in the House of Representatives. Palmer was Woodrow Wilson's floor leader at the 1912 Democratic nominating convention and was offered a position in the Cabinet following Wilson's election. He declined in favor of remaining in Congress, where he sponsored a number of progressive proposals including the Child Labor Act, which was adopted after Palmer left the House. Palmer supported labor interests and was instrumental in drafting the Underwood Tariff Bill. Palmer intended to run for governor of Pennsylvania in 1914, but was persuaded by Wilson to run for the U.S. Senate instead. The bid for the Senate seat failed badly and Palmer resumed his law practice. Palmer returned to Washington in 1916 to administer enemy-owned property in the United States, but Wilson soon promoted Palmer to the position of attorney general. He was required to address a number of difficult issues including labor strikes and the threat posed by political radicals, and he did so by invoking executive war powers. He obtained injunctions against striking unions under the Lever Act and designated J. Edgar Hoover to assess the strength of radical political organizations in the country. He used provisions of the Immigration Act of 1917 to deport aliens advocating violence against the government. The arrest of more than 3,000 such aliens eventually led to the deportation of many. These arrests, known as "Palmer Raids," were considered by some to be most serious violation of civil liberties in U.S. history. Palmer was in the running for the Democratic presidential nomination in 1920, but lost support before the party convention. Among other things, his actions against union strikers made convention delegates fearful of losing critical labor support. Although he remained active in Democratic politics, Palmer was never again prominent on the national political stage.

Populism

A grassroots political action movement that had its origin in the agrarian discontent in the late nineteenth century became known as populism. The movement resulted in the emergence of the Populist Party, which favored, among other things, government ownership of railroads, an expanded supply of paper currency, elimination of corporate monopolies, and a graduated income tax. Populists supported the use of government power to subject large businesses and commerce to extensive regulation. Although the Populist Party failed to displace either of the major parties, its agenda was substantially incorporated into the Democratic Party's platform in 1896 and was fully embraced by its presidential nominee William Jennings Bryan. The populist movement was successful in securing economic and social programs aiding agrarian interests and antitrust legislation.

Progressivism/Progressive Party

The Progressive Era began as populism collapsed in the early twentieth century. Progressivism was a largely urban and middle-class movement that targeted many of the same political and economic "evils" identified by the populists. Progressivism had significant influence on the country because it broadened and redefined the agenda left by the populists. The Progressive Party was organized as a means to nominate candidates for public office, including the presidency. Progressive Party candidates typically stood for liberal social, political, and economic reform. The party was first established when President William Howard Taft was renominated in 1912 and supporters of Theodore Roosevelt broke away from the Republican Party. Roosevelt's Progressive (nicknamed the "Bull Moose") Party candidacy won more popular votes than Taft, but lost to the Democratic candidate, Woodrow Wilson. The Progressive Party was reconstituted in 1924 and nominated Senators Robert M. La Follette of Wisconsin and Burton K. Wheeler of Montana for its national ticket. The party captured almost five million votes nationwide, but did not present serious opposition to Republican president Calvin Coolidge. The Progressive Party reappeared at the national level in 1948 with the unsuccessful presidential candidacy of Henry A. Wallace, who served as vice president during Franklin Roosevelt's third term.

Prohibition

The Eighteenth Amendment was proposed in late December 1917, ratified on 16 January 1919, and took effect on 1 January 1920. The Eighteenth Amendment provided that within a year of ratification, the "manufacture, sale, or transportation of intoxicating liquors within, the importation thereof into, or the exportation thereof from the United States and all territory subject to the jurisdiction thereof for beverage purposes is hereby prohibited." Congress and the states were given concurrent authority to enforce the amendment by appropriate legislation.

Attempts to prohibit production and use of intoxicating liquor had been a political issue long before the passage of the Eighteenth Amendment. In 1913 Congress responded to the growing prohibition sentiment by adopting the Webb-Kenyon Act, forbidding the shipment of liquor in interstate commerce into dry states. In 1917 Congress adopted Prohibition by statute in the Lever Act as a wartime food-control measure. The Volstead Act, passed in 1919 over President Woodrow Wilson's veto, provided the means to investigate and punish violators of the national prohibition policy. The act took its name from Representative Andrew J. Volstead of Minnesota, who introduced it. Prohibition became a highly partisan issue in the 1928 presidential election. Governor Al Smith, the Democratic candidate, opposed Prohibition, while the Republicans supported retaining Prohibition. Despite Smith's defeat, the movement to repeal Prohibition gained momentum, and when the Democrats returned to power in 1933, they submitted a constitutional amendment to the states repealing Prohibition (Kelly, Harbison, and Belz 1991, 463–464). The Twenty-first Amendment was proposed on 20 February 1933, ratified on 5 December 1933, and given immediate effect. Ratification of the Twenty-first Amendment marked the first time a constitutional amendment had ever been repealed. After the ratification of the Twenty-first Amendment, the Volstead Act expired automatically.

Roosevelt, Franklin D. (1882–1945)

Franklin Roosevelt was governor of New York and president of the United States for thirteen years. Roosevelt passed the New York Bar exam without completing his degree at Columbia Law School, and joined a prominent New York City law firm. He was urged to run for the New York state senate and, although he ran as a Democrat in a heavily Republican district, he won nonetheless. He was reelected to a second term in 1912. He worked on the presidential campaign of Woodrow Wilson in 1912, and he later became assistant secretary of the navy in the Wilson administration. After unsuccessfully running for vice president on the Democratic ticket in 1920, he became vice president of Fidelity and Deposit Company, a position he held until 1928. Despite infantile paralysis, which struck him in 1921, Roosevelt was elected governor of New York in 1928 and again in 1930. Roosevelt became the Democratic presidential nominee two years later, and easily defeated incumbent President Herbert Hoover. He took office at a time when the country was in the midst of a severe economic depression. Congress was in session for 104 days in the spring of 1933, during which a number of major pieces of Roosevelt-sponsored legislation were enacted. Following the midterm elections of 1934, Roosevelt successfully pressed for adoption of additional social legislation. Roosevelt was elected to a third term in 1940, a term that featured Roosevelt in the role of commander in chief. Roosevelt acquiesced to party leaders in 1944 and replaced Vice President Henry Wallace with Missouri senator Harry Truman. Roosevelt died less than three months after he began his fourth term and was succeeded by Truman. Achievements of the Roosevelt administration rank among the most important of any presidency in American history. He was responsible for the creation of new agencies that significantly and permanently expanded the role of the federal government. In addition, Roosevelt's political coalition brought about a long-term realignment that produced Democratic majorities in the Congress.

Roosevelt, Theodore (1858–1919)

Theodore Roosevelt was the twenty-sixth president of the United States. He was born in New York City in 1858 and educated by private tutors until he enrolled at Harvard in 1876. He was elected to the New York state assembly in the fall of 1880 but continued to study at Columbia Law School, a pursuit he subsequently abandoned in favor of politics. Although a Republican, Roosevelt proved to be something of a partisan maverick. Particularly troublesome to some Republicans was his advocacy of a number of progressive measures. Midway through Roosevelt's third term in the state assembly, his wife died during childbirth and he left public life for a time. Before an unsuccessful mayoral run in New York City in 1886, Roosevelt was a member and subsequently chairman of the U.S. Civil Service Commission in Washington. He returned to New York in 1895 to serve two years as president of the New York City Police Board, followed by a year in the Navy Department. When the Spanish-American War broke out, Roosevelt organized a unit nicknamed the "Rough Riders." At the conclusion of the war, Roosevelt was elected governor of New York. Roosevelt's independence alienated certain corporate interests, prompting some Republican leaders to end his tenure as governor by supporting his candidacy as William McKinley's running mate in 1900. The ticket was elected and less than a year after the election Roosevelt succeeded to the presidency when McKinley was assassinated.

Roosevelt was known as the "great trustbuster," but he supported a wider range of business regulation. Roosevelt was elected to a second term in 1904. During his second term, Roosevelt persuaded Congress to support such progressive measures as the Hepburn Railroad Rate bill, the Pure Food and Drug bill, and federal inspection of stockyards and packing houses. He oversaw expansion of the civil service and encouraged appointment of higher-quality applicants to second-tier bureaucratic positions. Roosevelt failed to transform his party into a significant agent for reform. Republican leaders were displeased with his stewardship theory of executive power and his use of the office as a "bully pulpit." Throughout his tenure, Roosevelt sought restrained use of the nation's natural resources. Much of Roosevelt's foreign policy was shaped by his view that an American-controlled canal should link the Atlantic and Pacific Oceans. His objective in limiting European influence in the region was the product of his resolve to maintain complete American control over the Panama Canal. Roosevelt believed the United States was obligated to act as the protector of the Western Hemisphere, a view that became known as the Roosevelt Corollary to the Monroe Doctrine. He sought to create a balance of power to enable the United States to protect its interests in the Philippines. Roosevelt was awarded the Nobel Peace Prize in 1905 for his efforts in facilitating mediation of the Russo-Japanese War. Roosevelt chose not to seek reelection in 1908, but decided to do so in 1912, even though Republican president William Howard Taft was seeking reelection. He ran as the candidate of the newly formed Progressive or "Bull Moose" Party, and his presence in the contest along with Taft swung the election to the Democratic candidate, Woodrow Wilson. He supported Charles Evans Hughes and the Republican ticket in 1916. Roosevelt was outspoken in his criticism of Wilson, and may have been the Republican nominee for president in 1920, had he not died the previous year.

Root, Elihu (1845–1937)

Root was a Cabinet member and U.S. senator born in Clinton, New York, in 1845. He graduated from New York University Law School in 1867 and was admitted to the New York State Bar. His practice specialized in civil matters and he became known for his extraordinary trial preparation and attention to detail. Root served as U.S. attorney from 1883 to 1885, and began an association with Theodore Roosevelt during Roosevelt's unsuccessful campaign for mayor of New York City in 1886. In 1899 President William McKinley appointed Root secretary of war. One of his responsibilities as secretary of war was administration of the territories acquired by the United States following the Spanish-American War. The most problematic of these territories was the Philippines. Root created a commission headed by William Howard Taft that replaced military rule in the islands in 1900. Following the death of Secretary of State John Hay in 1905, Root was appointed to the position by President Theodore Roosevelt. He was key to achieving Roosevelt's objective of improving relations between the United States and Latin America. Following an extensive tour of South America, Root cosponsored the Central American Peace Conference in 1907 out of which the Central American Court of Justice was established. Root had extremely good relations with the Senate and never lost a treaty ratification vote in the Senate during his tenure as secretary of state. Root resigned as secretary of state in 1909 after his election to the Senate. He was caught in the conflict between the Republican Party's progressive and conservative factions, which played out in the split between President Taft and Roosevelt at the Republican nominating convention in 1912. Root attempted to broker a reconciliation between the two, but was unable to do so. He eventually supported Taft at the cost of his friendship with Roosevelt. Root retired from the Senate at the end of his term in 1915. After leaving the Senate, Root was highly critical of President Woodrow Wilson's foreign policy. As a result, he was considered for the Republican presidential nomination in 1916, but the nomination went to Charles Evans Hughes instead. Root did not play a significant role in national politics thereafter. His work in international relations was recognized when he won the Nobel Peace Prize in 1912.

Rule of Reason

An approach used in reviewing practices that are subject to Sherman Anti-Trust Act regulation. The Sherman Act was passed in 1890, and the Supreme Court initially applied the act to any restraint of trade. The Court then departed from this approach, which had the effect of limiting the scope and effectiveness of the Sherman Act. The White Court, in *Standard Oil Co. v. United States* and *United States v. American Tobacco Co.* (1911) ruled that the act could regulate only those practices that operated to the prejudice of the public interest by "unduly" restraining trade. This rule-of-reason evaluation of business practices on an individual case basis was promonopoly in effect. The rule of reason was the Court's preferred approach in antitrust cases for more than two decades. The Court then moved to a position in which regulated practices were presumptively unreasonable under the Sherman Act. Proponents of the rule of reason, such as Chief Justice Edward D. White, argued that the approach gave effect to free market and probusiness objectives. Opponents, however, criticized the rule of reason as vague, lacking in substantive content, and ineffective in providing guidance for courts handling alleged Sherman Act violations.

Sheppard-Towner Maternity and Infancy Protection Act of 1921

The Sheppard-Towner Act made federal money available to states that operated infant and maternity health care programs in local hospitals. It was something of a forerunner of social welfare programs of the New Deal. A substantial level of controversy accompanied the initiative. The measure was criticized for "subsidizing procreation" and as a "dangerous intrusion by government into the affairs of the family" (Parrish 1992, 25–26). Reformers saw the act as a "triumph for feminism and progressivism," and they argued Sheppard-Towner would lower maternal and infant mortality rates. Even among reformers, however, there was anxiety that the law would "perpetuate gender stereotypes and draw attention away from the importance of birth control" (Parrish 1992, 142–143). The state of Massachusetts and a number of taxpayers sought to have the law declared unconstitutional, contending that it exceeded the authority of Congress and threatened state sovereignty. In *Massachusetts v. Mellon* (1923), a unanimous Supreme Court dismissed the challenge for lack of standing, but suggested that such federal grant-in-aid programs were not inherently coercive in nature. The Court concluded that initiatives like Sheppard-Towner "imposed no obligation [on the states] but simply extended an option which the state was free to accept or reject" (Kelly, Harbison, and Belz 1991, 460).

Sherman Anti-Trust Act of 1890

A federal antimonopoly law that forbade "every contract, combination . . . or conspiracy in the restraint of trade or commerce." The Sherman Act was a recognition by Congress that the government may need to intervene in a market-driven economy to preserve competition. Soon after its enactment in 1890, the act was limited by the Supreme Court's ruling in *United States v. E.C. Knight* (1895), in which the Court held that monopolies of manufacture could not be regulated under the federal commerce power because production was distinct from commerce. Enforcement of the act is provided through criminal penalties and/or civil remedies. Responsibility for enforcement is currently located in the Antitrust Division of the Department of Justice. The Court also restricted the reach of the Sherman Act by utilizing the "rule of reason" under which only some combinations in restraint of trade were prohibited. Congress enacted the Clayton Act and the Federal Trade Commission Act in 1914 to reinforce and clarify the Sherman Act.

Sinclair, Harry (1876–1956)

Sinclair was an oil producer born in Wheeling, West Virginia, in 1876. After a failed attempt to operate the family pharmacy, Sinclair began a new career in the oil industry in Kansas and Oklahoma and was highly successful as an oil producer for more than a decade. Sinclair sold his production properties in 1916 and began to create a conglomerate that would extract, refine, and market petroleum products. The new company, Sinclair Oil and Refining Corporation, then merged with the Sinclair Gulf Corporation, a corporation founded by Sinclair to take over oil fields in Mexico and the Southwest. Despite commendable public service in support of World War I, Sinclair is more often remembered for his involvement in the oil-lease scandal of the 1920s. In 1922 he formed the Mammoth Oil Company, which was intended to lease the naval oil reserves located in Teapot Dome, Wyoming. The following year, Congress determined that the lease secured through Secretary of the Interior Albert B. Fall had been obtained unlawfully, and the Supreme Court eventually invalidated the oil leases. Unlike Fall, who served a term of imprisonment for his role in the oil-lease scandal, Sinclair was acquitted of charges of conspiring to defraud the U.S. government. Sinclair returned to his job as board chairman of the Sinclair Consolidated Oil Corporation. During World War II, his company constructed a number of plants to process crude oil into products for use in the war. After the war, Sinclair expanded Sinclair Oil's operations in the suburbs and along major highways. Sinclair overcame his participation in Teapot Dome and is regarded as one of the most important magnates of the twentieth century.

Smith, Alfred P. (1873–1944)

Smith was governor of New York and the Democratic candidate for president in 1928. Smith was born in New York City in 1873 and later came to represent the city's diverse urban culture. He joined the Tammany Hall political organization and his first political job was in the jury commissioner's office. Smith won a seat in the state assembly in 1904, which he retained for more than a decade. Near the end of his assembly tenure, a fire at the Triangle Shirtwaist Co. killed more than 100 immigrant workers. This event altered Smith's political outlook and he became a leading spokesman for progressive causes. Two years later, Smith was elected president of New York City's board of aldermen in 1917. The following year, he was elected governor of New York. Smith was New York's "favorite son" presidential candidate at the Democratic National Convention of 1920, which eventually nominated James M. Cox. The election of 1920 placed Warren G. Harding in the White House, but also produced overwhelming Republican success across the board, including the defeat of Smith in his bid for reelection as governor. He regained the governorship in 1922, and was reelected to additional two-year terms in 1924 and 1926. He and William McAdoo seemed the leading contenders for the 1924 Democratic presidential nomination, but a deadlocked convention ultimately chose John W. Davis on the 103rd ballot. Although denied the 1924 nomination, Smith became the front-runner for his party's presidential nomination for 1928. He was nominated at the convention by Franklin Roosevelt who referred to Smith as the "happy warrior." Smith was nominated on the first ballot and ran with Senator Joseph Robinson of Arkansas on the vice presidential slate. The campaign was particularly rancorous with Smith's Catholic faith often in the spotlight. Republican Herbert Hoover won in the general election with more than 58 percent of the popular vote. Out of office, Smith became a successful businessman in New York City. By 1932 he had become part of the Democratic Party's conservative faction. Roosevelt, now the progressive governor of New York, was in the party's liberal wing. Smith received some support for the 1932 presidential nomination, but the convention delegates chose Roosevelt. Smith supported Roosevelt, but soon thereafter became a spokesman for the Liberty League, an organization formed to oppose much of the New Deal agenda and deny renomination to Roosevelt in 1936. In 1936 Smith supported the Republican candidate Alfred Landon and four years later backed Republican Wendell Willkie. Smith died in New York City in 1944.

Teapot Dome Oil-Lease Scandal

One of the most notorious government scandals in United States history was known as the Teapot Dome scandal. The scandalous acts occurred during the presidency of Warren G. Harding. Lengthy investigations by the Senate as well as a special commission concluded that there was serious wrongdoing on the part of Secretary of the Interior Albert B. Fall. Fall had persuaded Harding to move control of naval oil reserves from the Navy Department to his department in 1921. The following year Fall leased the reserves at Elk Hills, California, and Teapot Dome, Wyoming, to the private oil companies of Edward L. Doheny and Harry F. Sinclair without competitive bidding. For arranging the Elk Hills transfer, Fall received a "loan" of $100,000 from Doheny. Fall received over $300,000 in cash, bonds, and livestock from Sinclair for the Teapot Dome transfer. Fall was forced to resign his position in 1923, and would later join Sinclair's oil business. In 1927 the government was able to secure cancellation of the leases. Fall was convicted two years later of accepting a bribe, fined $100,000, and sentenced to a year in prison. Sinclair and Doheny were acquitted of criminal charges brought against them.

Tenth Amendment

The Tenth Amendment retains or reserves powers not assigned to the federal government for the states. It was added to the Constitution to diminish concerns of the states' rightists that the federal government established by the Philadelphia Constitution would substantially curtail state authority. The amendment was aimed at reiterating that the federal government could exercise only assigned powers. The final item of the Bill of Rights in the Constitution defines the principle of American federalism as: "The powers not delegated to the United States by the Constitution, nor prohibited by it to the states, are reserved to the states respectively, or to the people." The Tenth Amendment was added to the Constitution to make clear the position of the states in the Union. Although it was generally understood that the framers intended the states to retain all powers not prohibited by the Constitution or delegated to the national government, the people insisted upon an express provision to that effect. Initially developed to protect state initiatives that arguably entered the domain of the federal government, the Supreme Court later adopted the position that the "reserved" powers of the states were immune from powers exercised by the federal government or that the reserve clause precluded the federal government from entering regulatory domains.

Walsh, Thomas J. (1859–1933)

Walsh was a U.S. senator from Montana born in Two Rivers, Wisconsin, in 1859. He moved to Helena, Montana, in 1890 to practice law. Walsh unsuccessfully ran for a seat in Congress in 1906, but emerged as a leading progressive in the Democratic Party. In 1912 he won election to the U.S. Senate, and used his legal and oratorical skills to make an immediate and positive impression in Washington. He was a leading supporter of Woodrow Wilson in the presidential campaign of 1916 and strongly advocated such policy priorities as a graduated income tax, farm loans, and women's suffrage. Walsh supported Wilson's peace plans following World War I, including U.S. membership in the proposed League of Nations. As a member of the Senate Public Lands Committee, Walsh led the probe of the leases on public oil lands in the West, which exposed the details of the Teapot Dome oil-lease scandal. In 1927 the Supreme

Court agreed with the conclusions of his Senate committee and voided the leases. Walsh was considered for the Democratic presidential nomination in 1928, but Governor Alfred Smith of New York emerged as the party's nominee. Walsh fully embraced the New Deal agenda of Franklin Roosevelt, who in turn sought to have Walsh join his administration. Walsh was reluctant to leave the Senate, but ultimately agreed to become Roosevelt's attorney general. Roosevelt had supposedly promised to elevate Walsh to the Supreme Court at the earliest opportunity. Walsh died before he could become attorney general, however.

Wheeler, Burton K. (1882–1975)

Burton Wheeler was a U.S. senator from Montana. Wheeler earned his law degree at the University of Michigan before moving to Butte, Montana, where he began a law practice. Wheeler served in the U.S. House of Representatives for a term before becoming U.S. attorney for Montana, a position he held from 1913 to 1918. After an unsuccessful bid for governor of Montana in 1920, Wheeler was elected to the U.S. Senate in 1922 and served four terms. Wheeler was the running mate of Senator Robert La Follette on the Progressive Party ticket in 1924. He was one of the first Democrats to support Franklin Roosevelt for the 1932 Democratic presidential nomination, and was one of Roosevelt's principal political advisers in fashioning the New Deal program. Wheeler supported Roosevelt through the election of 1936, but parted company with him at the point the "court-packing" proposal was unveiled. Indeed, Wheeler led the Senate fight against the plan and was the Senate member to whom Chief Justice Hughes directed his letter opposing the proposal. Had Franklin Roosevelt not chosen to seek a third term in 1940, Wheeler might have been the Democratic presidential nominee. Wheeler was a progressive and an isolationist and opposed American involvement in World War II until the attack on Pearl Harbor. Prior to the Pearl Harbor attack, Wheeler led the opposition to such Roosevelt policies as lend-lease. His isolationism before Pearl Harbor was not well received in Montana and he was defeated in the Democratic Senate primary in 1946. Wheeler practiced law with his son in Washington, D.C., until his death in 1975.

White, Edward Douglass (1845–1921)

Edward D. White was the ninth chief justice of the United States. White attended Georgetown University until he joined the Confederate forces during the Civil War. At the conclusion of the war, he returned to New Orleans to practice law. He also became active in Democratic Party politics. He was elected to the Louisiana state senate in 1874, and his support of a successful gubernatorial candidate won him appointment to the Louisiana Supreme Court two years later. White was chosen to represent Louisiana in the U.S. Senate in 1888. When Justice Samuel Blatchford retired from the U.S. Supreme Court in 1894 President Grover Cleveland nominated White as his replacement. He became chief justice in 1910, a position he held until 1921. He was the first associate justice to be elevated to chief justice and in all served twenty-seven years on the Court. White was a Democrat at the time he first joined the Court, yet his nomination for chief justice came from the Republican William Howard Taft. White's extraordinary administrative skills appealed to Taft, but at least two other factors influenced the nomination. First, despite partisan differences, White and Taft shared very similar political views. Secondly, Taft wanted to be chief justice. White was sixty-five years old at the time of his nomination by Taft, and Taft may have hoped that the chief justiceship might become vacant once his service as president ended.

The main questions faced by the White Court included review of the Sherman Anti-Trust Act and other business practices that emerged during the industrial revolution. White was a political conservative and subscribed to the Social Darwinist ideology of the period. The majority opinions authored by White reveal a general resistance to progressive legislation, and he is perhaps best remembered for introducing the "rule of reason," which severely limited the reach of the Sherman Act. White had joined the Court's decision in *United States v. E.C. Knight Co.* (1895), which found that the Sherman Act could not extend to monopolies of production. White then wrote his views into law in *Standard Oil Co. v. United States* (1911), which held that only "unreasonable" restraints of trade were prohibited by the Sherman Act. White was also responsible for prolonging the use of the dual federalism concept until it was abandoned in the 1930s. White is recognized for leading a Court known for its high productivity and consensus, and he is generally ranked as one the Court's able if not great justices.

Whitney, Anita Charlotte (1867–1955)

Whitney was a political activist born in San Francisco, California, in 1867. She was the daughter of a California state legislator and the niece of Supreme Court Justice Stephen Field. Her family was wealthy and socially prominent, and she graduated from Wellesley College in 1889. Several years later Whitney became a social worker in New York City and her work exposed her to the plight of the poor. She returned to California in 1893, where she both taught school and worked in the slums of West Oakland. Persuaded that mere political and economic reforms were inadequate, Whitney joined the Socialist Party in 1914. She opposed U.S. involvement in World War I and advocated for the free speech rights of political radicals charged with sedition under the Sedition and Espionage Acts. She participated in the formation of the Communist Labor Party, an association that led to her arrest for violations of California's criminal syndicalism act. She was convicted for her organization of and membership in the Communist Labor Party and sentenced to a prison term. She carried her case all the way to the Supreme Court, but the Court ruled against her in *Whitney v. California* (1927). She was subsequently pardoned and resumed her advocacy of economic and social justice for workers and racial minorities. Whitney waged several unsuccessful campaigns for political office as a candidate of the Communist Party and remained fully engaged in the activities of the party until her death in 1955.

Wickersham, George W. (1858–1936)

Wickersham was U.S. attorney general and a prominent Republican Party leader. While studying civil engineering at Lehigh University in the mid-1870s, Wickersham became acquainted with prominent Philadelphia Republicans. He graduated from the University of Pennsylvania Law School and became a successful Wall Street attorney representing a number of major transportation and manufacturing companies. Wickersham became part of the Republican establishment in New York and was selected to serve as attorney general in 1909 by President William Howard Taft. During his tenure, he vigorously enforced the Sherman Anti-Trust Act, much to the dismay of the corporate community. Indeed, a number of historians suggest that his Sherman Act prosecutions contributed to Woodrow Wilson winning the presidential election in 1912. Wickersham returned to New York to resume his legal practice when Taft lost to Wilson. He was extensively engaged in state politics, serving as a delegate to New York's constitutional convention and as a member of a commission created by Governor Alfred Smith to reform state government. Wickersham returned to the national political stage during World War I and aligned himself with the internationalist wing of the Republican Party, which included such persons as Taft and Charles Evans Hughes. Following the war, Wickersham supported the country's participation in the League of Nations and urged American membership in the World Court. His final significant public involvement began in 1929 when he chaired the National Commission on Law Observance and Enforcement, a body assembled by President Herbert Hoover to examine the federal system of criminal justice. The body, known as the Wickersham Commission, issued an extensive report that addressed virtually every aspect of federal law enforcement. Wickersham died in New York City in 1936.

Wilson, Woodrow (1856–1924)

Wilson was the twenty-eighth president of the United States. He was born in Staunton, Virginia, in 1856 and was home schooled until he entered Davidson College in 1873. He continued his education at Princeton and the University of Virginia Law School. Wilson began a law practice in Atlanta, Georgia, but almost immediately gave it up to pursue graduate study at Johns Hopkins in constitutional and political history. His book, entitled *Congressional Government*, served as his doctoral dissertation and he was awarded his Ph.D. in 1886. Wilson taught history and political science at Bryn Mawr and Wesleyan University before joining the faculty at Princeton in 1890. In 1902 Wilson was chosen to serve as Princeton's president, a position he held until 1910. He was elected governor of New Jersey in 1910 on the strength, at least in part, of the Democratic political machine in the state. Once elected, Wilson developed an image of a progressive people's advocate. Two years later, Wilson was the Democratic candidate for president. In the election Wilson faced the incumbent president William Howard Taft, Theodore Roosevelt running as a splinter party (Progressive/"Bull Moose") candidate, and the Socialist Eugene Debs. The candidacies of both Taft and Roosevelt split the Republican vote and Wilson was elected. Wilson's domestic policy objectives were contained in his New Freedom program and featured aggressive executive leadership. In a manner drawing from the British parliamentary system, Wilson sought to influence Congress to an unprecedented degree, and used such devices as frequent news conferences to strategically develop public opinion. He utilized this approach to secure adoption of such New Freedom priorities as tariff reduction, intensified antitrust regulation, and banking reforms. His foreign policy was shaped by his view that the United States had a broad international mission. He sought, for example, to minimize European influence in the Caribbean and Latin America while trying to keep the United States out of the war in Europe. It was his success at keeping the United States out of war that led to his reelection in 1916. Wilson's efforts to keep the United States positioned as a neutral ultimately failed, and Congress declared war against Germany in May 1917. Wilson took decisive action on the war front as well as on the domestic front. Using authority conferred by such statutes as the Espionage Act, Trading with the Enemy Act, and the Sedition Act, the Wilson administration aggressively prosecuted political critics of the war. Wilson was able to mobilize the American economy in support of the war effort under such statutes as the Lever Act. He created agencies including the Food and Fuel Administration, Railroad Administration, and the War Industries Board to convert key industrial sectors for the war. These wartime actions gave Wilson unprecedented presidential power. In January 1918 he introduced his Fourteen Point program for a new world order that called for such objectives as open diplomacy and disarmament. He was extensively engaged in the Paris Peace Conference at the conclusion of World War I, which not only produced a formal treaty to end the hostilities, but also provided for the establishment of a League of Nations. Wilson returned to the United States with the treaty and, when it became clear that ratification would not occur without substantial modification, Wilson took the issue to the public. The Senate ultimately rejected the treaty on two occasions, and the exhausting campaign to win ratification took its toll on Wilson's health. He suffered a massive stroke, and although he completed his second term as president, he never recovered. His physical incapacity eroded his policy-making effectiveness. In addition, inflation and labor unrest were followed by an economic recession in 1920. Although Wilson was not a candidate in 1920, American voters used the presidential election to reject both Wilson and his progressive agenda by choosing Warren G. Harding and his promise of a "return to normalcy" instead of Wilson's reform agenda presidency. Wilson's public service ended when Harding was inaugurated and he lived the last three years of his life off the political stage. Wilson was awarded the 1919 Nobel Peace Prize for his efforts to establish the League of Nations.

References and Further Reading

Baum, Lawrence. 2001. *The Supreme Court.* 7th ed. Washington, DC: Congressional Quarterly Press.

Braeman, John, Robert H. Bremner, and David Brody, eds. 1968. *Change and Continuity in Twentieth Century America: The 1920s.* Columbus, OH: Ohio State University Press.

Clements, Kendrick A. 1992. *The Presidency of Woodrow Wilson.* Lawrence, KS: University Press of Kansas.

Fausold, Martin L. 1985. *The Presidency of Herbert C. Hoover.* Lawrence, KS: University Press of Kansas.

Ferrell, Robert H. 1998. *The Presidency of Calvin Coolidge.* Lawrence, KS: University Press of Kansas.

Goldberg, David J. 1999. *Discontented America: The United States in the 1920s.* Baltimore, MD: Johns Hopkins University Press.

Kelly, Alfred H., Winfred A. Harbison, and Herman Belz. 1991. *The American Constitution: Its Origins and Development.* Vol. 2. 7th ed. New York: W. W. Norton.

Kennedy, David M. 1999. *Freedom from Fear: The American People in Depression and War, 1929–1945.* New York: Oxford University Press.

Morison, Samuel Eliot, Henry Steele Commager, and William E. Leuchtenburg. 1980. *The Growth of the American Republic.* Vol. 2. New York: Oxford University Press.

Noggle, Burl. 1962. *Teapot Dome: Oil and Politics in the 1920s.* Baton Rouge, LA: Louisiana State University Press.

Parrish, Michael E. 1992. *Anxious Decades: America in Prosperity and Depression, 1920–1941.* New York: W. W. Norton.

Pritchett, C. Herman. 1984. *Constitutional Law of the Federal System.* Englewood Cliffs, NJ: Prentice-Hall.

Soule, George. 1947. *Prosperity Decade: From War to Depression 1917–1929.* New York: Rinehart & Co.

Trani, Eugene P., and David L. Wilson. 1977. *The Presidency of Warren G. Harding.* Lawrence, KS: Regents Press of Kansas.

Appendix: Term-by-Term Statistics

1921 Term (U.S. Reports 257–259)

Total Cases: 209

Total Opinions: 173

Vote Count	*Number*	*Percentage*
9–0	119	68.79
8–0	17	9.83
8–1	6	3.47
7–1	3	1.73
6–1	1	0.58
7–2	8	4.62
6–2	1	0.58
6–3	13	7.51
5–3	3	1.73
5–4	2	1.16

	Participation	Majority *Opinions*	*Concurring*	*Dissents*
Brandeis	168 (97.11%)	23 (13.29%)	3 (1.73%)	14 (8.09%)
Butler	–	–	–	–
Clarke	163 (94.22%)	20 (11.56%)	6 (3.47%)	13 (7.51%)
Day	171 (98.84%)	15 (8.67%)	0	4 (2.31%)
Holmes	173 (100%)	29 (16.76%)	1 (.58%)	9 (5.20%)
McKenna	173 (100%)	18 (10.40%)	0	11 (6.36%)
McReynolds	171 (98.84%)	20 (11.56%)	2 (1.16%)	12 (6.94%)
Pitney	166 (95.95%)	11 (6.36%)	2 (1.16%)	4 (2.31%)
Sanford	–	–	–	–
Stone	–	–	–	–
Sutherland	–	–	–	–
Taft	172 (99.42%)	27 (15.61%)	0	6 (3.47%)
Van Devanter	173 (100%)	10 (5.78%)	0	8 (4.62%)

1922 Term (U.S. Reports 260–262)

Total Cases: 304

Total Opinions: 225

Vote Count	*Number*	*Percentage*
9–0	205	91.11
8–0	3	1.33
8–1	4	1.78
7–2	10	4.44
6–3	2	0.89
5–3	1	0.44
5–4	0	

	Participation	Majority *Opinions*	*Concurring*	*Dissents*
Brandeis	224 (99.56%)	27 (12.00%)	2 (0.89%)	6 (2.67%)
Butler	153 (68.00%)	16 (7.11%)	0	0
Clarke	–	–	–	–
Day	–	–	–	–
Holmes	225 (100%)	30 (13.33%)	1 (0.44%)	6 (2.67%)
McKenna	225 (100%)	27 (12.00%)	0	2 (.89%)
McReynolds	225 (100%)	24 (10.67%)	1 (.44%)	6 (2.67%)
Pitney	–	–	–	–
Sanford	189 (84.00%)	10 (4.44%)	0	1 (0.44%)
Stone	–	–	–	–
Sutherland	223 (99.11%)	29 (12.89%)	0	7 (3.11%)
Taft	225 (100%)	46 (20.44%)	0	3 (1.33%)
Van Devanter	225 (100%)	16 (7.11%)	0	0

1923 Term (U.S. Reports 263–265)

Total Cases: 247

Total Opinions: 212

Vote Count	*Number*	*Percentage*
9–0	179	84.43
8–0	8	3.77
7–0	1	0.47
8–1	8	3.77
7–2	6	2.83
6–2	5	2.36
6–3	4	1.89
5–3	1	0.47
5–4	0	

	Participation	Majority *Opinions*	*Concurring*	*Dissents*
Brandeis	211 (99.53%)	25 (11.79%)	4 (1.89%)	11 (5.19%)
Butler	210 (99.06%)	25 (11.79%)	0	3 (1.42%)
Clarke	–	–	–	–
Day	–	–	–	–
Holmes	211 (99.53%)	27 (12.73%)	2 (.94%)	7 (3.30%)
McKenna	212 (100%)	18 (8.49%)	0	4 (1.89%)
McReynolds	211 (99.53%)	18 (8.49%)	3 (1.42%)	13 (6.13%)
Pitney	–	–	–	–
Sanford	211 (99.53%)	20 (9.43%)	0	2 (.94%)
Stone	–	–	–	–
Sutherland	205 (96.70%)	26 (12.26%)	1 (0.47%)	2 (0.94%)
Taft	209 (99.58%)	33 (15.57%)	1 (0.47%)	1 (0.47%)
Van Devanter	212 (100%)	20 (9.43%)	0	2 (0.94%)

1924 Term (U.S. Reports 266–268)

Total Cases: 255

Total Opinions: 230

Vote Count	*Number*	*Percentage*
9–0	153	66.52
8–0	53	23.04
7–0	1	0.43
8–1	9	3.91
7–1	4	1.74
7–2	4	1.74
6–3	3	1.30
5–3	1	0.43
5–4	2	0.87

	Participation	Majority *Opinions*	*Concurring*	*Dissents*
Brandeis	229 (99.57%)	31 (13.48%)	0	6 (2.61%)
Butler	228 (99.13%)	24 (10.43%)	0	3 (1.30%)
Clarke	–	–	–	–
Day	–	–	–	–
Holmes	230 (100%)	33 (14.49%)	0	2 (0.87%)
McKenna	89 (38.70%)	4 (1.74%)	0	1 (0.43%)
McReynolds	230 (100%)	33 (14.49%)	0	11 (4.78%)
Pitney	–	–	–	–
Sanford	230 (100%)	24 (10.43%)	0	3 (1.30%)
Stone	87 (37.83%)	11 (4.78%)	0	0
Sutherland	227 (98.70%)	27 (11.74%)	0	7 (3.04%)
Taft	230 (100%)	31 (13.48%)	0	5 (2.17%)
Van Devanter	230 (100%)	12 (5.22%)	0	2 (0.87%)

1925 Term (U.S. Reports 269–271)

Total Cases: 250

Total Opinions: 209

Vote Count	*Number*	*Percentage*
9–0	179	85.65
8–0	15	7.18
8–1	5	2.39
7–1	1	0.48
7–2	4	1.91
6–3	4	1.91
5–4	1	0.48

	Participation	Majority *Opinions*	*Concurring*	*Dissents*
Brandeis	208 (99.52%)	27 (12.92%)	2 (0.96%)	6 (2.87%)
Butler	209 (100%)	25 (11.96%)	0	1 (0.48%)
Clarke	–	–	–	–
Day	–	–	–	–
Holmes	206 (98.56%)	24 (11.48%)	1 (0.48%)	3 (1.44%)
McKenna	–	–	–	–
McReynolds	209 (100%)	21 (10.05%)	0	8 (3.83%)
Pitney	–	–	–	–
Sanford	209 (100%)	20 (9.57%)	2 (0.96%)	3 (1.44%)
Stone	202 (96.65%)	21 (10.05%)	0	4 (1.91%)
Sutherland	204 (97.61%)	17 (8.13%)	1 (0.48%)	4 (1.91%)
Taft	209 (100%)	37 (17.70%)	0	0
Van Devanter	209 (100%)	17 (8.13%)	0	1 (0.48%)

1926 Term (U.S. Reports 272–274)

Total Cases: 226

Total Opinions: 199

Vote Count	*Number*	*Percentage*
9–0	156	78.39
8–0	11	5.53
7–0	1	0.50
6–0	1	0.50
8–1	8	4.02
6–1	1	0.50
7–2	7	3.52
6–3	9	4.52
5–3	1	0.50
5–4	4	2.01

	Participation	Majority *Opinions*	*Concurring*	*Dissents*
Brandeis	197 (98.99%)	23 (11.56%)	7 (3.52%)	14 (7.04%)
Butler	196 (98.49%)	21 (10.55%)	2 (1.01%)	9 (4.52%)
Clarke	–	–	–	–
Day	–	–	–	–
Holmes	198 (99.50%)	25 (12.56%)	4 (2.01%)	11 (5.53%)
McKenna	–	–	–	–
McReynolds	198 (99.50%)	24 (12.06%)	0	10 (5.03%)
Pitney	–	–	–	–
Sanford	199 (100%)	16 (8.04%)	3 (1.51%)	3 (1.51%)
Stone	191 (95.98%)	30 (15.08%)	8 (4.02%)	9 (4.52%)
Sutherland	196 (98.49%)	19 (9.55%)	0	8 (4.02%)
Taft	198 (99.50%)	31 (15.58%)	0	2 (1.01%)
Van Devanter	198 (99.50%)	10 (5.03%)	0	2 (1.01%)

1927 Term (U.S. Reports 275–277)

Total Cases: 206

Total Opinions: 173

Vote Count	*Number*	*Percentage*
9–0	134	77.46
8–0	10	5.78
7–0	2	1.16
8–1	3	1.73
7–2	7	4.05
6–3	10	5.78
5–4	7	4.05

	Participation	Majority *Opinions*	*Concurring*	*Dissents*
Brandeis	173 (100%)	24 (13.87%)	1 (0.58%)	17 (9.83%)
Butler	173 (100%)	22 (12.72%)	1 (0.58%)	4 (2.31%)
Clarke	–	–	–	–
Day	–	–	–	–
Holmes	173 (100%)	20 (11.56%)	1 (0.58%)	17 (9.83%)
McKenna	–	–	–	–
McReynolds	173 (100%)	22 (12.72%)	0	9 (5.20%)
Pitney	–	–	–	–
Sanford	173 (100%)	20 (11.56%)	2 (1.16%)	7 (4.05%)
Stone	165 (95.38%)	24 (13.87%)	1 (0.58%)	14 (8.09%)
Sutherland	168 (97.11%)	9 (5.20%)	0	7 (4.05%)
Taft	173 (100%)	24 (13.87%)	1 (0.58%)	0
Van Devanter	172 (99.42%)	8 (4.62%)	1 (0.58%)	0

1928 Term (U.S. Reports 278–279)

Total Cases: 145

Total Opinions: 129

Vote Count	*Number*	*Percentage*
9–0	103	79.84
8–0	3	2.33
7–0	1	0.78
8–1	9	6.98
7–2	4	3.10
6–3	7	5.43
5–3	1	0.78
5–4	1	0.78

	Participation	Majority *Opinions*	*Concurring*	*Dissents*
Brandeis	129 (100%)	13 (10.08%)	3 (2.33%)	8 (6.20%)
Butler	128 (99.22%)	19 (14.73%)	1 (0.78%)	5 (3.88%)
Clarke	–	–	–	–
Day	–	–	–	–
Holmes	129 (100%)	17 (13.18%)	4 (3.10%)	7 (5.43%)
McKenna	–	–	–	–
McReynolds	129 (100%)	12 (9.30%)	4 (3.10%)	10 (7.75%)
Pitney	–	–	–	–
Sanford	129 (100%)	12 (9.30%)	0	4 (3.10%)
Stone	127 (98.45%)	19 (14.73%)	3 (2.33%)	5 (3.88%)
Sutherland	128 (99.22%)	15 (11.63%)	1 (0.78%)	3 (2.33%)
Taft	128 (99.22%)	18 (13.95%)	0	2 (1.55%)
Van Devanter	129 (100%)	4 (3.10%)	0	3 (2.33%)

1929 Term (U.S. Reports 280, Taft Cases Only)

Total Cases: 73

Total Opinions: 64

Vote Count	*Number*	*Percentage*
9–0	55	85.94
8–0	1	1.56
8–1	1	1.56
7–2	2	3.13
6–2	1	1.56
6–3	3	4.69
5–4	1	1.56

	Participation	Majority *Opinions*	*Concurring*	*Dissents*
Brandeis	64 (100%)	8 (12.50%)	1(1.56%)	5 (7.81%)
Butler	63 (98.44%)	9 (14.06%)	0	0
Clarke	–	–	–	–
Day	–	–	–	–
Holmes	64 (100%)	10 (15.63%)	0	6 (9.38%)
McKenna	–	–	–	–
McReynolds	64 (100%)	9 (14.06%)	1 (1.56%)	1(1.56%)
Pitney	–	–	–	–
Sanford	64 (100%)	6 (9.38%)	0	0
Stone	63 (98.44%)	8 (12.50%)	3 (4.69%)	3 (4.69%)
Sutherland	64 (100%)	8 (12.50%)	0	1 (1.56%)
Taft	64 (100%)	5 (7.81%)	1 (1.56%)	0
Van Devanter	64 (100%)	1 (1.56%)	1 (1.56%)	2 (3.13%)

Chronology

1918

January 7	*Selective Draft Cases* (245 U.S. 366).
January 8	Woodrow Wilson proposes Fourteen Points peace plan.
January 14	*Goldman v. United States* (245 U.S. 474).
February 24	Child Labor Tax Act levies heavy tax on goods produced by child labor.
March 21	Railroad Control Act is adopted.
April 5	War Finance Corporation is established to help banks finance operation of war industries.
April 8	National War Labor Board is established to settle labor disputes and prevent disruption of war production.
April 10	Webb-Pomerene (Export Trade) Act is passed that exempts export trade associations from antitrust laws while prohibiting unfair trade practices among themselves.
May 16	Sedition Act amends 1917 Espionage Act and sets criminal penalties for persons convicted of willfully making statements interfering with war effort.
May 20	Overman Act is adopted giving president authority to reorganize government agencies.
June 3	*Hammer v. Dagenhart* (247 U.S. 251).

1918, cont.

August	United States severs diplomatic relations with Russia.
November 5	Republicans gain control of U.S. House and Senate.
November 11	Germany signs armistice ending World War I.

1919

January 6	Theodore Roosevelt dies.
January 18	Paris Peace Conference starts.
January 29	Eighteenth Amendment ratified.
February 14	Wilson presents draft League of Nations Covenant to Paris Peace Conference.
March 10	*Frohwerk v. United States* (249 U.S. 204).
	Debs v. United States (249 U.S. 211).
May 21	Nineteenth Amendment providing for women's suffrage passes U.S. House by 304–89 vote.
June 4	Nineteenth Amendment passes U.S. Senate by 56–25 vote and is sent to states for ratification.
June 28	Versailles Peace Treaty signed in Paris.
July 1	First daily airmail service established between New York and Chicago.
August 1	Attorney General A. Mitchell Palmer organizes General Intelligence Division to combat political radicals.
September 9	Boston police strike begins.
September 25	President Wilson suffers stroke while campaigning for Paris Peace Treaty and League of Nations.
October 28	National Prohibition (Volstead) Act providing enforcement of Eighteenth Amendment passes over President Wilson's veto.

November 10	*Abrams v. United States* (250 U.S. 616).
November 19	Senate refuses to ratify Paris Peace Treaty.
December 15	*Hamilton v. Kentucky Distilleries & Warehouse Co.* (251 U.S. 146).

1920

January 2	Attorney General A. Mitchell Palmer orders raids against political radicals; more than 6,000 people are arrested and many deported. Arrests continue into May.
January 10	Treaty of Versailles goes into effect without U.S. acceptance.
January 16	Prohibition begins.
January 26	*Silverthorne Lumber Co. v. United States* (251 U.S. 385).
February 25	Oil and Coal Land Leasing Act is passed; provides foundation for oil-lease scandals.
February 28	Esch-Cummins (Transportation) Act is adopted, implementing return of railroads to private control following First World War and expanding Interstate Commerce Act of 1887 and power of Interstate Commerce Commission.
March 1	*United States v. United States Steel Corp.* (251 U.S. 417).
	Schaefer v. United States (251 U.S. 466).
March 8	*Eisner v. Macomber* (252 U.S. 189).
March 19	Treaty of Versailles fails last ratification vote in Senate on 49–35 vote.
April 1	"Red Scare" continues; five elected members of New York state legislature are expelled for Socialist Party affiliation.
April 7	50,000 railroad workers strike in Chicago.
April 9	Military draft for World War I ends.

1920, cont.

April 19	*Missouri v. Holland* (252 U.S. 416).
April 20	Grand Canyon National Park dedicated.
May 5	Nicola Sacco and Bartolomeo Vanzetti arrested in Massachusetts.
June 1	*Hawke v. Smith* (253 U.S. 221).
	Evans v. Gore (253 U.S. 245).
June 5	Immigration Act amended allowing for deportation of anarchists and aliens advocating political terrorism.
June 7	*National Prohibition Cases* (253 U.S. 350).
June 10	Federal Water Power Act is passed, creating Federal Power Commission with authority to license private industry to construct and operate power-generating facilities and transmission lines.
June 12	Warren Harding is nominated on tenth ballot at Republican nominating convention. Party endorses women's suffrage amendment.
June 28	Democrats nominate James M. Cox of Ohio for president.
August 26	Nineteenth Amendment is ratified.
November 2	Harding is elected president.
December 10	President Wilson is awarded Nobel Peace Prize.
December 13	*Gilbert v. Minnesota* (254 U.S. 325).

1921

January 3	*Duplex Printing Press Co. v. Deering* (254 U.S. 443).
January 4	War Finance Corporation is reactivated to assist farmers.
February 28	*United States v. L. Cohen Grocery Co.* (255 U.S. 81).
March 4	Harding inaugurated as president.

March 7	*Milwaukee Social Democratic Publishing Co. v. Burleson* (255 U.S. 407).
May 2	*Newberry v. United States* (256 U.S. 232).
May 16	*Dillon v. Gloss* (256 U.S. 368).
May 19	Chief Justice Edward Douglass White dies.
	Immigration Quota Act severely limits immigration to no more than 3 percent annually of each nationality.
May 21	Harding signs executive order transferring federal oil reserves from Navy Department to Interior Department, setting stage for Teapot Dome scandal.
May 27	Emergency Tariff Act is adopted, increasing rates on agricultural products.
June 1	*Burdeau v. McDowell* (256 U.S. 465).
June 10	Budget and Accounting Act signed, establishing Bureau of Budget and Office of Comptroller General.
	Taft Court era begins.
June 30	William Howard Taft nominated to replaced Edward White as chief justice.
July 14	Nicola Sacco and Bartolomeo Vanzetti are convicted of murder.
August 15	Packers and Stockyards Act becomes law, regulating activities of livestock processors to prevent unfair practices.
August 24	Futures Trading Act limiting speculative trading of wheat signed into law. Authority of War Finance Corporation broadened.
November 11	Tomb of Unknown Solider established at Arlington National Cemetery
November 23	Sheppard-Towner Act providing federal funding for promoting infant health is signed by President Harding.

1921, cont.

December 5	*American Steel Foundries v. Tri-City Central Trades Council* (257 U.S. 184).
December 19	*Truax v. Corrigan* (257 U.S. 312).
December 23	President Harding commutes prison terms of Eugene V. Debs and twenty-three other Socialists convicted under Espionage Act.

1922

January 30	*Cornelius v. Moore* (257 U.S. 491).
	Gillespie v. Oklahoma (257 U.S. 501).
February 2	James Joyce's novel *Ulysses* is published.
February 6	Conference for Limitation of Armament concludes.
February 15	Court of International Justice holds first session.
February 27	Nineteenth Amendment upheld by Supreme Court.
April 1	United Mine Workers coal strike begins.
April 7	Interior Secretary Albert Fall leases Teapot Dome oil reserve to oilman Henry Sinclair.
April 29	Senate votes to begin investigation of Sinclair oil leases.
May 1	*Stafford v. Wallace* (258 U.S. 495).
May 15	*Bailey v. Drexel Furniture Co.*(259 U.S. 20).
	Hill v. Wallace (259 U.S. 44).
May 26	Federal Narcotics Control Board is established to prohibit importation of illegal drugs.
May 30	Lincoln Memorial dedicated in Washington, D.C.
June 5	*United Mine Workers v. Coronado Coal Co.* (259 U.S. 344).

September 5	George Sutherland nominated to replace Justice John H. Clarke on Supreme Court.
September 19	President Harding vetoes Soldiers' Bonus Bill.
September 21	Fordney-McCumber Tariff Act establishes protectionist duties on imports.
September 22	Judicial Conference and Tenure Act passes, authorizing creation of conference of senior judges of judicial circuits.
November 7	Mid-term elections reduce Republican majority in House of Representatives by eighty-two seats and by eight seats in Senate.
November 21	Rebecca Latimer Felton of Georgia becomes first woman member of U.S. Senate.
November 25	Benito Mussolini gains dictatorial authority in Italy.
December 11	Justice Mahlon Pitney retires from Supreme Court.
	United States v. Lanza (260 U.S. 377).
	Pennsylvania Coal Co. v. Mahon (260 U.S. 393).
December 21	Pierce Butler Jr. is nominated to replace Justice William R. Day.
December 30	Lenin proclaims formation of Union of Soviet Socialist Republics.

1923

January 2	Interior Secretary Albert Fall resigns, effective on 4 March.
	Justice Butler joins Supreme Court.
January 14	First wireless phone call made from New York to London.
January 28	*Federal Trade Commission v. Curtis Publishing Co.* (260 U.S. 568).
January 29	Edward T. Sanford is nominated to Supreme Court to replace Justice Mahlon Pitney.
March 3	First issue of *Time* magazine published.
March 15	Senate rejects U.S. participation in International Court of Justice.

1923, cont.

March 23	Federal Intermediate Credit Bank Act passes, modifying Farm Loan Act of 1916 by creating intermediate credit banks that can make low-interest crop loans.
April 16	*Chicago Board of Trade v. Olsen* (262 U.S. 1).
April 19	*Adkins v. Children's Hospital* (261 U.S. 525).
May 2	First transcontinental airplane flight from New York to San Diego.
June 3	*Frothingham v. Mellon* (262 U.S. 447).
June 4	*Meyer v. Nebraska* (262 U.S. 390).
June 11	*Charles Wolff Packing Co. v. Court of Industrial Relations* (262 U.S 522).
August 2	President Harding dies in San Francisco.
August 3	Vice President Calvin Coolidge sworn in as president.
August 14	Coolidge holds first Cabinet meeting.
November 25	First transatlantic radio broadcast between United States and Great Britain.
December 15	Coolidge appoints Charles G. Dawes to head commission to develop reparations payment plan for Germany.

1924

January 7	*Dayton-Goose Creek Railway Co. v. United States* (263 U.S. 456).
January 21	Vladimir Lenin, leader of Russian Revolution, dies.
January 28	Senate calls for resignation of Navy Secretary Edwin Denby.
February 3	Woodrow Wilson dies.
February 18	Edwin Denby resigns.
March 12	Senate begins investigation of Attorney General Harry Daugherty.

March 26	Johnson-Reed Immigration Act adopted to further restrict immigration.
March 28	Attorney General Harry Daugherty resigns at request of President Coolidge after he withholds files from Senate investigators.
April 2	President Coolidge appoints Harlan Fiske Stone as attorney general.
April 14	*Jay Burns Baking Co. v. Bryan* (264 U.S. 504).
April 23	Congress adopts Soldiers' Bonus plan, which is vetoed by Coolidge.
May 10	J. Edgar Hoover appointed director of Bureau of Investigation, renamed Federal Bureau of Investigation in 1935.
May 19	U.S. House and Senate override President Coolidge's veto of Soldiers' Bonus Bill.
May 26	Immigration Quota Act amended to further reduce immigration.
June 9	*Michaelson v. United States* (266 U.S. 42).
June 12	Calvin Coolidge is nominated for president on first ballot at Republican nominating convention in Cleveland.
June 24	Democrats nominate John W. Davis of West Virginia for president.
June 30	Albert Fall, Henry Sinclair, and Edward Doheny are indicted by grand jury for alleged bribery and conspiracy to defraud government.
July 4	Progressive Party nominates Robert M. La Follette for president.
September 10	Nathan Leopold and Richard Loeb sentenced for murder.
October 25	Former Interior Secretary Albert Fall is convicted of taking bribe and sentenced to one year in prison.
November 4	Coolidge reelected president.

1925

January 5	Secretary of State Charles Evans Hughes resigns.
	Nellie Ross of Wyoming becomes first elected woman governor.
February 5	Harlan F. Stone is confirmed by Senate to replace Justice Joseph McKenna on Supreme Court.
February 13	Judicial Code Revision reduces number of cases that automatically come to Supreme Court on appeal and broadens Court's discretionary certiorari power.
March 2	*Ex parte Grossman* (267 U.S. 87).
	Carroll v. United States (267 U.S. 132).
	Buck v. Kuykendall (267 U.S. 307).
March 4	Coolidge is inaugurated for second term as president.
March 9	*Brooks v. United States* (267 U.S. 432).
April 10	F. Scott Fitzgerald's novel *The Great Gatsby* is published.
May 25	*Coronado Coal Co. v. United Mine Workers* (268 U.S. 295).
June 1	*Miles v. Graham* (268 U.S. 501).
	Pierce v. Society of Sisters (268 U.S. 510).
June 8	*Gitlow v. New York* (268 U.S. 652).
July 10	Trial of John T. Scopes begins in Tennessee; Scopes is charged with teaching evolution.
July 26	William Jennings Bryan dies.
August 8	40,000 Ku Klux Klan members rally in Washington, D.C.
December 10	Vice President Charles Dawes is awarded Nobel Peace Prize for developing plan for restructuring German economy and payment of war reparations debt.

1926

January 27	Senate approves United States participation in World Court by 76–17 vote.
May 3	*Colorado v. United States* (271 U.S. 153).
May 9	Richard E. Byrd becomes first flyer to reach North Pole.
May 20	Railway Labor Act is adopted, recognizing right to collective bargaining and establishing process for resolving labor disputes.
May 24	*Corrigan v. Buckley* (271 U.S. 323).
October 25	*Myers v. United States* (272 U.S. 52).
November 2	Democrats reduce Republican majorities in both U.S. House and Senate in mid-term elections.
November 22	*Village of Euclid v. Ambler Realty Co.* (272 U.S. 365).

1927

January 3	*Di Santo v. Pennsylvania* (273 U.S. 34).
January 17	*McGrain v. Daugherty* (273 U.S. 135).
February 11	Congress passes McNary-Haugen bill to allow government to purchase surplus farm commodities; Coolidge vetoes it.
February 23	Federal Radio Act signed into law. Statute establishes Federal Radio Commission to regulate radio industry.
February 28	*Tyson & Bros. v. Banton* (273 U.S. 418).
March 7	*Tumey v. Ohio* (273 U.S. 510).
	Nixon v. Herndon (273 U.S. 536).
March 17	Supreme Court rules that Teapot Dome and Elk Hills oil leases were entered into fraudulently and voids leases.
April 11	*Bedford Cut Stone Co. v. Journeyman Stone Cutters' Ass'n* (274 U.S. 37).

1927, cont.

May 2	*Buck v. Bell* (274 U.S. 200).
May 16	*Whitney v. California* (274 U.S. 357).
May 21	Charles A. Lindbergh lands in Paris after nonstop, transatlantic flight.
August 2	Coolidge announces that he will not seek reelection.
November 13	Holland Tunnel under Hudson River opens.
November 21	*Gong Lum v. Rice* (275 U.S. 78).

1928

April 9	*J.W. Hampton, Jr. & Co. v. United States* (276 U.S. 394).
May 3	Congress reenacts McNary-Haugen farm bill; Coolidge again vetoes it.
May 28	*Ribnik v. McBride* (277 U.S. 350).
June 4	*Olmstead v. United States* (277 U.S. 438).
June 15	Herbert Hoover is nominated for president at Republican National Convention in Kansas City, Missouri.
June 26	Democrats nominate Governor Alfred E. Smith of New York for president at Houston convention.
August 27	Kellogg-Briand Pact outlawing war is signed by fifteen nations in Paris.
September 8	League of Nations elects Charles Evans Hughes to Permanent Court of International Justice.
November 6	Herbert Hoover is elected president.

1929

January 15	Kellogg-Briand Pact ratified by Senate by 85–1 vote.

February 14 — St. Valentine's Day gangland massacre takes place in Chicago.

March 4 — Herbert Hoover inaugurated as president.

May 16 — Academy Awards for motion pictures are first presented.

May 20 — *Ex parte Bakelite Corp.* (279 U.S. 438).

President Hoover creates Wickersham Commission on Law Observance and Enforcement.

May 27 — *United States v. Schwimmer* (279 U.S. 644).

Pocket Veto Case (279 U.S. 655).

June 15 — Agricultural Marketing Act passes, setting up Federal Farm Board to assist in selling surplus agricultural commodities.

October 24–29 — Stock market crashes, marking first stage of Great Depression.

1930

February 3 — Chief Justice William Howard Taft leaves Supreme Court.

Taft Court era ends.

February 24 — Charles Evans Hughes becomes chief justice.

March 8 — Former Chief Justice William Howard Taft and Associate Justice Edward T. Sanford die.

April 28 — *Cochran v. Louisiana State Board of Education* (281 U.S. 370).

May 26 — *Baldwin v. Missouri* (281 U.S. 586).

June 2 — Justice Roberts replaces Justice Sanford.

June 17 — Smoot-Hawley Tariff signed by President Hoover.

July 3 — Veterans Administration established by Congress.

November 4 — Democrats gain control of U.S. House in mid-term elections.

1931

March 3	President Hoover vetoes Muscle Shoals bill, which would have allowed government to operate power plants.
May 18	*Stromberg v. California* (283 U.S. 359)
June 1	*Near v. Minnesota* (283 U.S. 697).
October	Al Capone jailed.

1932

January 22	Reconstruction Finance Corporation created to lend funds to aid in economic recovery.
March 3	Twentieth Amendment eliminating "lame duck" congressional sessions proposed by Congress.
March 23	Norris-LaGuardia Anti-Injunction Act is passed, denying federal courts authority to issue injunctions in labor disputes.
June 14	Republicans nominate President Hoover as their presidential candidate.
June 27	Democrats nominate New York governor Franklin D. Roosevelt as their presidential candidate.
July 21	Emergency Relief and Reconstruction Act is adopted, expanding power of Reconstruction Finance Corporation to make loans for public construction projects and to states to enable them to finance local relief projects.
July 22	Federal Home Loan Bank Act creates banking system designed to provide financial assistance to private homeowners.
November 8	Franklin D. Roosevelt is elected president.

Table of Cases

Abrams v. United States, 250 U.S. 616 (1919)

Adkins v. Children's Hospital, 261 U.S. 525 (1923)

Agnello v. United States, 269 U.S. 20 (1925)

Allgeyer v. Louisiana, 165 U.S. 578 (1897)

American Steel Foundries v. Tri-City Central Trades Council, 257 U.S. 184 (1921)

Anchor Lines v. Aldridge, 259 U.S. 80 (1922)

Ashwander v. Tennessee Valley Authority, 297 U.S. 288 (1936)

Bailey v. Drexel Furniture Co., 259 U.S. 20 (1922)

Bakelite Corp., Ex Parte, 279 U.S. 438 (1929)

Baldwin v. Missouri, 281 U.S. 586 (1930)

Barron v. Baltimore, 32 U.S. 243 (1833)

Barry v. United States ex rel. Cunningham, 279 U.S. 597 (1929)

Bedford Cut Stone Co. v. Journeyman Stone Cutters' Ass'n, 274 U.S. 37 (1927)

Berger v. New York, 388 U.S. 41 (1967)

Biddle v. Perovich, 274 U.S. 480 (1927)

Block v. Hirsh, 256 U.S. 135 (1921)

Brandenburg v. Ohio, 395 U.S. 444 (1969)

Brooks v. United States, 267 U.S. 432 (1925)

Brown v. Maryland, 25 U.S. 419 (1827)

Buchanan v. Warley, 245 U.S. 60 (1917)

Buck v. Bell, 274 U.S. 200 (1927)

Buck v. Kuykendall, 267 U.S. 307 (1925)

Bunting v. Oregon, 243 U.S. 426 (1917)

Burdeau v. McDowell, 256 U.S. 465 (1921)

Burke, Ltd. v. Blair, 265 U.S. 545 (1924)

Byars v. United States, 273 U.S. 28 (1927)

Carroll v. United States, 267 U.S. 132 (1925)

Casey v. United States, 276 U.S. 413 (1928)

Cement Manufacturers Protective Ass'n v. United States, 268 U.S. 588 (1925)

Charles Wolff Packing Co. v. Court of Industrial Relations, 262 U.S. 522 (1923)

Chastleton Corp. v. Sinclair, 264 U.S. 543 (1924)
Chicago Board of Trade v. Olsen, 262 U.S. 1 (1923)
Child Labor Case. See *Hammer v. Dagenhart*
Child Labor Tax Case. See *Bailey v. Drexel Furniture Co.*
Clark Distilling Co. v. Western Maryland Railway, 242 U.S. 311 (1917)
Cochran v. Louisiana State Board of Education, 281 U.S. 370 (1930)
Colorado v. United States, 271 U.S. 153 (1926)
Connally v. General Construction Co., 269 U.S. 385 (1926)
Coppage v. Kansas, 236 U.S. 1 (1915)
Corneli v. Moore, 257 U.S. 491 (1922)
Coronado Coal Co. v. United Mine Workers, 268 U.S. 295 (1925)
Corrigan v. Buckley, 271 U.S. 323 (1926)
Crescent Cotton Oil Co. v. Mississippi, 257 U.S. 129 (1921)
Crooks v. United States, 267 U.S. 432 (1925)
Cunard Steamship Co. v. Mellon, 262 U.S. 100 (1923)
Danbury Hatters Case. See *Loewe v. Lawlor*
Dayton-Goose Creek Railway Co. v. United States, 263 U.S. 456 (1924)
Debs v. United States, 249 U.S. 211 (1919)
Delaware, Lackawanna & Western Railroad Co. v. Yurkonis, 238 U.S. 439 (1915)
Dennis v. United States, 341 U.S. 494 (1951)
Di Santo v. Pennsylvania, 273 U.S. 34 (1927)
Dillon v. Goss, 256 U.S. 368 (1921)
Dorchy v. Kansas, 264 U.S. 286 (1924)
Duplex Printing Co. v. Deering, 254 U.S. 443 (1921)
Eisner v. Macomber, 252 U.S. 189 (1920)
Elkins v. United States, 364 U.S. 206 (1960)
Euclid, Village of v. Ambler Realty Co., 272 U.S. 365 (1926)
Evans v. Gore, 253 U.S. 245 (1920)
Everson v. Board of Education, 330 U.S. 1 (1947)
Fairchild v. Hughes, 258 U.S. 126 (1922)
Fairmont Creamery Co. v. Minnesota, 274 U.S. 1 (1927)
Farrington v. Tokushiga, 273 U.S. 284 (1927)
Federal Baseball Club of Baltimore, Inc. v. National League, 259 U.S. 200 (1922)
Federal Trade Commission v. Curtis Publishing Co., 260 U.S. 568 (1923)
Federal Trade Commission v. Gratz, 253 U.S. 421 (1920)
Fiske v. Kansas, 274 U.S. 380 (1927)
Flast v. Cohen, 392 U.S. 83 (1968)
Florida v. Mellon, 273 U.S. 12 (1927)
Frohwerk v. United States, 249 U.S. 204 (1919)
Frost v. Corporation Commission, 278 U.S. 515 (1929)

Frothingham v. Mellon, 262 U.S. 447 (1923)
Gambino v. United States, 275 U.S. 310 (1927)
Gilbert v. Minnesota, 254 U.S. 325 (1920)
Gillespie v. Oklahoma, 257 U.S. 501 (1922)
Girouard v. United States, 328 U.S. 61 (1946)
Gitlow v. New York, 268 U.S. 652 (1925)
Gold Clause Cases, 294 U.S. 240 (1935)
Goldman v. United States, 245 U.S. 474 (1918)
Gompers v. United States, 233 U.S. 604 (1914)
Gong Lum v. Rice, 275 U.S. 78 (1927)
Gouled v. United States, 255 U.S. 298 (1921)
Griswold v. Connecticut, 381 U.S. 479 (1965)
Grogan v. Hiram Walker & Sons, 259 U.S. 80 (1922)
Grossman, Ex parte, 267 U.S. 87 (1925)
Grovey v. Townsend, 295 U.S. 45 (1935)
Gruber, Ex parte, 269 U.S. 302 (1925)
Hamilton v. Kentucky Distilleries & Warehouse Co., 251 U.S. 146 (1919)
Hammer v. Dagenhart, 247 U.S. 251 (1918)
Harmon v. Tyler, 273 U.S. 668 (1927)
Hawke v. Smith, 253 U.S. 221 (1920)
Helvering v. Davis, 301 U.S. 619 (1937)
Hester v. United States, 265 U.S. 57 (1924)
Hill v. Wallace, 259 U.S. 44 (1922)
Hipolite Egg Co. v. United States, 220 U.S. 45 (1911)
Hitchman Coal & Coke Co. v. Mitchell, 245 U.S. 229 (1917)
Hoke v. United States, 227 U.S. 308 (1913)
Holden v. Hardy, 169 U.S. 366 (1898)
Home Building & Loan Ass'n v. Blaisdell, 290 U.S. 398 (1934)
Houston, East and West Texas Railway Co. v. United States, 234 U.S. 342 (1914)
Humphrey's Executor v. United States, 295 U.S. 602 (1935)
J. W. Hampton, Jr. & Co. v. United States, 276 U.S. 394 (1928)
Jacob Ruppert, Inc. v. Caffey, 251 U.S. 264 (1920)
James Everard's Breweries v. Day, 265 U.S. 545 (1924)
Jay Burns Baking Co. v. Bryan, 264 U.S. 504 (1924)
Katz v. United States, 386 U.S. 954 (1967)
Keller v. Potomac Electric Power Co., 261 U.S. 428 (1923)
Kiernan v. Portland, 223 U.S. 151 (1912)
Kilbourn v. Thompson, 103 U.S. 168 (1881)
Lambert v. Yellowley, 272 U.S. 581 (1926)
Liberty Warehouse Co. v. Grannis, 273 U.S. 70 (1927)

Liggett Co. v. Baldridge, 278 U.S. 105 (1928)
Lochner v. New York, 198 U.S. 45 (1905)
Loewe v. Lawlor, 208 U.S. 274 (1908)
Long v. Rockwood, 277 U.S. 142 (1928)
Macallen Co. v. Massachusetts, 279 U.S. 620 (1929)
Mahler v. Eby, 264 U.S. 32 (1924)
Maple Flooring Manufacturers Ass'n v. United States, 268 U.S. 563 (1925)
Marbury v. Madison, 5 U.S. 137 (1803)
Massachusetts v. Mellon, 262 U.S. 447 (1923)
McCray v. United States, 195 U.S. 27 (1904)
McCulloch v. Maryland, 17 U.S. 316 (1819)
McGrain v. Daugherty, 273 U.S. 135 (1927)
McLean v. Arkansas, 211 U.S. 539 (1909)
Meyer v. Nebraska, 262 U.S. 390 (1923)
Michaelson v. United States, 266 U.S. 42 (1924)
Miles v. Graham, 268 U.S. 501 (1925)
Miller v. Schoene, 276 U.S. 272 (1928)
Milwaukee Social Democratic Publishing Co. v. Burleson. See *United States ex rel. Milwaukee Social Democratic Publishing Co. v. Burleson*
Minersville School District v. Gobitis, 310 U.S. 586 (1940)
Missouri v. Holland, 252 U.S. 416 (1920)
Moore v. Dempsey, 261 U.S. 86 (1923)
Morehead v. New York ex rel. Tipaldo, 298 U.S. 587 (1936)
Muller v. Oregon, 208 U.S. 412 (1908)
Munn v. Illinois, 94 U.S. 113 (1877)
Myers v. United States, 272 U.S. 52 (1926)
National Prohibition Cases, 253 U.S. 350 (1920)
Near v. Minnesota, 283 U.S. 697 (1931)
Newberry v. United States, 256 U.S. 232 (1921)
New York ex rel. Bryant v. Zimmerman, 278 U.S. 63 (1928)
Nixon v. Condon, 286 U.S. 73 (1932)
Nixon v. Herndon, 273 U.S. 536 (1927)
Ohio ex rel. Popovici v. Agler, 280 U.S. 379 (1930)
Oliver Iron Mining Co. v. Lord, 262 U.S. 172 (1923)
Olmstead v. United States, 277 U.S. 438 (1928)
O'Malley v. Woodrough, 307 U.S. 277 (1939)
Ozawa v. United States, 260 U.S. 178 (1923)
Palko v. Connecticut, 302 U.S. 319 (1937)
Panhandle Oil Co. v. Mississippi, 277 U.S. 218 (1928)
Patton v. United States, 281 U.S. 276 (1930)

Pennsylvania Coal Co. v. Mahon, 260 U.S. 393 (1922)
Pierce v. Society of Sisters, 268 U.S. 510 (1925)
Pierce v. United States, 252 U.S. 239 (1920)
Plessy v. Ferguson, 163 U.S. 537 (1896)
Pocket Veto Case, 279 U.S. 655 (1929)
Pollock v. Farmers' Loan & Trust Co., 158 U.S. 601 (1895)
Porterfield v. Webb, 263 U.S. 225 (1923)
Postum Cereal Co. v. California Fig Nut Co., 272 U.S. 693 (1927)
Powell v. Alabama, 287 U.S. 45 (1932)
Prudential Insurance Co. v. Cheek, 259 U.S. 530 (1922)
Quaker City Cab Co. v. Pennsylvania, 277 U.S. 389 (1928)
Radice v. New York, 264 U.S. 293 (1924)
Railroad Commission v. Chicago, Burlington & Quincy Railroad, 257 U.S. 563 (1922)
Ribnik v. McBride, 277 U.S. 350 (1928)
Santa Clara County v. Southern Pacific Railroad, 118 U.S. 394 (1886)
Schaefer v. United States, 251 U.S. 466 (1920)
Schenck v. United States, 249 U.S. 47 (1919)
Second Employers' Liability Cases, 223 U.S. 1 (1911)
Selective Draft Law Cases, 245 U.S. 366 (1917)
Selzman v. United States, 268 U.S. 466 (1925)
Shelley v. Kraemer, 334 U.S. 1 (1948)
Shreveport Rate Case. See *Houston, East and West Texas Railway Co. v. United States*
Silverthorne Lumber Co. v. United States, 251 U.S. 385 (1920)
Smith v. Allwright, 321 U.S. 649 (1944)
Sonneborn Bros. v. Cureton, 262 U.S. 506 (1923)
Southern Railway Co. v. United States, 222 U.S. 20 (1911)
Southwestern Bell Telephone Co. v. Public Service Commission, 262 U.S. 276 (1923)
Springer v. Philippine Islands, 277 U.S. 189 (1928)
Stafford v. Wallace, 258 U.S. 495 (1922)
Standard Oil Co. v. United States, 221 U.S. 1 (1911)
Steward Machine Co. v. Davis, 301 U.S. 548 (1937)
Stromberg v. California, 283 U.S. 359 (1931)
Swift & Company v. United States, 196 U.S. 375 (1905)
Tagg Bros. & Moorhead v. United States, 280 U.S. 420 (1930)
Terrace v. Thompson, 263 U.S. 197 (1923)
Terral v. Burke Construction Co., 257 U.S. 529 (1922)
Texas Transport & Terminal Co. v. New Orleans, 264 U.S. 150 (1924)

Toyota v. United States, 268 U.S. 402 (1925)
Truax v. Corrigan, 257 U.S. 312 (1921)
Tumey v. Ohio, 273 U.S. 510 (1927)
Tutun v. United States, 270 U.S. 568 (1926)
Tyson & Bros. v. Banton, 273 U.S. 418 (1927)
United Mine Workers v. Coronado Coal Co., 259 U.S. 344 (1922)
United States v. American Tobacco Co., 221 U.S. 106 (1911)
United States v. Bhagat Singh Thind, 261 U.S. 204 (1923)
United States v. Bland, 283 U.S. 636 (1931)
United States v. Butler, 297 U.S. 1 (1936)
United States v. Carolene Products Co., 304 U.S. 144 (1938)
United States v. Classic, 313 U.S. 299 (1941)
United States v. Curtiss-Wright Corp., 299 U.S. 304 (1936)
United States v. Darby Lumber Co., 312 U.S. 100 (1941)
United States v. Doremus, 249 U.S. 86 (1919)
United States v. E.C. Knight Co., 156 U.S. 1 (1895)
United States v. L. Cohen Grocery Co., 255 U.S. 81 (1921)
United States v. Lanza, 260 U.S. 377 (1922)
United States v. Lee, 274 U.S. 559 (1927)
United States v. MacIntosh, 283 U.S. 605 (1931)
United States v. Reading Railroad Co., 253 U.S. 26 (1920)
United States v. Schwimmer, 279 U.S. 644 (1929)
United States v. Southern Pacific Co., 259 U.S. 214 (1922)
United States v. United Shoe Machinery Co., 247 U.S. 32 (1918)
United States v. United States Steel Corp., 251 U.S. 417 (1920)
United States ex rel. Milwaukee Social Democratic Publishing Co. v. Burleson, 255 U.S. 407 (1921)
Vigliotti v. Pennsylvania, 258 U.S. 403 (1922)
Village of Euclid v. Ambler Realty Co. See *Euclid, Village of v. Ambler Realty Co.*
Weaver v. Palmer Bros. Co., 270 U.S. 402 (1926)
Weeks v. United States, 232 U.S. 383 (1914)
West Coast Hotel v. Parrish, 300 U.S. 379 (1937)
West Virginia State Board of Education v. Barnette, 319 U.S. 624 (1943)
White River Lumber Co. v. Arkansas ex rel. Applegate, 279 U.S. 692 (1929)
Whitney v. California, 274 U.S. 357 (1927)
Williams v. Standard Oil Co., 278 U.S. 235 (1929)
Willing v. Chicago Auditorium Ass'n, 277 U.S. 274 (1928)
Wilson v. New, 243 U.S. 332 (1917)
Youngstown Sheet & Tube Co. v. Sawyer, 343 U.S. 579 (1952)

Glossary

Adversary proceeding A legal process that involves a contest between two opposing parties. Formal notice is served on the party against whom an action has been filed to allow that party an opportunity to respond. This system is generally regarded as the most effective means for the evaluation of evidence.

Advisory opinion An opinion of a court indicating how it would rule on an issue if the issue were presented in an actual case; an interpretation of law without binding effect. An advisory opinion offers a view on the legal effect of a law although no real case exists to present the legal question.

Affirmance An appellate court ruling that upholds the judgment of a lower court—that is, that the judgment of the lower court is correct and should stand.

Amicus curiae Latin, meaning "friend of the court." A person or group, not a party to a case, that submits a brief detailing its views on a case. The purpose of an *amicus* brief is to direct a court's attention to an issue or argument that might not be developed in the same way by the parties themselves.

Appeal A process by which a final judgment of a lower court ruling is reviewed by a higher court.

Appellant The party who seeks review of a lower court ruling before a higher court; the party dissatisfied with a lower court ruling who appeals the case to a superior court for review.

Appellate jurisdiction Authority of a superior court to review decisions of inferior courts. Appellate jurisdiction empowers a higher court to conduct such a review and affirm, modify, or reverse the lower court decision. Appellate jurisdiction is conveyed through constitutional or statutory mandate. Federal appellate jurisdiction is granted by Article III of the Constitution, which says that the Supreme Court possesses such jurisdiction "both as to law and fact, with such exceptions and under such regulations as the Congress shall make."

Appellee The party that prevails in a lower court and against whom an appeal of the judgment is sought; in some situations called a "respondent."

Assembly, right to A fundamental right provided by the First Amendment that the people are entitled peaceably to gather and petition the government for "redress of grievances." It includes the right to protest governmental policies, as well as to advocate particular, even distasteful, views. The government can impose regulations on the time, place, and manner of assembly, provided that substantial interests, such as preventing threats to public order, can be shown.

Balancing test A judicial decision-making approach by which interests on one side are weighed or balanced against interests on another. This approach is used most frequently when courts are reviewing individual rights issues. An individual's free speech interests, for example, may be balanced against a societal interest for national security to determine if the speech is protected from regulation or not. The test is based on the traditional idea that individual freedoms and governmental authority must be kept in equilibrium.

Brief A document containing arguments on a matter under consideration by a court. A brief submitted to a court by an attorney typically contains, among other things, points of law from previous rulings.

Case A general term for an action, cause, suit, or controversy at law.

Case law Precedent created as courts resolve disputes. Case law is judge-made law derived from rulings on a specific set of facts.

Case or controversy A constitutional requirement that disputes or controversies be definite and concrete, and involve parties whose legal interests are truly adverse. This requirement is contained in Article III of the U.S. Constitution, and establishes a bona fide controversy as a precondition for adjudication by federal courts.

Certification A process by which judges in one court state uncertainty about the rule of law to apply in a case and request instructions from a higher court.

Certiorari Latin "to be informed of, to be made certain in regard to." A writ or order to a court whose decision is being challenged on appeal to send up the records of the case to enable a higher court to review the case. The writ of certiorari is the primary means by which the U.S. Supreme Court reviews cases from lower courts.

Citizenship A legal status that entitles a person to all the rights and privileges guaranteed and protected by the Constitution of the United States. All persons born in the United States or to at least one parent who is an American possess U.S. citizenship. Others may obtain citizenship through naturalization, a process established by Congress.

Civil liberties Those liberties spelled out in a bill of rights or a constitution that guarantee the protection of persons, opinion, and property from the arbitrary interference of government officials. Civil liberties create immunities from certain governmental actions that interfere with an individual's freedom of action.

Civil rights Positive acts of government designed to protect persons against arbitrary and discriminatory treatment by government or individuals. Civil rights guarantees may be found in constitutions, but more frequently take the form of statutes.

Class action A legal action in which one or more persons represent both themselves and others who are similarly situated. All members of a class must share a common legal interest and meet particular requirements in order to proceed as a class or collective action.

Comity Legal principle that prompts a court to defer to the exercise of jurisdiction by another court. Comity is a rule of judicial courtesy rather than a firm requirement of law, and it suggests that a court that first asserts jurisdiction will not undergo interference by another court without its consent.

Commerce clause Provision found in Article I, Section 8 of the U.S. Constitution. The clause empowers Congress to "regulate commerce with foreign nations, and among the several states, and with the Indian tribes." Since the 1930s, the commerce power has been the basis for extensive federal regulation of the economy and, to a limited extent, federal criminal law.

Common law A body of principles that derive their authority from court judgments that are grounded in common customs and usages. Common law consists of principles that do not have their origin in statute and, as such, is distinct from law created by legislative enactments.

Concurrent jurisdiction Authority that is shared by different courts, and which may be exercised at the same time over the same subject matter.

Concurring opinion An opinion by a judge who agrees with the decision of the majority, but disagrees with the majority's rationale; an opinion by a judge who has arrived at the same conclusion as the majority, but for different reasons.

Conference A meeting of Supreme Court justices in which the justices conduct all business associated with deciding cases. Conferences are closed to all but the justices, and it is where the Supreme Court determines which cases will be reviewed, discusses the merits of cases after oral argument, and decides by vote which party to a case will prevail.

Constitutional court A federal court created by Congress under authority conveyed by Article III of the Constitution. Judges of constitutional courts serve for the duration of good behavior (life tenure), and are protected from having their salaries reduced by the legislature.

Declaratory judgment A ruling of a court that clarifies the rights of the parties or offers an opinion on a legal question, which is invoked when one of the parties seeks a declaration of his or her rights. It differs from a conventional action in that no specific order is issued nor is any relief or remedy granted.

Decree A judgment or order of a court.

de facto Latin for “in fact”; actual.

Defendant The party who is sued in a civil action or charged in a criminal case; the party responding to a civil complaint. A defendant in a criminal case is the person formally accused of criminal conduct.

de jure Latin for “by right.” A *de jure* action occurs as a result of law or official government action.

Demurrer An allegation by a defendant that even if the facts alleged by the plaintiff were true, their legal consequences are not such as to require an answer or further proceedings in the cause. Under contemporary rules of civil procedure, a motion to dismiss a case for failure to establish a claim is more commonly used to accomplish the same objective.

Dissenting opinion The opinion of a judge who disagrees with the result reached by the majority.

Diversity jurisdiction Authority conveyed by Article III of the U.S. Constitution empowering federal courts to hear civil actions involving parties from different states.

Due process Government procedures that follow principles of essential or fundamental fairness. Provisions designed to ensure that laws will be reasonable both in substance and in means of implementation are contained in two clauses of the Constitution of the United States. The Fifth Amendment prohibits deprivation of “life, liberty, or property, without due process of law.” It sets a limit on arbitrary and unreasonable actions by the federal government. The Fourteenth Amendment contains parallel language aimed at the states. Due process requires that actions of government occur through ordered and regularized processes.

Eighteenth Amendment Prohibited the manufacture, sale, transportation, importation, and exportation of intoxicating liquors. The amendment was ratified 16 January 1919 to take effect one year later. The amendment was repealed by the Twenty-first Amendment in 1933.

en banc French for "in the bench." A proceeding in which all the judges of an appellate court participate, as distinguished from a proceeding heard by a panel of three judges.

Enjoin, to To order a party to perform or refrain from a specified action. A party is enjoined by a court issuing an injunction or a restraining order.

Equity A system of remedial justice administered by certain courts empowered to order remedies based on principles and precedents developed by courts, especially when specific legal remedies are unavailable and a sense of fairness demands that something be done.

Exclusive power Authority that is assigned to either the national or state level of government, but not exercised by both.

Executive order A regulation issued by the president, a state governor, or some other executive authority for the purpose of giving effect to a constitutional or statutory provision. An executive order has the force of law and is one means by which the executive branch implements laws.

ex parte Latin for "only one side." Done for, in behalf of, or on the application of one party only.

Federal question An issue arising out of provisions of the U.S. Constitution, federal statutes, or treaties. A federal court has authority to hear federal questions under powers conferred by Article III of the U.S. Constitution.

Federalism A political system in which a number of sovereign political units join together, forming a larger political unit that has authority to act on behalf of the whole. A federal system or federation preserves the political integrity of all the entities composing the federation. Federal systems are regarded as "weak" if the central government has control over very few policy questions, and a "strong" system is one in which the central government possesses authority over most significant policy issues. Authority that is not exclusively assigned may be shared by the two levels and exercised concurrently. The supremacy clause of the U.S. Constitution requires that conflicts arising from the exercise of federal and state power are resolved in favor of the central government. Powers not assigned to the national government are "reserved" for the states by the Tenth Amendment.

Grand jury A panel of from twelve to twenty-three citizens who review prosecutorial evidence to determine if there are sufficient grounds to formally accuse an individual of criminal conduct. The charges a grand jury issues are contained in a document called an indictment.

Habeas corpus Latin for "you have the body." *Habeas corpus* was a procedure in

English law designed to prevent the improper detention of prisoners. The *habeas* process forced jailers to bring a detained person before a judge who would examine the justification for his or her detention. If the court found the person was being improperly held, it could order the prisoner's release by issuing a writ of *habeas corpus.*

Implied power Authority that is possessed by inference from expressed provisions of a constitution or statute. The intention is not manifested by explicit and direct words. Instead, the meaning is gathered by necessary deduction. Implied power is not conveyed by explicit language, but rather by implication or deduction from circumstances, general language, or the conduct of parties.

In camera Latin for "in chambers"; in private. A hearing conducted in a judge's chambers with no spectators present.

Incorporation Refers to the question of whether the federal Bill of Rights extends as a limitation on state governments. The issue largely has been resolved, but several schools of thought on the matter have existed historically. The most sweeping position was that all of the Bill of Rights provisions connected to the states through the Due Process Clause of the Fourteenth Amendment. The clause prohibits a state from denying liberty without due process. Those advocating total incorporation viewed the term liberty as an all-inclusive shorthand for each of the rights enumerated in the Bill of Rights. A second opinion rejected any structural linkage of due process to the Bill of Rights and held simply that the Due Process Clause requires states to provide fundamental fairness. Due process is assessed under this standard by criteria of immutable principles of justice, or, as suggested by Justice Benjamin N. Cardozo in *Palko v. Connecticut,* 302 U.S. 319 (1937), elements that are "implicit in the concept of ordered liberty." Application of such standards would occur on a case-by-case basis. The third opinion is a hybrid of the first two and is known as "selective" incorporation. The selective approach resembles the fundamental fairness position in that it does not view as identical those rights contained in the Bill of Rights and those rights fundamental to fairness. Unlike the fundamental fairness approach, however, the selective view holds that rights expressly contained in the Bill of Rights, if adjudged fundamental, are incorporated through the Fourteenth Amendment and are applicable at the state level regardless of the circumstances of a particular case.

Indictment A written accusation presented by a grand jury to a court, charging that a person has done some act or omission that by law is a punishable offense.

Injunction An order prohibiting a party from acting in a particular way or requiring a specific action by a party. An injunction allows a court to minimize injury to a person or group until the matter can otherwise be resolved, or it may prevent injury altogether. Failure to comply with an injunction constitutes a contempt of court. Once issued, an injunction may be annulled or quashed. An injunction may be temporary or permanent. Temporary injunctions, known as interlocutory injunctions, are used to preserve a situation until the issue is resolved through normal processes of litigation. A permanent injunction may be issued upon completion of full legal proceedings.

In re Latin for "in the matter of." The usual manner of entitling a judicial proceeding in which there are no adversary parties as such, but some issue requiring judicial action.

Judgment of the court The final conclusion reached by a court—the outcome as distinguished from the legal reasoning supporting the conclusion.

Judicial activism An interventionist approach or role orientation for appellate decision making that has the appellate courts playing an affirmative policy role. Judicial activists are inclined to find more constitutional violations than those who see a more restrained role for courts; activists are more likely to invalidate legislative and executive policy initiatives. Judicial activism is seen by its critics as legislating by justices to achieve policy outcomes compatible with their own social priorities.

Judicial notice The act by which a court recognizes the existence and truth of certain facts. These facts are recognized by the court's own initiative, and not offered as evidence by either party.

Judicial review The power of a court to examine the actions of the legislative and executive branches with the possibility that those actions could be declared unconstitutional. The power of judicial review was discussed extensively at the Constitutional Convention of 1787, but it was not included in the Constitution as an expressly delegated judicial function. The Supreme Court first asserted the power of judicial review in *Marbury v. Madison*, 5 U.S. 137 (1803).

Judicial self-restraint A view of appellate court decision making that minimizes the extent to which judges apply their personal views to the legal judgments they render. Judicial self-restraint holds that courts should defer to the policy judgments made by the elected branches of government.

Jurisdiction Jurisdiction defines the boundaries within which a particular court may exercise judicial power; it defines the power of a court to hear and decide cases. The jurisdiction of federal courts is provided in Article III of the Constitution in the case of the Supreme Court, and in acts of Congress in the case of the lower federal courts. Federal judicial power may extend to classes of cases defined in terms of substance and party as well as to cases in law and equity stemming directly from the federal Constitution, federal statutes, treaties, or those cases falling into the admiralty and maritime category. Federal judicial power also extends to cases involving specified parties. Regardless of the substance of the case, federal jurisdiction includes actions in which the federal government itself is a party, between two or more states, between a state and a citizen of another state, between citizens of different states, between a state and an alien, between a citizen of a state and an alien, and where foreign ambassadors are involved. State constitutions and statutes define the jurisdiction of state courts.

Jurisprudence A legal philosophy or the science of law. A term used to refer to the course or direction of judicial rulings. Jurisprudence draws upon philosophical thought, historical and political analysis, sociological and behavioral evidence, and legal experience; it is grounded on the view that ideas about law evolve from critical thinking in a number of disciplines. Jurisprudence enables people to understand how law has ordered both social institutions and individual conduct.

Jus belli Latin for the "law of war"; it applies directly to wartime. *Jus belli* addresses the rights and legal obligations of those nations engaged in warfare as well as the status of neutral nations.

Justiciable Describes a matter that may be appropriate for a court to hear and decide.

Laissez-faire An economic theory that advocates that the government ought not to interfere with the dynamics of a free market economy—government should stay out of economic matters. Those subscribing to the laissez-faire view reject any form of government control or regulation of the economy. The decisions of the U.S. Supreme Court from the 1890s through 1937 frequently reflected laissez-faire values.

Legislative court A court created by Congress under authority of Article I of the U.S. Constitution. Legislative courts may be assigned administrative functions in addition to or instead of judicial functions. Such courts facilitate development of some level of specialization in a court system. Judges of federal legislative courts may be granted life tenure by Congress, but do not have the same level of protection as judges of Article III or constitutional courts.

Liberty of contract A laissez-faire doctrine used to free private agreements from governmental regulation. The liberty-of-contract concept holds that individuals have a right to assume contractual obligations affecting their personal affairs. This includes the right of employers and employees to agree about wages, hours, and conditions of work without government interference. The concept was a central element of substantive due process, in which the courts closely examined the reasonableness of governmental regulations. The liberty-of-contract concept was used to strike down laws establishing minimum wages and maximum hours of work.

Litigant A party to a lawsuit.

Mandamus Latin for "we command." A writ issued by a court of superior jurisdiction to an inferior court or governmental official commanding the performance of an official act.

Martial law Military government established over a civilian population during an emergency. Under martial law, military decrees supersede civilian laws and military tribunals replace civil courts. Martial law can be invoked by the president when necessary for the security of the nation. State governors, as commanders in chief of state militias, may declare martial law during an emergency occasioned by internal disorders or natural disasters.

Mootness A question presented in a lawsuit that cannot be answered by a court either because the issue has resolved itself or conditions have so changed that the court is unable to grant the requested relief.

Motion A request made to a court for a certain ruling or action.

Natural law Laws considered applicable to all persons because they are basic to human nature. Applies to all nations and people; contrasts with positive law.

Naturalization Legal procedure by which an alien is admitted to citizenship. Congress is authorized by Article I, Section 8 of the Constitution to establish uniform rules for naturalization. An individual over eighteen years of age may be naturalized after meeting certain qualifications. These include: 1) residence in the United States for five years; 2) ability to read, write, and speak English; 3) proof of good moral character; and 4) taking an oath of allegiance administered by a federal judge. The residence requirement is lowered for spouses of citizens and for aliens who serve in the armed services. Minors become citizens when their parents are naturalized.

Nineteenth Amendment Extended the right to vote to women. The amendment was ratified in August 1920.

Obiter dictum Latin for "a remark by the way." *Dicta* are statements contained in a court's opinion that are incidental to the disposition of the case. *Obiter dicta* often are directed to issues upon which no formal arguments have been heard, thus the positions represented in *dicta* are not binding on later cases.

Opinion of the Court The statement of a court that expresses the reasoning or *ratio decidendi* upon which a decision is based. The opinion summarizes the principles of law that apply in a given case and represents the views of the majority of a court's members. Occasionally the opinion of a court may reflect the views of less than a majority of its members and is then called a plurality opinion.

Order A written command issued by a judge.

Original jurisdiction The authority of a court to hear and decide a legal question before any other court. Original jurisdiction typically is vested with trial courts rather than appellate courts, although Article III of the Constitution extends very limited original jurisdiction to the United States Supreme Court. Trial courts are assigned specific original jurisdiction defined in terms of subject matter or parties.

***Per curiam* opinion** Latin for "by the court." An unsigned written opinion issued by a court.

Petitioner A party seeking relief in court.

Plaintiff The party who brings a legal action to court for resolution or remedy.

Plurality opinion An opinion announcing a court's judgment and supporting reasoning in a case, but which is not endorsed by a majority of the justices hearing the case.

Pocket veto A special presidential veto power that can be exercised at the end of a congressional session. Bills not signed by the president within a specified time do not become law. A pocket veto cannot be overridden by Congress, but can be reintroduced at a subsequent legislative session.

Police power Authority that empowers government to regulate private behavior in the interest of public health, safety, and general welfare. In the American constitutional system, police power resides with the state and not the federal government. The police power enables states and their respective local units of government to enact and enforce policies deemed appropriate to serve the public good. It is a comprehensive power, and substantial discretion is possessed by the states for its exercise. It is limited by various provisions of the U.S. Constitution and state constitutions, however, and must conform to the requirements of due process.

Political question An issue that is not justiciable or that is not appropriate for judicial determination. A political question is one in which the substance of an issue is primarily political or involves a matter directed toward either the legislative or executive branch by constitutional language. The political question doctrine is sometimes invoked by the Supreme Court, not because the Court is without power or jurisdiction, but because the Court adjudges the question inappropriate for judicial response. In the Court's view, to intervene or respond would be to encroach upon the functions and prerogatives of one of the other two branches of government.

Preemption doctrine Holds that federal laws supersede or preempt state laws in certain policy areas. The preemption doctrine is grounded in the supremacy clause of Article VI of the Constitution, and applies where the federal regulatory interest is so dominant or pervasive as to allow no reasonable inference that room is left for states to act. Congress may state explicitly such a preemptive interest, or the courts may interpret the intent of Congress fully to occupy the field.

Preferred position doctrine Holds that legislative enactments that affect First Amendment rights must be scrutinized more carefully than legislation that does not. The preferred position doctrine says that certain legislative activity deserves priority consideration because it affects fundamental rights such as free speech. The burden is clearly on the state to demonstrate justification for limiting a preferred position freedom. The preferred position doctrine is attributed to Justice Harlan Fiske Stone who said in a footnote to his opinion in *United States v. Carolene Products Co.*, 304 U.S. 144 (1938), that a lesser presumption of constitutionality exists when legislation "appears on its face to be within a specific prohibition such as those of the first ten amendments."

Prior restraint A restriction placed on a publication before it can be published or circulated. Prior restraint typically occurs through a licensure or censorship process or by a full prohibition on publication. Censorship requirements involve a review of materials by the state for objectionable content. Prior restraint poses a greater threat to free expression than after-the-fact prosecution because government restrictions are imposed in a manner that precludes public scrutiny, and the First Amendment prohibits prior restraint in most instances. Although government censorship is generally suspect, prior restraint may be justified if a publication threatens national security, incites overthrow of the government, is obscene, or interferes with the private rights of others.

Procedural due process Fundamental fairness in the means by which governmental actions are executed. Procedural due process demands that before any deprivation of liberty or property can occur, a person must be formally notified and provided an opportunity for a fair hearing. Procedural due process must also be accorded persons accused of crimes, and must include access to legal counsel, the ability to confront witnesses against him or her, and a trial by jury.

Quash To annul, vacate, make void, or totally do away with.

Recusal The process by which a judge is disqualified from participating in the hearing or review of a case. Disqualification may be initiated by a party(ies) to a case or by the judge himself or herself when a judge's participation might be inappropriate because of self-interest or bias.

Remand, to To send a case back to an inferior court for additional action. Appellate courts send cases back to lower courts with instructions to correct specified errors.

Removal jurisdiction The power to transfer a cause, before trial or final hearing, from one court to another.

Republicanism (Guaranty Clause) Government by representatives chosen by the people. A republic is distinguished from a pure democracy where the people make policy decisions themselves rather than through an elected representative. Article IV, Section 4 of the Constitution provides that the national government shall guarantee to each state a "republican form of government."

Respondent The party against whom a motion or appeal is filed.

Reversal An action by an appellate court setting aside or changing a decision of a lower court. The opposite of affirmance.

Right A power or privilege to which a person is entitled. A right is legally conveyed by a constitution, statute, or common law. A right may be absolute, such as one's right to believe, or it may be conditional so that the acting out of one's beliefs will not injure other members of a community.

Ripeness A condition in which a legal dispute has evolved to the point where the issue(s) it presents can be determined by a court. Ripeness is an issue that requires a court to consider whether a case has matured or developed into a controversy worthy of adjudication.

Separation of powers The principle of dividing the powers of government among several coordinate branches to prevent excessive concentration of power. The principle of separation of powers is designed to limit abusive exercise of governmental authority by partitioning power and then assigning that power to several locations. The distribution of powers embodied in the U.S. Constitution functionally distinguishes between government and people, and between legislative, executive, and judicial branches. Although the Constitution creates three separate branches, it also assigns overlapping responsibilities that make the branches interdependent through the operation of a system of checks and balances.

Sovereignty The supreme power of a state or independent nation free from external interference. Sovereignty is exercised by government, which has exclusive and absolute jurisdiction within its geographical boundaries.

Standing The requirement that a real dispute exists between the prospective parties in a lawsuit before it can be heard by a court. As a result, courts typically are unable to respond to hypothetical questions. If a party does not have standing to sue, the matter is not justiciable.

Stare decisis Latin for "let the decision stand." *Stare decisis* holds that once a principle of law is established for a particular fact situation, courts should adhere to that principle in similar cases in the future. The case in which the rule of law is established is called a precedent. *Stare decisis* creates and maintains stability and predictability in the law. Precedents may be modified or abandoned if circumstances require, but the expectation is that rules from previously adjudicated cases will prevail.

State action An action taken by an agency or official of government. The state action concept is used to determine whether an action complained of has its source in state authority or policy. The concept is critically important in cases presenting allegations of discrimination. The equal protection clause typically cannot be applied to private acts of discrimination. Rather, it requires conduct that occurs "under color" of governmental authority.

Stay, to To stop, suspend, or hold in abeyance.

Substantive due process Fundamental fairness in the content or substance of government policy. Substantive due process review requires courts to examine the reasonableness of legislative enactments—that laws be fair and reasonable in substance as well as application. Substantive due process is distinguished from procedural due process.

Summary judgment A decision by a court made without a full hearing or without receiving briefs or oral arguments.

Taxing power Article I, Section 8 of the U.S. Constitution permits Congress to "lay and collect taxes, duties, imposts and excises" and to provide for the "common defense and general welfare" of the United States. The scope of federal power to tax and spend has depended, at least in part, on the Supreme Court's interpretation of the "general welfare" phrase.

Tenth Amendment Provision added to the U.S. Constitution in 1791 that retains or "reserves" for the states powers not assigned to the federal government. The Tenth Amendment has frequently been used to limit the actions of the federal government.

Twenty-first Amendment Repealed the Eighteenth Amendment, which had prohibited the manufacture, sale, transportation, importation, or exportation of intoxicating liquors. The amendment authorized the states to regulate intoxicating liquors as they wished. The amendment was ratified in December 1933.

Vacate To void, rescind, annul, or render void.

Vested right A right that so completely applies to a person that it cannot be impaired by the act of another person. Such rights must be recognized and protected by the government.

Warrant A judicial order authorizing an arrest or search and seizure.

Writ A written order of a court commanding the recipient to perform certain specified acts.

Annotated Bibliography

Books and Articles

Abels, Jules. *In the Time of Silent Cal.* New York: G. P. Putnam's Sons, 1969.

Provides useful background on Coolidge and the decade in which he was on the national stage.

Abraham, Henry J. *Justices, Presidents, and Senators: A History of the U.S. Supreme Court Appointments from Washington to Clinton.* Rev. ed. Lanham, MD: Rowman and Littlefield, 1999.

Written by a preeminent constitutional scholar, this volume provides an analysis of the process used to select Supreme Court justices. Abraham discusses every nomination, successful or not, the motivations and expectations of the nominating president, the Senate review, and characterizes the on-bench performance of each justice.

Baker, Liva. *The Justice of Beacon Hill: The Life and Times of Oliver Wendell Holmes.* New York: HarperCollins, 1991.

A comprehensive discussion of Holmes's professional and private life; the definitive biography of Holmes.

Baum, Lawrence. *The Supreme Court.* 7th ed. Washington, DC: Congressional Quarterly Press, 2001.

A comprehensive discussion of the Supreme Court as an institution. It covers, among other things, the selection of Supreme Court justices, the cases the Court decides, the decision-making process, and the Court's societal impact.

Belknap, Michal R. "Mr. Justice Pitney and Progressivism." *Seton Hall Law Review* 16 (1986): 381–425.

Excellent summary of Pitney's jurisprudence.

Braeman, John, Robert H. Bremner, and David Brody, eds. *Change and Continuity in Twentieth Century America: The 1920s.* Columbus, OH: Ohio State University Press, 1968.

A collection of twelve essays focusing on various social, political, and cultural issues of the 1920s.

Burner, David. "Pierce Butler." In *The Justices of the Supreme Court, 1789–1995.* Leon Friedman and Fred L. Israel, eds. New York: Chelsea House Publishers, 1995a.
Extended essay on one of the Court's most conservative justices and his Supreme Court career.

———. "John H. Clarke." In *The Justices of the Supreme Court, 1789–1995.* Leon Friedman and Fred L. Israel, eds. New York: Chelsea House Publishers, 1995b.
Essay contains biographical information on Clarke and a helpful analysis of his Supreme Court career.

———. "James C. McReynolds." In *The Justices of the Supreme Court, 1789–1995.* Leon Friedman and Fred L. Israel, eds. New York: Chelsea House Publishers, 1995c.
Essay contains biographical information and discussion of McReynolds's almost reactionary jurisprudence.

———. "Edward Terry Sanford." In *The Justices of the Supreme Court, 1789–1995.* Leon Friedman and Fred L. Israel, eds. New York: Chelsea House Publishers, 1995d.
Brief but informative essay on the judicial career of Edward Sanford.

———. "George Sutherland." In *The Justices of the Supreme Court, 1789–1995.* Leon Friedman and Fred L. Israel, eds. New York: Chelsea House Publishers, 1995e.
Excellent essay on one of the Court's so-called Four Horsemen and his intellectual leadership of the conservative bloc.

———. "Willis Van Devanter." In *The Justices of the Supreme Court, 1789–1995.* Leon Friedman and Fred L. Israel, eds. New York: Chelsea House Publishers, 1995f.
Extended essay containing biographical information and an overview of Van Devanter's jurisprudence.

Carter, Paul A. *The Uncertain World of Normalcy: The 1920s.* New York: Pitman, 1971.
A collection of informative essays on a number of topics, which contribute to a fuller understanding of the 1920s.

Chandler, Ralph C., Richard A. Enslen, and Peter G. Renstrom. *Constitutional Law Dictionary: Governmental Powers.* Santa Barbara, CA: ABC-CLIO, 1987.
Summaries of Supreme Court decisions dealing with institutional authority. Volume also contains brief biographical entries on leading justices and provides a brief discussion of selected legal terms and concepts.

Clements, Kendrick A. *The Presidency of Woodrow Wilson.* Lawrence, KS: University Press of Kansas, 1992.
In this volume in the American Presidency Series from the University Press of Kansas, Clements offers a detailed account of Wilson's domestic and foreign policy record as president.

Currie, David P. *The Constitution in the Supreme Court: The Second Century, 1888–1986.* Chicago: University of Chicago Press, 1990.
The second of two volumes that critically represent the constitutional decisions

of the Supreme Court from 1888–1986. Currie breaks the second century at 1941, focusing on the rise and fall of substantive due process through the end of the 1930s and the evolution of individual rights protection thereafter.

Cushman, Barry. "Mahlon Pitney." In *The Supreme Court Justices: A Biographical Dictionary.* Melvin I. Urofsky, ed. New York: Garland, 1994.

Summarily represents Pitney's Supreme Court voting record and his more notable opinions.

Cushman, Clare, ed. *The Supreme Court Justices: Illustrated Biographies, 1789–1995.* Washington, DC: Congressional Quarterly Press, 1993.

A volume produced by the Supreme Court Historical Society under the direction of Clare Cushman. Each justice is profiled in a five-page essay that provides biographical background information. Although this book does not intend to assess the jurisprudence of each justice, it does provide a brief description of the justices' most significant opinions.

Danelski, David J. *A Supreme Court Justice Is Appointed.* New York: Random House, 1964.

A three-part discussion of the appointment of Pierce Butler to the Supreme Court. The first part provides background on Butler to the point of his nomination. The second part focuses on his selection by President Harding, the role of Chief Justice William Howard Taft in the selection process, and Senate confirmation. The third part is an analysis of the process in the Butler case and the consequences of his joining the Court.

———. "Pierce Butler." In *The Supreme Court Justices: A Biographical Dictionary.* Melvin I. Urofsky, ed. New York: Garland, 1994.

Brief discussion of Butler's path to the Supreme Court written by the author of a detailed monograph on Butler's nomination to the Court. Briefly represents Butler's very conservative jurisprudence.

Daugherty, Harry M., in collaboration with Thomas Dixon. *The Inside Story of the Harding Tragedy.* Freeport, NY: Books for Libraries Press, 1932/1971.

An account of the scandals that occurred during the Harding presidency. Daugherty, U.S. attorney general from 1921–1924, was a central figure in the scandals.

Epstein, Lee, Jeffrey A. Segal, Harold J. Spaeth, and Thomas Walker. *The Supreme Court Compendium: Data, Decisions, and Developments.* Washington, DC: Congressional Quarterly Press, 1994.

A comprehensive collection of information about the Supreme Court including institutional history, decision-making processes, cases, caseload, and impact. It also provides valuable information about the justices, such as background, characteristics, opinions, and voting patterns.

Fausold, Martin L. *The Presidency of Herbert C. Hoover.* Lawrence, KS: University Press of Kansas, 1985.

Provides something of Hoover's background, but focuses on the four years of the Hoover presidency. The dominating event is the economic Depression, which began with the stock market crash in October 1929. Fausold traces Hoover's response to the emergency and his defeat in the presidential election of 1932.

Ferrell, Robert H. *The Presidency of Calvin Coolidge.* Lawrence, KS: University Press of Kansas, 1998.

Chronicles the Coolidge presidency and the performance of the Coolidge administration across the predominant domestic and foreign policy issues of the period.

Freund, Paul A. "Oliver Wendell Holmes." In *The Justices of the Supreme Court, 1789–1995.* Leon Friedman and Fred L. Israel, eds. New York: Chelsea House Publishers, 1995.

A brief essay containing biographical information and a representation of Holmes's jurisprudence.

Friedman, Leon, and Fred L. Israel, eds. *The Justices of the Supreme Court, 1789–1995.* New York: Chelsea House Publishers, 1995.

A superb five-volume set containing extended essays on all of the Supreme Court's justices. Each essay provides biographical background information, but also includes substantial discussion of the justices' jurisprudence. Earlier editions of these volumes also contain a sample of two or three of each justice's major opinions.

Goldberg, David J. *Discontented America: The United States in the 1920s.* Baltimore, MD: Johns Hopkins University Press, 1999.

A valuable account of the decade of the 1920s. Goldberg features the conflicts among a variety of economic, ethnic, and religious population subgroups, and the collapse of progressivism in the years following World War I.

Goldman, Sheldon. *Constitutional Law: Cases and Essays.* 2d ed. New York: HarperCollins, 1991.

Conventionally fashioned constitutional law casebook, but with two unusually valuable features. First, Goldman develops in Chapters 2 and 3 the political and historical context of the Supreme Court from 1789 to the present. Second, he discusses each justice as he or she joined the Court, the characteristics of the group interactions of each Court era, and the voting patterns of each individual justice.

Hall, Kermit L., ed. *The Oxford Companion to the Supreme Court of the United States.* New York, NY: Oxford University Press, 1992.

A comprehensive single volume with informative entries on the Supreme Court, its principal decisions, and the justices.

Hamm, Richard F. "Williams Rufus Day." In *The Supreme Court Justices: A Bio-*

graphical Dictionary. Melvin I. Urofsky, ed. New York: Garland, 1994a.
Short essay on Day's Supreme Court voting record.

———. "Joseph McKenna." In *The Supreme Court Justices: A Biographical Dictionary.* Melvin I. Urofsky, ed. New York: Garland, 1994b.
Briefly represents McKenna's undistinguished and somewhat erratic twenty-seven years on the Supreme Court.

Hicks, John D. *Republican Ascendancy: 1921–1933.* New York: Harper & Row, 1960.
An excellent discussion of the political, social, and economic scene in the 1920s; a critical examination of a decade most notable for "evaded responsibilities and opportunities missed."

Israel, Fred L. "Mahlon Pitney." In *The Justices of the Supreme Court, 1789–1995.* Leon Friedman and Fred L. Israel, eds. New York: Chelsea House Publishers, 1995.
Useful essay on the jurisprudence of one of the Court's more obscure justices.

Johnson, John W. "Harlan Fiske Stone." In *The Supreme Court Justices: A Biographical Dictionary.* Melvin I. Urofsky, ed. New York: Garland, 1994.
Excellent short essay on Stone's judicial philosophy and his Supreme Court record.

Kelly, Alfred H., Winfred A. Harbison, and Herman Belz. *The American Constitution: Its Origins and Developments.* Vol. 2. 7th ed. New York: W. W. Norton, 1991.
An excellent two-volume narrative on the evolution of American constitutional law.

Kennedy, David M. *Freedom from Fear: The American People in Depression and War, 1929–1945.* New York: Oxford University Press, 1999.
One of the volumes in the Oxford history series on the United States, this volume is a comprehensive narrative of the period. It is particularly valuable in representing the Roosevelt presidency and his responses both to the Great Depression and World War II.

Mason, Alpheus T. *Harlan Fiske Stone: Pillar of the Law.* New York: Viking, 1956.
The most authoritative work on Stone, the volume provides essential insights into the Supreme Court as an institution as well as Justice Stone.

———. *William Howard Taft: Chief Justice.* New York: Simon and Schuster, 1964.
The leading discussion of Taft and his decade as chief justice. Mason focuses on Taft as judicial reformer and the political lobbying that was required to achieve his reform objectives.

———. *The Supreme Court from Taft to Burger.* 3d ed. Baton Rouge: Louisiana State University Press, 1979.
An overview of the several Supreme Court eras beginning with the Taft Court of the 1920s. Mason identifies the principal characteristics of each Court and discusses what he finds to be the most significant aspects of the jurisprudence of each.

———."Louis D. Brandeis." In *The Justices of the Supreme Court, 1789–1995.* Leon Friedman and Fred L. Israel, eds. New York: Chelsea House Publishers, 1995a.
Extended essay containing biographical background on Brandeis plus a brief analysis of his distinguished Supreme Court record.

———. "William Howard Taft." In *The Justices of the Supreme Court, 1789–1995.* Leon Friedman and Fred L. Israel, eds. New York: Chelsea House Publishers, 1995b.
An informative essay on Taft's political and judicial career by the author of the definitive monograph on Taft.

McDevitt, Br. Matthew. *Joseph McKenna: Associate Justice of the United States.* New York: Da Capo Press, 1974.
In this reprinted doctoral dissertation, McDevitt provides the only comprehensive biographical source on McKenna.

McLean, Joseph E. *William Rufus Day: Supreme Court Justice from Ohio.* Baltimore, MD: Johns Hopkins University Press, 1946.
The only substantial biographical work on Day and his almost twenty years on the Supreme Court.

Milkis, Sidney M., and Michael Nelson. *The American Presidency: Origins and Development, 1776–1993.* 2d ed. Washington, DC: CQ Press, 1994.
Traces the institutional evolution of the presidency, beginning with the executive under the Articles of Confederation through to the modern presidency.

Morison, Samuel Eliot, Henry Steele Commager, and William E. Leuchtenburg. *The Growth of the American Republic.* Volume 2. New York: Oxford University Press, 1980.
Excellent narrative discussion of the growth and development of the United States.

Murphy, Paul L. *The Constitution in Times of Crisis 1918–1969.* New York: Harper and Row, 1972.
An insightful discussion of the effects of the Supreme Court's decisions from the conclusion of World War I into the turbulent decade of the 1960s.

Murphy, Walter F. "In His Own Image: Mr. Chief Justice Taft and Supreme Court Appointments." In *Supreme Court Review.* Philip B. Kurland, ed. Chicago: University of Chicago Press, 1961.
Excellent discussion of the political activities of Taft during his tenure as chief justice, and a discussion of his substantial influence on President Warren Harding's Supreme Court nominations.

Noggle, Burl. *Teapot Dome: Oil and Politics in the 1920s.* Baton Rouge, LA: Louisiana State University Press, 1962.
Describes the factors and personalities that led to the oil-lease scandal, its discovery, and the Senate investigation that led to criminal prosecutions. Noggle

concludes with a brief discussion of the impact ("residue" in his words) of the high-level corruption.

Parrish, Michael E. *Felix Frankfurter and His Times: The Reform Years.* New York: Free Press, 1982.

A revealing discussion of Frankfurter's years on the Harvard Law School faculty, his "boys"— students who later made their marks in Washington after Harvard Law—and his role in Franklin Roosevelt's "inner circle."

———. *Anxious Decades: America in Prosperity and Depression, 1920–1941.* New York: W. W. Norton, 1992.

A comprehensive discussion of the twenty years between the world wars.

Paschal, Joel Francis. *Mr. Justice Sutherland: A Man against the State.* New York: Greenwood, 1969.

An excellent representation of Justice Sutherland and his jurisprudence. Paschal suggests that while he was on the Court (1922–1938), no other justice "spoke for the majority in so many great cases."

Post, Robert C. "William Howard Taft." In *The Supreme Court Justices: A Biographical Dictionary.* Melvin I. Urofsky, ed. New York: Garland, 1994.

Informative essay on Taft's Supreme Court career with particular focus on his judicial reform initiatives and the administrative skills he demonstrated as chief justice.

Pritchett, C. Herman. *Constitutional Law of the Federal System.* Englewood Cliffs, NJ: Prentice-Hall, 1984.

Pritchett provides a concise commentary of the American federal system, its organization and powers.

Rodell, Fred. *Nine Men: A Political History of the Supreme Court of the United States from 1790 to 1955.* New York: Vintage Books, 1955.

Overview of the Court's history with brief sketches of the justices serving prior to 1955.

Schlesinger, Arthur M., Jr. *The Crisis of the Old Order, 1919–1933.* Boston: Houghton Mifflin, 1957.

Schlesinger discusses the period following the end of World War I and the beginning of the Roosevelt years. He effectively examines the decade of "normalcy" and relative prosperity that immediately preceded the Great Depression.

Shoemaker, Rebecca Sheppard. "Willis Van Devanter." In *The Supreme Court Justices: A Biographical Dictionary.* Melvin I. Urofsky, ed. New York: Garland, 1994.

Brief essay on Van Devanter's judicial career and his influence in the Supreme Court's conferences.

Soule, George. *Prosperity Decade: From War to Depression 1917–1929.* New York: Rinehart, 1947.

In this one of nine volumes on the economic history of the United States, Soule suggests that the prosperity for which the decade of the 1920s is known was only a limited prosperity for many sectors of the nation's economy.

Stratton, David H. *Tempest over Teapot Dome: The Story of Albert B. Fall.* Norman, OK: University of Oklahoma Press, 1998.

A balanced analysis of the Teapot Dome oil-lease scandal through the character of Interior Secretary Albert Fall, the central figure in the affair.

Strum, Philippa. *Louis D. Brandeis: Justice for the People.* Cambridge, MA: Harvard University Press, 1984.

One of the most valuable biographies of Brandeis. Extensive discussion of his legal practice prior to appointment to the Supreme Court and an insightful representation of his more than two decades on the Court.

———. "Louis Dembitz Brandeis." In *The Supreme Court Justices: A Biographical Dictionary.* Melvin I. Urofsky, ed. New York: Garland, 1994.

Unusually informative essay on Brandeis's jurisprudence, featuring the time he shared on the Court with Justice Oliver Wendell Holmes Jr.

Swindler, William F. *Court and Constitution in the Twentieth Century: The Old Legality, 1889–1932.* Indianapolis, IN: Bobbs-Merrill, 1974.

One of an excellent two-volume narrative on the historical evolution of the Supreme Court.

Trani, Eugene P., and David L. Wilson. *The Presidency of Warren G. Harding.* Lawrence, KS: Regents Press of Kansas, 1977.

A brief review of the three-year Harding presidency; the historical context of the early 1920s, Harding's modest domestic agenda in the pursuit of returning to "normalcy," and Harding's place in history.

Urofsky, Melvin I., ed., *The Supreme Court Justices: A Biographical Dictionary.* New York: Garland, 1994.

A collection of essays about each of the 107 justices who have served on the U.S. Supreme Court. The essays contained in this volume were prepared by an extremely distinguished collection of authors and provide valuable analysis, albeit summarily, of the jurisprudence of the justices.

Urofsky, Melvin I., and Paul Finkelman. *A March of Liberty: A Constitutional History of the United States.* Vol. 2. 2d ed. New York: Oxford University Press, 2002.

A superb two-volume narrative on the history and development of the U.S. Constitution.

Warner, Hoyt Landon. *The Life of Mr. Justice Clarke: A Testament to the Power of Liberal Dissent in America.* Cleveland, OH: Western Reserve University Press, 1959.

In this, the only biography on Clarke, Warner provides a valuable account of the development of Clarke's political and constitutional philosophy. Although

Clarke served on the Court only briefly, Warner suggests that he played a valuable role as spokesman for the liberal minority.

Watts, James F., Jr. "William R. Day." In *The Justices of the Supreme Court, 1789–1995.* Leon Friedman and Fred L. Israel, eds. New York: Chelsea House Publishers, 1995.

Lengthy essay containing a comprehensive analysis of Day's Supreme Court record.

White, G. Edward. *The American Judicial Tradition: Profiles of Leading American Judges.* Oxford, UK: Oxford University Press, 1976.

This volume contains a number of group and individual portraits of selected Supreme Court justices. Particularly valuable to an understanding of the Stone Court are the chapters on the Four Horsemen of the 1930s, a comparative examination of Hughes and Stone as chief justices, on Jackson's jurisprudence, and a profile of Black and Frankfurter as members of the Warren Court.

———. "Oliver Wendell Holmes, Jr." In *The Supreme Court Justices: A Biographical Dictionary.* Melvin I. Urofsky, ed. New York: Garland, 1994.

An excellent essay on Holmes and his unique contributions to the Supreme Court and American constitutional law.

Wolf, Michael Allan. "George Sutherland." In *The Supreme Court Justices: A Biographical Dictionary.* Melvin I. Urofsky, ed. New York: Garland, 1994.

Represents the conservative jurisprudence of the justice who long led the substantive due process fight.

Internet Sources

New Internet sites are introduced frequently. Readers who use the sites listed below are encouraged to explore the countless number of links to other sites that are provided in virtually every site you visit.

There are a number of excellent sites with information about the U.S. Supreme Court, some of which are listed below. The full text of Court decisions is available from some of these sites, but generally limited to cases decided since approximately 1900.

Emory University School of Law (2 sites)

Electronic Reference Desk

http://www.law.emory.edu/LAW/refdesk/toc.html

Initial menu offers several useful categories of information including federal and state laws in the United States, and selected representation of laws from over seventy other countries. This site contains a reference option as well as sections on law by subject, law schools, legal periodicals, legal career information, and selected law firms.

Federal Courts Finder

http://www.law.emory.edu/FEDCTS

This site links the user to all federal appellate courts. Supreme Court links connects the user to the Legal Information Institute site. Excellent source for U.S. Court of Appeals decisions. Click any of the circuits on the U.S. maps to access rulings covering the last several years.

Federal Judicial Center

http://www.fjc.gov/

Homepage for the Federal Judicial Center, the research and education agency of the federal judicial system. Contains links to other courts, including the new Supreme Court site, and the newly added link to the History of the Federal Judiciary site which contains a biographical database of all federal judges since 1789, histories of the federal courts, and other historical materials related to the federal judicial branch.

Federal Judiciary Homepage

http://www.uscourts.gov/

This page is maintained by the Administrative Office of the U.S. Courts and is a good source of information on the federal courts. The site contains a number of links to other valuable court/law-related sites. There is also a link featuring recent developments regarding the federal courts, including the latest on the status of federal judicial vacancies.

Federal Legal Information Through Electronics (FLITE)

wysiwyg://14/http://www.fedworld.gov/supcourt/index.htm

This site contains the full text of about 7,500 U.S. Supreme Court decisions from 1937 to 1975. Cases can be retrieved by case name or key word. Links are provided to other sites such as the Cornell University site.

Findlaw

http://www.findlaw.com/

An extraordinarily valuable and comprehensive site. Among other things, the site has federal and state cases and codes; U.S. and state resources; news and references; a legal subject index; and links to bar associations, lawyers, and law firms. Decisions of the U.S. Supreme Court back to 1893 can be accessed as can federal courts of appeals rulings.

Jurist: The Legal Education Network

http://jurist.law.pitt.edu/supremecourt.htm

The Pittsburgh University Law School guide to the U.S. Supreme Court is an online introduction to the "jurisprudence, structure, history and justices of America's highest court." Links the user to sites containing Supreme Court decisions (e.g., Cornell, Findlaw), news about the Court, biographies of the justices, the Court's procedures, and the latest media coverage of the Court.

Legal Information Institute (LII)
http://www.law.cornell.edu/index.html

Cornell Law School site containing Supreme Court decisions since 1990, U.S. and state constitutions and codes, law by source or jurisdiction including international law, and "law about" pages providing summaries of various law topics. The site has a "current awareness" page that contains news about the Court. LII provides a free e-mail service that distributes syllabi of Supreme Court decisions within hours of their release.

Lexis-Nexis Academic Universe
http://web.lexis-nexis.com/universe/

Lexis-Nexis is a subscription database that covers a wide range of news, business, and reference information. Free access can be obtained to Lexis-Nexis through Academic Universe, which is available through most educational institutions.

National Center for State Courts
http://www.ncsc.dni.us

A comprehensive site with extensive information on state courts, state judges, and state court caseloads. Links are provided for information about federal courts and international courts.

Oyez Project
http://oyez.nwu.edu/

Northwestern University multimedia database that allows users to hear oral arguments from selected cases, obtain summaries of more than 1,000 Court opinions, biographical information on all the justices who have served on the Court, and a virtual-reality tour of the Supreme Court building.

Supreme Court
http://supremecourtus.gov/

A newly accessible site that overviews the Supreme Court as an institution, its functions, traditions, procedures, court rules, docket, and calendar. There is also information available on the justices and the Supreme Court building. "Plug in" capability is required to access information from this site.

Westlaw
http://westlaw.com/

Westlaw is one of the largest and most comprehensive legal and business databases available on the Internet. Subscription is required for access, but prospective subscribers are able to fully explore the site on a "trial" basis.

Yahoo Law
http://dir.yahoo.com/Government/Law/

Yahoo is a search engine with a separate and extensive listing of law-related sites. An easy-to-use and comprehensive searching device.

Other Resources

A number of newspapers provide good coverage of the U.S. Supreme Court. Among the best are the *New York Times* at http://www/nytimes.com, and the *Washington Post* at http://www.washpostco.com.

Index

Peter G. Renstrom is a professor of political science at Western Michigan University. He is also a coauthor of ABC-CLIO's *The Constitutional Law Dictionary* (1987) and author of *Constitutional Law and Young Adults* (1992), *Constitutional Rights Sourcebook* (1999), and *The Stone Court* (2001).

www.ingramcontent.com/pod-product-compliance
Ingram Content Group UK Ltd.
Pitfield, Milton Keynes, MK11 3LW, UK
UKHW050947290926
15470UKWH00005B/1690

9 781576 072806